# EPIPLOKE:

Rhythmical Continuity
and
Poetic Structure in Greek Lyric

# EPIPLOKE:

## Rhythmical Continuity
### and
## Poetic Structure
## in Greek Lyric

# THOMAS COLE

PUBLISHED BY THE DEPARTMENT OF THE CLASSICS

Harvard University

Distributed by Harvard University Press

Cambridge, Massachusetts
London, England

1988

To Helena and Celia

PA
415
.L9
C6
1988

Loeb Classical Monographs
In Memory of James Loeb

Cover design by Jennie Bush/Designworks

**Library of Congress Cataloging in Publication Data**
Cole, Thomas, 1933-
   Epiploke: rhythmical continuity and poetic structure in Greek
lyric/Thomas Cole
      p.      cm. — (Loeb classical monographs)
   Includes index.
   1. Greek language—Metrics and Rhythmics. 2. Greek poetry-
-History and criticism.   I. Title.   II. Series.
PA 415. L9C6 1988                             87-30467
881'.01'09—dc19                                CIP
ISBN 0-674-25822-3

# PREFACE

Students first learning to read or write Greek and Latin hexameters are taught that every line must consist of six feet: a concluding spondee (or trochee) preceded by five dactyls, one or more of which may also be replaced by spondees. A little later they wil learn that a line may be generated in strict accordance with these rules and still not constitute an acceptable hexameter—the notorious

> sparsis hastis longis campus splendet et horret

for example, or the only marginally superior

> poste recumbite vestraque pectora pellite tonsis.

Word end has to occur at certain places within the line, and not occur at others; and this means that every hexameter is a succession, not only of feet, but of phrases as well, certain combinations of which occur over and over again. A third stage of sophistication is reached when each verse takes shape in the conscious mind of hearer or composer almost exclusively in terms of such phrases, with rhythmical instinct seeing to it that the dactyl-and/or-spondee count comes out right. The same process repeats itself when one is seeking to master the art of trimeters or elegiacs.

With all but the simplest and most familiar of lyric stanzas the situation is quite different. As is only proper in a discipline felt to be remote and recondite, students are expected to work at the ''stage-three'' level without ever having gone through stages one and two. It is rather as if they had been provided with a labeled catalogue of the sequences of longs and shorts whose beginnings and ends coincide most frequently with word boundary in the Virgilian corpus, and then told to compose, or analyze, Virgilian hexameters by combining by combining two or more such phrases. Hemiepes ($-\cup\cup-\cup\cup-$) + paroemiac ($\overline{\cup\cup}-\cup\cup-\cup\cup--$) will obviously account for

> arma virumque cano + Troiae qui primus ab oris,

and dactylic tetrameter (''Almanicum'') + adonic ($-\cup\cup--$) for

> ducite ab urbe domum mea carmina + ducite Daphnim.

But are the two combinations metrically equivalent? And what is to prevent their ingredients being linked together in a different way:

arma virumque cano—ducite Daphnim?

Absurd as such questions would be for anyone who has mastered stage one of hexameter versification, they are ubiquitous and, for the most part, unanswerable in the study of Greek lyric as it is now conducted and has been conducted, by and large, since Alexandrian times.

The present work departs from the prevailing pattern by attempting to provide some sort of lyric analogue to stage one. The analogue suggested differs from the model in three ways: (1) In place of the hexameter, with its 12 to 17 syllables, one usually has various forms of "hypermeter," longer units which may contain as many as several hundred syllables (569, in the anapests of the comic poet Mnesimachus [fr. 4 Kock] is the attested maximum); (2) Within such continuous movements ambiguous transitional passages may permit modulation from one rhythm to another in such a way that exact demarcation or segmentation is impossible; and (3) Homogeneous rhythmical movement, when it occurs, is often "cyclical" rather than "metrical" in character. Longs and shorts succeed each other in an order that recurs exactly, depending on the type of rhythm involved, every 3, 4, 7 or 8 quantities, but without regular articulation into verbal phrases which would allow one version of the resulting cycle (dactylic $-\cup\cup$, for example, as against anapestic $\cup\cup-$) to be regarded as fundamental or primary.

These modulating (2) or cyclical (3) sequences of fused and interlocking units are the "interweaves" (*epiplokai*) to which the title of this book refers. They provide, it is argued, a kind of rhythmical ground over which the "stage three" phrase structures catalogued by traditional metrics are superimposed (harmoniously at times, contrapuntally at other times). And, for large areas of Greek lyric, an understanding of their character is essential if the identification and analysis of such phrases structures is not to be totally capricious and arbitrary. Exactly how large and how important those areas are is for the reader himself to decide. To that end, I have attempted to base my argument on as complete and conscientious a survey of the evidence as is possible.

The term *epiploke* is an ancient one; and the phenomenon, or phenomena, to which it refers has been sporadically noted or commented upon by earlier scholars. They have always, however, had a limited problem or a limited goal in mind: explaining the interrelation of particular verse forms, for example (Heliodorus, Jean Irigoin, L. E. Rossi); or establishing the presumed presence of a given rhythmical *Leitmotif* in passages whose phrase structure seemed to demand a rather different analysis (Walter Headlam and George Thomson); or arguing for certain revisions in inherited nomenclature and notation (Paul Maas, A. M. Dale). The elevation of *epiploke* to a cardinal principle of Greek versification is an innovation, for which only I can claim the credit or bear the blame.

In other respects my indebtednesses are many—most extensively, as a glance at the citations of modern scholarship will show, to the published work of A. M. Dale. All or part of the manuscript was read at various stages by Ann Bergren, Michael Gagarin, Richard Garner, Bruno Gentili, Eric Havelock, Joel Lidov and L. E. Rossi; their criticisms have saved me from a number of obscurities and errors. C. J. Herington's friendly but firm intervention, at a penultimate stage in the process, is largely responsible for such legibility as the book possesses, though credit here should be shared with Gary A. Bisbee, who coped long and valiantly with the nightmarish problems of format and notation. To all of these—and, above all, to George Goold and Gregory Nagy, whose interest and support ultimately made publication possible—my warmest thanks.

CONTENTS

ABBREVIATIONS

## 1. *Rythmici* and *metrici*

AQ = Aristides Quintilianus, *De musica* (ed. R. P. Winnington-Ingram)

Conomis = N. C. Conomis, "The Dochmiacs of Greek Drama," *Hermes* 92 (1964) 23–50

Dale = A. M. Dale, *Collected Papers* (Cambridge 1969)

DH = Dionysius of Halicarnassus, *De compositione verborum* (ed. H. Usener and L. Radermacher)

Fraenkel = E. Fraenkel, "Lyrische Daktylen," *RhM* 82 (1917–18) 161–97 and 321–52

Fuehrer = R. Fuehrer, "Beiträge zur Metrik und Textkritik der griechischen Lyriker," *NachGött* (1976) 112–261

Gentili = B. Gentili, *Metrica greca arcaica* (Messina 1950)

*GL* = *Grammatici Latini* (ed. B. Keil)

*GV* = U. von Wilamowitz-Moellendorff, *Griechische Verskunst* (Berlin 1921)

Haslam = M. Haslam, "Stesichorean Metre," *QuadUrb* 17 (1974) 7–57

Heph = *Hephaestionis enchiridion cum commentariis veteribus* (ed. M. Consbruch)

Korzeniewski = D. Korzeniewski, *Griechische Metrik* (Darmstadt 1968)

Koster = W. J. W. Koster, *Traité de métrique grecque*[4] (Leiden 1966)

Kraus = W. Kraus, "Strophengestaltung der griechischen Tragödie," *SBWien* 231.4 (1957)

*LMGD* = A. M. Dale, *The Lyric Metres of Greek Drama*[2] (Cambridge 1968)

Maas = P. Maas, *Greek Metre* (Eng. transl., Oxford 1962). (References are to sections)

Nagy = G. Nagy, *Comparative Studies in Greek and Indic Meter* (Cambridge, Mass. 1974)

Parker = L. P. E. Parker, "Porson's Law Extended," *CQ* 60 (1966) 1–25

Pohlsander = H. A. Pohlsander, *Metrical Studies in the Lyrics of Sophocles* (Leiden 1964)

*RS* = Aristoxenus, *Rhythmica Stoicheia* (ed. R. Westphal, *Aristoxenus von Tarent* 2 [Leipzig 1893] 75–107)

Schroeder     =   O. Schroeder, *Aeschyli cantica*[2], *Sophoclis cantica*[2], *Euripidis cantica*[2] or *Aristophanis cantica*[2] (Leipzig 1916, 1923, 1928 and 1930)

Snell     =   B. Snell, *Griechische Metrik*[4] (Göttingen 1982)

Webster     =   T. B. L. Webster, *The Greek Chorus* (London 1970)

West     =   M. L. West, *Greek Metre* (Oxford 1982)

White     =   J. W. White, *The Verse of Greek Comedy* (London 1912). (References are to sections)

## 2. *Poetae*

Unless otherwise indicated, non-dramatic lyric is cited in the line or fragment numberings of Lobel and Page (*Poetarum Lesbiorum Fragmenta* [Oxford 1955]), Page (*PMG* = *Poetae Melici Graeci* [Oxford 1962], *SLG* = *Supplementum Lyricis Graecis* [Oxford 1974]), Snell (Pindar and Bacchylides), and Powell (*Collectanea Alexandrina* [Oxford 1925]); elegy and iambus in the numberings of West (*Iambi et Elegi Graeci* [Oxford 1971–72]); and dramatic lyric in those of the *OCT* or, for fragments, Lloyd-Jones (Aeschylus), Radt (Sophocles), Diggle (the *Phaethon* of Euripides), Nauck (other Euripidean fragments), Kassel and Austin (comedy), Snell (minor tragedians) and Snell-Radt (tragic *adespota*). Pindaric and Bacchylidean references are regularly to the position of a line within strophe and antistrophe or epode (e.g., *O*1e3 = *Olympian* 1, epode, line 3 [in Snell's numbering]).

When reference is made to two or more passages in strophic response but only one such passage is actually quoted, the passage is either the first to appear in a poem (Pindar and Bacchylides) or the one referred to first.

## I: DEMARCATION AND SYNAPHEIA

‖  = "prosodic demarcation"—i.e., rhythmically significant instance of prosodic break (an interruption in the flow of sound or some other modification in delivery sufficiently pronounced that when it occurs between vowels they do not coalesce). Syllables not separated by prosodic break—i.e., those part of the same flow of sound—are said to be in prosodic "synapheia."

⌒  = rhythmically significant "verbal synapheia" or "bridge." (Adjacent syllables which are part of the same word or closely cohering word group are said to be in verbal synapheia).

|  = "verbal demarcation," i.e., rhythmically significant boundary between words or word groups. (Noted by superscripts and subscripts [ ', , ] when confined to, respectively, strophe or antistrophe).

## II. SYLLABLES AND QUANTITIES

Syllables ending in a short vowel and in prosodic synapheia with what follows are short. All others are long—i.e., all those ending in a long vowel, all closed syllables,[1] and, presumably, all followed by prosodic break, where bringing the flow of sound to a close would have had the same effect as a final consonant in closing and so lengthening a syllable.[2] Syllable lengths and the members of the ordered sequence of temporal "quantities" which syllables supply to create a given rhythm are desig-

---

[1] Cf. M. Lejeune, *Traité de phonétique grecque* (Paris 1945) 258–59.

[2] This inference is supported, for poetry, by the total absence of prosodic demarcation within repeating rhythmical series at a place where the pattern, insofar as it is ascertainable, calls for a short quantity (cf. Maas 33); and for the prose of Demosthenes, at any rate, by the failure of final ⌣ ⌣ ⌣ to constitute an exception to Blass' law prohibiting more than two consecutive short syllables (see D. M. McCabe, *The Prose Rhythm of Demosthenes, HSCP* 85 [1981] 312).

nated as follows:[3]

| | | |
|---|---|---|
| – | = | long quantity (i.e., one necessarily long by the requirements of the rhythm) or, in referring to a particular instance of a given rhythm, a long quantity supplied by a long syllable |
| ◡ | = | necessarily short quantity, or short quantity supplied by a short syllable |
| × | = | rhythmically unregulated, or "anceps" quantity |
| ×̆ | = | anceps supplied by a short syllable ("short" anceps) |
| ×̄ | = | anceps supplied by a long syllable ("long" anceps) |
| ◡̆◡̆ | = | single long quantity supplied by two short syllables ("resolved" long) |
| ◡◡‿ | = | two consecutive shorts supplied by a single long syllable ("contracted" double short) |
| . | = | "syncopated" quantity—i.e., one supplied by a pause or a protraction of the syllable that supplies the quantity immediately preceding |
| ◡⌐ | = | "protracted" syllable (syllable supplying a long quantity and the one following it) |
| ◡ ◡ , ◡ , – | = | (when printed as superscripts) two short syllables, or single long or short syllable (without specification of the type of quantity supplied) |
| ( ) | = | (when enclosing one of the above symbols) feature present in some instances of the rhythm under examination but not in other (e.g., ⁽◡̆⁾ = occasional or frequent, but not obligatory, resolution) |

Superscripts and subscripts may indicate, when used together, equivalent variations: $\frac{-\times}{\times -}$ etc.

## III. SEQUENCES

| | | |
|---|---|---|
| ×× | = | aeolic base (×× in Sappho and Alcaeus; elsewhere ⁽×̆×̆⁾ varied occasionally by ⁽×̆×̆⁾ and [in Euripides and Timotheus] – ◡ ◡) |

---

[3] Readers familiar with the work of Paul Maas may prefer to think of quantities as elements; but element is a purely descriptive term, permitting one to distinguish different types of equivalence empirically verifiable in a written poetic text (responsion of single long syllable to double short [elementum biceps] or single long to single short [elementum anceps] etc.). A quantity is any one of the minimal constant components of a temporal design that is assumed to have been actually perceived by the poet and his audience.

---

an = anapest $\cup\cup$ᵕ ( )

(The glossary of metrical symbols:)

an = anapest

do = dochmiac

D = – ᴗ ᴗ – ᴗ ᴗ – in prosodiac rhythm

E = – ᴗ – × – ᴗ – in the iambo-trochaic sequence |(×)– ᴗ – × – ᴗ –(×)|

A = – ᴗ ᴗ – ᴗ – or – ᴗ ᴗ – × – in aeolic

B = – × – ᴗ ᴗ – in aeolic

— = (when different symbols appear above and below) rhythmically ambiguous sequence

ˆ, ˆˆ = terminal or initial shortening by, respectively, one or two quantities of the sequence designated by the letter symbol immediately preceding or following

= = strophic response between the sequences printed or identified by symbols or line numbers in what immediately precedes or follows

+ = boundary between rhythmically discontinuous portions of a poem or stanza

⦙ = boundary between discrete, isolable units (whether metra or cola)

Superscripts and subscripts used simultaneously may indicate two sequences to both of which a given observation in the text applies.

# PART ONE: BASIC FORMS OF EPIPLOKE

# CHAPTER ONE: COLON, METRON, EPIPLOKE

Metricians' quarrels, like the study of Greek metrics itself, have displayed a remarkable constancy over the past two thousand years. "Metrists" and "colometrists" continue to dispute the field between them, very much as in the days of Hephaestion and Terentianus Maurus. For the former, the metron was and remains the minimal structural element in all Greek poetry. The latter tend (and tended) to confine such analyses to the familiar dactyls, anapests, trochees and iambs of verse composed for recitation rather than singing. Sung verse, on the other hand, is/was in their view a collection of poetic "limbs" or cola rather than metra: rhythmical phrases which are usually longer than metra and which, unlike metra, need not be of the same length and character to appear in the same passage. Cola articulate the larger entities in which they occur; they do not always measure them out into equal or equivalent parts.

Ancient metrists worked from a list of nine or ten trisyllabic or tetrasyllabic "prototypes," convinced that one or another of these, with or without equivalent variants, would account for even the most recalcitrant of verse forms. They thus saw the asclepiad as a succession of three "antispastic" metra ($\cup--\cup$), the first allowing certain substitutions (indicated by parentheses below) and the last replaced by an "equivalent" $\cup-\cup-$:

$$(\bar{\cup} \quad \overset{\times}{\underline{}}) \; - \; \cup \; \mid \; \cup \; - \qquad - \; \cup \; \mid \; \cup \; - \; \cup \; -$$
$$\text{Mae ce nas a} \quad \text{ta vis} \quad \text{e di} \quad \text{te re gi bus}$$

($\mid$ indicates division between metra or cola. For this and the other symbols used here and in what follows, see Introductory Note).

Ancient colometrists viewed the asclepiad in quite different fashion, as a combination of two cola identical to those which compose the pentameter of the elegiac couplet, but with $-\times$ or $\cup-$ substituted for $-\cup\cup$ at the start of the first, and $\cup-$ for $\cup\cup-$ at the end of the second:

$$\text{pentameter:} \quad - \; \cup \; \cup \; - \; \cup \; \cup \; - \; \mid \; - \; \cup \; \cup \; - \; \cup \; \cup \; -$$
$$\text{asclepiad:} \quad \overset{\cup}{\underline{}} \; \bar{\times} \quad - \; \cup \; \cup \; - \; \mid \; - \; \cup \; \cup \; - \; \cup \quad -$$

The two halves of the pentameter were in turn regarded as derived from the penthemimeral segment of the hexameter—hence the name "derivationist" often applied to this sort of analysis, which sought to trace all cola back to the segments of hexameter and iambic trimeter bounded by the beginning or end of a verse and one of its regular caesurae or diaereses.

Analogues to both analyses of the asclepiad have their contemporary defenders, although the colometry of the moderns prefers in general to trace cola back to some hypothetical syllable- or accent-counting ancestor of pre-Greek times rather than to trimeter or hexameter; and though modern "metrometry" at its most original and characteristic conceives of the metron as a musical bar, identifiable by the number of beats it contains rather than the presence of a particular sequence of long and short quantities.

If the two types of analysis have persisted, side by side, virtually unchanged, for over two thousand years, one of the reasons is surely that they reflect essentially identical approaches to their subject. Both conceive Greek verse as a mosaic of discrete pieces, each one maintaining its separate identity, character and coloration through all the combinations in which it appears. It makes little difference whether these pieces are metra set out in even rows, or cola thrown together in less regular, more heterogeneous fashion. The basic rhythm component is the isolable unit, whatever name one chooses to give it.

Widespread and persistent as this shared conception continues to be, it is, arguably, not the best way of looking at the rhythms of Greek poetry, and certainly not the only way. A possible alternative is attested, at least in rudimentary form, as early as the first century A.D., in the work of the metrician Heliodorus, and may well be considerably older. It will be presented in the pages which follow, together with a summary account of the fairly large body of evidence suggesting that it is superior, for large areas of Greek poetry, to its metrist/colometrist competitor. Later chapters deal in greater detail with the evidence as it pertains to particular rhythmical techniques and genres (Part One) and particular authors and periods (Part Two).

Heliodorus—or the metrician from whom his views derive—takes as his starting point the observation that certain rhythmical types stand in a particularly close relationship to each other, sufficiently close to suggest that they are not types, but sub-types. To isolate and identify a fundamental rhythmical genus (*anōtaton genos*: Heph 257.6–7) one must learn to regard related species as constituent parts of larger wholes. In each instance the related species are those which may, in theory, be generated from each other by transferring a long or short from one end of a foot or metron, or foot or metron series, to the other. Thus, to name the most frequently encountered examples, such transfers will convert a dactylic metron ($-\cup\cup$) or metron series into an anapestic foot ($\cup\cup-$) or series, an iambic metron ($\times-\cup-$) or series into trochaic ($-\cup-\times$) and choriambic ($-\cup\cup-$) into ionic ($\cup\cup--$):

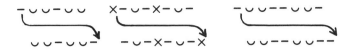

Pure ionic and choriambic are both relatively rare, but the relationship remains even in the more frequently encountered compounds which either may form with iambic or trochaic. Just as the "pure" choriambic dimeter $(- \cup \cup -- \cup \cup -)$ may become ionic $(\cup \cup -- \cup \cup --)$ by transfer of a long quantity from one end to the other, so the "mixed" iambo-choriambic sequence $- \cup \cup - \times - \cup -$ becomes, by the same transfer, a mixed ionic form, the so-called "anaclastic" dimeter or "anacreontic":

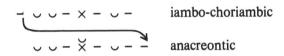

iambo-choriambic

anacreontic

In describing these relationships readers familiar with modern poetry would probably speak of falling and rising versions of identical rhythmical types. Ancient texts speak of an "interweaving" (*epiploke*) of two metrical types, or refer to the members of one metron pair (dactylic and anapestic for example) as parts of one "interweave," iambic and trochaic as parts of another, etc.

Surviving reports of the theory (confined to nomenclature and a few examples)[1] are meagre enough that it is difficult to know exactly what to make of it, and modern scholars have tended to make very little of it indeed. They take note of epiploke, if they take note at all, in passing—as an "occasional phenomenon in Greek metric" (*LMGD* 41; cf. Dale 49–50, 95) or as a purely theoretical way of relating metron types. Nor can we be sure that Heliodorus himself would have ever regarded it as much more than that. But whatever the "interweave" metaphor might have meant for him, it makes perfect sense in itself. Rhythm is a single fabric in which rise and fall are constantly being interwoven through a pattern of alternating or cyclical recurrence. A dactylic (iambic, choriambic) movement phase is beginning during the closing portion of each anapestic (trochaic, ionic) phase, and vice versa:

---

[1] The principal ancient discussions are *GL* 6.94.4–29 (containing the analysis of iambo-choriambic dimeter and anacreontic), and Heph 257.6–18. The term *epiploke* itself fluctuates slightly in meaning, referring sometimes to the process of interweaving or the state of interwovenness (*GL* 6.63.11–16), sometimes to the fabric that results (Heph *loc. cit.*), sometimes to the actual process of quantity transfer by which one sub-species may be generated from another (*GL* 6.75.3–4, 84.1–4, 122,27–32).

dactyl          dactyl          dactyl

anapest          anapest          anapest

Double shorts and single longs are here conceived as creating by their alternation a movement which can possess shape and form even when it is without internal demarcation—like the perpetual succession of good and evil in men's lives which the word *rythmos* designates when first attested (Archilochus 128.7). When the measuring stick of metre is applied to this temporal phenomenon, a rectilinear spatial analogue is introduced and, somewhat inappropriately, the idea of segmentation. For segmentation is the simplest means, given such a model, of indicating equivalence or correspondence between parts of a pattern. The interwoven segments of epiploke are one possible alternative to this model; another would be to represent rhythm, not as straight movement along a segmented line:

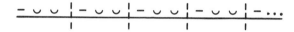

but as cyclical movement along an unsegmented closed curve—the circumference of a clock face, for example, marked with shorts at 12 and 4 and a long at 8. The dactylic day begins at eight and the anapestic one at noon, which does not prevent the morning, noon and night of the former and the noon, night and morning of the latter from being different, overlapping versions of the same diurnal rhythm—as is the much rarer night, morning and noon produced by "amphibrachic" ( ᵕ – ᵕ ) rising at 4 p.m.

By virtue of its ability to indicate the relationship of cycles and corresponding phases within cycles without creating demarcation or grouping, such a diagram may well be truer to the early Greek sense of time, whose passage was often felt as a non-linear, periodic phenomenon, like the procession of seasons and stars by which it was measured.[2] Given, however, the incorrigibly rectilinear format of ancient and modern writing, the interwoven or interlocking segments of epiploke are probably as practical a means as any of suggesting the phenomenon of undemarcated recurrence:

---

[2] Cf. F. M. Cornford, *The Unwritten Philosophy* (Cambridge 1953) 4–5.

iambo-choriambic     iambo-choriambic

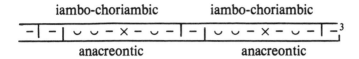

anacreontic          anacreontic

or, when simple identification of a type is involved:

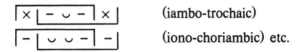     (iambo-trochaic)

(iono-choriambic) etc.

The labeled segments must, of course, be understood as indicating a potential rather than an actual way of organizing the rhythmical line, just as the unbroken clock circumference indicated the absence of any single uniform type of demarcation rather than the absence of demarcation altogether. Word end recurring at intervals of eight quantities creates a series of verbal demarcations that make Arist. *Eq.* 551 (ἵππι' ἄναξ Πόσειδον . . . = 581 (Ὦ πολιοῦχε Παλλάς . . .) ff. unambiguously iambo-choriambic in its strophe and, almost as unambiguously, anacreontic in its antistrophe:

| ὦ χαλκοκρότων ἵππων κτύπος | καὶ χρεμετισμὸς ἀνδάνει | καὶ κυανεμβόλοι θοαὶ | μισθοφόροι τριήρεις |
|---|---|---|---|
| 551–55 | | | |
| – – – ∪ ∪ –    ×–    ∪ – | – ∪ ∪ –   ×–    ∪ – | – ∪ ∪ – × – ∪ – | – ∪ ∪ – ∪ – – |
| 581–85 | | | |
| ὦ τῆς ἱερωτάτης | ἀπασῶν | πολέμῳ τε καὶ ποιηταῖς δυνάμει | θ' ὑπερφερούσης μεδέουσα |
| | | | χώρας |

It is only in the anticipated or remembered texture of the poet's entire song that the two rhythms are likely to remain interwoven—as closely as are Pallas and Poseidon in the life of the city he celebrates.

For metrists and colometrists, of course, Aristophanes' rhythm must be either iambo-choriambic or anacreontic, not both; and this leads to a dilemma: one or the other set of demarcations must be selected as basic—a series of colon or metron diaereses (divisions) separating rhythmical units—and the other dismissed as comprising only colon or metron caesurae (cuts) within units.[4] Epiploke provides the simplest and most

[3] For a similar means of designating rhythmical relationships in modern music, see G. W. Cooper and L. B. Meyer, *The Rhythmic Structure of Music* (Chicago 1960) 6–7 and *passim*.

[4] For this extension of the notion of caesura from metra to cola, see the first edition of *LMGD* (Cambridge 1949) 59, with n. 2. The phenomenon is variously designated "overlap" (J. D. Denniston, "Greek Lyric Metre: Some Main Problems," *ProcClassAss* 42 [1945] 11–19), "Wortübergreifen" (Kraus 27), "colon-continuum" (Korzeniewski 9) and "dovetailing" (Maas 59). Cf. Pohlsander 147–56 and L. E. Rossi's review of Korzeniewski

natural way of avoiding the dilemma in passages of this sort, and as such it deserves a place in any discussion of the rhythmical procedures used in Greek poetry. The essential question to be posed is not whether it occurs, but how often, or—equally important—how far below the surface of any rhythmical utterance does the multiple potentiality represented by epiploke lie? Is it present—when present—at the level of specific verse design—hexameter, sapphic strophe, the rhythm of a given Pindaric ode—to be actualized in different ways in the particular lines, stanzas or triads that are instances of the design.[5] Or is it present merely in the overall rhythmical system of Greek—as a set of potentialities only one of which, as a rule, is used by poets when they produce a specific verse form from that system? Is epiploke a property of rhythmical discourse at the level of *parole*, or merely at that of *langue*?

Like all dead languages, Greek rhythmical idiom is more extensively understood at the level of *langue* than of *parole*, and it is here that the investigation will begin, leaving *parole* for the concluding section of the chapter and the detailed studies of specific topics and periods which follow.

## i. The Greek rhythmical system

All the basic units which Greek poets employ regularly and in homogeneous repetition to form a single independent movement such as the stanza or, in stichic verse, the repeated line contain, at most, eight and, at least, three quantities. Longer sequences are always analyzable as compounds of simpler types, and no two-quantity sequence ever serves as the basis for an entire movement. There is a single five-quantity or "pentadic" unit (the dochmiac: $\times--\times-$) and, except for sporadic experiments (below, 83), a single hexadic unit (the dipodic anapest $\smile\smile^{(\simeq)}\smile\smile^{(\simeq)}$ , distinguished from the shorter $\smile\smile^{)}-$ by the resolvability of its long quantities, greater frequency of contraction, and a tendency to be preceded and followed immediately by word end). Rhythmical selection seems to have been arbitrary here; elsewhere, however, there is evidence that it was not.

For every three-, four-, seven- or eight-quantity sequence attested there is another linked to it in "Heliodoran" fashion; but no two such pairs are ever parts of the same cycle. And the rhythms thus represented by a single pair apiece comprise almost all the ways of arranging three,

---

(*RFIC* 97 [1969] 318).

[5] The verse design-verse instance distinction is that drawn by R. Jakobson; see "Linguistics and Poetics" (in T. A. Sebeok, ed., *Style in Language* (Cambridge, Mass. 1960) 364–66.

four, seven or eight quantities into a cyclically recurring pattern that are possible without violating certain basic rules of Greek versification. Those rules call for long quantities which always appear singly or in pairs and alternate with double shorts or single "non-long" quantities (⌣̅), whether short or anceps.[6] (The short-anceps contrast is less fundamental than the others in that no two cola or metra are ever distinguished from each other solely by the fact that one has a short at a position where the other has an anceps. Non-longs usually appear as shorts when in a penultimate or antepenultimate position, otherwise as anceps).

Two three-quantity cycles are possible without violating these rules. One of them is represented by Heliodorus's dactyls and anapests, the other by additional sub-types not mentioned by him but interrelated in the same way:

$$1) \ldots \cup \overline{- \underline{\cup \ \cup} -} \ \cup \ \cup \ - \ \cup \ \cup \ - \ \cup \ldots$$

with *dactyl* labelling the first unit and *anapest* the one below.

$$2) \ldots - - \ \aleph \ - \overline{- \underline{\cup} - -} \ \aleph \ - - \ \aleph \ldots$$

with *cretic* labelling the overlined unit and *bacchius* the one below.

Alongside these "triadic" cycles,[7] there are two possible "tetradic" ones, each of them represented by one of Heliodorus's pairs:

$$3) \ldots \aleph \ - \overline{\times \underline{- \cup -} \times} \ - \ \aleph \ - \ \aleph \ - \ldots$$

with *iambic* labelling the overlined unit and *trochaic* the one below.

[6] For similar accounts of these basic "rules," see West 18–19 and Dale 49–51. In the notation (*ibid.*, 63; *LMGD* 117) which accompanies Dale's system, double short is, in effect, designated by d, single short by s, anceps by ⌣̲ or s̄ , double long by | between instances of d and/or s̄), and single long by the absence of | before or after d or s̄). Initial ∪– and ∪∪– must accordingly be distinguished from –∪– and –∪∪– by carets (s = –∪–, ˆs = ∪–, d = –∪∪–, ˆd = ∪∪–). The existence of initial and terminal double long is not allowed for—an arbitrary decision—as is the assumption that the first quantity in a pair of longs must always conclude a rhythmical unit. But the system has the great merit of calling attention to what seem to have been fairly strict limits on the store of rhythmical "raw materials" available to the Greek poet.

[7] Epiplokai are here classified by reference to the number of quantities—three, four, seven or eight—in the recurring cycles which compose them, not, as in Heliodorus, the number of sub-types recognized within a given genus (dactylic and anapestic, or iambic and trochaic, in the two "dyadic" epiplokai; choriambic, "antispastic" and "major" and "minor" ionic [text, 17] in the one "tetradic" epiploke).

choriambic

4) ... ∪ - ‾ ∪ ∪ ‾ - ∪ ∪ - - ∪ ...

ionic

All but one of the possible octadic types are represented:

iambo-choriambic

5) ... 𐑒 - ‾ ∪ ∪ - × - ∪ ‾ - ∪ ∪ - 𐑒 - ∪ - - ∪ ∪ ...

anacreontic

6) ... ∪ - ‾ ∪ ∪ - - ∪ ∪ ‾ - ∪ ∪ - - ∪ ∪ - - ∪ ∪ ...

7) ... 𐑒 - x - ∪ - x - ∪ - x - 𐑒 - 𐑒 - 𐑒 - 𐑒 - 𐑒 ...

8) ... ∪ - x - ∪ ∪ - ∪ ∪ - x - ∪ ∪ - ∪ ∪ - 𐑒 - ∪ ...

9) ... 𐑒 - ‾ x - ∪ ∪ - ∪ - - 𐑒 - ∪ ∪ - 𐑒 - - 𐑒 - ...

10) ... ∪ - ‾ x - x - ∪ ∪ - - 𐑒 - 𐑒 - ∪ ∪ - - 𐑒 ...

11) ... 𐑒 - - 𐑒 - - 𐑒 - 𐑒 - - 𐑒 - - 𐑒 - 𐑒 - - ...

(6) and (7) are simply doublings of the tetradic pairs ‾ ∪ ∪ - - and x - ∪ - x. (8) is represented by two sequences to which the name prosodiac is often given in ancient sources:[8] cf. the triple - ∪ ∪ - ∪ ∪ - × of A. *Ag.* 720–22 = 730–32:

ἐν βιότου προτελείοις    - ∪ ∪ - ∪ ∪ - ×
ἄμερον εὐφιλόπαιδα    - ∪ ∪ - ∪ ∪ - ×
καὶ γεραροῖς ἐπίχαρτον    - ∪ ∪ - ∪ ∪ - ×

or the double × - ∪ ∪ - ∪ ∪ - of Pindar's 12th *Pythian*:

αἰτέω σε φιλάγλαε, καλλίστα βροτεᾶν πολίων    × - ∪ ∪ - ∪ ∪ - × - ∪ ∪ - ∪ ∪ -

‾ x - ∪ ∪ - ∪ - - (9) is a pair consisting of the most frequently attested forms of two aeolic cola, so called because first attested in the aeolic dialect poems of Sappho and Alcaeus. They are the glyconic (- × - ∪ ∪ - ∪ -) and x - ∪ ∪ - ∪ - -, the variously named "paraglyconeus" (Koster 233–34), "choriambic enoplian" (*LMGD* 136) or

---

[8] Cf., for example, the metrical scholia to Pind. *I I* (p. 158.7 and 15 Irigoin). *Enoplios*, attested as a rhythmical term at Ar. *Nub.* 651 (text, 10, with n. 12), has a better claim to being the earliest name for such sequences; but it has been taken over by modern scholars to designate such a variety of forms that a less ambiguous piece of ancient nomenclature is preferable here.

"Hagesichorean" (West 30). $\overline{\text{–×–×– ◡◡ – –}}$ (10) comprises the so-called choriambic dimeter (–×–×– ◡◡ –) and the nameless ×–×– ◡◡ – – (found, for example, at E. *HF* 795–96 = 812–13), two additional aeolic types, both of which may appear in strophic responsion with the corresponding segments of (9).

Heptadic cycles are less well represented:

12)   – ଃ – $\overline{\text{× – ◡◡ – ◡ – ×}}$ – ◡◡ – ଃ – ଃ –
13)   ◡ ◡ – – ◡◡ – ◡◡ – – ◡◡ – ◡◡ –
14)   – ଃ – – ଃ – ଃ – ଃ – – ଃ – ଃ – ଃ – – ଃ
15)   – ଃ – – ◡◡ – – ଃ – – ◡◡ – – ଃ – – ◡

×– ◡◡ – ◡ – is the familiar telesillean of Greek drama, – ◡ ◡ – ◡ – × the sequence labeled in certain contexts "aristophaneus." Like (9) they are first attested in Sappho and Alcaeus (cf., for the latter, the repeated – ◡ ◡ – ◡ – × – ◡◡ – ◡ – × of Sappho 112). They may be called "heptadic aeolic" to distinguish them from the two octadic types (9 and 10).

Plausible reasons can be given for the avoidance of the four possible forms (11, 13–15) which are not attested as the basis of continuous, independent rhythmical movements. 11 and 15 may well have been felt as too irregular: compounds of shorter rhythms of unequal length:

$$\overset{\text{cretic} \quad \text{dochmiac}}{11) \ldots ଃ – – ଃ – \overline{\text{– ◡ –}} \; \overline{\text{◡ – – ◡ – – ◡ –}} \; ଃ – – \ldots}$$
$$\underset{\text{bacchiac} \quad \text{dochmiac}}{}$$

$$\overset{\text{choriambic} \quad \text{cretic}}{15) \ldots – ଃ – \overline{\text{– ◡ ◡ – –}} \; \overline{\text{◡ – –}} \; ◡ ◡ – – ଃ – – ◡ \ldots}$$
$$\underset{\text{ionic} \quad \text{bacchiac}}{}$$

and 13 and 14 as too jerky and abrupt, each one a succession of discontinuous segments composed from a single such rhythm:

13)   . . . ◡ ◡ – (◡ ◡) – ◡ ◡ – ◡ ◡ – (◡ ◡) – ◡ ◡ – ◡ ◡ . . .
          (dactylo-anapestic)
14)   . . . – ◡ – (×) – ◡ – × – ◡ – (×) – ◡ – × – ◡ – (×) –
          (iambo-trochaic)[9]

---

[9] Such an analysis—or, alternatively, interpretation as syncopated versions of the octadic ×– ◡ – ×– ◡ – × or ×– ◡◡ – ◡◡ – × (prosodiac)—is the one usually suggested by the contexts which show consecutive instances of – ◡ ◡ – ◡◡ – or – ◡ – × – ◡ – (cf., for example, the Aeschylean passages discussed in the text [161–62] or the elegiac couplet, where the two

The whole "system" may be the result of accident, but it is rather more likely to reflect, to some degree, the work of design, operating over the course of time to utilize fully a set of possibilities within which the fundamental rhythmical category was the cycle or epiploke, not the discrete metrical or colometric unit. The process was complete by, at the latest, the early fifth century. (The last of the forms to be attested [bacchiac, choriambic and aeolic $-\mathrm{x}-\mathrm{x}-\cup\cup--$] are all found in Anacreon or Pindar). But some of the development must postdate the early years of the sixth century, when Lesbian poets were still using, instead of (9), a form $(\overline{\mathrm{x}\mathrm{x}}-\cup\cup-\cup-\mathrm{x})$ which contained the prohibited succession of two non-long quantities. The one major irregularity of the system, the occasional presence (in post-Lesbian verse) of $\mathrm{x}-$ rather than $-\mathrm{x}$ as a version of this "aeolic base" in both $(\overline{\mathrm{x}\mathrm{x}})-\cup\cup-\cup--$ (9) and $(\overline{\mathrm{x}\mathrm{x}})-\mathrm{x}-\overline{\cup\cup--}$ (10), may reflect the lingering influence of an earlier manner.

Whatever its origin, the system corresponds more closely than any based on metra or cola to the earliest attested stratum in Greek rhythmical terminology—i.e., to that present in pre-Hellenistic texts or in the nomenclature used by the one school of later theorists (the *rhythmikoi* or *mousikoi*) which draws on the work of pre-Hellenistic musicologists (Aristoxenus in the fourth century and, possibly, Damon in the fifth). With the exception of *trochaios* (Plato, *Rep.* 3.400b, Arist. *Rhet.* 3.8 1408b36) and, possibly, *krêtikon* at Cratinus 237, no term from this stratum refers to one member of a pair of sub-types in contradistinction to the other. The *iamboi* or *iambeia* of Aristotle include both iambic and trochaic,[10] and his paeon ($-\cup\cup\cup$ or $\cup\cup\cup-$; cf. *Rhet.* 3.8 1409a12–16) is similarly inclusive of both bacchiac $\cup\,\overset{=}{\cup}-$ and cretic $-\,\cup\,\overset{=}{\cup}$ or $\overset{=}{\cup}\,\cup\,-$. The same applies to Plato's *daktylos* (*Rep.* 3.400b), which is defined only by reference to the equality of its "up" ($\cup\cup$) and "down" ($-$) parts and so, presumably, either $-\cup\cup$ or $\cup\cup-$;[11] and both $-\cup\cup-\cup\cup-\mathrm{x}$ and $\mathrm{x}-\cup\cup-\cup\cup-$ are instances of the *rhythmos kat'enoplion* first mentioned at Ar. *Nub.* 650–51.[12] Finally, *bakcheios* seems to have been the name used

---

instances of $-\cup\cup-\cup\cup-$ that compose the pentameter are most naturally seen as disconnected segments—*hemiepe*—taken from the preceding hexameter).

[10] On the meaning of these and related terms in early contexts, see K. J. Dover, "The Poetry of Archilochus," *Entretiens Hardt* 10 (1963) 186–87.

[11] The *anapaistoi* of Ar. *Eq.* 504 and *Pax* 735 are not an alternate way of designating $\cup\cup-$ which distinguishes it from $-\cup\cup$ but, presumably, a reference to the totally different, hexadic form (text, 6).

[12] $\mathrm{x}-\cup\cup-\cup\cup-$ is the form designated by most later references (e.g. the scholia to Ar. *Nub.* 651 and Bacchius p. 316.6–7 von Jan), but Aristophanes seems to have $-\cup\cup-\cup\cup-\mathrm{x}$ in mind as well. Strepsiades is to learn from Socrates the art of distinguishing rhythms *kata daktylon* from those *kat'enoplion*—i.e. dactylo-anapestic from a compound form (the *enoplios*

by the *rhythmikoi* for a class of rhythm which included ionic, choriambic and octadic aeolic (cf. *GL* 6.93.23, 90.26, 127.25–27 and 149.30–35; Bacchius 101 p. 316.1–2 von Jan; AQ 1.16 p. 36.6–24). The inclusiveness of this term, as well as the absence of any special designation for heptadic aeolic, suggests a late fifth-century origin for most of the nomenclature. Iono-choriambic was by then felt as sufficiently close to octadic aeolic to permit occasional strophic responsion (E. *Su.* 1000 = 1023, *Or.* 813 = 824; Ar. *Vesp.* 531 = 636) between ⅹ– ◡ – – ◡ ◡ – or – ◡ ◡ – ⅹ– ◡ – and – ⅹ– ◡ ◡ – ◡ – or – ⅹ– ⅹ– ◡ ◡ –; and heptadic aeolic had become quite rare, virtually confined in the new style of Euripides to prosodiac contexts and perhaps not clearly distinguished from prosodiac.

Not all of these identifications are certain; and even if they were, it would not necessarily follow that the users of a given term would have regarded the different sequences it designated as linked by epiploke.[13] But the nomenclature does suggest that, for Greeks at a time when the composition of lyric verse was still part of a living tradition, rhythmical typology possessed the underlying simplicity of the system set forth above, not the complexity of later metrist and colometrist handbooks, ancient or modern.

To the evidence drawn from the internal structure and distribution of rhythmical sub-types one should add that from the norms that govern combination and modulation. Passage from one member of a pair to the other is common, so long as there is no break in the epiploke to which they belong:

|  | bacchiac |
|---|---|
| τίνα θεόν, τίν' ἤρωα, τίνα δ'ἄνδρα κελαδήσομεν; | ◡ ͌͌ – ◡ – – ◡ ͌͌ – ◡ ͌͌ – ◡ – |
| —Pind. *O2s2* | cretic |

---

*synthetos* of Damon: cf. Plato, *Rep.* 3.400b) in which what might be mistaken for regularly recurring contraction creates apparent tripodies:

‖– ◡ ◡ – ◡ ◡ – x̅ ‖ – ◡ ◡ – ◡ ◡ – x̅ ‖ – ◡ ◡ – ◡ ◡ – x̅ ‖ – ◡ ◡ – . . .

(so Gentili 55–56; cf. later descriptions of the hexameter of the form – ◡ ◡ – ◡ ◡ – ◡◡̅ ◡ ◡ – ◡ ◡ – ◡◡̅ as *katenoplion* [Heph 340.14–15], or composed of two *periodoi dōdecasēmoi* [GL 6.73.23–34]—i.e., two units each of which, like the enoplion – ◡ ◡ – ◡ ◡ –x̅, is equivalent in time value to twelve short syllables).

[13] The various types of paeonic and "bacchiac" rhythm may, for example, have been felt as composed of feet of equal duration—equivalent to five short syllables in the former instance (text 117, with n. 133) and to six or twelve in the latter, depending on whether the recurring unit was a four-quantity one (choriamb, ionic metron) or an eight-quantity one (glyconic, choriambic dimeter).

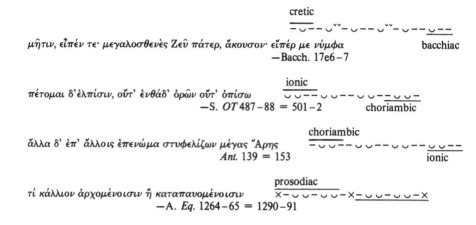

μῆτιν, εἶπέν τε· μεγαλοσθενὲς Ζεῦ πάτερ, ἄκουσον· εἴπέρ με νύμφα          bacchiac
—Bacch. 17e6–7

πέτομαι δ᾽ἐλπίσιν, οὔτ᾽ ἐνθάδ᾽ ὁρῶν οὔτ᾽ ὀπίσω
—S. OT 487–88 = 501–2          choriambic

ἄλλα δ᾽ ἐπ᾽ ἄλλοις ἐπενώμα στυφελίζων μέγας Ἄρης
Ant. 139 = 153          ionic

τί κάλλιον ἀρχομένοισιν ἢ καταπαυομένοισιν
—A. Eq. 1264–65 = 1290–91

A liberal use of the concepts of procephaly, acephaly, hypercatalexis and catalexis (i.e., initial or terminal lengthening or shortening, by one quantity, of metra or cola) will reduce such sequences to metric or colometric form: acephalous cretic or catalectic bacchiac pentameter in the first example, hypercatalectic choriambic or procephalic ionic tetrameter in the fourth etc. But the procedure is an artificial one, except where the forms are found in a single context alongside a preponderance of regular ones; and it fails to explain why preferred forms of "lengthening" and "shortening" are usually those which produce the other rhythm in a given pair of subtypes. "Acephalous" choriambic (i.e., ionic) and "hypercatalectic" iambic (i.e., trochaic) are quite common but "acephalous" ionic (‿−−...) and "hypercatalectic" trochaic (...−‿−×−) are isolated curiosities.

The only apparent exceptions are certain terminal rhythms that are not shortenings but clausular modifications of a normal sequence and appear in conjunction with both sub-types. Hence the terminal ‿−⁻ which, in iambo-trochaic, replaces the ×−‿ one would expect were the rhythm continuing in normal fashion at that point:

−‿−‿−⁻          "ithyphallic" (trochaic)
×−‿−‿−⁻          catalectic dimeter (iambic)

and the similar −‿‿−⁻ that appears as a terminal variant on aeolic −‿‿−‿, whichever sub-type of the rhythm is involved:

glyconic          glyconic          glyconic
−×−∪∪−∪− −×−∪∪−∪− −×−∪∪−∪− −×−∪∪−⁻          —Anacreon
                                                          13/358
×−∪∪−∪−− ×−∪∪−∪−− ×−∪∪−∪−− ×−∪∪−⁻
paraglyconeus     paraglyconeus     paraglyconeus

τίς σοί ποτε τᾶς ἀπλάτου
κοίτας ἔρος, ὦ ματαία,
σπεύσει θανάτου τελευτάν;          — E. *Med.* 151–54 =
μηδὲν τόδε λίσσου                   176–79


(The superscript ⁻ represents the length of the final syllable in ∪−⁻ or
−∪∪−⁻, long because of the ensuing prosodic demarcation at the end of
a movement [see Introductory Note], but supplying a quantity which
could have been felt as either long or anceps).

If it is impossible through use of catalexis and related concepts to determine the location of any single set of unit boundaries within such
sequences, it is equally impossible to locate a single point of transition
when one sub-type passes into a sub-type in a different epiploke. Such
transitions are very frequent between iambic or trochaic and all sub-types
except dactylic and anapestic, and the resulting "mixed" forms often
exhibit the same sort of pairing as do the pure ones. But the apparent
mechanism for modulation is the same in every instance: ∪−, or some
longer sequence shared between the two types of epiploke, seems to act as
a transitional segment:


iambic          cretic

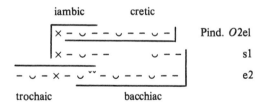

| | | |
|---|---|---|
|× − ∪ − − − ∪ − − ∪ − | | Pind. *O2*e1 |
|× − ∪ − − ∪ − − | | s1 |
|− ∪ − × − ∪ ⁓ − ∪ − − − ∪ − − | | e2 |

trochaic          bacchiac


iambic          heptadic aeolic ("telesillean"—i.e., with "telesillean" close)

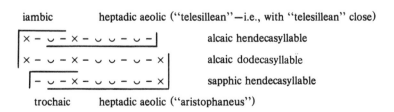

| | |
|---|---|
|× − ∪ − × − ∪ ∪ − ∪ − | | alcaic hendecasyllable |
|× − ∪ − × − ∪ ∪ − ∪ − × | | alcaic dodecasyllable |
|− ∪ − × − ∪ ∪ − ∪ − × | | sapphic hendecasyllable |

trochaic          heptadic aeolic ("aristophaneus")

iambic         octadic aeolic ("glyconic")

$$\boxed{\times - \cup - \times \times - \cup \cup - \cup -}$$ Alcaeus D12/70

$$|\times - \cup - - \times - \cup \cup - \cup - \times|$$ S. *Aj.* 601 = 614, 625 = 636

$$\boxed{- \cup - \times \times - \cup \cup - \cup - \times}$$ Sappho 123; cf. E. *Hcld.* 898–99 = 907–8

trochaic     octadic aeolic ("paraglyconeus")

Sequences such as ×– ‿ –: ‿ – – or ×– ‿ –: ‿ ‿ – – or – ‿ –×:–×– ‿ ‿ – ‿ –, in which it is possible to isolate a distinct iambic or trochaic opening followed by bacchiac, or ionic or glyconic, simply do not occur, or if they do, occur in contexts where other analyses are more likely.

Modulation may also lead into the iambo-trochaic clausula ‿ – ‾ mentioned earlier, but the transitional segment continues to be the same regardless of what sub-type of the other rhythm precedes:

|  |  | choriambic |  |
|---|---|---|---|
| δακρυόεσσαν τ'ἐφίλησεν αἰχμήν | | $\overline{- \cup \cup - - \cup \cup - \cup -^{\,-}}$ | —Anacreon 37/382 |
| | | iambo-trochaic | |
| προσέβα τόνδε πάγον πατρῷας | | $\underline{\cup \cup - -} \,\overline{\cup \cup - \cup -^{\,-}}$ | —A. *PV* 130 = 146 |
| | ionic | | |

"trochaeo-" prosodiac

οἷς γὰρ ἄν σεισθῇ θεόθεν δόμος ἄτας $\quad \boxed{- \cup - \times - \cup \cup - \cup \cup - \times}$
οὐδὲν ἐλλείπει γενεᾶς ἐπὶ πλῆθος ἕρπον $\quad | - \cup - \times - \cup \cup - \cup \cup - \cup -^{\,-}$
S. *Ant.* 583–85 = 595–96 $\qquad\qquad$ iambo-trochaic

"iambo-" prosodiac

σπουδαί τε δεσποίνας ὅ τε καιρὸς ἄπεισι τόλμας $\quad \overline{\times - \cup - \times - \cup \cup - \cup \cup - \cup -^{\,-}}$
E. *Ion* 1061–62 = 1048–49 $\qquad\qquad$ iambo-trochaic

"telesillean"

πλήρης μὲν ἐφαίνετ' ἀ σελάννα $\quad \overline{\times - \cup \cup - \underline{\cup - \cup -^{\,-}}}$
Sappho 154.1 $\qquad\qquad$ iambo-trochaic

"aristophaneus"

αἰέναον σέβοντι $\quad \boxed{- \cup \cup - \cup - \times}$
πατρὸς Ὀλυμπίοιο τιμάν $\quad | - \cup \cup - \underline{\cup - \cup -^{\,-}}$
Pind. *O* 14s12 $\qquad\qquad$ iambo-trochaic

"glyconic"

cui dono lepidum novum libellum? $\quad \overline{- \times - \cup \cup - \underline{\cup - \cup -^{\,-}}}$
Catullus 1.1 $\qquad\qquad$ iambo-trochaic

"paraglyconeus"

μὴ μή μ' ἀνέρῃ τίς εἰμι    $\boxed{\times - \cup \cup - \cup - \times}$

μηδ' ἐξετάσῃς πέρα ματεύων    $-- \cup \cup - \cup - \cup -^-$

S. OC 210-11                    iambo-trochaic

Parallel arrangement of long and short quantities has been the only cri-
terion offered up to this point for rhythmical identity, but other criteria
exist and reinforce the basic argument. They include corresponding rules
governing resolution, contraction and various forms of "free" responsion;
identical preferences, when such exist, as to where word end should be
avoided within a metron or colon; and identical restructions on the use of
suppressed or "syncopated" quantities. Such correspondences are especially well documented in iambic and trochaic; hence the decision of a
number of modern scholars to treat the caesurae, diaereses, bridges and
resolutions of iambic trimeter and trochaic tetrameter together—for
descriptive convenience if for no other reason.[14] Such divergences as do
exist, here and within other pairs of sub-types, tend to be confined to
specific genres or periods—the trimeter and tetrameter of Aristophanic
and post-Aristophanic comedy, for example,[15] or the iambo-trochaic and
iono-choriambic lyric of the Hellenistic age. All such exceptions are compatible with the assumption that when metron rather than epiploke is the
fundamental rhythmical category it is as the result of innovation at a relatively late stage in the development of the forms involved.

The coherence and correlations which point to the existence of epiploke
as a basic organizing principle on Greek verse are extensive enough to
serve as a point of departure for a detailed reexamination and reevaluation
of what is known about actual rhythmical practice. Convenience and
economy in the presentation of the simple facts of versification are likely
to be enhanced by such a reexamination; and if these were the only considerations one might well be tempted to proceed on the basis of a
revised, expanded version of the notational system proposed by Paul Maas
for the mixed prosodiac form known as dactylo-epitritic.[16] Designating the
$- \cup -$ segment of iambo-trochaic by e, $- \cup - \times - \cup -$ by E, and the
$- \cup \cup - \cup \cup -$ of prosodiac by D, and using these symbols in conjunction

---

[14] Cf., for example, the studies of the applicability of Porson's law to various verse types
cited and synthesized by Parker (1ff.), or the detailed examination of the norms of iambic
and trochaic verse (in their Plautine form) offered by C. Questa, *Introduzione alla metrica di
Plauto* (Bologna 1967) 187-206.
[15] The differences become minimal once again in Plautus and Terence, as well as in the
analyses of certain Latin grammarians (cf. *GL* 6.134.12-30).
[16] In his review (*BPhW* 1911, 328) of the first edition of Schroeder's *Euripidis cantica*. Cf.
*Greek Metre* 55.

with one for anceps, Maasian notation is able to show quite clearly the close relationship of all the most common pure and mixed prosodiac sequences:

| | | |
|---|---|---|
| $-\cup\cup-\cup\cup-\times$ | D $\times$ | (prosodiac) |
| $\times-\cup\cup-\cup\cup-$ | $\times$ D | (prosodiac) |
| $-\cup-\times-\cup\cup-\cup\cup-\times$ | e$\times$ D $\times$ | (cf. E. *Hec.* 906–7 = 915–16) |
| $\times-\cup-\times-\cup\cup-\cup\cup-$ | $\times$e$\times$ D | (iambelegus) |
| $-\cup\cup-\cup\cup-\times-\cup-\times$ | D $\times$ e $\times$ | (elegiambus) etc. |

Following a suggestion of A. M. Dale, one could use similar notation for heptadic aeolic:

| | |
|---|---|
| $-\cup\cup-\cup-\times$ (A) | (aristophaneus) |
| $\times-\cup\cup-\cup-$ (A) | (telesillean) |
| $-\cup-\times-\cup\cup-\cup-\times$ (A) | (sapphic hendecasyllable) |
| $\times-\cup-\times-\cup\cup-\cup-$ (A) | (alcaic hendecasyllable) |
| $\times-\cup-\times-\cup\cup-\cup-\times$ (A) | (alcaic dodecasyllable) etc.[17] |

An analogous $\times\times-\cup\cup-\cup-\times$ (A) along with $\times\times-\times-\cup\cup-\times$ (B) or the like could be used for octadic aeolic, $\times\times$ designating the aeolic base in both its Lesbian ($\times\times$) and later ($\underset{\times}{\times}\bar{\times}$) forms. The $-\cup\cup-$ of octadic aeolic is sometimes called a nucleus, and extending the term to the entire six-quantity sequence in which it appears would provide a convenient way of referring to all the rhythms under discussion here. Octadic aeolic shows the "double" base $\times\times$ either preceding or surrounding the nucleus; heptadic aeolic shows the "single" base $\times$ before or after the sequence, and similarly for the other basic forms:

---

[17] Dale's own notation (*LMGD* 177, Dale 93) is $\smile$ s $\smile$ ds for alcaic and s $\smile$ ds $\smile$ for sapphic (above, n. 6).

|  | base | nucleus | base |
|---|---|---|---|
| octadic aeolic | ×× | – ∪ ∪ – ∪ – (A) / – × – ∪ ∪ – (B) | or × |
| heptadic aeolic | × | – ∪ ∪ – ∪ – (A) | × |
| prosodiac | × | D | × |
| iono-choriambic | – | ∪ ∪ – | – |
| iambo-trochaic | × | – ∪ – | × |
| bacchio-cretic | – | ∪ – | – |
| dactylo-anapestic | – | ∪ ∪ | – |

Exclusive use of such a system, however, has the disadvantage of suggesting that the letter-designated segments are basic units, capable of combining with each other either directly or with an intervening ××, – or ×, the last of which is sometimes relegated to the subsidiary role of "link" anceps. In so far as units exist at all, however, they are two- and three-symbol combinations such as × D and ×– ∪ ∪ – ∪ –× (A). Like the colon and metron terminology which it seeks to supplant, Maasian notion continues to work with a rectilinear model and runs the same risk of introducing an inappropriately rigid segmentation. The cycle and interweave models are probably a better means of suggesting the nature of the rhythmical phenomenon involved, and are also better able to accommodate those cases (isolated in some genres, rather less isolated in others) where a rhythmical movement begins or ends within a "nuclear" segment. Here the Maasian system must resort to the same notions of acephaly and catalexis criticized earlier; with the other models one can simply specify an additional point at which the cycle may, atypically, begin, or add another strand to the epiploke. Ancient theory actually posited the existence of two such additional strands in one type of tetradic epiploke, related to ionic and choriambic in the same way as those are to each other:

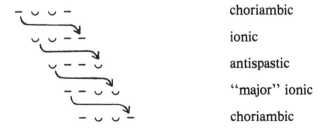

choriambic

ionic

antispastic

"major" ionic

choriambic

Only one significant modification of either model is called for—as a means of underlining the way compound rhythms seem to be just as resistant to segmentation as simple ones. If pure movement proceeds along a single circle, a compound movement such as mixed iono-choriambic or mixed aeolic is a clockwise back and forth between the circumferences of two tangent circles:

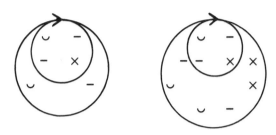

Passage from the iono-choriambic or aeolic outer circle to the iambotrochaic inner one is effected via the ∪ – common to both. There is no single point of transition just as there is no single point on the individual circles at which a given cycle ends and another begins. Such relationships are harder to diagram with the segments of epiploke, but their character can be suggested verbally. Extending Heliodorus's notion of what is in effect a "primary" and "total" epiploke involving every quantity in each of two interwoven series of metra, one can posit a "secondary" epiploke between epiplokai. This type is "partial" as well as secondary, involving only the ∪ – (or some longer segment) that is common to both rhythms:

| iambo-trochaic | | iambo-trochaic | |
|---|---|---|---|
| – × – ∪ – × – | ∪ – × – ∪  ∪ – ∪  ∪ – × – | ∪ – × – ∪ – × – | . . . etc. |
| | prosodiac | | |

The variety and frequency of such combinations (to be discussed in later chapters) is very great, but in every instance the modulatory mechanism involved is essentially the same.

## *ii. Verse design and verse instance*

When a specific verse design is generated from one or more of the rhythmical matrices just described, it is not inevitable that it retain the potentiality for different types of segmentation that was characteristic of basic categories in the parent system. The Hellenistic forms just mentioned are a sufficient proof of that. But it is equally clear that such retention can and does occur. The passage cited earlier from Aristophanes (above, 5) is one instance. E. *Hyps.* I.ii.11–15 = I.iii.11–15 is another.

Its pattern may be written as follows:

|-ᴗᴗ-ᴗᴗ-ₗᴗᴗ-ᴗᴗ'-ᴗᴗ-ᴗᴗ-ₗᴗᴗ-ᴗᴗ'-ₗᴗᴗ-ᴗᴗ-ₗᴗᴗ-ᴗᴗ'-ₗᴗᴗ-ᴗᴗ-ᴗᴗ-ᴗᴗ'-ₗᴗᴗ-ᴗᴗ-|

with the symbols ' and ₗ designating verbal demarcation confined to, respectively, strophe and antistrophe. S. *OT* 1088–97 = 1100–1109 is almost equally certain: mostly trochaic combined with prosodiac (or, in the last line, heptadic aeolic) in the strophe and iambic in the same combination in the antistrophe:

$$-\cup\underset{D}{\cup\cup-\cup\cup}-_{\lambda}\times^{\lambda}-\cup-\times$$
$$-\cup-\times-\cup-|-\cup-_{\lambda}\times^{\lambda}\underset{D}{-\cup\cup-\cup\cup}-_{\lambda}\times^{\lambda}-\cup-$$
$$-\cup-\times-\cup-\times|$$
$$-\cup-\times-\cup-_{\lambda}\times^{\lambda}\underset{D}{-\cup\cup-\cup\cup}-_{\lambda}\times^{\lambda}-\cup-\cup-$$
$$\times-\cup\underset{A}{\cup-\cup}-_{\lambda}\times^{\lambda}-\cup--^{18}$$

| | |
|---|---|
| οὐ τὸν Ὄλυμπον ἀπείρων | ὦ Κιθαιρών |
| οὐκ ἔσῃ τὰν αὔριον \| πανσέληνον | μὴ οὐ σ'ἐμὲ καὶ πατριώταν\|Οἰδίπου |
| καὶ τροφὸν καὶ ματέρ' αὔξειν \| | |
| καὶ χορεύεσθαι πρὸς ἡμῶν | ὡς ἐπίηρα φέροντα \|τοῖς ἐμοῖς τυράννοις· |
| ἰήιε Φοῖβε, σοὶ δὲ | ταῦτ' ἀρέστ' εἴη |

| | |
|---|---|
| Πανὸς ὀρεσσιβάτα πατρὸς πελασθεῖσ' | |
| ἤ σέ γ'εὐνάτειρά τις \| Λοξίου; | τῷ γὰρ πλάκες ἀγρόνομοι\|πᾶσαι φίλαι. |
| εἴθ' ὁ Κυλλάνας ἀνάσσων \| | |
| εἴθ' ὁ Βακχεῖος θεὸς | ναίων ἐπ' ἄκρων ὀρέων \|σ'εὕρημα δέξατ' ἐκ του |
| | νυμφᾶν Ἑλικωνίδων \|αἷς πλεῖστα συμπαίζει |

To these should probably be added two of the most common stichic forms. The dactylic opening of the hexameter is followed by anapestic demarcation at the penthemimeres, or "amphibrachic" demarcation (...ᴗ-ᴗ|ᴗ-ᴗ...) *kata triton trochaion*; and the trimeter has a comparable choice between the penthemimeral trochaic -ᴗ-×| or the contrasting -×-ᴗ| two quantities later.[19]

---

[18] On the rhythm ×-ᴗ--⁻, an equivalent to the ×-ᴗ-ᴗ-⁻ of the preceding line, see text, 41.

[19] Demarcation at the hephthemimeres or *kata triton trochaion* introduces, of course, a third preferred position for word end (over and above initial dactylic/iambic and medial anapestic/trochaic) for which there is no parallel in the lyric forms cited. Either the techniques of recited and sung verse diverge at this point, or one has here, as in the Lesbian aeolic base (text, 10), a relic of an earlier, freer manner. That the expected, anapestic alternative to dactylic demarcation in the hexameter is in some sense more "recent" than its "amphibrachic" competitor follows from the argument in Nagy (82–93) for the "non-inherited" character of epic formulae ending at the penthimemeral caesura with a third-person aorist or imperfect verb form; and both penthimemeral demarcations are, until the

The colometrist and metrist dilemma in such passages (above, 5) is usually solved by assuming that, in case of competing demarcations, only one (at most) represents diaeresis; and that this is the one which continues the rhythm with which a movement opens, or is found most frequently throughout the attested instances of a given design. These principles produce an analysis that is choriambic for the Aristophanes passage, dactylic for Euripides, and trochaic up until the final line of Sophocles, where there is a shift to iambic. There is, however, a certain arbitrariness about both criteria and, more important, a difficulty analogous to that raised earlier in connection with the notion of intial and terminal lengthening or shortening. Like those lengthenings and shortenings, the demarcations relegated to the status of caesura regularly produce sequences identical to the ones encountered in the other sub-type of the epiploke involved. And the usual reasons given for caesura—inability to achieve complete coincidence between rhythmical and verbal-syntactical boundaries, quest for variety, desire to weld the rhythmical units of a verse more closely together by not permitting them to be separated by word end—are not sufficient to explain why ionic $|\ \cup\cup-x-\cup--|$ is a more satisfactory alternative to $|-\cup\cup-x-\cup-|$ than, say, $|--\cup\cup-x-\cup|$, or why trochaic $-\cup-x|$ rather than the nameless $\cup-x-|$ is the preferred caesural rhythm in iambic.

Comparable problems arise even when it is different portions of a design rather than different instances of the design that display contrasting demarcation. The connection between the two situations is well illustrated by a series of passages closely allied in their rhythm to Ar. *Eq.* 551 = 581ff.:

1)          $-\cup\cup-x-\cup|--\cup\cup-x-\cup-'-_,\cup\cup-x-\cup-'-_,\cup\cup-x-\cup-$      $'-_,\cup\cup-\cup-$
                                                 Ar. *Eq.* 551 = 581ff.

2)          $-\ \cup\cup-x-\cup--\ |\cup\cup-x-\cup-$      $-\cup\cup-\cup-^-$
                                                  A. *Sup.* 562–64 = 571–73

3)          $-\ \cup\cup-x-\cup--\ |\cup\cup-x-\cup--$
                                                  Anacreon 53/398

4)          $-\ \cup\cup-x-\cup--\ |\cup\cup-x-\cup--|\cup\cup--\cup\cup-\cup-^-$
                                                  Anacreon 1/346.1

5)          $x-\cup--\cup\cup-x-\cup--$
                                                  A. *Pers.* 977 = 991

6)          $x-\cup--\cup\cup-x-\cup--$    $|\cup\cup-x-\cup-|$      $-\cup\cup-\cup-^-$
                                                ∼ *PV* 132–33 = 148–49

7)          $x-\cup--|\cup\cup-x-\cup--$   $|\cup\cup-x-\cup--|\cup\cup--\cup\cup-\cup-^-$
                                                  128–30 = 143–45

---

advent of Alexandrian archaism and eclecticism, the ones which poets increasingly favor (cf. the statistics in West 40, 82, 98, 153 and 159).

8)              - ⏑ ⏑ - x - ⏑ - - ⏑ ⏑ - | - ⏑ ⏑ - x - ⏑ -         - | ⏑ ⏑ - ⏑ - ‾

E. Rh. 360–62 = 370–72

9)        - ⏑ ⏑ - x - ⏑ - - | ⏑ ⏑ - x - ⏑ - '-ₗ⏑ ⏑ - x - ⏑ -      - | ⏑ ⏑ - ⏑ - ‾

S. Ph. 687–90 = 703–706

10)      - ⏑ ⏑ - x - ⏑ - - | ⏑ ⏑ - x - ⏑ - - | ⏑ ⏑ - x - ⏑ - - | ⏑ ⏑ (-)- ⏑ ⏑ - ⏑ - ‾

El.1066–69 = 1078–81

11)    x - ⏑ - - ⏑ ⏑ - x - ⏑ - - | ⏑ ⏑ - x - ⏑ - | - ⏑ ⏑ - x - ⏑ - -ₗ⏑' ⏑ - x - ⏑ - -ₗ⏑' ⏑ (-)- ⏑ ⏑ - ⏑ - ‾

1058–61 = 1070–73

12)        x - ⏑ - - ⏑ ⏑ - x - ⏑ - - |

⏑ ⏑ - - ⏑ ⏑ - - ⏑ ⏑    - - ⏑ ⏑ - x - ⏑ - - | ⏑ ⏑ - x - ⏑ - - | ⏑ ⏑ - x - ⏑ - - | ⏑ ⏑ - x - ⏑ - - |

⏑ ⏑ - x - ⏑ - - |

⏑ ⏑ - x - ⏑ - - |

A. PV 397–405 = 406–14

13)         x - ⏑ - - ⏑ ⏑ -      - |

           ⏑ ⏑ - x - ⏑ - - |

     ⏑ ⏑ - - ⏑ ⏑ - -    | ⏑ ⏑ - x - ⏑ - - |

⏑ ⏑ - - ⏑ ⏑ - | - ⏑ ⏑ - - ⏑ ⏑ - - ⏑ ⏑ -

A. Sept. 720–25 = 728–32

Analyzing these passages in terms of epiploke is fairly easy. The basic rhythm is iono-choriambic $\overline{- ⏑ ⏑ - x - ⏑ - -}$, usually terminally modified into - ⏑ ⏑ - ⏑ - ‾ (above, 14) or, adding a cycle of pure iono-choriambic, - ⏑ ⏑ - - ⏑ ⏑ - ⏑ - ‾. (10 and 11 show the same terminal rhythm with the apparent omission of one quantity: . . . ⏑ ⏑ (-)- ⏑ ⏑ - ⏑ - ‾). All movements begin with - ⏑ ⏑ -. . . or the x - ⏑ -. . . that appears four quantities further on (or back) in the epiploke. Internal demarcation, by contrast, is largely ionic, occasionally (1, 6, 8, 9, 11) replaced by, or responding with, choriambic or something rarer (the | - - ⏑ ⏑. . . of 1, or the | ⏑ - x - ⏑ - - ⏑ | of 11:

κηδομένους ἀφ' ὧν τε βλάστωσιν     - ⏑ ⏑ - x - ⏑ - - ⏑
ἀφ' ὧν τ' ὄνασιν εὕρωσι          ⏑ - x - ⏑ - - ⏑
τάδ' οὐκ ἐπ' ἴσας τελοῦμεν         ⏑ (-)- ⏑ ⏑ - ⏑ - ‾

(1060–62)

In colometric terms, however, most of the passages are problematic. The two main criteria for determining the character of a demarcation are in conflict: frequency of occurrence suggests that internal . . . x - ⏑ - - | ⏑ ⏑ -. . . is diaeresis; its relation to the initial iambic or choriambic of every movement suggests that it is caesura. Accepting the former alternative involves giving three different analyses to the sequence - ⏑ ⏑ -, depending on whether it opens a choriambic colon, is divided between two ionic cola, or contains the end of a "hypercatalectic" choriambic colon and the beginning of an ionic one. Accepting the latter leaves the reasons for the existence and positioning of caesura as obscure as they were when caesura stood in strophic response to diaeresis. And the way the

passages, when taken in conjunction with the – ∪ ∪ – × – ∪ – | – ∪ ∪ –
× – ∪ – | – ∪ ∪ – ∪ – ‾ of, say, Ar. *Nub.* 563–64 = 595–97, exhibit a gra-
dual transition from pure choriambic internal demarcation to the insistent,
repeated ionic of 12, naturally raises the question whether the ratio of
ionic and choriambic demarcation in such contexts is determined by basic
verse design at all. Were the genre more abundantly attested, it might be
evident that the choice between ionic and choriambic demarcation was
rather like that between long and short anceps. The fact that in certain
contexts and certain writers responsion between long and short anceps is
rare, or that one form is greatly preferred over the other does not establish either variety as the basic one or necessitate assigning passages which
contain one form to a different rhythm from passages which contain the
other. Whether the absence of demarcation in one of the two usual positions should be taken (as in 1 and 11 above) as an instance of irregular
demarcation, or simply as an absence of demarcation altogether,[20] is
difficult to decide with the limited evidence at our disposal. But the
matter is, for present purposes, of secondary importance.

Verse designs with shifting demarcation are not confined to mixed
iono-choriambic. They occur wherever the rhythmical system allows
epiploke—everywhere, that is, except in dochmiacs and dipodic anapests
(above, 6):

| | | | |
|---|---|---|---|
| ὡς ποιμὰν ἀγροβάτας | × – × –̅ᴮ ∪ ∪ – | | |
| ἀλλ' ἤ που πταίων ὑπ' ἀνάγκας | × × – × – ∪ ∪ – × | | |
| βοᾷ τηλωπὸν ἰωάν | × – × – ∪ ∪ – × | S. Ph. 205–7 = 214–16 |

| | | |
|---|---|---|
| ἤ Φρύγα καλλιπνόων | D | |
| αὐλῶν ἱερῶν βασιλῆα | × D × | |
| Λυδὸν ὃς ἄρμοσε πρῶτος | D × | |
| Δωρίδος ἀντίπαλον | D | |
| μούσας † νομοαιολον ὄρφνᾳ | × D × | |
| πνεύματος εὔπτερον αὔραν | D × | |
| ἀμφιπλέκων καλάμοις | D | Telestes 2/806 |

---

[20] The usual situation within many of the dactylo-epitritic sequences of Pindar: see L. E.
Rossi, "La metrica come disciplina filologica" *RFIC* 94 (1966) 195–99.

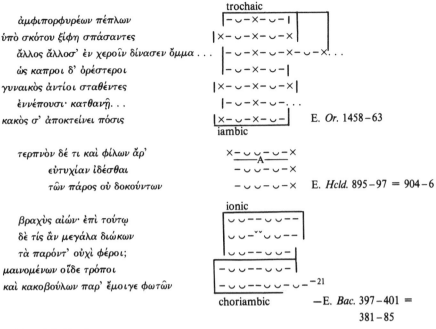

trochaic

ἀμφιπορφυρέων πέπλων

ὑπὸ σκότου ξίφη σπάσαντες

ἄλλος ἄλλοσ᾽ ἐν χεροῖν δίνασεν ὄμμα . . .

ὡς κάπροι δ᾽ ὀρέστεροι

γυναικὸς ἀντίοι σταθέντες

ἐννέπουσι· κατθανῇ. . .

κακὸς σ᾽ ἀποκτείνει πόσις          E. Or. 1458–63

iambic

τερπνὸν δέ τι καὶ φίλων ἄρ᾽

εὐτυχίαν ἰδέσθαι

τῶν πάρος οὐ δοκούντων          E. Hcld. 895–97 = 904–6

ionic

βραχὺς αἰών· ἐπὶ τούτῳ

δὲ τίς ἂν μεγάλα διώκων

τὰ παρόντ᾽ οὐχὶ φέροι;

μαινομένων οἵδε τρόποι

καὶ κακοβούλων παρ᾽ ἔμοιγε φωτῶν

choriambic          —E. Bac. 397–401 =
                         381–85

τοῦτ᾽ ἐκεῖν᾽· ἰώ, ξύνοικοι,

τάδε τέρα θεάσασθε· τὸν ἀλεκτρυόνα μου

συναρπάσασα φρούδη Γλύκη

cretic          bacchiac                                              cretic

iambo-trochaic                                          iambo-trochaic

—Ar. Ran. 1342–44

dactylic                    dactylic

ὑψηλῶν ὀρέων κορυφὰς

anapestic

ἐπὶ δενδροκόμους,

ἵνα τηλεφανεῖς σκοπιὰς ἀφορώμεθα          —Ar. Nub. 279–81[22]

The last passage was probably heard as an echo, with variation, of the pure dactylic that immediately precedes:

[21] Cf., earlier in the stanza, ⏑⏑−−⏑⏑−|−⏑⏑−|−⏑⏑−−⏑⏑−|−⏑⏑−−⏑⏑−− ⏑⏑−|−⏑⏑− (375–78 = 391–94) where all the verbal breaks indicated may not have the same demarcative function, but the shift from opening ionic to some sort of choriambic is clear.

[22] Demarcation following epi and hina (so most editors) would make the sequence uniformly dactylic, but at the price of a highly anomalous concentration of cola (two here and one in the antistrophe [arrêtôn hina] ) ending in prepositives.

ἀρθῶμεν φανεραὶ δροσερὰν φύσιν  – ‿‿– ᴗ ᴗ– ᴗ ᴗ– ᴗ ᴗ |– ‿‿– ‿‿|– ᴗ ᴗ– ᴗ ᴗ– ᴗ ᴗ– ᴗ ᴗ
  εὐάγητον,
    πατρὸς ἀπ᾽ Ὠκεανοῦ βαρυαχέος

Both echo and variation are underlined by the placing of punctuation, which coincides in the strophe (above) with the second of the two internal demarcations (whether dactylic or anapestic) in each sequence, and in the antistrophe with the first:

– ‿‿– ᴗ ᴗ– ᴗ ᴗ– ᴗ ᴗ |– ‿‿– ‿‿|– ᴗ ᴗ– ᴗ ᴗ– ᴗ ᴗ– ᴗ ᴗ
ἔλθωμεν λιπαρὰν χθόνα Παλλάδος,
    εὔανδρον γᾶν
      Κέκροπος ὀψόμενοι πολυήρατον
– ᴗ ᴗ– ‿‿– ᴗ ᴗ– | ᴗ ᴗ– ᴗ ᴗ– |ᶜ ᴗ– ᴗ ᴗ– ᴗ ᴗ– ᴗ ᴗ– ᴗ ᴗ
οὗ σέβας ἀρρήτων ἱερῶν,
    ἵνα μυστοκοδόκος
      δόμος ἐν τελεταῖς ἁγίαις ἀναδείκνυται
                                                        −299−304[23]

[23] Comparable passages (cf. *LMGD* 40−41) are often longer, though rarely with more than two demarcation shifts:

– ᴗ ᴗ– ᴗ ᴗ– ᴗ ᴗ– ᴗ ᴗ|– ᴗ ᴗ– ᴗ ᴗ– |ᴗ ᴗ– ᴗ ᴗ– |ᴗ ᴗ– ᴗ ᴗ– |
                      ᴗ ᴗ– ᴗ ᴗ– ᴗ ᴗ– ᴗ ᴗ– |ᴗ ᴗ– ᴗ ᴗ– ᴗ ᴗ– ᴗ ᴗ|– ᴗ ᴗ–
ᴗ ᴗ– ᴗ ᴗ– ᴗ ᴗ|– ᴗ ᴗ– ᴗ ᴗ

                                                        S. *OC* 229ff.

– ᴗ ᴗ– ᴗ ᴗ– |ᴗ ᴗ– ᴗ ᴗ– |ᴗ ᴗ– ᴗ ᴗ– |ᴗ ᴗ– ᴗ ᴗ–

                                                        E. *Ph.* 830−31

– ᴗ ᴗ– ᴗ ᴗ– |ᴗ ᴗ– ᴗ ᴗ– |ᴗ ᴗ– ᴗ ᴗ– ᴗ ᴗ– ᴗ ᴗ– |
                      ᴗ ᴗ– ᴗ ᴗ– ᴗ ᴗ– ᴗ ᴗ–

                                                        1488−91

– ‿‿– ᴗ ᴗ– ᴗ ᴗ– ᴗ ᴗ– |ᴗ ᴗ– ᴗ ᴗ– |(‿‿)– ᴗ ᴗ–

                                                        A. *Pers.* 882−84 = 891−93

ᴗ ᴗ– ᴗ ᴗ– ᴗ ᴗ– ‿‿|– ‿‿– ᴗ ᴗ– |ᴗ ᴗ– ᴗ ᴗ– ᴗ ᴗ– ᴗ ᴗ–

                                                        E. *Phaeth.* 83−85 = 91−93

– ‿‿– ‿‿– ‿‿– ‖ᴗ ᴗ– ‖ᴗ ᴗ– ‖‿‿– |ᴗ ᴗ– ᴗ ᴗ– |ᴗ ᴗ– ᴗ ᴗ– |ᴗ ᴗ– ᴗ ᴗ

                                                        Or. 1453−56

                      ᴗ ᴗ– ᴗ ᴗ– |ᴗ ᴗ– ᴗ ᴗ– ᴗ ᴗ– ‿‿|– ᴗ ᴗ– ‿‿|
                                                        1007−11
          – ᴗ ᴗ– ᴗ ᴗ– |          ᴗ ᴗ– ᴗ ᴗ– |ᴗ ᴗ– ᴗ ᴗ
                                              |– ᴗ ᴗ– ᴗ ᴗ– ᴗ ᴗ– ᴗ ᴗ

All such passages are characterized by highly regular sequences of longs and shorts in conjunction with varying patterns of verbal demarcation. When the latter sort of variety exists in conjunction with modulations at irregular intervals into different types of rhythm, the diaeresis-caesura dilemma is likely to be resolved in favor of the former, with the result that the third possibility represented by epiploke seems less attractive or necessary. In fr. 6 of the dithyrambist Telestes, for example,

| | | |
|---|---|---|
| πρῶτοι παρὰ κρατῆρας Ἑλλάνων ἐν αὐλοῖς | 1 | ×–∪–×–∪–×–∪–– |
| συνοπαδοὶ Πέλοπος Ματρὸς ὀρείας | 2 | ∪∪––∪∪––∪∪–× |
| Φρύγιον ἄεισαν νόμον. | 3 | ⁀∪–×–∪– |
| τοὶ δ' ὀξυφώνοις πηκτίδων ψαλμοῖς κρέκον | 4 | ×–∪–×–∪–×–∪– |
| Λύδιον ὕμνον. | 5 | –∪∪–– |

contrast is clearly intended as the Greek instrumentation of the first line gives way to the Asiatic song and performers of the second and third; and this gives some support to the highly heterogeneous analysis produced by positing consistent diaeresis:

| | | |
|---|---|---|
| 1 | ×–∪–×–∪–×–∪–× | iambic trimeter "hypercatalectic" |
| 2 | ∪∪––∪∪––∪∪–– | ionic trimeter |
| 3 | ⁀∪–×–∪– | "lecythion" (i.e., catalectic trochaic dimeter) |
| 4 | ×–∪–×–∪–×–∪– | iambic trimeter |
| 5 | –∪∪–⁀⁀ | "adonic" (i.e., dactylic dipody) |

To accept this analysis, however, is to ignore the possibility that lines 4–5 are identical to the opening seventeen quantities of 1–2 and that the final quantity of 2 may, in conjunction with what follows, be identical to the opening of 1 and 4:

| | |
|---|---|
| 2–3 | . . . ×|⁀⁀∪–×–∪– |
| 1,4 | ×–∪–×–∪–. . . |

If these parallels are considered significant, one may continue to prefer analysis by epiploke, as a means of accommodating diversity within a compound movement that persists unbroken from iambic through ionochoriambic (with ionic demarcation) back to iambic at the end of the third line, at which point—whether by way of continuation or the beginning of a new movement—the first seventeen quantities are repeated, now with

---

The three shifts in the last passage may have a special purpose: the subject of the chorus is the reversals in the history of the house of Atreus and their celestial counterparts.

iambo-choriambic demarcation instead of ionic.

One's final decision here will probably depend, to some extent, on the relative importance attached, in general, to two fundamentally different approaches to rhythmic analysis. For the metrist or colometrist, the whole character of a rhythmical design derives from the character of the separate phrases out of which, by a largely additive process, it is put together. Even in isolation each of these must strike the ear as possessing a certain formal identity, and in a poetic context the listener must be able to pick them out from amid structures of a different character. If caesura is used extensively, the process is further complicated by the failure of verbal and rhythmical structure to coincide, for then phrases must be identified against the competing background created by articulations of a totally different character. There is usually a limit in the proliferation of phrase types beyond which it is assumed that such contrapuntal structures are not allowed to go. But whether a lyric poet produces a profusion of clearly recognizable motifs, or makes more sparing use of motifs partially obscured by the interplay between verbal and rhythmical patterns, his repertory of phrases or motifs is what determines the basic character of his work.

The approach is, to use the vocabulary of contemporary analysis, an essentially "paradeigmatic" one. The metrist or colometrist concentrates on detaching individual sequences from their context, identifying them by reference to a basic model and establishing the range within which variation and contrapuntal interplay with patterns of a different character is possible without obscuring the connection of instance to paradigm. One thinks of Seidler's "classic" study of the dochmiac and its thirty-two varieties.

Epiploke's concerns are, by contrast, basically "syntagmatic": the rhythmical sequence as related to, and modified by, contiguous sequences in a particular environment. When separated from their surroundings by verbal demarcatton, such sequences may continue to be called cola; but in order to function structurally they do not need the same clear relationship to an identifiable model as do their homonymous counterparts in metric and colometric analysis. They exist in relation to each other as integrating segments of a single or compound epiploke. The latter does not embody a rival system of demarcation but is rather a means of locating and interrelating cola within the realm of rhythmical time in the same way as a scale locates and interrelates the intervals of a melody within the realm of musical pitch. It lends itself freely to whatever articulation is imposed upon it. At the same time, by virtue of being itself without internal demarcation it can serve to unify an entire context in which cola appear. Once impressed on the ear, it continues to create the expectation, as each new quantity is heard, that the next one in the series is going to follow, and this persists until modulation or the end of a movement. Epiploke is compatible with a capacity for long, sustained rhythmical lines that is, to a modern ear, at any rate, more characteristic of music than poetry; and given the importance of song, dance and instrumental accompaniment in the performance of Greek poetry, its presence there would not be surprising.

Metric and colometric composition, by contrast, suggest, not music, but the stanzaic or free-verse forms of Renaissance and post-Renaissance lyric, where the feeling for the identity and discreteness of rhythmical units is powerfully reinforced by their visual demarcation on the printed page, and where the visual lay-out of the page may well be an essential prerequisite for a reader's coping with rhythmical complexity and diversity. If "the great age of metrical variation in English poetry almost exactly coincides with the age of printing,"[24] it may be no accident that the age of ancient colometry coincides, almost as exactly, with the great age of Alexandrian editions of the Greek poets. The very word *kōlon* is first attested in a different context—as a designation for the rhetorical units of prose (Arist. *Rhet.* 3.9 1409b13, *Rhet. ad Alex.* 27 1435b40 and 28 1436a6).[25] Its application to the rhythmical units of lyric verse was, so far as we know, the work of Aristophanes of Byzantium (c. 250–180 B.C.), who was also the first to assign to each of those units its separate line of written text. And Aristophanes lived in a century whose most complex and original achievements in lyric rhythm were the pattern poems of Simmias (pp. 109ff. Powell), composed more for eye than for ear.

A view of the nature of Classical verse is not necessarily incorrect for being first attested in Aristophanes of Byzantium. But neither is it a view that deserves the virtual monopoly of metrical studies which it has enjoyed since first propounded. With its emphasis on rhythmical vocabulary at the expense of rhythmical syntax, it runs the risk of reducing the latter to a set of cliches, reusable in much the same way in all the contexts in which they appear. Such cliches certainly exist in Greek—to such an extent, in fact, that the entire history of Greek lyric can be most succinctly described as the abandonment of one set of cliches—those inherited from a pre- or proto-Greek period in the history of Indo-European verse—and their eventual replacement by another: the fossilized hendecasyllables and anacreontics, sapphics and alcaics, which were the final legacy of Greek lyric versification to the rhythmical repertory of the West. The new cliches were, however, developed in the course of a period of

---

[24] P. Fussell, Jr., *Poetic Metre and Poetic Form* (New York 1965) 136.

[25] The Peripatetic critic Demetrius, writing (if the early dating of *On Style* is accepted) in the second quarter of the third century, still seems to know only of metra: ὥσπερ ἡ ποίησις διαιρεῖται τοῖς μέτροις οἷον ... ἑξαμέτροις ἢ τοῖς ἄλλοις, οὕτω καὶ τὴν ἑρμηνείαν τὴν λογικὴν διαιρεῖ καὶ διακρίνει τὰ καλούμενα κῶλα (1).

intense expansion and system building on the basis of the old, a process which resulted in the creation—to a degree unparalleled before or since—of an entire rhythmical language within which the stereotyped rhythmical phrase plays a distinctly limited role. A thorough investigation of epiploke—one that seeks to determine not simply the usefulness of the concept, but the limits of its usefulness—will inevitably include a certain number of borderline cases; but it will be an investigation of what was most characteristic and original in the formal structure of Greek lyric during the period of its greatest brilliance.

# CHAPTER TWO: TETRADIC RHYTHM
## (IONO-CHORIAMBIC, IAMBO-TROCHAIC)

All passages composed in "tetradic" rhythm thus far considered, whether iambic, trochaic, ionic, choriambic or some compound form, bring into play one or more of the following techniques:

1) total epiploke (above, 18) of iambic with trochaic and of ionic with choriambic:

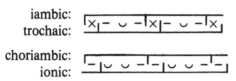

           iambic:
          trochaic:

       choriambic:
         ionic:

2) partial epiploke (*ibid.*) of iono-choriambic with iambo-trochaic (utilized in the frequently attested transitions from one to the other via the shared segment ‿ –:

     iambo-trochaic       iambo-trochaic
        × – ‿ – – ‿ ‿ – × – ‿ –
          iono-choriambic)

3) use of ‿ –‾ (above, 13–14), a clausular modification of iambo-trochaic ×– ‿, as one way of bringing a movement to a conclusion following the "nuclear" segment (above, 16–17) – ‿ – or ‿ ‿ –.

Three further techniques remain to be considered. They all operate in exactly the same way, no matter what sub-type of tetradic rhythm is involved:

i) Equivalence, and so the possibility of strophic responsion, between any two segments of tetradic rhythm whose patterns diverge for no more than the duration of a single cycle. (I.e., – ‿ ‿ –×– ‿ – may respond to – ‿ ‿ – – ‿ ‿ – or ×– ‿ –×– ‿ – but not to ×– ‿ – – ‿ ‿ –, etc.).

ii) Contraction and

iii) Syncopation. A single syllable sometimes appears in place of the two which supply the short quantity in the ‿ – segment of tetradic rhythm and the quantity preceding, or the long and the quantity following. The procedure is known as contraction ( $\smile\smile$ ) when both quantities are short; otherwise one speaks of the second of the two quantities as "syncopated."[26] It was probably supplied by a pause in the vocal line or by "protraction" of the syllable supplying the quantity which precedes. The sequences which result are the following (protracted syllables are written as ⌐, syncopated quantities—however supplied—as .):

| | | |
|---|---|---|
| x⁻.⁻x, | x – ◡ ⁻.,x⁻.⁻. | (iambo-trochaic) |
| – ◡◡ – –, | – ◡ ◡ ⁻. | (pure iono-choriambic) |
| – ◡⁻. ◡ ◡ –, | ◡ ◡ ⁻.⁻ ◡ – | (mixed iono-choriambic) |

All of these procedures have been noted at one time or another as characteristic of one or more sub-species of tetradic rhythm. The possibility of their applicability to all types has been ignored—largely, as I shall try to show, because of the application of metrist principles to texts which can be analyzed more simply and consistently as pieces of epiploke.

## i. Equivalence

"Choriambic" substitution in iambic and iambic substitution in choriambic are universally recognized rhythmical procedures—however much their frequency may vary from poem to poem and genre to genre: once every three lines in Anacreon 43/388, once every three or four thousand in the spoken trimeters of Greek drama.

The phenomenon is exactly paralleled in ionic and trochaic. Thus the mixed "dimeters" discussed in the preceding chapter (above, 3–5) yield the following examples:

"iambic" or "choriambic" substitution:

| | | | | |
|---|---|---|---|---|
| Ar. *Vesp.* 637 = 532 | x – ◡ – x – ◡ – | = | – ◡ ◡ – x – ◡ – | |
| 527 = 632 | | | – ◡ ◡ – x – ◡ – | = | – ◡ ◡ – – ◡ ◡ – |

---

[26] The inaccuracy of the musical term syncopation as applied to such phenomena has been pointed out by Rossi (above, [n. 4] 318); but the term is sanctioned by usage and readily understood as referring to what would properly be called hold or rest (presumably distinct in performance but not distinguishable in transmitted texts).

"ionic" and "trochaic" substitution:

Ar. *Th.* 111-12 =
116-17 = 123-24    – ⌣ – × – ⌣ – –    =  ⌣ ⌣ – × – ⌣ – –
*Ran.* 327 = 343         ⌣ ⌣ – × – ⌣ – –    =    ⌣ ⌣ – – ⌣ ⌣ – –
E. *Bac.* 530 = 549

To these may be added the two attested instances of another dimeter, the so-called "Cleomachean" (Heph 35.12 – 13):

τίς τὴν ὑδρίην ἡμῶν      – – ⌣ ⌣ – – ⌣͡⌣
ἐψόφησ'; ἐγὼ πίνων      – × – ⌣ – – ⌣͡⌣

Substitution appears, but in conjunction with "major" ionic demarcation (above, 17):

– – ⌣ ⌣ – – ⌣͡⌣ =      – × – ⌣ – – ⌣͡⌣      (Heph 35.12 = 35.13)
⌣ ⌣ – – ⌣ ⌣ – –   =   ⌣ ⌣ – × – ⌣ – –      (*Bac.* 549 = 530)
– ⌣ ⌣ – – ⌣ ⌣ –   =   – ⌣ ⌣ – × – ⌣ –      (*Vesp.* 632 = 527)

Such correlations notwithstanding, substitution in mixed ionic (major or minor) is usually analyzed in such a way as to minimize or ignore its similarity to what is found in choriambic. In minor ionic the only equivalence usually considered is that between ⌣ ⌣ – ×̆ – ⌣ – – (the normal form of the so-called anacreontic) and ⌣ ⌣ – – ⌣ ⌣ – –. The former is seen as derived from the latter by a process of "anaclasis" (i.e., metathesis of the fourth and fifth quantities):

Ionic anaclasis is a notion inherited from ancient metrism (see, most extensively, *GL* 6.93.11 – 94.6) or, more precisely, "isometrism." The one ionic form divisible into exactly equal metra is taken as a primary type and ⌣ ⌣ – ⌣ – ⌣ – – derived from it by metathesis, even though the theory leaves unclear the origin and status of the alternate form ⌣ ⌣ – – – ⌣ – – (i.e., ⌣ ⌣ – ×̄ – ⌣ – –) that is found occasionally in fifth-century drama (as well as, more likely than not, Anacreon),[27] and can even stand in strophic

---

[27] Cf. 1/346.4.3, a line ending – – – ⌣ – – in a poem where all other lines endings, insofar as they are preserved, are compatible with the pattern ⌣ ⌣ – ⌣ – ⌣ – ¯. If the poem is stichic, it is far more likely, given the convivial, erotic subject matter, to be in ionic trime-

responson with ◡ ◡ – ◡ – ◡ – – (Ar. *Ran.* 328 = 345) or ◡ ◡ – – ◡ ◡ – –
(*ibid.*, 336 = 353). For mixed ionic that conforms to the theory one must
go to verse composed in the Hellenistic or post-Hellenistic period:[28]
Catullus 63, for example, or Lucian's *Podagra* 30–53. There ◡ ◡ – – –
◡ – – is totally absent, unknown to the poets, perhaps, or consciously
rejected by them (as it is at *GL* 6.95.10–17) for being a sign of *inconditae
compositionis.*

A different metrist interpretation of mixed ionic underlies a freer type
of composition, equally well attested in the Hellenistic period and equally
un-Classical. Here the starting point seems to have been the three
equivalent forms already cited:

$$- \; ◡ \; - \; \times \quad - \; ◡ \; - \; -$$
$$◡ \; ◡ \; - \; \times \quad - \; ◡ \; - \; -$$
$$◡ \; ◡ \; - \; - \quad ◡ \; ◡ \; - \; -$$

These were seen in metrist terms as implying the existence of:

$$- ◡ - \times$$
$$◡ ◡ - \times \qquad \begin{array}{c} - ◡ - - \\ ◡ ◡ - - \end{array}$$
$$◡ ◡ - -$$

i.e., a combination of two separate metra in which any of the three versions of the first could be succeeded by either version of the second.
Hence such departures from Classical practice as

$$◡ ◡ - \overset{◡◡}{-} \qquad - ◡ - -$$
$$- ◡ - \overset{◡}{\times} \qquad ◡ ◡ - -$$
$$◡ ◡ - \overset{◡}{\times} \qquad ◡ ◡ - -^{29}$$

---

ters or tetrameters ([◡ ◡ – –]◡ ◡ – – ◡ ◡ – × – ◡ – ⁻) than *encomiologi* (– ◡ ◡ – ◡ ◡ – × –
◡ – ×) the only other possibility among stichic forms attested for Anacreon (46–48 /
391–93; 71/416; cf. Heph 51.1). The rarity of long anceps in Anacreon's mixed ionic is
paralleled by the rarity of the corresponding |– ◡ ◡ – x̄ – ◡ –) in what survives of his mixed
choriambic (38/383, 40–44 / 385–89). For the possibility of ionic | ◡ ◡ – x̄ – ◡ – in the
Danae fragment of Simonides as well (*PMG* 38/543.8–10) see Fuehrer, 160, and below,
Appendix III, B6.

[28] Sappho 134 also conforms, but a single line provides little grounds for speculating about
the character of mixed ionic before Anacreon (cf. below, n. 159).

[29] Attested in the transmitted text of Aristophanes at *Vesp.* 281 and 314 (cf. MacDowell *ad
loc.*) where, however, it produces violation of responson and is usually removed, following
Hermann, by emendations which can be supported on other than metrical grounds: elimination of an awkward *ge* by changing ἀνόνητον ἄρα σ'ὦ θυλάκιον γ' εἶχον ἄγαλμα to . . . ἄρ'
ὦ θυλάκιον σ'εἶχον in 314; removal of the late form χθεσινόν in favor of χθιζινόν at 281.

and, once it was assumed that the order of metra was reversible:

$$- \cup -^{\smile\smile} \quad | \quad - \cup - -$$

(All the certain examples—see Table I, B—involve either short anceps or resolved long, since it is only when one or the other of these is present that $\cup \cup - -$ is distinguishable from $\cup \cup - \times$ and $- \cup - -$ from $- \cup - \times$).

Hellenistic choriambic, by contrast, continued to follow classical lines, because there metron division produced units ($| - \cup \cup - |$, $| \times - \cup - |$) capable of being substituted for each other regardless of what preceded or followed. It is only by thinking of the transition back and forth between iono-choriambic and iambo-trochaic as proceeding independently of any division into metra or cola that one can obtain a formula capable of generating all those forms—and only those forms—attested in the fifth century for both mixed ionic and mixed choriambic:

iambo-choriambic

iambo-trochaic:

iono-choriambic:

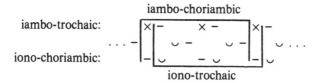

iono-trochaic

The positioning and frequency of $\times -$ and $- \cup$ within any sequence may vary, provided responding segments do not show consecutive instances of $\times -$ corresponding to $- \cup$, but transition from one to the other must always be via the $\cup -$ printed on the middle line.

The same formula will also generate all the sequences in the earliest attested samples of the most common major ionic form, that invented or given currency in the early third century by Sotades and named after him:

$$\begin{array}{llll} \times - & \times - & \times - & \times \\ - & \quad \cup - & \quad \cup - & \quad \cup - \\ - \cup & - \cup & - \cup & - \end{array}$$

Here, however, a different set of factors has led, both in Hellenistic practice and modern analyses influenced by it, to an elimination of the close links between sub-species of iono-choriambic.

The Sotadean in its earliest form ignores the single-cycle limit on the substitution of iambo-trochaic for iono-choriambic that holds in Classical verse: $- \times - \cup - \times - \cup - \times - \cup -^{-}$ and $- - \cup \cup - - \cup \cup - - \cup \cup -^{-}$ are felt as equivalents. At the same time, however, it restricts iambo-trochaic in a different way—through elimination of long anceps (cf. the parallel elimination of $\cup \cup - \bar{\times} - \cup - -$ in one form of Hellenistic minor ionic [above,

## TABLE I: HELLENISTIC AND LATER IONIC (MINOR)

A. Non-classical metron forms

1) ⏖‒̈- and ⏖‒̈

    Plaut. *Ps.* 1274–75: ⏑ ⏑ – – ⏑ ⏑ – – | ⏖‒̈- | ⏑ ⏑ –̈ | ⏖‒̈-

    *Tr.* 448–52: ⏑ ⏑ – – | ⏑ ⏑ – – ‖ ⏖‒̈- | ⏖‒ – ⏑ ⏑ – – | ⏑ ⏑ – – | ⏑ ⏑ – – ‖ ⏑ ⏑ – – ⏖‒̈ | ⏖‒
    – | ⏖‒̈- | ⏑ ⏑ –̈ | ⏑ ⏑ – – | ⏑ ⏑ –̈ | ⏖‒̈-

    *Ru.* 185–90:    ⏑ ⏑̈ | ⏖‒ – | ⏑ ⏑̈ | ⏑ ⏑ – – | ⏑ ⏑ – – ⏑ ⏑ – × |̈ ⏑ – – | ⏑ ⏑ – – | ⏖‒̈-
    | ⏖‒ – – ⏖‒ – – | ⏑ ⏑ – – | ⏑ ⏑ – – |    ⏑ ⏑ – – | ⏖‒̈- | ⏖‒ – – | ⏑ ⏑ – – | ⏑ ⏑ – – ⏖‒ – – ⏖‒̈- |
    ⏑ ⏑ – – | ⏖‒̈-

    *POxy* ii.219 (below, C)

2) ⏖‒× 

    First attested in the second quarter of the fourth century, if PHib 2.174 ( = TrGF 60F1h fr.I col.
    2.14 is correctly attributed to the younger Astydamas; otherwise confined to Hellenistic and post-
    Hellenistic instances of

    a) anacreontic ( ⏖‒× – ⏑ – – ) and galliambic ( ⏖‒× – ⏑ – – | ⏖‒× – ⏑ – ) Catullus 63 (11
       instances); Lucian *Podagra* 30–53 (10 instances);[1] Seneca, *Med.* 849–50, 853, 856–57; Ana-
       creontea *passim*

    b) (–) –̱ × – ⏑ ⏑ × – ⏑ – × (on the form, see *GV* 146–51); *IG* 9.1.883; *PBerl* 10525; *POxy* 2331
       (S9 Heitsch; line 19 shows the unusual ⏖‒ – – ⏑ ⏑ – × – ⏑ – ‾ ); Synesius 4

3) × – ⏑ – (?)

    Posited as an alternative form of ionic metron (e.g., in *GV* 146–51) but fairly easily removed from
    all the passages in which it is alleged to appear: by scanning – – ⏑ – ⏑ – ⏑ – ⏑ – ‾ as ⏖‒× –
    ⏑ – × – ⏑ – ‾ rather than as × – ⏑ – × – ⏑ – ⏑ – ‾; by emendation (τοῦτ' Εὔοδος βροτοῖς{ι} πᾶσι
    παραινῶ) in *IG* 9.1.883.1 (above 2b) and by rejecting at *PBer* 10525.15 (*ibid.*) the anomalous
    πρόπειε and the supplement μέθνε in favor of, e.g., ἔγχει} καὶ πρόπ{ε}ι' ἐ<ς> πολὺ παραμείνας.

B. Non-classical combinations of metron forms

    1) ⏑ ⏑ –̈ |̱ – ⏑ – –      Isyllus of Epidaurus 52 (p. 134 Powell), Anacreontea 40.8, 44.13, 46.1 and 12
                              Mesomedes 11.1–2 (if correctly scanned at *GV* 605)

    2) ⏑ ⏑ – × |̱ ⏑ ⏑ – –    Isyllus 47 and 60; Anacreontea 14.14 and 28.6; Synesius 9.49 and 100

    3) – ⏑ – × |̱ ⏑ ⏑ – –    *POxy* ii.219.17 and 20 (below, C)

    4) – ⏑ –̈ |̱ – ⏑ – –    Isyllus 42, Laevius 26.2 (unless *sive* is twice emended to give *seu femina seu*
                            *mas est* ( ⏖‒̈ ⏖‒ – – ); *Frgm. Grenfellianum* 12 (p. 177 Powell):
                            παράπεμψον ἔτι με νῦν πρὸς ὃν ἡ Κύπρις ( ⏑ ⏑ – × |̈ ⏑ –̈ |̱ – ⏑ –).

C. Most of the above, plus ⏑ – ×, a headless version of ⏑ ⏑ – × or – ⏑ – ×, are
found in the *ionicos tetrametros effrenatos* (Crönert, *RhM* 64,444) of *POxy* ii.219
(pp. 182–83 Powell):

| | | | | |
|---|---|---|---|---|
| Ἀπορο]ῦμαι ποῦ βαδίσω· ἡ ναῦς μου ἐ<ρ>ράγη. | ⏑ ⏑ – – | ⏖‒̈- | ⏖‒× | – ⏑ – | 15 |
| τὸν κ]α [τ]α [θ]ύμιον ἀπολέσας ὄρνιθά μου κλαίω | ⏖‒̈× | ⏑̈ ⏑̈ –̈ | ⏖‒× | – ⏑ – | |
| Ἀλλὰ φ]έρε τὸ ἐρνίον, τροφὴν αὐτοῦ, περιλάβω, | ⏖‒̈× | – ⏑ – × | ⏖‒× | ⏑̈ ⏑ – | |
| τοῦ μ[αχ]λίμου, τοῦ ἐπεραστοῦ, τοῦ Ἑλληνικοῦ· | ⏖‒̈- | ⏖‒̈- | ⏖‒× | – ⏑ – | |

---

[1] Counting line 39 (κλάζει δὲ βριθὺ σάλπιγξ Dindorf: βρίθουσα *codd.*).

χάρ[ιν τ]ούτου ἐκαλούμην μέγας ἐν τῷ βίῳ          ◡ – –      ◡◡˘˘–      ◡◡˘˘×      – ◡ –

καὶ [ἐλ]εγόμην μακάριος ἀνδράσι τοῖς φιλοτρόφοις          ◡◡˘˘×      – ◡˘˘×      ◡◡˘˘×      ˘˘ ◡ –      20

Ψυχομαχῶ· ὁ γὰρ ἀ[λ]έκτωρ ἠστόχηκέ μου,          ◡◡˘˘–      ◡˘˘–      ◡◡˘˘–×      – ◡ –

καὶ θακοθαλπάδος ἐρασθεὶς ἐμὲν ἐγκατέλιπε.          ◡◡◡–×      – ◡˘˘–      ◡◡˘˘×      ˘˘ ◡ –

'Αλλ' ἐπιθεὶς λίθον ἐμα[υ]τοῦ ἐπὶ τὴν καρδίαν          ◡◡˘˘–      ◡˘˘–      ◡◡˘˘×      – ◡ –

καθ[η]συχάσομαι· ὑμε[ι]ς δ' ὑγιαίνετε, φίλοι.          ◡ – ×      ◡ ◡ – –      ◡◡˘˘×      ˘˘ ◡ –      24

(The form ◡ – ×, if it is not—like the author's permissiveness with regard to hiatus—the result of simple incompetence, may stem from a metrist reinterpretation of the "antispastic" iono-choriambic openings discussed in the text (99): ◡ – – ◡ ◡ – –… taken as ◡ – – ¦ ◡ ◡ – – ¦… with a subsequent use of ◡ – – medially as well as initially).

32]). The result is the frequent appearance of − ∪ − ∪, a sequence which by itself, in metrist isolation, was naturally heard as a trochee with short anceps − ∪ − ×̆ rather than as the anonymous − ×̆ − ∪; and this led— equally naturally—to the introduction of a corresponding − ∪ − x̄ (first securely attested in Greek in the 2nd century A.D.: see Table II, C3).

Further innovation came once the rhythm was felt, not as part of the same epiploke as minor ionic:

minor

∪ ∪ − − ∪ ∪

major

but as an inversion of it:

| 1 | 2 | 3 | 4 | |
|---|---|---|---|---|
| ∪ | ∪ | − | − | minor |
| − | − | ∪ | ∪ | major |
| 4 | 3 | 2 | 1 | |

For at this point it was natural to produce new forms in major through the inversion of mixed as well as pure minor:

| 1 | 2 | 3 | 4 | | 5 | 6 | 7 | 8 | |
|---|---|---|---|---|---|---|---|---|---|
| ∪ | ∪ | − | ∪ | \| | − | ∪ | − | − | minor |
| − | − | ∪ | − | \| | ∪ | − | ∪ | ∪ | major |
| 8 | 7 | 6 | 5 | | 4 | 3 | 2 | 1 [30] | |

One of these new forms, ∪ − ∪ ∪, appears along with the trochaic − ∪ − x̄ in Hephaestion's analysis of the metre. Together they enable him, in conjunction with the original − − ∪ ∪ and − ∪ − ∪, to produce ionic scansion of a number of sequences beginning × − ∪ ∪ that are more plausibly classified as aeolic.[31] The other new form, − − ∪ −, appears along with

---

[30] The parallel between ∪ ∪ − ∪ and ∪ − ∪ ∪ is implicit in Heph 146.23–24 and 148.20–21, where similar language is used in reference to major ionics in which the first quantity is "shortened" and minor ionics in which the last quantity is short rather than long (cf., also, 111.1–4). There is nothing comparable on the relation of − ∪ − − to − − ∪ −; but, with the possible exception of Plotius Sacerdos, in an obscure passage (*GL* 6.540.14–541.10), no ancient theorist recognizes the existence of the major ionic form − − ∪ − at all. The tradition followed by the poets who use it was evidently an eccentric one, of which no trace is found in surviving handbooks.

[31] E.g., the telesillean (Heph 35.8–11), the Sapphic × − ∪ ∪ − ∪ − ∪ − ⌣̄ (35.17–21; cf. text, 14) and the Sapphic or pseudo-Sapphic × − ∪ ∪ − ∪ − × (37.5 = *PMG* 976).

– ∪ – x̄ and the two original ones in the Sotadeans preserved in Stobaeus, as well as contracted (⌣̄)– ⌣̄⌣̄ and – – – ∪ (presumably the – x – ∪ already mentioned, but with long anceps). Contraction is more frequent and appears in conjunction with resolution to produce –⌣̆⌣̆ ⌣̄⌣̄ as well as the Stobaean ⌣̆⌣̆– ⌣̄⌣̄ in the six Sotadeans quoted by Athanasius from the prologue to the *Thaleia* of his rival Arius (Table II, C5). Otherwise Arius's versification follows the Stobaean pattern.

Contraction, like long anceps, is totally absent from Sotades himself and his close imitators (cf. *GL* 6.370.1480–83 [Terentianus Maurus] where the Sotadean is said to exclude successions of three long syllables—hence, presumably, the contracted – – ⌣̄⌣̄). Other theorists, however, (cf. AQ 1.27 p. 50.10–11 and *GL* 6.89.31–90.10) allowed contraction, and it appears occasionally, together with long anceps but without any trace of the Hellenistic innovations – ∪ – –, – – ∪ – and ∪ – ∪ ∪, in a group of texts which seem to occupy a middle position between Sotades and Stobaeus in the spectrum of major ionic (see Table II, B and, for a further discussion of the most important text in this group, the Dictaean Zeus hymn, below 197–99). *POxy* 2331 (Table I, A2b) occupies a similar middle position in minor ionic, showing as it does a solitary instance of long anceps in what is otherwise an example of more strict Hellenistic practice (above, 32).

The Hephaestionic, Stobaean and Arian forms of major ionic have little in common with minor ionic and choriambic, just as they have little in common with anything in Classical verse at all (hence the understandable decision of some metricians—cf., Gentili 69–85, *LMGD* 96[1]—to view major ionic as a totally Hellenistic development). As practiced by Sotades himself, however, major ionic is simply a third example along with minor ionic and choriambic of the persistence of a single type of compound epiploke through different demarcative patterns. And there are a number of possible Classical instances: the expanded "Sotadean" of S. *Aj.* 1202 = 1216ff., for instance:

$$\text{– – ∪ ∪ – – ∪ ∪ – – ∪ ∪ – – ∪ ∪ – –}$$

οὔτε γλυκὺν αὐλῶν ὄτοβον δύσμορος οὔτ' ἐννυχίαν τέρψιν ἰαύειν,

or the expanded "Cleomachean" of 399–400 = 416–17:

οὔθ' ἀμερίων ἔτ' ἄξιος βλέπειν τιν'    – – ∪ ∪ – x – ∪ – x – ∪ | – x – ∪ – – ⌣̄⌣̄
εἰς ὄνασιν ἀνθρώπων

(see, further, below 192–97). Rather than deny all connection between such passages and later developments by making the Sotadean the unique brainchild of an Alexandrian *doctus poeta*, it may make more sense to

## TABLE II: HELLENISTIC AND LATER IONIC (MAJOR)

(cf. F. Koch, *Ionicorum a maiore historia* [Bonn 1926] 24–43)

| Author | Number of lines attested (Sotadeans unless otherwise indicated) | Metron forms employed |
|---|---|---|
| A1 Sotades (fr. 1–4b, pp. 238–39 Powell) | 10 | (͜)(͜) ∪ ∪ and (͜) ∪ (͜) ∪ |
| 2 Lucian, *Podagra* 113–24 | 12 | '' |
| 3 Moschion (cf. Koch, p. 29) | 9 | '' |
| 4 *POxy* iii, p. 41, 88–91 (p. 181 Powell) | 4 | '' |
| 5 Laevius 22 (*Venus amoris altrix* genetrix cup<p> iditatis . . .); Varro *Menipp.* 489 Buecheler | 2 catalectic decameters | '' |
| 6 Varro *Menipp.* 19, 85, 112, 322, 342, 400, 438 Buecheler | 10 | '' |
| 7 Petronius 23 and 132 | 13 | '' |
| 8 Martial 3.29 | 2 | '' |
| 9 Terentianus Maurus 85–278, 1457–1579, 2013–60, 2072–92 | 386 | '' |
| B1 Dictaean Zeus hymn (pp. 160–61 Powell) | 7 tetrameters | '' − − ∪͜∪ |
| 2 Cleomachus (*ap.* Heph 35.15–16) | 2 cleomacheans | '' '' |
| 3 DH 4 p. 16.13–14 | 2 | '' ''1 ∪∪−∪͜∪ and |
| | | _∪∪ ∪͜∪ |
| 4 Maximus the Decurion (Koch p. 30) | 23 | '' '' '' −x̄(͜) ∪ |
| 5 Plautus, *Amph.* 168–72 | 5 | '' ''2 |
| 6 Ennius, pp. 217–18 Vahlen | 5 | '' |
| C1 Accius, fr. 19 | 1 | '' __ − ∪ −x̄3 |
| 2 Varro, *Menipp.* 2–3 Buecheler | 2 tetrameters | '' '' |
| 3 *POxy* 3010 (2nd cent. A.D.; cf. *BICS* 18 [1971] 54) | 20 | '' '' '' |
| 4 Stobaeus 1.1, 3.1, 22; 4.34, 39, 44, 51, 52; pp. 240–43 Powell | 63 | '' '' '' '' '' |
| 5 Arius, prologue to the *Thaleia* (*ap.* Athan. *Contr. Ar.* 1.5 = Migne 26.20c–21a)4 | 6 | (∪͜∪∪) − ∪ − '' '' '' '' '' '' |
| 6 Hephaestion | | '' '' '' ∪−∪∪ |

---

[1] Transposing κεῖτο to follow ὁ in ὡς ὁ πρόσθ' ἵππων καὶ δίφρου κεῖτο τανυσθείς. The line as transmitted is a simple Sotadean rescanning of *Il.* 13.393 (with one instance of −∪−x̄ or −x̄−∪), whereas context leads one to expect a rearrangement of Homer's *synthesis onomatōn*.

[2] Scanning *dives operis* in 170.

[3] *non ergo aquila ita uti praedicant sciciderat pectus*, with a highly anomalous final −∪−x̄−¯ (cf. West 144). Transposition of *aquila* to the penultimate position would produce a more normal −x̄ˇˇ∪−∪− ∪ˇˇ∪ˇˇ∪−¯. Additional metron forms are posited in Lachmann's rescanning and rewriting of the fragments of the *Didascalica* as Sotadeans; but the only such fragments still accepted as verse by Accius' most recent editor (fr. 7–8, 10, 12, 15 Buechner) are better taken as Saturnians constructed in the highly regular manner of the roughly contemporary Naevius epitaph: cf. *YCS* 21 (1969) 61–64.

[4] Text as in Koster, 364. Against the non-ionic scansions sometimes offered, see West, *Journal of Theological Studies* 33 (1981) 98–99. West himself (*ibid.*, 100–105) scans as acatalectic tetrameters (as in B1 and C2 above) in an effort to extend ionic analysis to Athanasius' citations (*loc. cit.* and *Syn.* 15) from sections of the *Thaleia* other than the prologue. But this requires extensive emendation, the positing of additional metron forms (∪−∪−, ∪∪−∪, −∪∪−∪) not elsewhere attested in major ionic, and a neglect of features of technique (avoidance of hiatus, regular diaeresis between the second and third metron of each line) which set the prologue citations apart from the rest and suggest that the latter, if they be verse at all, are composed in a different, as yet unidentified metre.

locate the decisive break with Classical practice differently: not with the poet who made an unusual type of iono-choriambic demarcation the basis of a stichic form and radically increased the number of permissible substitutions within it, but with those among his successors, whoever they were, who first decided to abandon close imitation of their model and compose in accordance with what they conceived to be the metrist principles on which that model was constructed. Their methods, it may be noted, have continued in use almost to our own day. Just as minor ionic – ◡ – – yielded major ionic – – ◡ – by inversion, so in the 19th century the reverse of the process was to create out of major ionic – ◡ – × a minor ionic × – ◡ – (see Table I, A3) that still appears in the scansion of some pieces of Classical lyric[32] — a striking testimony to the perennial attractiveness of "metrism."

## ii. Contraction

Contraction is attested in both Classical ionic and Classical choriambic:

| | |
|---|---|
| κισσῷ τε στεφανωθείς | ◡◡– – ◡ ◡ – – |
| Διόνυσον θεραπεύει | ◡ ◡ – – ◡ ◡ – – |

—E. *Bac.* 81–82 = 96–98

κρυπτομένα δ' ἐν τυμβήρει θαλάμῳ    – ◡ ◡ – – ◡◡– – ◡ ◡ –

—S. *Ant.* 946 = 957

but only in the pure forms of both rhythms and rarely even there. In Hellenistic times the situation changes sharply. Contraction disappears from choriambic altogether (except in certain aeolic sequences occasionally analyzed as containing choriambs—e.g., the × × – ◡◡– ◡ – ◡ – ‾ of
Catullus 55). In ionic, however, it is more frequent. Beside the – – ◡◡ of the Cleomachean and the (post-Sotadean) Sotadean (Table II, B and C) one finds numerous examples (Table I, A2) of the mixed ionic ◡◡– ×̆ – ◡ – –:

iam iam dolet quod egi, iam iamque paenitet    ◡◡– ×̆ – ◡ – – | ◡◡– ×̆ – ◡ –

—Catullus 63.73

And in pure ionic sequences contraction may even be immediately followed and preceded by resolution:

[32] E.g., Ar. *Th.* 114–15 and 120 (probably corrupt), Sappho 133 and Alcman 50 (see text, 000), and A. *Sup.* 164 (Table III).

nimis ex discipulina ⏑ ⏑ – – ⏑ ⏑ – –
quippe ego qui probe Ionica perdidici. ⏔ˇ – ⏑ ⏑ –ˇˇ ⏔ ˇˇ –

—Plautus *Ps.* 1274–75

(if the second line is correctly scanned and reflects contemporary Greek practice).[33]

Once again, the change seems to reflect metrist principles. The result of contraction in choriambic would be a single long syllable spanning the boundary between the "arsis" and "thesis" of the metron—i.e., the two halves, "choree" (– ⏑) and iamb (⏑ –), out of which, as its (Hellenistic or post-Hellenistic) name indicates, the choriamb was felt to be composed. In ionic, on the other hand, contraction only affects the two quantities contained within the "lesser" of the two parts into which Hellenistic theory analyzed the sequence ⏑ ⏑ – – (called the "ionic beginning from the lesser" [*iōnikos ap'elassonos*] to distinguish it from – – ⏑ ⏑, the ionic "beginning from the greater" [*apo meizonos*]).

Refusal to divide a single syllable between metron parts is paralleled by reluctance, in the pure forms of ionic cited, to divide a word between metra. The three Plautine passages which can be identified with some plausibility as containing ionic subject to frequent resolution and contraction show 31 metron diaereses out of a possible 39 (Table I, A 1).[34]

This Hellenistic concern not to obscure divisions between metra or their identifying parts stands in sharp contrast with the Classical concern not to obscure the character of a whole epiploke—by contractions and resolutions which would allow, for example, ⏔– – ⏑ ⏑ – – and ⏔ˇ– ⏑ ⏑ –ˇˇ ⏔ˇ– to be heard as dactylo-anapestic – ⏔– ⏑ ⏑ – – and – ⏑ ⏑ – ⏑ ⏑ – ⏑ ⏑ – ⏑ ⏑ –, or ⏔– × – ⏑ – – as iambo-trochaic × – ⏑ – ⏑ – ¯. It is only when, as in a special type of ionic to be considered later (below, 94) there is intentional playing on the ambiguity of initial | ⏔– – ⏑ ⏑ –. . . and aeolic | × × – ⏑ ⏑ –. . . that contraction becomes frequent. Elsewhere it is more important to establish the pattern of an epiploke than

[33] Alleged Classical parallels are better taken as instances of syncopation: *Hipp.* 732 = 742 as – ⏑ ⏑ –. ⏑ ⏑ – – ⏑ ⏑ – – (text, 47) rather than ⏔ˇ – ⏑ ⏑ – – ⏑ ⏑ – – (*LMGD* 129–30), S. Ph. 1178–79 as ⏑ ⏑ –. ⏑ ⏑ –. ⏑ ⏑ – – ⏑ ⏑ –. ⏑ ⏑ – – (*LMGD* 130) rather than ⏑ ⏑ – ˇˇ⏔ˇ – ⏔ˇ – ⏑ ⏑ – – (*GV* 341), and Ar. *Av.* 1374 and 1376 as ⏑ ⏑ –. ⏑ ⏑ –. ⏑ ⏑ (ˇˇ)– ⏑ ⏑ – (more in line with the rest of Cinesias's utterances in this scene, none of which containers fewer than fourteen quantities, than the alternative ˇˇ⏔ˇ – ⏑ ⏑ (ˇˇ)– ⏑ ⏑ –).

[34] Other possible Plautine examples are discussed in F. Leo, "Die plautinischen Cantica und die hellenistische Lyrik," *AbhGött* N.F. i. 7 (1897) 37–49. But the verse form posited there is very amorphous—allowing unrestricted resolution and contraction, all the peculiarities of Hellenistic ionic noted in the text (32–33), and in addition the modern invention × – ⏑ – (text, 39). Accidental conformity to its rules is thus fairly easy.

to underline through demarcation the groupings within it. In the Hellenistic passages cited, on the other hand, the grouping seems to be more important than the patterning—almost as if, once boundaries between units were impressed on the ear, any internal patterning of the right length would be acceptable to the audience. Something similar occurs in Classical practice as well—when recurring demarcation at intervals of five or six quantities seems to become crucial for establishing the identity of dochmiacs or metric anapests, and frequent use of resolution, contraction and long anceps obscures the inner patterning of the segments so demarcated. But dochmiac and metric anapests are the two Classical genres (above, 6, 22) from which epiploke is largely or totally absent.

## iii. Syncopation

Most metricians recognize syncopation of either short or anceps as a frequent procedure in the trochaic and iambic of drama; and their view is supported by occasional instances of strophic responsion between – ◡ – ✕ – ◡ – and – ◡ – – ◡ – (i.e., syncopated – ◡ –.– ◡ – and non-syncopated – ◡ – ✕ – ◡ –), final – ◡ – ◡ – ‾ and – ◡ – – – ‾ (i.e., – ◡ – ◡ – ‾ and – ◡ –.– ‾) and, more dubiously, – ◡ – and – – (– ◡ – and –.–).[35] There exist, moreover, a very large number of passages in which iambic and trochaic forms are used alongside others identical to them except for the fact that they seem to be missing a short or anceps at one or two points. Here, even in the absence of the guarantee provided by responsion, syncopation is a reasonable hypothesis.

Whether the apparently missing or "syncopated" quantity was supplied by pause or protraction (above, 30) is difficult to decide in many cases; but protraction certainly seems the better explanation when, as often occurs, the syllables supplying the adjoining quantities are in the same word. As to the question of whether the protracted syllable supplied the syncopated quantity and the one preceding or the syncopated quantity and the one following, the usual answer is different for iambic from what it is for trochaic. In iambic it is assumed to be the quantity following, largely on the basis of two pieces of fairly late evidence. One is the so-called Seikelos inscription, a poetic text with musical and metrical notation dating from the second century A.D. which contains several instances of the metra ✕ – .‾ and .‾–.‾:

---

[35] See the examples collected in West, 103–4, to which may be added –⦗✕⦘– at Ar. *Av.* 1560 = 1701, *Ran.* 1486 = 1495, *Vesp.* 342–43 = 374–75 and –⦗◡⦘– at E. *IA* 253 = 265 and Ar. *Lys.* 264 = 279.

ὅσον ζῆς, φαίνου                     × – ‿́ . ‿́ . ‿́
(p. 38 Jan)

The other consists of the lines

ἔνθα δὴ ποικίλων ἀνθέων ἄμβροτοι λείμακες     ×– ‿ –.‿́‿ –.‿́‿ –.‿́‿ –.‿́‿ –
βαθύσκιον παρ' ἄλσος ἀβροπαρθένους           ×– ‿ –×– ‿ –×– ‿ –
εὐιώτας χόρους ἀγκάλαις δέχονται              .‿́‿ –.‿́‿ –.‿́‿ –– ‿ –

which appear, so scanned, in a Hellenistic treatise on rhythm (*POxy* 2687 ii.10–14 = *PMG* 926a; cf., also, ii.18–19 = *PMG* 926b and *POxy* 2436.6–8).

The same papyrus (ii.3–7) gives – ‿ –. as an instance of syncopated trochaic, and analogy posits two further forms: –.–× and –.–. to match the three (.– ‿ –, ×–.– and .– .–) attested for iambic. Protraction is thus assumed to display a symmetrical but opposite pattern in the two rhythms:

iambic:     ×  – .– .– .– .–  ‿ –
trochaic:          .– .– .– .– .–  ‿ –

The result is always, as in contracted ionic, the supplying by a single syllable of one of the two halves, arsis or thesis, into which Hellenistic theory divided the metra involved. And *POxy* 2687 recognizes the existence of a similar protraction in choriambic, supplying the "choree" half of the four complete metra in

φίλον Ὥραισιν ἀγάπημα θνατοῖσιν ἀνάπαυμα μόχθων     ‿ ‿ ––‿ ‿˘˘––‿ ‿ ––‿ ‿˘˘––‿ ‿ ––

–iii.3–5 = PMG 926c

The compatibility of all three types of protraction–iambic, trochaic and choriambic–with metrist theory is clear; and once more Classical procedure, so far as it can be determined, does not quite fit the theory. The passage just quoted shows two instances of resolution immediately preceding a protracted syllable. Yet such resolution never occurs in Classical syncopated iambic: there are no instances of the sequence ×– ‿˘˘.– ‿ –, which would be the closest iambic parallel to choriambic – ‿ ‿˘˘ –‿ ‿ –, and none of ×˘˘.– either.[36] What one does find is .˘˘‿ – or ×–.˘˘, i.e.,

[36] See *LMGD* 73–74, and the earlier discussions in W. Christ, *Metrik der Griechen und Römer*[2] (Leipzig 1879) 358 and 392, and R. Westphal and H. Gleditsch, *Allgemeine Theorie der griechischen Metrik* (Leipzig 1889) 198. This exclusion of ˘˘. has recently been denied

resolution replacing rather than preceding the protracted syllable of the posited .‒ ᴗ ‒ or ×‒.‒. And it is difficult to see how two short syllables could have been thus given the value of short plus long or anceps plus long. Protraction will only work as an explanation in such passages if one assumes that syncopation in Classical iambic followed the same pattern as that attested and reconstructed for trochaic: ×‒ᴗ‒.‒.‒ . If the protracted syllable always supplies the syncopated quantity and the one preceding it, the pattern of resolution makes sense. ×‒.ᵛᵛ and . . .ᴗ‒. ᵛᵛ ᴗ ‒ are allowed, but ×ᵛᵛ ᴗ ‒ and . . .ᴗᵛᵛ×‒ ᴗ ‒ are prohibited; for both the latter contain a pair of short syllables which would have to supply the time value of the following short or anceps as well as that of the long which they "resolve." (Supplying of a syncopated anceps or short by a pause would be equally impossible following resolution, since pause would inevitably lengthen the syllable preceding, producing the impossible sequences × ᴗ ‒ ᴗ ‒ and . . .ᴗ ᴗ ‒×‒ ᴗ ‒ as syncopations of ×ᵛᵛ ᴗ ‒ and . . .ᴗᵛᵛ×‒ ᴗ ‒).

The absence of any instances of immediately preceding resolution is obviously irrelevant in arguing against the possibility of an initial |.‒ ᴗ ‒ in iambic; but analogy, and the absence of free responsion between initial ×‒ and ‒ in iambo-trochaic, suggests that the same analysis should be applied initially as well as internally. The syllable sequence ‒ ᴗ ‒ is always either a "trochaeo-iambic" ‒ ᴗ ‒ or a trochaic ‒ ᴗ ‒., never an iambic .‒ ᴗ ‒.

Reconstruction of Classical technique points here as elsewhere to a common body of iambo-trochaic procedures operating regardless of the demarcation involved in a particular passage. And the frequency with which different quantities or quantity sequences are syncopated seems equally unaffected by demarcation:

---

(J. Diggle, *Studies on the Text of Euripides* [Oxford 1981] 18–21). But of the six "certain or very probable" instances Diggle adduces, only E. *An.* 1204–5 = 1219 is in a context that clearly calls for iambo-trochaic analysis, and there a lacuna in the antistrophe makes scansion uncertain. The reconstruction

1204–5:     ‒ ᴗ  ‒.ᵛᵛᴗᵛᵛ×‒ᴗ×    ‒|ᴗ‒ᵣᴗᵛᵛ
1219:       <‒ ᴗ >‒.ᵛᵛᴗ‒×‒ᴗ‒×<‒‒ᴗ‒.‒ᴗᵛᵛ>

removes the ᵛᵛ. posited by Diggle's

1204–5:     ‒ ᴗ‒.ᵛᵛᴗᵛᵛ ᴗ‒⁻ +  ‒‒‒|ᴗ‒‒ᴗᵛᵛ
1219:       ‒ ᴗᵛᵛ.‒ᴗ‒ᴗ‒⁻ + <‒‒‒ᴗ‒‒ᴗᵛᵛ>

as well as an intruding molossus ¦ dochmiac and a series of consecutive responsions between resolved and unresolved longs (‒.ᵛᵛᴗᵛᵛ = ᵛᵛ.‒ ᴗ ‒) that has no parallel elsewhere in syncopated iambo-trochaic.

- ⏑ -.- ⏑ -    (the most frequent form, both in iambic and trochaic)
-.-.- ⏑ -    (less frequent and usually preceded, when not initial in a movement, by |⏓, .| or ⏓|)
-.-×- ⏑ -    (rare, even when preceded by |⏓, .| or ⏓|, except in late Euripides)[37]

- ⏑ -.-.- is rarer still, unless clausular - ⏑ --⁻ is so interpreted (i.e., as - ⏑ -.-.- rather than, as suggested above [41], - ⏑ -.-⁻). But the analysis - ⏑ -.-.- requires - ⏑ - ⏑ -.- for the closely related - ⏑ - ⏑ -⁻,[38] and the latter is already attested in Archilochus (188–92) and Sappho (117), authors in whose work there is no strong evidence for syncopation of any sort. Terminal -⁻ would, moreover, lose some of its distinctive clausular effect if it were a -.- capable of being heard initially or medially as well.

The mechanics of syncopation are, of course, crucial for the way large portions of tragic iambic and trochaic are read and heard. In particular they are crucial for the way the difference between syncopated forms of the two rhythms is heard. Anceps is the quantity most often syncopated, and a protracted syllable supplying this quantity and the one preceding necessarily results in the elimination of the possibility of "iambic" word end (. . . ⏑ -|×-. . .) at the point in the verse where syncopation occurs. By the same token it increases the likelihood of "trochaic" word end (. . .-. |- ⏑) and so can impart, when used frequently, a certain trochaic drift to a passage, however resolutely iambic a course is set by the overall demarcative pattern. A natural result is the existence of iambic cola that suggest uncertainty and tension because of an inner pull in the opposite directton; and, correspondingly, of a kind of "hyper-trochaic" in which intensification accompanies regularization. Thus the heavily syncopated parodos of the *Agamemnon* passes from trochaic to iambic as the resignation and awe of the Zeus hymn give way to the anguish and indecision of the wait at Aulis. The modulation is strikingly introduced at the end of the last two trochaic stanzas, coinciding in the strophe:

[37] A. *Pers.* 550–55 = 560–63 (text, 177) and, perhaps, *Ch.* 735 (καὶ γαῖα κόνις . . .) = 743 (αἰῶνα δ' ἐς τρίτον . . .) are isolated trochaic instances from earlier tragedy. Iambic |×-.-×- ⏑ - is better attested (e.g., at *Ch.* 44 = 56) but still uncommon; see T. C. W. Stinton, "More Rare Verse Forms," *BICS* 22 (1975) 84ff.

[38] Cf. Ar. *Av.* 459 = 547, where the two forms are in responsion; and such passages as E. *Su.* 781–89 (clausular ×- ⏑ -.-⁻ in the same context as three instances of - ⏑ - ⏑ -⁻ [785 = 795, 801 = 814, 810 = 823]) and A. *Su.* 139–40 = 149–50 (terminal ×- ⏑ -.-⁻ + - ⏑ - ⏑ -⁻ anticipating - ⏑ - ⏑ -⁻ + - ⏑ -.- ⏑ -×- ⏑ - at the strophe end following).

δαιμόνων δέ που χάρις                        – ◡ – × – ◡ –

βιαίως σέλμα σεμνὸν ἡμένων        × – . – . – ◡ – × – ◡ –

(182–83)

with an oxymoronic movement from *charis* to the *bia* that is to dominate the rest of the ode;[39] and in the antistrophe with what begins as a purely physical movement to the scene of violence and its back-flowing waters:

Χαλκίδος πέραν ἔχων                          – ◡ – × – ◡ –

παλιρρόχθοις ἐν Αὐλίδος τόποις.        × – . – . – ◡ – × – ◡ –

(190–91)

but soon becomes an almost audible anticipation of the back-blowing contrary winds and conflicting wills of the iambic lines immediately following:

πνοαὶ δ' ἀπὸ Στρυμόνος μολοῦσαι           × – ◡ – . – ◡ – ◡ – ‾

κακόσχολοι, νήστιδες, δύσορμοι            × – ◡ – . – ◡ – ◡ – ‾

βροτῶν ἄλαι, ναῶν τε καὶ πεισμάτων ἀφειδεῖς   × – ◡ – × – ◡ – . – ◡ – ◡ – ‾

παλιμμήκη χρόνον τιθεῖσαι                 × – . – . – ◡ – ◡ – ‾

(192–96)

Hellenistic ears, trained to hear iambic as syllables grouped into metra (× – ◡ –⌐× – ◡ –) and sub-grouped into arsis and thesis (⌐× – : ◡ –⌐) may have found the colon opening

$$× \overset{\rule{1em}{0.5pt}\phantom{x}}{–} : . \overset{\rule{1em}{0.5pt}\phantom{x}}{–} | . – : ◡ –$$

used twice here in the space of five lines almost as disquieting as the poet's theology: similar in its effect, perhaps, to one form of syncopation in the modern, musical sense:

¾  πα - λ ι ρ - ρ ό χ - θοις ἐν Αὐλ-ίδος τό-ποις

The new technique found in the Seikelos epitaph and *POxy* 2687 reduces the rhythm to a more comfortable matter of holds and rests, as in trochaic; but the transformation may have taken some time to complete. The puzzling statement (*ibid.*, i.33 and iii.12–14) that protraction is more suitable to trochaic than to iambic is hard to square with either Classical or

[39] On the distinctively Aeschyulean—and, probably emphatic—character of this juxtaposition, see C. J. Herington, *The Author of the Prometheus Bound* (Austin and London 1970) 61.

Hellenistic practice as attested, but may reflect a transitional period when the original iambic forms had fallen into disuse and not yet been replaced by new ones created, on the analogy of those already existing in trochaic, to ensure the coincidence of syllable boundary with arsis, thesis and metron boundary.

In syncopation, as in contraction (above, 40–41) Classical practice is less concerned with such boundaries than it is with the short and long contrast that, independently of metrical demarcation, produces the flow of the rhythm. Syncopation is only used when the deviation from rhythmical regularity which it involves results in an accentuation of this contrast—i.e., when short or short anceps plus long is the expected sequence and one hears instead short plus extra-long or long reinforced by a succeeding pause. The same reinforcement is also heard in iono-choriambic, where syncopation exactly parallels the − ∪ −.− ∪ − of iambo-trochaic:

'Aσίας ἀπο γᾶς          ∪ ∪ − . ∪ ∪ − .
ἱερὸν Τμῶλον ἀμείψασα θοάζω   ∪ ∪ − − ∪ ∪ − − ∪ ∪ − −
                                        —E. Bac. 64–65

and even stands on one occasion (Ar. Vesp. 283 = 277) in strophic responsion with it:

διὰ τοῦτ' ὀδυνηθείς =      ∪ ∪ − . ∪ ∪ − × =
εἶτ' ἐφλέγμηνεν αὐτοῦ      − ∪ − . − ∪ − ×

Examples also occur in mixed and catalectic sequences:

πίσυνοι λεπτοδόμοις πείσμασι λαοπόροις τε μηχαναῖς
                    ∪ ∪ − − ∪ ∪ − − ∪ ∪ − . ∪ ∪ − × − ∪ −
                                        —A. Pers. 105 = 114

'Ω χθονία βροτοῖσι φάμα      − ∪ ∪ − × − ∪ − −
κατά μοι βόασον οἰκτρὰν      ∪ ∪ − × − ∪ − −
ὄπα τοῖς ἔνερθ' 'Ατρείδαις    ∪ ∪ − × − ∪ − −
ἀχόρευτα φέρουσ' ὀνείδη      ∪ ∪ − . ∪ ∪ − ∪ − ‾
                                        —S. El. 1066–69 = 1078–81

the latter a syncopated, lengthened version of Anacreon 1/346.1 (above, 20).

Neither type of context is ever analyzed in this fashion by ancient metricians. The moderns are inconsistent, recognizing the technique when, as in the four passages just cited, it appears in conjunction with ionic demarcation, but ignoring its possibility in choriambic:

Λαβδακίδαις ἐπίκουρος ἀδήλων θανάτων      – ◡ ◡ –. ◡ ◡ –. ◡ ◡ – – ◡ ◡ –
                                          —S. OT 496–97 = 510–11

(usually "ionicized" by demarcation after *Labdakidais*, thereby obscuring
the way the final colon, rhetorically demarcated in both strophe and antistrophe, is a doubly syncopated version of the – ◡ ◡ – – ◡ ◡ – – ◡ ◡ – –
◡ ◡ – with which the stanza begins—see below, 195);

ἀ νεότας μοι φίλον αἰεί, τὸ δὲ γῆρας ἄχθος      – ◡ ◡ – – ◡ ◡ – –| ◡ ◡ – ◡ –⁻
βαρύτερον Αἴτνας σκοπέλων ἐπὶ κρατὶ κεῖται      ⏑ ◡ ◡ – – ◡ ◡ –. | ◡ ◡ – ◡ –⁻
                                               —E. HF 637–40 = 655–58[40]

(where a new movement is usually assumed to begin with ἐπὶ κρατί);

ἠλιβάτοις ὑπὸ κευθμῶσι γενοίμαν      – ◡ ◡ –. ◡ ◡ – – ◡ ◡ – –
                                     —E. Hipp. 732 = 742

(ionicized into ⏖̆– ◡ ◡ – – ◡ ◡ – – in spite of the unparalleled character
of the contraction plus resolution posited [above, 39–40] and the pres-
ence of a similarly syncopated | ◡ ◡ –. ◡ ◡ – – ◡ ◡ –. . . . two cola later);[41]

ματρὸς ἐμᾶς ἢ διδύμοισι γάλακτος παρὰ μαστοῖς      – ◡ ◡ – – ◡ ◡ –. ◡ ◡ – – ◡ ◡ – –
ἢ πρὸς ἀδελφῶν <δίδυμ'> οὐλόμεν' αἰκίσματα νεκρῶν      – ◡ ◡ – –< ◡ ◡ >–. ◡ ◡ – – ◡ ◡ – –
                                               —E. Ph. 1526–29

(where choriambic analysis is supported by the parallel with the – ◡ ◡ –
– ◡ ◡ – – ◡ ◡ – – ◡ ◡ – – ◡ | ◡ – – ◡ ◡ – – ◡ ◡ – – ◡ ◡ – – ◡ ◡ – of 1519–
22 and the presence of two other pairings of long iono-choriambic movements elsewhere in the same passage [1508–18 and 1539–42]).

When a corresponding syncopation of a "base" quantity (above,
16–17) occurs in the mixed ◡ ◡ –.– ◡ – rather than the pure ◡ ◡ –
. ◡ ◡ – the situation is just the reverse. ◡ ◡ –.– ◡ – is regularly so
analyzed when it appears in conjunction with choriambic demarcation—as,

[40] The same sequence at E. IT 392–93 = 407–8 and, longer by a cycle and with different
location of syncopation, (– ◡ ◡ –. ◡ ◡ – – ◡ ◡ – – ◡ ◡ – ◡ –⁻) E. El. 725. The context in
both passages is less indicative, however, and the scansion for the second requires emendation of the responding 711; cf. Denniston ad loc.
[41] On the close of the colon and the text of its opening see text, 93 with n. 94. A similar
alternation between ionic and choriambic demarcation is found in the second and penultimate cola of A. Sept. 321 = 333ff.:

. . .–. | ◡ ◡ –. ◡ ◡ – – ◡ ◡ – – |
| – ◡ ◡ –. ◡ ◡ – – ◡ ◡ – |

for example, in the trimeter ‿ ∪ ∪ -. - ∪ - ∪ - ¯ that closes a number of stanzas composed largely of syncopated iambo-trochaic (A. *Sup.* 375 = 386, *Pers.* 283 = 289, *Sep.* 784 = 791, E. *Sup.* 1130 = 1137). In conjunction with ionic demarcation, however, it tends to be emended away or given a different scansion:

ἐρεθίζων πλανάτας                                    ∪ ∪-.-∪--

ἰαχαῖς τ' ἀναπάλλων                                  ∪ ∪-.∪ ∪--

τρυφερὸν πλόκαμον⁴² εἰς αἰθέρα ῥίπτων    ∪ ∪-.ͮ∪--∪∪-×

ἅμα δ' ἐπ' εὐάσμασιν ἐπιβρέμει τοιάδε·      ͮ∪-×ͮ∪ͮ-∪∪-

                                                            —E. *Bac.* 148-51

πλανάτας ἐρεθίζων, τρυφερόν <τε> Wilamowitz; πλόκ[αμ]ον Burges; βόστρυχον Earle

    ὅρα, βλέπ' εἰ καίρια φθέγγῃ.                 ×-∪-.-∪-.-¯

    τὸ δ' ἀλώσιμον ἐμᾷ φροντίδι, παῖ,        ∪ ∪-.ͮ∪--∪ ∪-.

    πόνος ὁ μὴ φοβῶν κράτιστος.               ͮ∪-×-∪-×

                                                            —S. *Ph.* 862-64

(taken by the manuscripts and modern editors as ×- ∪ -- ∪ -¦-- ∪ ∪- ∪ ∪¦∪ -- ∪ ∪- ∪ ∪¦×- ∪- ∪- ¯, in spite of the rhetorical demarcation, which suggests that the first line should be a separate rhythmical movement: catalectic trimeter with two syncopations,⁴³ the first of them matched by a corresponding syncopation in the line that follows).

Once again, modern practice is guided by metrist assumptions. Ionic ∪ ∪ =.¦ ∪ ∪ -- is possible, but not choriambic - ∪ ∪ =¦. ∪ ∪-. And since this same ionic ∪ ∪=.¦ ∪ ∪ -- will not yield ∪ ∪=.- ∪ -- by anaclasis, ∪ ∪ -.-∪-- must be taken, in Hellenistic fashion (above, 42), as ∪ ∪-.=∪-, an analysis which requires choriambic metron division:

----
⁴² The text is supported by the parallel with the next colon (even closer if one follows Elmsley in deleting *ep'*). Cf., also, E. *Ph.* 1517 (μονομάτορος ὀδυρμοῖς [∪ ∪-.ͮ∪--] in an iono-choriambic context, regularized by Wilamowitz's μονομάτορσιν into ∪ ∪--∪ ∪--), the variously emended E. *El.* 727 = 737 (below, n. 89), and, perhaps, ∪ ∪-.ͮ∪ͮ- |∪ ∪--∪ ∪|ͮ-∪ ∪-- echoing ∪ ∪-×-∪-×|-.-×ͮ∪|-×ͮ∪-× two lines earlier in *Or.* 1479-84.

⁴³ Or better, perhaps, ×-∪-.-∪-×-, echoing the colon close that prevails in the stanza preceding (below, Appendix V). For similar instances of ionic syncopation see S. *Inachus* 16-19 (a quadruple ∪ ∪--∪-, usually taken as an anomalous dochmiac rather than the ∪ ∪-.-∪- which ∪ ∪-×-∪- in the line following would suggest (cf. Ar. *Nub.*, 1206-8: ∪ ∪-.-∪ͮ|×-∪-.-∪-|×-∪-.-∪-) and A. *Pers.* 659-62 = 666-70, where the analysis -∪∪-×-∪--|∪ ∪--∪ ∪--∪ ∪--|∪ ∪-.-∪--|∪ ∪-∪-¯ favored by the context (text, 174-76) is usually ignored or dismissed.

∪ ∪ –|⌣.= ∪ –, not ∪ ∪ –. ⊤⌣=∪ –.
A different problem interferes with the recognition of the other type of iono-choriambic syncopation. – ∪ –. ∪ ∪ – is externally identical with aeolic x̆x̆ – ∪ ∪ – or –x̆ – ∪ ∪ –, and in most of its occurrences this is certainly the way – ∪ – ∪ ∪ – should be analyzed. Yet there is little reason to doubt the ionic analysis proposed (*LMGD* 125) for Ar. *Ran.* 326 = 342ff. (– ∪ –. ∪ ∪ – – ∪ ∪ – – followed by normal trimeters and dimeters); and at E. *Bac.* 576ff. the usual analysis of ⌣⌣∪ – ∪ ∪ – – as aeolic x̆x̆ – ∪ ⌣ – destroys the close parallel between the centrally demarcated ionic lines of Bacchus and the trochaic ones of the chorus:

| | | |
|---|---|---|
| Δι. | ἰώ, | exclamation *extra metrum* |
| | κλύετ' ἐμᾶς, κλύετ' αὐδᾶς, | ⌣⌣∪ –.\| ∪ ∪ – – |
| | ἰὼ βάκχαι, ἰὼ βάκχαι. | ⌣⌣– –\| ⌣⌣– –[44] |
| Xo. | τίς ὅδε, τίς, πόθεν ὁ κέλαδος | ⌣⌣∪ –.\|⌣⌣∪⌣⌣× |
| | ἀνά μ' ἐκάλεσεν Εὐίου; | ⌣⌣∪⌣⌣×\|– ∪ – |
| Δι. | ἰώ, ἰώ, πάλιν αὐδῶ, | ⌣⌣∪ –.\| ∪ ∪ – – |
| | ὁ Σεμέλας, ὁ Διὸς παῖς. | ⌣⌣∪ –.\| ∪ ∪ – – |
| Xo. | ἰώ, ἰώ, δέσποτα, δέσποτα, | ⌣⌣∪ –. \|– ∪ ∪ – – ∪ ∪[45] |
| | μόλε νῦν ἡμέτερον ἐς | ⌣⌣∪ –.⌣⌣∪ –. |
| | θίασον, ὦ Βρόμιε Βρόμιε | ⌣⌣∪ –. \|⌣⌣∪⌣⌣× |

The passage (cf. Murray *ad loc.*) recalls several in Aeschylus in which a series of verbally demarcated repetitions of ⌣⌣∪ – are followed by ∪ ∪ – – or ∪ ∪ –×; cf. *Ch.* 807–8:

| | |
|---|---|
| τὸ δὲ καλῶς κτίμενον ὦ μέγα ναίων | ⌣⌣∪ –.\|⌣⌣∪ –.\| ∪ ∪ –× |
| στόμιον, εὖ δὸς ἀνιδεῖν δόμον ἀνδρός | ⌣⌣∪ –.\|⌣⌣∪ –.\| ∪ ∪ – –, |

perhaps, since it is a mesodic passage, intended to be heard as a partial echo of the unambiguous ionic beginnings of the two preceding mesodes (789–91 and 827–29).

The ionic – ∪ –. ∪ ∪ – of these passages has an iambo-choriambic counterpart in the second major rhythmical movement of *Rhesus* 360 = 370ff.:

---

[44] For monosyllabic scansion of ἰώ (however pronounced) cf. E. *Or.* 976, with the parallels cited by di Benedetto *ad loc.*; and, for double contraction in an ionic dimeter, E. *Bac.* 537.
[45] Perhaps an intruding pair of dactyls, perhaps an example of the irregular trochaic to be discussed later (text, 213 ).

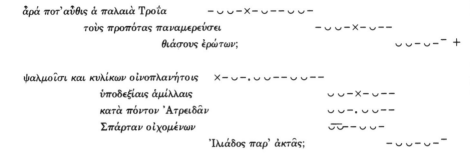

ἀρά ποτ'αὖθις ἀ παλαιὰ Τροΐα    – ∪ ∪ – × – ∪ – – ∪ ∪ –
 τοὺς προπότας παναμερεύσει    – ∪ ∪ – × – ∪ – –
  θιάσους ἐρώτων;    ∪ ∪ – ∪ – ⁻ +

ψαλμοῖσι και κυλίκων οἰνοπλανήτοις    × – ∪ –. ∪ ∪ – – ∪ ∪ – –
 ὑποδεξίαις ἀμίλλαις    ∪ ∪ – × – ∪ – –
 κατὰ πόντον 'Ατρειδᾶν    ∪ ∪ –. ∪ ∪ – –
 Σπάρταν οἰχομένων    ᴖᴖ – – ∪ ∪ –
  'Ιλιάδος παρ' ἀκτᾶς;    – ∪ ∪ – ∪ – ⁻

Here the analysis × – ∪ –. ∪ ∪ – is supported by the parallel syncopation
two cola later, as well as by the close similarity between the second movement and the first: identical except for the reversed order of iambic and
choriambic at their beginnings and the presence, in one, of four cycles of
pure ionic (| ∪ ∪ –. ∪ ∪ – – | ᴖᴖ – – ∪ ∪ – | –) not found in the other. The
same sequence × – ∪ –. ∪ ∪ – introduces a pair of iono-choriambic movements at S. *Aj.* 1211[46] and should probably, if the text is correct, be given
the same analysis.

The syncopation – ∪̆ – belongs, strictly speaking, to pure iambo-
trochaic, but its appearance in conjunction with a preceding ∪ ∪ – × is
worth noting, as providing a final set of parallels between choriambic and
ionic. The most striking are at E. *Bac.* 73 = 88ff. and 105 = 120ff. The
former begins with two identical movements that are syncopated versions
of the mixed "choriambo-ionic" examined earlier (above, 20–22):

   ὦ μάκαρ ὅστις εὐδαίμων    – ∪ ∪ – ×̆ –. – –
   τελετὰς θεῶν εἰδὼς    ∪ ∪ – ×̆ –. – –
   βιοτὰν ἁγιστεύει    ∪ ∪ – ×̆ –. – – +
   καὶ θιασεύεται ψυχάν    – ∪ ∪ – ×̆ –. – – etc.

The opening rhythm of the two tricola is then echoed, with choriambic
demarcation, in the – ∪ ∪ – × – ∪⁀| – ∪ ∪ – ∪ – ⁻ with which the second
passage closes, as well as in what may be one or more instances of
| – ∪ ∪ – ×̆ –. – |

---

[46] The strophe (1199) has × – ∪ – – ∪ ∪ – at this point, but is more easily brought into line
with the antistrophe (by Hermann's ἐκεῖνος οὐ[τε] στεφάνων) than vice versa. The responsion × – ∪ –. ∪ ∪ – = × – ∪ – – ∪ ∪ – is conceivable, but much harder to parallel in iono-
choriambic than iambo-trochaic (above, n. 35).

ὦ Σεμέλας τροφοὶ Θῆβαι,  – ∪ ∪ – × – . – –
στεφανοῦσθε κισσῷ·  ∪ ∪ – × – . – (or ∪ ∪ – ∪ – ⁻)
βρύετε, βρύετε χλοήρει  ⌣⌣∪ ∪⌣⌣× – . – ‖ (or ⌣⌣∪ ∪⌣⌣∪ – ⁻)
μίλακι καλλικάρπῳ  – ∪ ∪ – × – . – (or – ∪ ∪ – ∪ – ⁻)
καὶ καταβακχιοῦσθε δρυὸς  – ∪ ∪ – × – ∪⌣⌣
ἢ ἐλάτας κλάδοισι.  – ∪ ∪ – ∪ – ⁻

Other instances of <u>– ∪ ∪ – × – . – –</u> variously demarcated, include the following:

|  |  |
|---|---|
| – ∪ ∪ – × – . – – ∪ ∪ – ∪ – ⁻ | A. *Sup.* 631 = 644 |
| – ∪ ∪ – × – . – \| – ∪ ∪ – × – . – – ∪ ∪ – ∪ – ⁻ | *Ch.* 387–89 = 412–14 |
| – ∪ ∪ – × – . – \| – ∪ ∪ – × – . – \| – ∪ ∪ – × – . – ' – ₁∪ ∪ – ∪ – ⁻ | Ar. *Vesp.* 533–36 = 638–41 |
| – ∪ ∪ – × – ∪ – – \| ∪ ∪ – × – . \| – – ∪ ∪ – ∪ – ⁻ | A. *Sup.* 814–16 = 822–24 |
| – ∪ ∪ – × – . – – | S. *Tr.* 947 = 950, *Fr. adesp.* 127.9.10 |
| ∪ ∪ – × – . – – | E. *Bac.* 72, *Cyc.* 510 = 518 |
| ∪ ∪ –   – ∪ ∪ – × – . – – | *Cyc.* 510 = 518 |
| – ∪ ∪ –   – ∪ ∪ – × – . – – ∪ ∪ – | *Bac.* 86–88 = 102–4 |

and ionic and choriambic versions, with further syncopations, may appear side by side at E. *Alc.* 269 and 271:

κλίνατ', οὐ σθενῶ ποσίν. πλησίον Ἄιδας. – ∪ – × – ∪ – \| – ∪ ∪ – –
  σκοτία δ' ἐπ ὄσσοις νὺξ ἐφέρπει ∪ ∪ – × – . – . – ∪ – ×

                   (269)

τέκνα, τέκν',         – ∪ – \| – ∪ ∪ – ‖

οὐκέτι δή,         – ∪ ∪ – . – . – . – ×

οὐκέτι δὴ μάτηρ σφῷν ἔστιν.   (271)

if one can accept a highly unusual accumulation of syncopations in 271.[47] In the parallel ionic and trochaic sequences of A. *Eu.* 321–22 = 334–35 – . – is separated by intervening iambo-trochaic from ∪ ∪ –:

---

[47] The nearest possible tragic parallel for the accumulation is E. *Alc.* 595 = 604, where neither text nor the analysis – ∪ – . – . – . – ∪ – × is certain (see Dale *ad loc.*). From comedy, however, there is Ar. *Lys.* 1260–61, where – . – . – ∪ – ∪ – ⁻ seems to be echoed in the quadruply syncopated – . – . – . – . – ⁻ that immediately follows, just as – \| ∪ ∪ – × – . – . – ∪ – × is echoed by the following \| – ∪ ∪ – . – . – . – × in the *Alcestis passage*. – ∪ – ∪ – ⁻ seems to stand in a similar relationship to a succeeding – . – . – ⁻ at A. *Sup.* 140–42 = 150–52 and E. *IT* 403–4 = 417–18.

μᾶτερ, ἁ μ'ἔτικτες, ὦ μᾶτερ νύξ,     – ∪ – × – ∪ –.–.– –
ἀλαοῖσι καὶ δεδορκόσιν ποινάν     ∪ ∪ – × – ∪ – × –.– ×⁴⁸

The reverse of these rhythms, | –. – – ∪ ∪ –. . . or | × –. – – ∪ ∪ –. . . is
very rare, the one or two possible examples being in ambiguous contexts:

'Ασιήτιδα γαῖαν          ∪ ∪ –. ∪ ∪ – ×̆
    Εὐρώπας διαμείψας          –. – – ∪ ∪ – –
                                   –E. IT 396–97 = 411–12⁴⁹

Like 'Ασίας ἀπὸ γᾶς (above, 46) the opening phrase has the oriental
associations that often go with ionic in tragedy, but this is hardly decisive
in analyzing what could just as easily be aeolic, ending in – ∪ ∪ – ∪ – ×
—A—
– ∪ ∪ –.
    —A—
The rarity is not surprising, given the rarity of the corresponding | × –
. – × – ∪ –. . . and | –. – × – ∪ –. . . in iambo-trochaic (above, 44). What
is surprising is the rarity of the non-syncopated ionic counterpart to | –. –
– ∪ ∪ – ×̲ |:

              οὐκ ἀείδω τὰ παλαιά,          – ∪ – – ∪ ∪ – ×
        καινὰ †γὰρ ἄμα† ⁵⁰ κρείσσω.          – ∪ – – ∪ ∪ – –
              νέος ὁ Ζεὺς βασιλεύει          ∪ ∪ – – ∪ ∪ – –
        τὸ πάλαι δ' ἦν Κρόνος ἄρχων          ∪ ∪ – – ∪ ∪ – –
                                   Timotheus 20/796.1–4

given the frequency of the parallel choriambic | × – ∪ – – ∪ ∪ – (see Table
III). The contrast between ionic and choriambic is much sharper here
than anywhere else in Classical rhythmical practice, and it raises the question whether, even before the Hellenistic period, the two types were not
more distinct than the theory of epiploke would suggest—built up, on the
one hand, from a free combination of choriambs and iambs and, on the
other, from longer minimal units beginning with ∪ ∪ – ( ∪ ∪ – – ∪ ∪ – –,

⁴⁸ ἀλαοῖσι (responding to ἐπέκλωσε) is usually scanned ∪ – – ∪ and taken as a Homerism
(cf. Od. 10.493 and 12.267 μᾶντῖος ἀλαοῦ). But even if Aeschylus was familiar with the
phrase in this form rather than in the variant version μάντηος ἀλαοῦ (with metrical lengthening of -ος) an anomalous epic ἀλαοῦ is a weak parallel for tragic ἀλαός. For the colon close
× –. – – or × –. – ×, cf. A. Ag. 246–47 = 256–57 (× – ∪ –. – ∪ – × –.ˈ– –ˌ∪ ∪ – ∪ –⁻) and
E. IA 301 (˘ ∪ –. – ∪ – × –. – × | –. –. – ∪ – × – ∪ –).
⁴⁹ For another possibility (equally uncertain), cf. E. Hipp. 554 = 564 (below, n. 244).
⁵⁰ The words have often been emended: perhaps γὰρ τᾶσματα (ἄσματα Schneidewin),
which would give to the first two lines the same sort of repetition and contrast (ἀείδω :
ᾄσματα; παλαιά : καινά found in the third and fourth (βασιλεύει : ἄρχων; νέος : πάλαι).

⌣ ⌣ – × – ⌣ – – etc.).

The possibility certainly exists, but alternative explanations for the contrasting patterns of usage are at least as likely. They may, for example, have something to do with the general reluctance, more pronounced in trochaic than in iambic, to allow word end within a colon immediately following the sequence – ⌣ – x̄.[51] A comparable prohibition involving – ⌣ – –, the mixed iono-choriambic counterpart to this sequence, might be expected to operate more strongly in iono-trochaic than in iambo-choriambic; and if so, the constraints it imposed would be much more serious than in pure trochaic. Ionic tends, to a greater degree than trochaic, to subdivide cola into four-quantity groups by word end, but lacks any variant form which, like the trochaic – ⌣ – x̆, would allow initial – ⌣ – – to constitute such a group. Rather than accept the rhythmical "bridge" (see Introductory Note) – ⌣ – –͡, or iconoclastically ignore it (οὐκ ἀείδω τὰ παλαιά), poets may have preferred, by and large, to confine – ⌣ – – to colon close.[52] The result is a rhythm less flexible than choriambic, but the contrast is no more striking than that between, say, the three tragedians' handlings of a single type such as syncopated iambo-trochaic. It does not constitute an argument against the fundamental unity of tetradic rhythm strong enough to carry weight in the face of the remarkable consistency with which seemingly disparate phenomena in four rhythmical types are correlated through positing the fairly simple set of techniques listed at the beginning of the chapter:

1 and 2) total or partial epiploke,
   3) clausular ⌣ – ⁻ ,
   4) interchangeability, subject to certain restrictions, of iono-choriambic – ⌣ and iambo-trochaic × –,
5 and 6) contraction or syncopation affecting the short in the sequence ⌣ – and the quantity preceding, or the long in the sequence and the quantity following.[53]

---

[51] Iambic cola opening with × – ⌣ – x̄ | or closing with x̄ | – ⌣ – are significantly more common than their trochaic counterparts (– ⌣ – x̄ |... and ...x̄ | – ⌣ – ×), both in the iambo-trochaic portions of Pindaric and Bacchylidean dactylo-epitritic and in the dimeters and trimeters of tragic lyric (see Parker, 4–8 and 11–12).

[52] Medial occurrences of – ⌣ – – are even rarer than initial ones, the only certain instances being Anacreon 66/411 and Ar. *Ran.* 330 = 347.

[53] The extreme rarity of consecutive syncopations (– . – . ⌣ ⌣ – ) in mixed iono-choriambic (perhaps at E. *Alc.* 396 = 409, if the rhythm is ionic) by contrast with the relative frequency (text, 44) of the iambo-trochaic counterpart (– . – . – ⌣ –) might be a further argument against the unity posited here. But in iambo-trochaic such syncopation involves durational equivalents: short and (since the anceps following a syncopated short quantity is almost never long) short anceps. Whatever considerations made a succession of two equivalent departures from rhythmical regularity acceptable need not have applied when the successive syncopated quantities were different, as they are in the – ⌣ – ± ⌣ ⌣ – of iono-choriambic.

## TABLE III: THE DEMARCATIONS |×–◡–◡◡–... AND |–◡–◡◡–...

A. |×–◡––◡◡–...     B. |×–◡–.–◡–...     C. |(–◡–×)–◡–◡◡–...     D. |–◡–.◡◡–...

**A.** |×–◡––◡◡–...

Anacr. 67|412:
×–◡––◡◡◡–◡–

Pind. N7s4:
×–◡–◡◡–̈◡–◡–

e1:
×–◡–◡◡––◡–

**A.**

Pers. 977 = 991:
×–◡–◡◡–×–◡–
1017 = 1030:
×–◡–◡◡–×–◡–

Sep. 720 = 727:
×–◡–◡◡–◡–

Sup. 524 = 531:
×–◡–◡◡–
782 = 791:
×–◡–◡◡◡–

Ag. 141:
×–◡–◡◡–◡–

PV 128 = 143,
133 = 148, 397 = 406:
×–◡–◡◡–×–◡––
131 = 146: ×–◡–◡◡–◡◡–

**S.**

Aj. 705 = 718:
×–◡––◡–◡–

Ant. 781–82 = 791–92:
×–◡––◡–|×–◡–◡◡–◡–×
785 = 795:
×–◡–◡◡–◡–◡–×–
806 = 823:
×–◡––◡–
839 = 857:
×–◡–◡◡–×–◡–×

**C.** |(–◡–×)–◡–◡◡–...

P5s10:
–◡–◡◡–̈–̈◡◡––◡–

256 = 262:
◡̈◡̈◡̈◡◡◡̈◡̈
×–◡–.◡–◡–◡–◡–◡–

164:
–◡◡–.◡◡–◡◡–

141:
–◡–◡◡–×|
–̈◡–.◡–.◡–

Eu. 358–59:
◡◡–×◡◡––◡◡––◡–◡–̈(?)

1199 = 1211:
×–◡–.◡◡–

375 = 390:
◡–×–◡◡◡–◡◡––|×E'

**D.** |–◡–.◡◡–...

Ag. 1018–19:
◡̈◡–.|◡◡–.|◡◡–.◡◡–.|◡◡––[1]

Ch. 807–8:
◡̈◡–.|◡◡–.|◡◡–.|◡◡–×
◡̈◡–.|◡◡–.|◡◡–.|◡◡––

Eu. 328–30 and 372–74:
◡̈◡–.|◡̈◡–.|◡◡––
◡̈◡–.|◡◡–.|◡◡–.◡◡–
◡̈◡–.|◡̈◡–.|◡◡––

[1] Followed by an (or ◡◡–.◡◡–)|an an^; cf. ◡◡–––◡◡–|◡◡–––◡◡––|◡◡––––◡◡–– + an an^ at Pers. 694–96 = 700–702.

OT 463 = 473:
x–∪–∪–×
El. 1058 = 1070:
x–∪–∪–×–∪–
Tr. 116–18 = 126–28:
x–∪–∪∪–|
x–∪–∪–|x–∪–∪∪–
Ph. 1099, 1136 = 1159,
1137 = 1160
x–∪–∪∪–
E.
Med. 431 = 439:
x–∪–∪–∪–
Hipp. 58:
x–∪–∪–×
128 = 138:
x–∪–∪∪–
Sup. 977:
x–∪–∪–∪–
HF 352–53 = 368–69:
x–∪–∪∪–∪– +
x–∪–∪∪–∪–
763–65 = 772–75:
x–∪–∪–|x–∪–∪∪–∪–
x–∪–∪–|x–∪–∪∪–|×E´
IT 425 = 442:
x–∪–∪–∪–

Ion 1074 = 1091:
x–∪–∪–∪–
Hel. 1338–39 = 1353–54:
x–∪–∪–|x–∪–∪∪–
1451–52 = 1465–66:
x–∪–∪–|x–∪–∪∪–∪–
1454 = 1468:
x–∪–∪–
1457 = 1471:
x–∪–∪–

OT 1209 = 1218:
–∪–(∪)∪∪–×–∪–²
Tr. 517:
–∪–∪∪–
893:
∪∪–∪∪–|E×⁴

Ph. 1181–85:
–∪∪–∪∪–|∪∪–|∪∪–.
–∪∪–|∪∪–
1172–75:³
x–∪–×–∪–|x–∪–×|
–∪.∪∪–∪∪–∪–

1340–41 = 1356–57:
–∪–∪∪–.|–∪–∪∪–

²If one scans πάτρι in the strophe and deletes ὡς in the antistrophe.
³With Hartung's deletion of ἐμοί. Cf. the very similar 1185.
⁴Best so taken, however one handles the break in the continuity of iambo-trochaic created by the × Eˆ that follows E × (cf. LMGD 75 and, for problems posed by other analyses of the first colon, Parker, CQ [1968] 255). Insertion of a second μεγάλαν would restore continuity (ἔτεκεν ἔτεκεν μεγάλαν | ἃ νέορτος ἅδε νύμφα [∪∪–×∪∪∪–∪–∪–] <μεγάλαν> δόμοισι τοῖσδ᾽ Ἐρινύν [∪∪–×∪∪∪––]) and make the stanza end with an echo of the immediately preceding –∪∪–,∪∪∪∪–.|∪∪–×–∪–∪– (πρὸς θανάτῳ θάνατον ἀνύσασα μόνα | ῾στονόεντος ἐν τομᾷ σιδάρου).

Or. 814 = 826:
×−∪−−∪∪−−

Ar.
Ach. 1150:
×−∪−−∪∪−∪−
Vesp. 526 = 631:
×−∪−−∪∪−
1450−61 =
1462−73 (5 times)
Nub. 515:
×−∪−−∪∪−×
571 = 603:
×−∪−−∪∪−
700 = 804:
×−∪−−∪∪−
949−50 = 1025−26:
×−∪−−∪∪− (twice)
Lys. 321 = 355ff.:
×−∪−−∪∪− (6 times)
Eccl. 969−70 =
973−74:
×−∪−−∪∪− (twice)
Aristonous, Hymn. Apoll. 29 (p. 163 Powell):
×−∪−−∪∪− (= ××A and ××B)

Rhes. 363 = 373:
×−∪−.∪∪−−∪∪−−

Or. 813 = 825:
−∪−−∪∪−−(= ×B)
834:
−∪−−∪∪−
1431:
−∪̆∪̆−∪∪− (?)

Bac. 151:
∪∪−×̆∪̆∪̆−∪∪−
1340−41 = 1356−57:
−∪−−∪∪−.|−∪−−∪∪−

Pax 342−45:
−−×−∪−−∪∪−×|E

Th. 110 = 119 = 125, 316:
(∪̆)∪̆∪̆−∪∪−
109, 1044:
(∪̆)∪̆∪̆−∪∪−×

Timotheus 20|796.1:
−∪−−∪∪−×
26|802.3:
−∪−−∪∪−−

PMG 845.1:
−∪−−∪∪−−
853:
−∪−×−∪−−∪∪−×|−[−]⁵∪−−∪∪−×

Frgm. Grenfellianum 11:
−∪̆∪̆−×̆∪̆∪̆−⁶

576, 580, 581:
−∪̆∪̆−.|∪∪−−

Ran. 326 = 342:
−∪−∪−−∪∪−−|−∪−∪∪−−

⁵ πρὶν [καὶ] μολεῖν κεῖνον ἀνίστω.
⁶ ἄστρα φίλα καὶ συνέρωσα πότνια νύξ μοι.

# CHAPTER THREE: PROSODIAC AND HEPTADIC AEOLIC

Metrist interpretation of tetradic rhythm pervades most ancient and modern discussions of the forms it was intended to explain. Its most extravagant application, however, has been to a different rhythm altogether: a form of mixed prosodiac which admits linkage to ionochoriambic as well as iambo-trochaic. Linkage may occur either through the same ᴗ– that is part of the transitional segment in ordinary mixed prosodiac:

θεομήστωρ δ' ἐπικλήσκετο Πέρσαις     iono-choriambic
θεομήστωρ δ'         ᴗ ᴗ – – ᴗ ᴗ –. ᴗ ᴗ – – | ᴗ ᴗ–×|– ᴗ ᴗ – ᴗ ᴗ – ᴗ – ‾
    ἔσκεν, ἐπεὶ στρατὸν εὖ ποδούχει     prosodiac
                        –A. Pers. 655–66 = 649–50

                                  prosodiac
γᾶς δόσις οὐτιδανοῖς         – ᴗ ᴗ – ᴗ ᴗ –|– ᴗ ᴗ – ᴗ – ‾
    ἐν ῥοθίοις φορεῖται         iono-choriambic
                                –Sept. 361–62 = 350–51

or through the segment – ᴗ. In contexts where – ᴗ plays this role it can also link iono-choriambic with iambo-trochaic. Thus the – ᴗ –×  – ᴗ ᴗ – – ᴗ – that appears eight times in the dactylo-epitritic of Pindar and Bacchylides (see Table IV) may be analyzed as:

        iambo-trochaic     iambo-trochaic
        – ᴗ –× – ᴗ ᴗ – – ᴗ –
               iono-choriambic

to which prosodiac analogues, also from Pindar, are N11e4:

                           prosodiac      iambo-trochaic
ἐν τ' ἀέθλοισιν ἀριστεύων ἐπέδειξεν βίαν    – ᴗ ᴗ – ᴗ ᴗ –× – ᴗ ᴗ – – ᴗ –
                               iono-choriambic

and *N*5e5:

iambo-trochaic          prosodiac

$$\overline{\times - \cup - \times} \overline{- \cup \cup - - \cup \cup - \cup \cup - \times - \cup -}$$

iono-choriambic          iambo-trochaic

πύκταν τέ νιν καὶ παγκρατίου φθέγξαι ἑλεῖν Ἐπιδαύρῳ διπλόαν (52)

This method of joining iono-choriambic to other rhythms may be called "trochaic" modulation to distinguish it from the "iambic" modulation (via ⏑−) dealt with hitherto. As the name suggests, it is a mirror image of the other. Moving counter-clockwise rather than clockwise on the tangent circles drawn in Chapter One (above, 18) will generate a piece of mixed iono-choriambic with trochaic modulation, and reversing the order of the quantities in a segment of iono-choriambic or prosodiac constructed one way will produce a segment constructed the other way. The ×−⏑− −⏑⏑−×−⏑− of A. *Pers.* 1017 = 1030 is an exact inversion of the −⏑−×−⏑⏑−−⏑−× of Pind. *O*13e3 and fr. 122s3; as is ×−⏑−× −⏑⏑−⏑⏑−−⏑⏑−×−⏑⏑−⏑⏑−× (S. *Tr.* 520−23) of ×−⏑⏑− ⏑⏑−×−⏑⏑−|−⏑⏑−⏑⏑−×|−⏑−×... (Pind. *I*3e1−3).[54]

When iono-choriambic introduced by either type of modulation is a third ingredient in mixed prosodiac, the result can easily be a great variety of eight-quantity segments: not only prosodiac $\overline{\times - \cup \cup - \cup \cup - \times}$ and iambo-trochaic $\overline{\times - \cup - \times - \cup - \times}$, but $\overline{\times - \cup \cup - - \cup - \times}$, $\overline{\times - \cup - - \cup \cup - \times}$ etc. In an effort to reduce as many as possible of these to equivalence, 19th-century metrists took over and reapplied the entire repertory of choriambic and major and minor ionic forms provided in the post-Classical theory and practice of the ancients. The assumption was that all such sequences were dimeters (major ionic followed by choriamb, minor ionic followed by major ionic etc.) and that either metron of a dimeter could exhibit any of the variant forms attributed to it by ancient analysis without the dimeter losing its identity. Hence equations such as the following:

---

[54] This analysis will not explain passages in which ×−⏑⏑− is followed by ×−⏑− rather than by −⏑− or −⏑⏑−⏑⏑−. But no such transitions are securely attested. Of the instances sometimes alleged for Pindar, two are in contexts too brief to allow certainty as to structure (frs. 126 and 168), and a third (−⏑⏑−|x̄−⏑⏑−×−⏑−×−⏑− at *O*6e3 is more plausibly taken as −⏑⏑−| ⏑⏑⏑⏑−×−⏑−..., a repeat of the similarly demarcated portion of the preceding line (−⏑−×−⏑−×−⏑⏑−|⏑⏑⏑−⏑⏑−×−⏑⏑−). Mixed prosodiac here shows the modulations into dactylo-anapestic discussed later in the chapter (text, 66−69), and the presence of that rhythm, together with the contracted ⏑⏑⏑ common in dactylo-anapestic but rare in prosodiac, gives a suitably epic flavor to the context where it first appears: Adrastos's memorial *epos*, spoken on the battlefield over the vanished Amphiraus and modeled, according to the scholiast, on a hexameter from the *Thebaid*.

## TABLE IV: IONO-CHORIAMBIC IN COMBINATION WITH PROSODIAC

A. *Trochaic modulation* (– ∪ – × – ∪ ∪ –... etc.)    B. *Iambic modulation* (– ∪ – – ∪ ∪ –... etc.)

1a. *Pindar and Bacchylides* (| – ∪ . . .)

| | | |
|---|---|---|
| *O*6e2: | – ∪ – × – ∪ – ×$^{D ∪ ∪ -}_{- ∪ ∪ D}$× – ∪ ∪ – | |
| 11s3: | – ∪ – × – ∪ ∪ – | |
| 12s2: | – ∪ – × D × – ∪ ∪ – | |
| s4,e6 | – ∪ – × – ∪ – × – ∪ ∪ – | |
| 13s8 | – ∪ – . – ∪ – × – ∪ ∪ – | |
| e3 | – ∪ – × – ∪ ∪ – – ∪ – × | |
| *P*1s2 | – ∪ – × – ∪ ∪ – – – ∪ – × D × – | *P*4e4: – ∪ ∪ – × – ∪ – × – ∪ – × D |
| 4e6 | – ∪ – × – ∪ – × – ∪ ∪ – | (or ^^^D × – ∪ – . . .?) |
| *N*8s2 | – ∪ – × – ∪ – × – ∪ – × – ∪ ∪ – | |
| e6 | – ∪ – × – ∪ ∪ – – × D × | |
| *N*11s5 | – ∪ ∪ – – ∪ – . – ∪ – × – ∪ ∪ – | |
| e4 | D × – ∪ ∪ – – ∪ – | |
| *I*1s6 | – ∪ – × D . – ∪ ∪ – – ∪ – × – ∪ – | |
| e3 | D × – ∪ – × – ∪ ∪ – | |
| 2e4 | – ∪ – × – ∪ – × – ∪ ∪ – | |
| 5s2 | – ∪ – × – ∪ – × – ∪ ∪ – | |
| s6 | – ∪ – × – ∪ ∪ – – ∪ – × – ∪ – × | |
| e4 | – ∪ – . – ∪ ∪ – | |
| e5 | – ∪ – × – ∪ – × – ∪ ∪ – | |
| 6s2 | – ∪ – × – ∪ – × – ∪ ∪ – | |
| 6 | D × – ∪ – × – ∪ ∪ – | |
| *Dith.* 2s7 | D × – ∪ ∪ – | *Dith.* s6 – ∪ ∪ – × – ∪ – × – ∪ – |
| fr. 122s3 | – ∪ – × – ∪ ∪ – – – ∪ – × | (or ^^^D × – ∪ – . . .?) |
| 124a,s3 | – ∪ – × – ∪ ∪ – – – ∪ – × – ∪ – × | |
| 227 | – ∪ – × – ∪ ∪ – | |
| Bacch. 11s5–7 | D × D . – ∪ – × – ∪ ∪ – | fr. 4.32: ∪ ∪ – × – ∪ – × ( = – – ∪ – × – ∪ – ×) |
| 14e3 | – ∪ – × – ∪ ∪ – – – × D × | 10s10  – ∪ – . ∪ ∪ – ( = – ∪ – . – ∪ –) |

1b. *Pindar and Bacchylides* (| × – ∪ . . .)

| | | |
|---|---|---|
| *P*3s4 | × – ∪ – × – ∪ – × – ∪ ∪ – | |
| *N*1e4 | × – ∪ – . – ∪ ∪ – | |
| *N*5e4 | × – ∪ – × – ∪ ∪ – D × – ∪ – | |
| *I*1e4 | × – ∪ – × – ∪ ∪ – – – ∪ – × – ∪ – × | |
| 3e1 | × D × – ∪ ∪ – | |
| *Hymn*1s5 | × – ∪ – × – ∪ ∪ – | |
| fr. 42 | × – ∪ – × – ∪ – × – ∪ ∪ – | |
| 193 | × – ∪ ∪ – – – ∪ – × D . – ∪ – | |
| Bacch. 5e1 | × – ∪ ∪ – – – ∪ – × – ∪ – × – ∪ – × | 19s8:  × D – ∪ ∪ – × – ∪ – × – ∪ – ∪ – ‾ |

2. *Drama and later lyric*

A.
*Pers.* 650–51 = 655–56
∪ ∪ – – ∪ ∪ – – – ∪ ∪ – – | ∪ ∪ – × | D ∪ – ‾
*Sept.* 349–51 = 360–62
D × | D | – ∪ ∪ – ∪ – ‾
     725–26 = 732–33
∪ ∪ – – ∪ ∪ – – ∪ ∪ – . | D ∪ – ‾
     781–82 = 788–89
D | ⏒ ∪ ∪ ⏒ × – + D | – ∪ ∪ – . – ∪ – ∪ – ‾
*Supp.* 524–26 = 531–33
× – ∪ – | ∪ ∪ – × D × D ∪ – ‾
     543–46 = 552–55
– ∪ ∪ D – ∪ ∪ – – ∪ ∪ –
– ∪ ∪ – – ∪ ∪ – – ∪ ∪ – – ∪ ∪ – ∪ – ‾

*Supp.* 40–42 = 49–51:
  D. | D. – ∪ – × – ∪ – × | – ∪ ∪ – D ∪ ∪ – ‾
  73–76 = 82–85:
  × E. | D.     – ∪ ∪ – D | × E^

(TABLE IV, continued)

(column A)

S.
*Ant.* 357–60 = 368–70:
   x–ᴗ–.–ᴗ–|x–ᴗ–.–ᴗ–.|–ᴗᴗ–
*OT* 1086 = 1098:
   –ᴗᴗ––ᴗ–x–ᴗ–x–ᴗ–

E.
*Alc.* 572–74 = 582–84:
   x–ᴗ–x–ᴗᴗ–|–ᴗ–ᴗ–⁻

Ar.
*Vesp.* 274 = 282:
   –ᴗᴗ––ᴗ–x|–ᴗᴗ––ᴗ–x ( = Dx|Dx)
*Av.* 924–25:
   –ᴗᴗ––ᴗ–xDx⁝ ᴗ–
936–39:
   ⁝ᴗ–x–ᴗᴗ–|–ᴗ–.–ᴗᴗ–|⁝ᴗ–x⁝ᴗ–x–ᴗᴗ–
(Pindaric pastiche)
Flamininus Paean 1–2 (p. 173 Powell)
   x–ᴗ–x–ᴗᴗ– D x–ᴗ–x

(column B)

*Ch.* 808–10
   ⁝ᴗ–.|⁝ᴗ–.|ᴗ ᴗ–x|Dx|D.|Dᴗ–
*Ag.* 689–90 = 707–708
   ᴗ ᴗ–xD–ᴗ ᴗ––
*PV* 131–32 = 147–48
   x–ᴗ––ᴗ ᴗ–.|Dᴗ–⁻
533–45 = 542–44
   D.|ᴗ̄ᴗ–x–ᴗ–x–ᴗ–ᴗ–⁻

*Aj.* 222–26 = 246–50:
   –ᴗ ᴗD|xE^ + –ᴗᴗ–ᴗ ᴗD|–ᴗᴗ––ᴗᴗ––

*El.* 856–57 = 867–70
   x–ᴗ–xD|–ᴗ ᴗ–ᴗ–⁻
*Tr.* 520–23
   x–ᴗ–xD–|ᴗ ᴗ–xDx
517–19
   –ᴗ– –ᴗ ᴗ–.|–.–.Dx
   (or . . .|–ᴗ̄ᴗ̄Dx)
*Alc.* 909–10 = 933–34:
   ^Dx + ᴗ̄ᴗ̄ᴗ̄ᴗ––|ᴗ ᴗ–ᴗ–
*Hipp.* 58–60: ⁼^D⁼⁼⁼
   x–ᴗ––ᴗ ᴗ–x|D.|Dx
*Med.* 846–47 = 856–57
   xD|–ᴗ ᴗ–x–
*Ph.* 1515–16
   ᴗ ᴗ–xD|–ᴗ ᴗ––ᴗ ᴗ–
*Rhes.* 244 = 255
   D.|ᴗ ᴗ–.|Dx
349–50 = 358–59
   –ᴗ–xD–ᴗ ᴗ–ᴗ–⁻
527 = 546
   ^D.|ᴗ ᴗ–x–ᴗ–. . .(?)
*TGrF* 2.127.1–2
   x–ᴗ––ᴗ ᴗ––ᴗ ᴗ–.|Dᴗ–⁻
482 Dᴗ ᴗ–
   x D x|     .D–|ᴗ ᴗ––ᴗ ᴗ–.|ᴗ ᴗ–x–ᴗ–x
   –ᴗ ᴗD

*Vesp.* 273–74 = 281–82
   –ᴗ ᴗ––ᴗ ᴗ––ᴗ ᴗ–x|–ᴗ ᴗ–. . .
*Av.* 539 = 451ff.
   ^D.|ᴗ ᴗ–x–ᴗ–|x–ᴗ–.–⁻
   ^D.|ᴗ ᴗ–x–.–.|–ᴗ–.–⁻
*Th.* 327–30:
   x–ᴗ––|ᴗ ᴗ––ᴗ ᴗ–xDxDx|E^
*PMG* 1018b5–6:
   –ᴗ––ᴗ ᴗ–xDx–ᴗ–x
   929b3–5: ᴗ ᴗ–x–ᴗ–.|D–‖ᴗ ᴗ––ᴗ ᴗ––

x– ᴗ ᴗ – ᴗ ᴗ – = x̄ – ᴗ – – ᴗ ᴗ –    (i.e., major ionic x– ᴗ ᴗ + choriamb =
                                    major ionic – – ᴗ – + choriamb)

– ᴗ ᴗ – ᴗ ᴗ –x = – ᴗ ᴗ – – ᴗ –x   (   choriamb + minor ionic ᴗ ᴗ –x =
                                    choriamb + minor ionic – ᴗ –x)

x̄ – ᴗ –x– ᴗ – = x– ᴗ ᴗ – – ᴗ –   (   major ionic – – ᴗ – + iamb =
                                    major ionic x– ᴗ ᴗ + iamb)

These were defended, where possible, by appeal to "free" responsion—
i.e., passages in the transmitted texts of drama and lyric which showed
one side of an equation in strophic response with the other.

Such analyses are now dismissed as a historical curiosity, though more
on textual than metrical grounds. The *Responsionsfreiheiten* once adduced
in their support have been, if not totally eliminated, at least so reduced in
number by the studies of Maas[55] that no one would now venture to base a
whole theory on them. With isolated passages the situation is different;
and here the metricization of prosodiac continues. Isolation of ionic as
the basic unit of movement in A. *Ag.* 685–93 = 705–10:

τὰν δορίγαμβρον ἀμφινεικῆ θ' Ἑλέναν; ἐπεὶ πρεπόντως

                    – ᴗ ᴗ –x|– ᴗ – –|ᴗ ᴗ –x|– ᴗ – –

ἐλένας ἔλανδρος ἐλέπτολις ἐκ τῶν ἀβροπήνων

                    ᴗ ᴗ –x|– ᴗ ᴗ –|ᴗ ᴗ – –|ᴗ ᴗ – –

προκαλυμμάτων ἔπλευσε Ζεφύρου γίγαντος αὔρᾳ

                    ᴗ ᴗ –x|– ᴗ – –|ᴗ ᴗ –x|– ᴗ – –

requires that the second line be taken as a tetrameter with a highly
anomalous ᴗ̃ᴗ̃– as its second metron. A different analysis is suggested,
however, by the exact parallel between the

ἐπεὶ πρεπόντως                     x– ᴗ – –|ᴗ ᴗ –x– ᴗ ᴗ – ᴗ ᴗ–. . . .
    ἐλένας ἔλανδρος ἐλέπτολις ἐκ . . .

of this passage and the opening of A. *Sup.* 524–26 = 531–33:

55 "Die neuen Responsionsfreiheiten bei Pindar und Bacchylides," *Jahresberichte des philo-
logischen Vereins* (1914) 289–320 and (1921) 1–31.

ἄναξ ἀνάκτων μακάρων    ×– ◡ – – ◡ ◡ – | ×– ◡ ◡ – ◡ ◡ – | ×– ◡ ◡ – ◡ ◡ – ◡ – ‾
μακάρτατε καὶ τελέων
                 τελειότατον κράτος, ὄλβιε Ζεῦ

where the possiblity of a different demarcation has led most editors to
take the first | ×– ◡ ◡ – ◡ ◡ – | as a prosodiac × D (above, 15) identical to
the beginning of the × D ◡ – ‾ which follows it. Both ways of demarcat-
ing are correct, for neither represents the sole or inevitable one for the
rhythm present in both passages: a transition via "iambic" modulation
from mixed iono-choriambic into prosodiac (followed, in the *Agamemnon*
passage, by return to iono-choriambic). To let the overall ionic demarcation of that passage determine one's view of the basic character of the
rhythm is to follow 19th-century metrist theory in its decomposition of
prosodiac – ◡ ◡ – – ◡ ◡ –× into choriamb + minor ionic.

It is also to obscure the probable purpose of the rhythmical modulation,
which is not simply to underline the peculiar way in which a string of
heroic-sounding epithets is being applied to Helen—an anomalous "ionic"
◡◡˘– might do that—but also to suggest wherein the peculiarity lies.
Prosodiac, "the favored rhythm of hymns, dirges and encomia" (West
76), gives a brief taste of the sort of rhythmical environment in which
such epithets would *not* be peculiar. Helen and her triple antonomasia
must be truly scanned if one is to feel just how and to what extent she
was truly named. And something similar occurs in the antistrophe. One
must get a hint—through the – ◡ ◡ – ◡ ◡ – of prosodiac—of the predominantly dactylo-anapestic rhythms of epithalamia in order to savor fully the
contrast with the new *hymnoi* the Trojans were soon to learn:

ὑμέναιον, ὃς τότ' ἐπέρρεπε γαμβροῖσιν ἀείδειν·    ◡ ◡ –×– ◡◡ – ◡ ◡ – – ◡ ◡ – –
μεταμανθάνουσα δ' ὕμνον Πριάμου πόλις γεραιὰ    ◡ ◡ –×– ◡ – – ◡ ◡ –×– ◡ – –
πολύθρηνον μέγα που στένει                       ◡ ◡ – – ◡ ◡ –×– . . .

A close parallel to *Ag.* 687 = 706 (cf. Denniston-Page *ad loc.*) appears
at E. *Ph.* 1515:

      τίς ἄρ' ὄρνις ἢ δρυὸς ἢ ἐλάτας       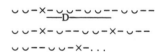
      ἀκροκόμοις ἀμφὶ κλάδοις ἑζομένα      – ◡ ◡ – – ◡ ◡ – – ◡ ◡ –

though there the reasons for introducing prosodiac are unclear; and Ar.
*Th.* 327 – 30 offers another example:

χρυσέα τε φόρμιγξ     ×-∪--|∪∪--∪∪-×-∪∪-
ἰαχήσειεν ἐπ' εὐχαῖς ἡμετέραις
τελέως δ' ἐκκλησιάσαιμεν 'Αθην[αι]ῶν   —D—∪∪-×ᴰ×
                                            -∪-∪-‾
εὐγενεῖς γυναῖκες.


In both passages, as in that from the *Agamemnon*, the introduction of prosodiac rhythm does not necessarily mean the introduction of the most common prosodiac demarcations (D ×|D and D|× D). The "ionic" grouping of quantities into fours or multiples of four (the catalectic "trimeter" ∪∪-×|-∪∪-|∪∪- in Euripides, the acatalectic ∪∪-×|- ∪∪-|∪∪-×| in Aristophanes, and the "tetrameter" ∪∪-×|- ∪∪-|∪∪--|∪∪-- in Aeschylus) is clearly suggested in the text and should not be ignored. To do so is to "colometrize" prosodiac, and this is as much of a distortion as the "metricization" discussed earlier. The rhythm continues to be an epiploke and so capable, even when three different components are involved, of taking on different demarcational patterns without changing its fundamental character. Even the *Suppliants* passage cited above is probably better represented, following verbal and (in the strophe) rhetorical demarcation as:

ἄναξ ἀνάκτων          ×-∪--
μακάρων μακάρτατε       ∪∪-×-∪∪
καὶ τελέων τελειότατον κράτος ὄλβιε Ζεῦ   -∪∪-×-∪∪-∪∪-∪-‾
                                         —D—        —D—

The opening of the second colon is ionic, that of the third suggests choriambic. There is no reason to posit a series of fixed units separated by diaeresis: iambo-choriambic dimeter |× D |× D ∪-‾. The whole is very similar, except for the "choriambic" opening of the third line, to what appears in Aristophanes:

Aristophanes:  ×-∪--|∪∪--∪∪-×-∪∪-|∪∪-   ×-∪∪-∪∪-×|-∪-∪-‾
Aeschylus:   ×-∪--|      ∪∪-×-∪∪|-∪∪-   ×-∪∪-∪∪-      ∪-‾;

and a similar epiploke, with uniform, rhetorically reinforced "iambo-choriambic" grouping, appears at S. *Tr.* 520–23

ἦν δὲ ἀμφίπλεκτοι κλίμακες   ×-∪- ×-∪∪|‾ᴰ‾-∪∪--∪∪-×-∪∪|‾ᴰ‾-∪∪-×
ἦν δὲ μετώπων ὀλόεντα πλήγματα
καὶ στόνος ἀμφοῖν

Such partial assimilation of prosodiac to iono-choriambic through demarcations in a mixed epiploke is almost inevitable once modulation between the two forms occurs. When iono-choriambic follows prosodiac through iambic modulation the concluding – ∪ ∪ – of $\underline{\phantom{x}}$∪∪$\underline{\phantom{x}}$–∪∪– will be heard as choriambic as well as prosodiac, and when it modulates into prosodiac in the same way it will itself be heard retrospectively as containing the conclusion of –∪∪–∪∪–:

prosodiac$\underline{\phantom{xxx}}$

– ∪ ∪ – ∪ ∪ – – ∪ ∪ – – ∪ ∪ –

iono-choriambic

iono-choriambic

– ∪ ∪ – – ∪ ∪ – × – ∪ ∪ – ∪ ∪ –

prosodiac

Iono-choriambic introduced by trochaic modulation has even less of an independent identity. It is hardly ever found outside prosodiac contexts[56] and never more than two or three times in a poem or for as many as two cycles in succession. Assimilation accordingly proceeds further, but in a single direction. – ∪ ∪ – is probably felt as a shortened version of a prosodiac cycle, succeeding iambo-trochaic via the same modulatory sequence (– ∪ – × – ∪ ∪ –. . .) but replaced by iambo-trochaic once again four quantities earlier than would be necessary in the case of prosodiac. – ∪ ∪ – – ∪ – is thus a kind of half-way house between prosodiac – ∪ ∪ – ∪ ∪ – and iambo-trochaic – ∪ – × – ∪ –; and this position is reflected in such freedoms of response as do seem to occur in the rhythm:

– ∪ ∪ – ∪ ∪ – ≡ – ∪ ∪ – – ∪ –

– ∪ ∪ – – ∪ – ≡ – ∪ – × – ∪ –

There are two fairly certain instances of the first at Ar. *Vesp.* 274–75 = 281–82 and several probable ones (in Pindar and Bacchylides)[57] of both

[56] Ar. *Eccl.* 898–99 (|– ∪ – × – ∪ – × |– ∪ – × – ∪ ∪ – – ∪ – × | in the midst of trochaic) is the only instance of which I am aware. 909–10 may contain another (κἀπὶ τῆς κλίνης ὄφιν εὕροις <τε> καὶ προσελκύσαιο βουλομένη φιλῆσαι: – ∪ – × – ∪ ∪ – – ∪ – × – ∪ – × | – ∪∪ – ∪ – ×, but should perhaps be more extensively emended (e.g., by Wilamowitz's deletion of εὕροις καί) to produce a closer parallel to the aeolic (Table V) of the similar movements that precede.

[57] Often emended, following Maas (above, n. 55), but not always with good reason. See, for a balanced view of the problem, Fraenkel 345–46, *GV* 433–34 and Fuehrer 245ff. Particularly questionable is Maas's assumption that, even where prosodic demarcation does not occur, a normally short syllable may, if it ends in a consonant and concludes a word, be lengthened (306). This form of lengthening is plausible in the sequence – ∪ ∪ – ∪ ∪ –,

types. But $- \cup - \times - \cup -$ $=$ $- \cup \cup - \cup \cup -$ is not securely attested anywhere. Prosodiac and iambo-trochaic do not respond to each other, but
either may on occasion respond to a special form of mixed iono-
choriambic that is identical with iambo-trochaic in one of its segments and
reminiscent of prosodiac in the other.

There is no comparable evidence suggesting that the iambically modulated $- \cup - - \cup \cup -$ had a corresponding intermediate position between
$- \cup - \times - \cup -$ and $- \cup \cup - \cup \cup -$; and assimilation there would have been,
in any case, less close. The only possible counterpart, among iambically
modulated sequences, is a much remoter one, not involving prosodiac at
all: iono-choriambic $\cup \cup - \times - \cup -$ is intermediate between $- \cup - \times - \cup -$
and $\cup \cup - - \cup \cup -$, if the presence of the responsions

$$\cup \cup - - \cup \cup - \ = \ \cup \cup - \times - \cup -$$
$$\cup \cup - \times - \cup - \ = \ - \cup - \times - \cup -$$

(above, 30–31) and the absence of $- \cup - \times - \cup - \ = \ \cup \cup - - \cup \cup -$ is indicative.

Whatever the character and degree of assimilation involved, passage
between iambo-choriambic, iono-choriambic and prosodiac is largely
independent of the demarcation of a given passage. $- \cup - \times - \cup \cup -$ may
be a partial exception, since the general rarity, in all rhythms except
dactylo-anapestic, of demarcation following a double short seems to have
limited the use of $|\times - \cup - \times - \cup \cup|$ and $|\times - \cup \cup - - \cup -|$ (where tetradic
grouping would have isolated $\times - \cup \cup$ as a quasi-metron). One neverthe-
less finds "iambo-prosodiac" $|\times - \cup - \times - \cup \cup -|$:

ἔτλα δὲ σοῖσι μηλονόμας        $\times - \cup - \times - \cup \cup - | - \cup - \cup -^-$
     ἐν δόμοις γενέσθαι

          E. *Alc.* 573–74 = 583–84

(see Table IV, 1b) alongside the more common "trochaeo-choriambic"
$|- \cup - \times - \cup \cup -|$.[58]

---

whose dactylic character might justify what could have been felt as similar to the lengthening
*in arsi* of the hexameter. But three of the apparent freedoms of response removed by
Maas involve positing this license in the sequence $(\times) - \cup - (\times)$ (*P* 3.6 [cf. Turyn *ad loc.*], *P.*
4.184 and Bacchylides 11.114) and Snell applies the principle to three more (*O* 6.28 and 77,
and Bacchylides 10.10). Except in Bacchylides 11 (on which see Fuehrer 245, with n. 74)
assumption of free response between $- \cup - \times$ and $- \cup \cup -$, or (in Bacchylides 10) $- \cup -$
and $\cup \cup -$ is less improbable than the lengthening posited by Maas.

[58] For the term, cf. Parker 17, where A. *Sup.* 42 (Table IV) is described as a "long
trochaeo-choriambic verse," and *LMGD* 191, on $- \cup \cup -$ as "a sort of anaclasis of $- \cup -^{\cup}$."
Both formulizations "metricize" the rhythm under discussion, unnecessarily in my view.

Of the two means of linking iono-choriambic to mixed prosodiac, trochaic modulation via – ⏑ is the one preferred in early choral lyric (Table IV). All but excluded from non-prosodiac passages, it must have increased the integrity and homogeneity of Pindaric and Bacchylidean dactylo-epitritic as a genus apart, rarely combinable with other rhythms in a single poem. Its exclusion, by and large, from drama in favor of the more widely prevalent iambic modulation via ⏑ – probably had just the opposite effect. There iambic modulation takes its place alongside other non-Pindaric, non-Bacchylidean features (clausular ⏑ – ‾, free use of short anceps) which have parallels outside prosodiac and facilitate the inclusion of prosodiac within the same stanza or the same movement as extended segments from other rhythms. Trochaic modulation appears occasionally, but it is enough of an oddity that at Ar. *Av.* 936–39 it can serve as a Pindaric signpost, pointing the way to the pastiche that is to follow:

τόδε μὲν οὐκ ἄ[ε]κουσα φίλα          ⏑̈⏑– × – ⏑ ⏑ –

Μοῦσα δῶρον δέχεται,                      – ⏑ –. – ⏑ ⏑ –

τὺ δὲ τεᾷ φρενὶ μάθε Πινδάρειον ἔπος.   ⏑̈⏑ – × ⏑̈⏑ – × – ⏑ ⏑ –

(For the syncopated quantity in the second line, see below, 70–71).

Iono-choriambic, however introduced, is one of the few ingredients in mixed prosodiac not paralleled in heptadic aeolic,[59] perhaps because its presence would not have had the same assimilatory effect there which it has in prosodiac. Any regular piece of prosodiac can be "aeolized" by replacing a double with a single short: the familiar Archilochean dicolon, for example:

Ἐρασμονίδη Χαρίλαε,          × —— D —— × | – ⏑ – ⏑ – ‾

χρῆμά τοι γελοῖον              (fr. 168)

---

[59] S. *Ant.* 139–40 = 153–54 and E. *IA* 175–76 = 196–97 are the only possible instances of direct transition from iono-choriambic to heptadic aeolic: – ⏑ ⏑ – – ⏑ ⏑ – – ⏑ ⏑ – – ⏑ ⏑ – × | – ⏑ ⏓ – ‾ and ᴗᴗ – – ⏑ ⏑ – × – ⏑ ⏑ – ⏑ – . But the former is often taken as ending in . . . ⏑ ⏑ – – + – ⏑ ⏑ – –, and the latter may begin with aeolic – ×̄ – ⏑ ⏑ – rather than the continuation of the preceding ionic (text, 99) just suggested. What is sometimes analyzed as × – ⏑ ⏑ – ⏑ – – ⏑ ⏑ – at S. *Tr.* 517–18 is better taken as iono-choriambic, analogous syntactically and rhythmically to what follows:

517–19:    × – ⏑ –.‖ (or × – ⏑ – +)
            – ⏑ – – ⏑ ⏑ –   .| – . – . ‾ ⏑ ⏑ D ‾ ⏑ ⏑ – × (or .| – ᴗᴗD ×)

520–23:    × – ⏑ – ×   – ⏑ ⏑̣ | – ⏑ ⏑ – ———D——— – ⏑ ⏑ – × – ⏑ ⏑̣ | – ⏑ ⏑ – ×

into the Cratinean parody:

'Ερασμονίδη Βάθιππε,                     ×–∪∪–∪–×–∪–∪– ‾
τῶν ἀωρολείων                              ‾‾A‾‾                    (fr. 11)

But assimilation to tetradic rhythm is much easier when a double cycle of one rhythm is equivalent in length to a single cycle of another—prosodiac– ∪ ∪ – ∪ ∪ –× to "trochaeo-choriambic" – ∪ ∪ – – ∪ –× for example—and this parity does not exist when the single cycle contains seven quantities rather than eight.[60] In its absence one obvious reason for introducing a third ingredient into a mixed epiploke would disappear.

By contrast, heptadic aeolic shares with prosodiac a totally different type of modulation, one whose effect is to replace a 4-4 grouping of quantities within an octadic cycle with a 3-3-2 or 2-3-3 grouping:

mixed prosodiac
‾‾‾D‾‾‾
– ∪ –×–∪ ∪– ∪ ∪ – ∪ ∪ –×– ∪ –×– ∪ –
dactylo-anapestic
‾‾D‾‾

mixed prosodiac
λαὸν ἵππαιχμον θάμα δὴ καὶ 'Ολυμπιάδων φύλλοις ἐλαιᾶν χρυσέοις
—Pind. N1e3

Here the inner movement of prosodiac – ∪ ∪ – ∪ ∪ – is felt as a dactylo-
‾‾D‾‾
anapestic – ∪ ∪ – ∪ ∪ – and so extended for a cycle before the passage proceeds on in normal prosodiac fashion. Both D segments will be heard with the surrounding iambo-trochaic as a part of mixed prosodiac, and with each other as dactylo-anapestic. The close of the alcaic stanza involves a similar expansion into dactylo-anapestic of an aeolic rhythm heard in the first two lines of the stanza:[61]

[60] The assimilation, if it existed at all, opeated sporadically and inconsistently, linking ×–∪∪–‾ to ×–∪–×– by free response at Ar. *Nub.* 1304 = 1312 and, possibly, 1350 = 1396 (see Dover *ad loc.*); ×–∪∪–∪–× to ×–∪–×–∪–× or ×–∪––∪–× in the same manner at Ar. *Pax* 951–53 = 1034–36; and ×–∪–×–∪– or ×–∪––∪– (*PMG* 935.19) to adjoining instances of ×–∪∪–∪– in the Epidaurian hymn to the Magna Mater.

[61] Cf. the similar relationship between ×–∪∪–∪–×|–∪–×–∪–× and a preceding ×–∪∪–∪∪–∪–× at Simonides 59/564.3, and between –∪∪–∪– and –∪∪–∪∪–∪– in *Hipp.* 161–63 (text, 76).

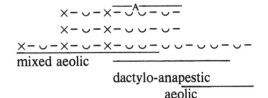

mixed aeolic
dactylo-anapestic
aeolic

The – ∪ ∪ – segment is heard both as the beginning of aeolic – ∪ ∪ – ∪ – and the beginning or end of dactylo-anapestic – ∪ ∪ – ∪ ∪ –.
Since modulation occurs in such passages either via the ambiguous segment – ∪ ∪ – or a longer one beginning and ending with – ∪ ∪ –, it will be called "choriambic" modulation to distinguish it from the "iambic" and "trochaic" varieties. Its presence may produce an interlude of dactylo-anapestic within aeolic or prosodiac (as in *N*1e3 and the alcaic stanza), or dactylo-anapestic can precede or follow. Instances of initial dactylo-anapestic, variously demarcated, are

ἠρά σε Ταυροπόλα Διὸς Ἄρτεμις        – ∪ ∪ – ∪ ∪ – ∪ ∪ – ∪ ∪
   ὦ μεγάλα φάτις, ὦ                                – ∪‿∪ – ∪ ∪ –. | E
        μᾶτερ αἰσχύνας ἐμᾶς                                  ――D――
   ὤρμασε πανδάμους ἐπὶ βοῦς ἀγελαίας        × – ∪ – ×      D       ×
                                                                        –S. *Aj.* 172–75 = 182–85

ἰότατι γάμων ὅτε τὰν ὁμοπάτριον ἔδνοις        ∪ ∪ – ∪ ∪ – ∪ ∪ – ∪‿∪ – ∪ ∪ – ×
        ἄγαγες Ἡσιόναν πιθὼν δάμαρτα κοινόλεκτρον       D       | × E ×
                                                                        –A. *PV* 559–60 = 550–51

Κρ, ἀ σκοπέλοις ἐπ' ἐμοῖς τὸν ἐλαιοφυῆ πάγον
        θάσσει        – ∪ ∪ – ∪ ∪ – ∪ ∪ – ∪ ∪ – ∪ – | × – ∪ – ×̈ – ∪ – × – ∪ – +
                                    ――A――
Ιω.        λέγεις μοι σκολιὰ κ' οὐ σαφῆ τάδε.
Κρ. παρ' ἀηδόνιον πέτραν        ∪ ∪ – ∪ ∪ – × – | × – ∪ – ∪ –  ̅ +
        Φοίβῳ                                    ――A――

Ιω.        τί Φοῖβον αὐδᾷς;        – ∪ ∪ – ∪ ∪ – × – | × – ∪ – × – ∪ – × – ∪ – +
Κρ. κρυπτόμενον λέχος εὐνάσθην        ――A――
Ιω.        λέγ' ὡς ἐρεῖς τι κεδνὸν εὐτυχές τέ μοι        –E. Ion 1479–85[62]

────────────

[62] Cf., for other aeolic examples, Table VI, and for prosodiac, E. *Med.* 993–94 = 999–1000 (∪ ∪ – ∪ ∪ – ∪ ∪ – ∪ ∪ – × D ), *Tr.* 825–30 (– ∪ ∪ – ∪ ∪ – ∪ ∪ – ∪ ∪ |D ‖ × – ∪ –.– ∪ –.– ∪ – × – ∪ –), *Hcld.* 774–76 = 781–83 (D × + ∪ ∪ – ∪ ∪ – ∪ ∪ – ∪ ∪ – × – ∪ –.– ∪ – ∪ –  ̅), S. *Tr.* 497 = 507ff., where the ∪ ∪ – ∪ ∪ – ∪ ∪ – ∪ ∪ – × – ∪ – of the first and third cola looks forward to the D × | – ∪ – × D × of 501–2 = 512–13; and Ar. *Ran.* 675–85 = 706–16:
                        – ∪ ∪ – ∪ ∪ – ∪ ∪ – ∪ ∪ |D .– ∪ – +
                                            D ᵎ× ₁ D .– ∪ – ∪ –  ̅
                        ∪ ∪ – ∪ ∪ – ∪ ∪ – ∪ ∪ – ₗ×ᵎ D ᵎ. D .– ∪ – ∪ –  ̅
        ∪ ∪ – ∪ ∪ – ∪ ∪ – ∪ ∪ – | ∪ ∪ – ∪ ∪ – ∪ ∪ – ∪ ∪ D ₗ×ᵎ – ∪ – ∪ –  ̅

(The Maasian symbol E [above, 15] is here used for iambo-trochaic
– ∪ – × – ∪ – in the sequence |(×)– ∪ – × – ∪ –(×)|. The variant
$\frac{- ∪ ∪ - × -}{A}$ replaces $\frac{- ∪ ∪ - ∪ -}{A}$ occasionally in both heptadic and octadic
aeolic).

The reverse order, aeolic or prosodiac into dactylo-anapestic, is rarer,
perhaps because aeolic and prosodiac, unlike dactylo-anapestic, can lead
without a break into iambo-trochaic, which was felt as supplying a better
clausular rhythm (cf. Korzeniewski 145). The modulation appears, how-
ever, at E. *Ph.* 350–51 (× D | ×–∪∪––∪∪–∪∪–∪∪|–∪∪–∪∪–
∪∪–∪∪|–∪∪–∪∪–) and at Pind. *P2s5–6*:

εὐάρματος Ἱέρων εν ᾇ κρατέων          ×–∪⌣×–×⁼–∪∪–

τηλαυγέσιν ἀνέδησεν Ὀρτυγίαν στεφάνοις   ×–∪⌣×–×⁼–∪∪–∪∪–

                                        dactylo-anapestic

where ×–×–∪∪– designates an occasional variant on the more common
×–∪∪–∪–, to which it is related in the same way as octadic
××–×–∪∪– to ××–∪∪–∪– (above, 9; cf. the responson
×–∪∪–∪–×|–∪–∪–– at S. *Tr.* 960–61 = 969–70). The end of the
first pair of stanzas in S. *Ant.* 338–75 is less clear:

θεῶν τε τὰν ὑπερτάταν          × E ᵎ×ᵢ–∪∪–∪∪–∪∪–∪∪
   Γᾶν ἄφθιτον ἀκαμάταν ἀποτρύεται
   ἰλλομένων ἀρότρων ἔτος εἰς ἔτος     –∪∪–∪∪–∪∪–∪∪ +
ἱππείῳ γένει πολεύων          –.–.–∪–∪–

The analysis is supported, however, by the way the same prosodiac passing
into dactylo-anapestic continues to accompany the high tide of human progress into the beginning of the following pair of stanzas:

σοφόν τι τὸ μηχανόεν          ×–∪∪–∪∪–
τέχνας ὑπὲρ ἐλπίδ' ἔχων          ×–∪∪–∪∪–|⌣⌣'–∪∪–∪∪–∪–
   τοτὲ μὲν κακὸν ἄλλοτ' ἐπ' ἐσθλὸν ἕρπει,

then disappears, except for a final, almost abortive suggestion (the iono-
choriambic ×–∪∪– discussed above) as the subject moves from civilization to civilization and its discontents:

νόμους παρείρων χθονός,

    θεῶν τ' ἔνορκον δίκαν    x–∪–.–∪–|  x–∪–.–∪–.|  –∪∪–

ἄπολις ὅτῳ τὸ μὴ καλὸν    ὑψίπολις·

    ξύνεστι τόλμας χάριν.    x⁽ᵕ̃⁾∪–x–∪–|  x–∪–.–∪–.

μήτ' ἐμοὶ παρέστιος    –∪–x–∪–|  x–∪–x–∪–.|  –∪–x

    γένοιτο μήτ' ἴσον φρονῶν

        ὃς τάδ' ἔρδοι.

Most of the syncopations in this passage are typical of what appears in the iambo-trochaic sections of prosodiac or heptadic aeolic, where the phenomenon shows the same variety as it does in iambo-trochaic itself. Thus, to quote only instances of the Archilochean dicolon (above, 67) and its aeolic counterpart (respectively, xD x E^ and x A x E^, where E^ designates –∪–∪–‾, a clausular variant on E) one finds:[63]

ἐκλακτισάτω τις, ὅπως

    ἰδόντες ἄνω σκέλος ὥζωσιν οἱ θεαταί    x D |x D . E ^

at Ar. *Vesp.* 1525–27 ( = x D |x D  x E ^ at 1520–22), x A ₁x'–∪–.–‾ immediately following a non-syncopated x D ₁x'E ^ at S *OT* 1094–97 = 1106–9: above, 19), as well as

| | | |
|---|---|---|
| ἢ γᾶς ὑπὸ κεῦθον ἄφαντον | xD x\|– ∪ –.–‾ | 272–73 |
|   ἐξαμαυρωθῶ | | —E. *Phaeth.* |
| Ἑλλάδι κουροτρόφον | D \|x–.‥̈∪–‾ | |
|   Φρυγῶν πατρίδι πένθη | | *Tr.* 566–67 |
| ἔβασαν ἔβασαν ἄμεικτον | xDx\|– ∪ – ∪ –‾ + | |
|   αἶαν, ἔνθα κούρᾳ | | |
|   δίᾳ τέγγει | –.–.–‾ | *IT* 404 = 414 |

The syncopations A ., .A , D . and .D (or, as in the *Antigone* passage, .–∪∪–) are more problematic than .–∪–, –∪–. and (x)–.–(x), since they have no exact parallel in iambo-trochaic. Analogy is in favor of positing them, however; and one of them, at least, (D.) is guaranteed by

---

[63] Cf., for instances outside the dicolon, *PMG* 755.1–4 (Euripides' epinician for Alcibiades): ≂∪–‖x–∪–x\|–∪–.–‾ + –.–.–∪–x\|–∪–.–‾ + D x D), A. *Pers.* 131 = 136 (most naturally scanned as x–.–.–∪–x–.– . D), E. *Tr.* 272–76 (Table VII) and 511–15 = 531–35 (text, 74), and *Phaeth.* 231–33 = 240–42 (D x–∪–x\|–∪–.–.– x\| D).

responsion. [64] A . is very likely in S. *Aj.* 196–98:

ἐχθρῶν δ' ὕβρις ὧδ' ἀτάρβητα        ×–∪∪–∪–.–‾
                                                    ‾‾A‾‾
ὁρμᾶτ' ἐν εὐανέμοις βάσσαις        ×–∪–.–∪–.–‾
πάντων καχαζόντων        ×–∪–.–‾

in view of the parallel syncopations in the two succeeding lines. There is
similar evidence for . A ^ (i.e., .–∪∪–‾, the clausular variant on
.–∪∪–∪–: cf. above, 12) in S. *OC* 1057–58 = 1072–73:
    ‾‾A‾‾

αὐτάρκει τάχ' ἐμμείξειν βοᾷ
        τοῦσδ' ἀνὰ χώρους        –.–.–∪–×–∪–.|‾‾∪‿×‾‾
                                                                    A

The sequence closes a stanza which contains two unsyncopated instances
of terminal ×–∪‿–‾ and itself looks very much like a triply syncopated
            ‾A‾
version of the stanza close at *OT* 895–96 = 908–10:

εἰ γὰρ αἱ τοιαίδε πράξεις τίμιαι,        –∪–×–∪–×–∪–|×–∪‿–‾
        τί δεῖ με χορεύειν;                                          ‾‾A‾‾

The rarity of verbal synapheia between two instances of ‾∪‿∪‾∪∪‾ is
                                                                          ‾D‾
also relevant here, suggesting as it does either separate rhythmical movements or syncopation located in such a way as to produce normal demar-
cation, following an anceps (D . |D), rather than an anomalous –∪∪–
∪∪–.–|∪∪–∪∪– or the like. ‾∪‿∪‾∪–‾∪∪‾∪‾ without such
                                                    ‾‾‾A‾‾‾    ‾‾A‾‾
demarcation is more common, but not in heptadic aeolic contexts (below,
88).
    Such syncopations, if they exist, are rarer in heptadic aeolic than in pro-
sodiac; continuous sequences are, as a rule, longer; and there is a certain
preference for demarcation before rather than following anceps (see, for a
catalogue of the attested examples, Table V). Otherwise the two rhythms
closely parallel each other. They may appear in the same context, sometimes as part of different movements (cf. *OT* 1096–97 = 1108–9: above,
19), sometimes within a single movement, in which case transition can be
either via iambo-trochaic:

---

[64] At Ar. *Av.* 1525–27 = 1520–22 and Bacch. 5s11–13 (× D ⊻–∪–×–∪–‖× D× D ⊻–
∪–×–∪–). The latter passage is often emended, but cf. Snell *ad loc.*

# TABLE V: HEPTADIC AEOLIC

| A: Pure sequences (usually ending ×A^, and with—unless otherwise indicated—the prevailing demarcation |×A|) | B: Combined with iambo-trochaic (the numerous examples from early lyric are not listed) | C: Preceded by dactylo-anapestic (◡◡–◡◡–◡◡–◡◡–| unless otherwise indicated) | D: Combined with prosodiac and iambo-trochaic |
|---|---|---|---|
| Sappho 112: A×A×A×‖A×Ax | PV 571–72: | OT 470–72 = 480–82 | Stesichorus 46|223: |
| A. | A×|Ax–◡– | |×A^ + E^ | D|×D|×Dx–◡–|×E|×Dx|A×|A |
| S | 580–81 = 599–600: x–◡–×A|×E^ | fr. 808: | 23|200: |
| Aj. 199–200 | Aj. 408–9 = 426–27: | ◡◡–◡◡–◡◡–|×A | ×D|×D|×A^ |
| OT 467–69 = 477–79 | ×E×A^ | | (or...|x–◡–◡–...?) |
| | OT 866–72 = 876–82 | | Pindar O 13s6: |
| | ×B,|–◡–x–◡–◡– + | | ×Bx–◡–×D.–◡- |
| | x–◡–x–◡◡– A| | | N8s1: B×–◡–x|D |
| | 883–88 = 897–903: | | fr. 127: x–◡–◡D×A^ |
| | ×A×|E|×A×|E|×A×|E | | ×D|×E^ |
| | 892–96 = 906–10: | | A. fr. 37.1–3: |
| | x–◡–,–◡–|×A×–◡–x(?) | | ...–◡|D×|A×|A×|E |
| | +–◡–x–◡–x–◡–x|A^ | | (reading γαί[ωα]ς) |
| | Tr. 637–39 = 644–46: | | Aj. 180–81 = 190–91: |
| | ^B×–◡–|×B|×E^ | | –◡–×D .|–◡–×A^ |
| | 953–61 = 962–70: | | 957–60 = 911–13: |
| | ×A|x–◡–x–◡–◡– + | | x–◡–x|D|×E^ |
| | |×E|×A×|E + | | D|×A^ |
| | |×A|×E^ (=×B|×E^) | | OT 1092–97 = 1104–9: |
| | El. 480–85 = 495–500 | | Ex|E₁×'D₁×'E^ + |
| | A×|E(?) | | ×A₁×'–◡–.–. |
| | ×E×|–◡–◡– | | Tr. 633–35 = 640–43: |
| | ×E×|–◡–◡– | | ×A×|E|×D×|–◡–x| |
| | ×A×E^ | | –◡–––– |
| | Ph. 716–17 = 728–29: | | |
| | x–◡–×A|×A^ | | |
| | OC 1044–48 = 1059–63: | | |
| | ×A|×A|×A|×E|×A^ | | |
| | 1055–58 = 1070–73: | | |
| | –◡◡–x–◡–|×A^ | | |
| | –,–◡–x–◡–.|A^ | | |

E.
Hcld 895–97 = 904–6:
×A×|A×|A×
×A×|A×|A×

Ar.
Eq. 1111–50
Pax 856–57 = 910–11
860–61 = 914–15
Av. 1731–34 = 1737–40
Ran. 451–54 = 457–59
Eccl. 289–310
fr. 9
A×|A×|A×|A×|A×(?)
A×|A×|A×|A
A×|A×|A×|A
Eupolis 163 Kock
Hermippus 58 Kock
PMG935 (exc. ⏑–⏑–⏑–⏑–
in line 19 and ⏑⏑A in 21)

Alc. 989–94 = 1005–8:
×A×|B +
×A× + ×A× + ×A×|B⏑–⏑–
Hipp. 1379–86:
⏑–|⏑–⏑–⏑–|⏑–×A˘ + ×E×|E
⏑–||μοl⏑–|–⏑–×A.|E
1143–46 (?):
x˘⏑–×|A˘
E˘ + x˘⏑–⏑–(–.)E˘
(×A˘+E˘ or ×A.|E˘)

Ph. 1543–45:
...˘⏑–(or ×–⏑–:
νέκῦν ἐνερθ(εν)|)|×A˘

Bac 875–76 = 895–96:
...×–⏑× A˘

Ach. 840–41 = 846–47 = 852–53 = 858–59;
Nub. 1345–50 = 1391–96, 1303–4
Pax 954–55 = 1037–38: (×–⏑–)×E×A˘
Eccl. 909–10
...–×⏑–×|A×
900–902 = 903–5 = 906–8
–⏑–˘⏑–(.–⏑–)×|E×|A×
Nub. 1102–5: ×E|×E|×–⏑–×A×

Cratinus 11: ×A×|E˘

Alc. 89–91 = 101–4:
–⏑–D|×D|×D×|
–⏑–⏑–×
Hipp. 161–62:
×E×A×–⏑–D–⏑–˘
121–24 = 131–34:
D×D×– + ×e×A×
HF1075–77:
×–⏑–×D|D×D×|A˘
894–95: ×E×A.|˘⏑–×–
×E×|D×|–⏑–×–
Tr. 1081–86 = 1100–1104:
D|×D× + ×–⏑˘×|
–⏑–×A|×A˘
IT401–5 = 416–19: ×A× +
×D×|E
Hel. 1109–10 = 1124–25:
×B×–⏑–D–⏑–⏑–˘
1495–1502 = 1479–86: ×D× +
×D.|B.||–.–×||×B|
×B|×–⏑–×|E|×E˘
Or. 180–84 = 201–5:
do do|×–⏑–⏑–⏑–⏑–⏑A×|D¹
1246–57 = 1266–57:
×A|×–⏑–⏑– do|
(cf. 1255–57 = 1275–77:
do do|×D×D×–)
Phaeth. 227–30 = 236–39:
×–⏑–|D×–⏑–|
–⏑–×–×–⏑–|×A×
Pax 781–90 = 804–11:
D×|D×–⏑–×A×A×A×|
–⏑–⏑–⏑–×
or D
Lys. 1299–1300:
×E|×B×|D|×–⏑–×–⏑–.–˘
Cratinus 62: ×A|×D|×E˘
PMG744.1–3 (Ion of Chios)
871.5–7 D×|A˘ + A˘
917b:...|×A|×D×|...×D×–⏑–×|A
Bias 35 Diehl:
×A×|D|×A + B.|B.|E˘
Cercidas 4.4 Diehl D|×A˘
4.11 D|×–⏑×A˘

1 Aeolic without prosodiac may follow dochmiac (or bacchio-cretic: text, 112–14) at Ph. 1536–38
⏑–|⏑–|⏑–|⏑–––|⏑–⏑–⏑–|×A˘ and bacchio-cretic at 1543–45 (column B).

ὦ ναύλοχα καὶ πετραῖα

   θερμὰ λουτρὰ καὶ πάγους       ×−∪∪−∪−×| E
                              A
   Οἴτας παραναιετάοντες          × D ×
   οἵ τε μέσσαν Μηλίδα παρ' λίμναν    −∪− ×−∪∪−×−
                                        A
                                 −S. *Tr.* 633–36 = 640–43

μηδὲ Μελάνθιος οὗ δὴ πικροτάτην ὄπα γηρύσαντος ἤκουσ'   D × D × −∪− ×
ἡνίκα τῶν τραγῳδῶν τὸν χορὸν εἶχον ἀδελφός τε καὶ αὐτός, ἄμφω

                       −∪∪−∪−×−∪∪−∪−×−∪∪−∪−×
                         A       A       A
Γοργόνες ὀψοφάγοι βατιδοσκόποι Ἅρπυιαι   −∪∪−∪∪−∪∪−∪∪−×−
                                          A
                                    −Ar. *Pax* 804–11 = 782–90 [65]

or directly, via the same transitional ∪− which allows modulation in mixed prosodiac and mixed iono-choriambic:

   κλέωα τὸν Ἀμύκλαις σιὸν           × E
     καὶ Χαλκίοικον Ἀσάναν          ×−×−∪∪−×
                                  B
     Τυνδαρίδας τ' ἀγασώς,           D
   τοὶ δὴ παρ' Εὐρώταν ψιάδδοντι   ×−∪−×−∪−.−⁻
                                       −Ar. *Lys.* 1299–1300

At times the ambiguous −∪∪−−− (i.e., $\overline{−∪∪-\overset{\times}{\underset{A}{}}−}$ or $\overline{−∪∪-\underset{D}{}∪∪-}$) provides the basis for a rhythmical movement that can be taken as either prosodiac or aeolic:

   πᾶσα δε γέννα Φρυγῶν           D . |−∪−. −. −×
      πρὸς πύλας ὡρμάθη
   πεύκα ἐν οὐρείᾳ               −∪∪−×−
   ξεστὸν λόχον Ἀργείων          ×−∪∪−−−
   καὶ Δαρδανίας ἄταν            ×−∪∪−−−
      θεᾷ δώσων                  ×−. −×
                         −E. *Tr.* 531–35 = 511–14[66]

---

[65] The passage, part of a Stesichorean parody, recalls in its metre Stesichorus 46/223: D |×
D |× D ×−∪−|× E |×D ×|−∪∪−∪−×|−∪∪−∪− and so gives some metrical reason
for not emending the close of the latter into prosodiac (West, *Philologus* 110, 152) or detaching its penultimate −∪∪−∪−× as a separate movement (Haslam 38).

[66] −−− ∪∪⁓ is similarly ambiguous between D and $-×\underset{B}{-}∪∪-$. Cf. S. *Tr.* 638–39 =
645–46 (×−−−∪∪−|× E ⁀), which closes the passage cited in the text, and E. *HF* 135–37
(−∪−. −∪−|×−−−∪∪−×|E ˆ at the end of trochaics).

On other occasions a different type of ambiguity is created by the sequence ∪ ∪ − ∪ ∪ − ∪ − (or ∪ ∪ − ∪ ∪ − × −), which contains both the ∪ ∪ − ∪ ∪ − of D and the − ∪ ∪ − ∪ − or − ∪ ∪ − × − of A, and appears as a variant on initial (×) D or (×) ⁻∪∪⁻ₐ⁻∪⁻ at the beginning of both pro-sodiac and aeolic passages (see Table VI).[67] The frequency with which this initial sequence is prefaced by dactylo-anapestic suggests that it be taken as itself an instance of dactylo-anapestic leading into aeolic, though there is reason to believe that, by Hellenistic times at any rate, it had come to be felt as ×̆⁻∪∪̆⁻∪⁻ₐ, with the anomalous resolution of initial anceps that is found in the tragic trimeter.[68] Terminal − ∪ ∪ − ∪ ∪ − ∪ − ⁻ can be similarly ambiguous: prosodiac D followed by clausular ∪ − ⁻, or AX extended at its beginning into dactylo-anapestic. When such ambiguity is present the sequence may be designated as ⁼∪∪ᴰ⁼∪∪⁻∪−⁻.

Transitions between aeolic and prosodiac, with ᴬthe obscuring of rhythmical identity which often results, are frequent in Euripides, rare in Sophocles. Demarcation is not affected by the transitions, however, show-ing the same tendency to appear before or after anceps that it shows when aeolic and prosodiac appear separately or in combination with iambo-trochaic. Other demarcations (see above, 17) are rare, but one must allow for the possibility of their occurrence. S. *Tr.* 637 = 644 (Table V, B) seems to begin with the second quantity in the sequence − × − ∪ ∪ − (the rhythm is written as ^B), and the initial | ∪ ∪ − of Pindar *P*9s1 and 3 and *O*7s1 and 6 (i.e., the fifth, sixth and seventh quantities of D)[69] may appear along with other, still rarer types, at E. *Hipp.* 161–69:[70]

---

[67] The name enoplion sometimes attached to these sequences suggests, misleadingly, that there is such a thing as an independent "enoplion" movement, capable of forming the basis for continuous composition. As the table shows, enoplia immediately preceded or followed by other enoplia are rare (two Pindaric and three Euripidean examples), and when they occur they are always separated by demarcation. This suggests that the second enoplion in the series is the beginning of a new piece of epiploke, containing, like its predecessor, an ini-tial variant on, or introduction to, the continuous prosodiac or aeolic that follows.

[68] Cf. *PMG* 935.21, Theocritus, *Ep.* 17 and Callimachus fr. 228 (Table VI).

[69] All four lines contain foreshortened anticipations of more normally demarcated sequences heard later in their respective poems:

| | | |
|---|---|---|
| ∪ ∪ − × − ∪ − × | D | *O*7s1,6 |
| − ∪ ∪ − ∪ ∪ − × − ∪ − × | D | s5, e5 |
| ∪ ∪ − × | D × | *P*9s1,3 |
| − ∪ ∪ − ∪ ∪ − × | D (×) | s4,6 |

[70] Prosodiac analysis is the only one which allows uniform scansion to the − − − ∪ ∪ − that appears in every line of the stanza except the last. Without the deletion of τᾷ the first line will be a catalectic × − ∪ −. − ∪ − ∪ − ⁻ followed by − ∪ ∪ − ∪ − × − ∪ ∪ −∪∪ − ∪ − ×.

## TABLE VI: ∪∪A (×) and (where noted) Longer Variants (∪∪−∪∪A × etc.)

| A. Alone or initial leading into iambo-trochaic (often ambiguous with prosodiac) | B. Initial leading into prosodiac or (where noted) heptadic aeolic | C. Initial leading into octadic aeolic or (where noted) other rhythms | D. Initial and repeated or echoed partially in subsequent movements | E. Non-initial |
|---|---|---|---|---|
| Stesichorus 67\|244 (cf. *GL* 6.256.9);<br>∪−∪∪−∪∪A×<br><br>Pindar<br>*N*3s8: ∪∪A×E˘<br>*I*7s1 ∪∪A∪−˘<br>*Pae*9s8 ∪∪A<br>4s1 ∪∪−∪∪−A<br><br>A. *PV* 545–49 = 552–58<br>∪∪−∪∪A∪−˘<br>∪∪A×−∪−×<br>∪∪A×\|E×<br>167 = 185:<br>∪∪−∪−∪∪−∪∪−∪∪−∪∪<br>−∪∪   A×<br><br>E.<br>*Hipp.* 755 = 769 and<br>*Hec.* 653–54: ∪∪A×E˘<br>655, 927 = 937: ∪∪A∪−˘<br>*Med.* 645–46 =<br>655–56: ∪∪A×\|E˘<br>648 = 658<br>*Alc.* 435 = 457<br>442 = 452 } ∪∪A(∪)−˘<br>400 = 412<br>*Hyps.* 64.94<br>*Rhes.* 901 = 912 | *N*10s1<br>*P*10s6: ∪∪A×B˘<br><br>*S. Ant.* 1115–17 = 1126–28<br>∪∪A×−∪−×\|−∪−×A<br>*Tr.* 647 = 655<br><br>*Hipp.* 756 = 770<br>*Hec.* 905 = 914 | 910–13 = 919–21 | *N*3e5: ∪∪A +<br>∪∪A−∪−<br>fr. 105.4–5<br>∪∪A∪−−∪− +<br>∪∪A×−∪−×<br>106.1–3<br>∪∪A∪− +<br>∪∪A+∪∪A<br>Bacch. 16e6–8<br>¯A\|A +<br>∪∪−∪∪A +<br>∪∪A−∪∪−∪−<br>∪∪−∪∪A˘ | E. Non-initial |

*Tr.* 282–83:
⏑⏑A×|–⏑–.–⁓

*HF* 1198:
⏑⏑–⏑–|⏑⏑A×

*Ion* 1479–85:
–⏑–⏑–⏑⏑A|
×–⏑×–⏑×⏑–
⏑⏑A|×–⏑⏑–
–⏑⏑A|×–⏑–×–⏑–×–⏑–
1078–79 = 1094–95: ⏑⏑A×|E⁓

*Hel.* 657, 680, 681: ⏑⏑A.–⁓

*Ar.*
*Th.* 1020–21: ⏑⏑A×|E⁓
fr. 516
⏑⏑–⏑–⏑–⏑|
⏑⏑–A×

Callimachus 228:
⏑⏑–⏑⏑A×
(= ×–⏑⏑–⏑⏑A×)

*Andr.* 1014 = 1022
*Tr.* 832 = 852

*El.* 733–76 = 743–46

*Ion* 1486–87:
⏑⏑A|do do

*Hel.* 1114 = 1138 and
1342 = 1358

*IA* 582

*Cycl.* 52–54
(sequel uncertain)

*Telephus* 149.3–8 (?)
⏑⏑ A×–|⏑–⏑⏑–×|
–⏑–×D⏑–⁓
×A×–⏑– ×–⏑– .––

*PMG* 769.1, 813.1 and
8–9 (⏑⏑–⏑–⏑–⏑⏑A)
Aristonous, *Hymn to Vesta*
(p. 164 Powell)

*Andr.* 1034–35 =
1044–45(?)[1]
⏑⏑A+⏑⏑A×⏑–
⏑⏑A+⏑⏑A×⏑–
–⏑–⏑–⏑A
⏑⏑A×
699–701 = 713–15
–⏑–⏑⏑A+
⏑⏑A+
⏑⏑A+
⏑⏑A

*El.* 167–68 = 190–91:

*Ion* 458–60 = 478–80:
⏑⏑A⁓+
××B|⏑⏑–⏑–A⁓⁓
468–71 = 488–91
⏑⏑A+
⏑⏑A+
⏑⏑–⏑–⏑–⏑–⏑⏑––|⁓A⁓

*Hel.* 1120–21 = 1132–36:
⏑⏑A+
⏑⏑–⏑–⏑–⏑–⏑–|×E⁓

*IA* 177–79 = 198–200:
⏑⏑–⏑–⏑A+
⏑⏑A×A
1049–53 = 1071–75
⏑⏑A.|×B+
⏑⏑A×|×B|××A⁓

*Hcld.* 371–73:
××A××A+⏑⏑A⁓
748–50 = 759–61:
××A××A+⏑⏑A⁓+
–⏑⏑A⁓
755–57 = 766–68:
××A××A+⏑⏑A⁓+
××A⏑–
355–57 = 364–66:
××A⁓+
⏑⏑–⏑–⏑–⏑⏑A×

*HF* 380–82 = 394–96:
××–⏑–⏑–⏑–A⁓+
⏑⏑–⏑–|
⏑⏑–⏑–|⏑⏑A⁓

*PMG* 935.21
|⏑⏑A| amid instances of
|⏑⏑A| used *kata*
*stichon*
Theocritus, *ep.* 17: ⏑⏑A⁓
(= ×A⁓)
following trimeter or tetrameter

[1] Scanning κτέανον in 1035 and deleting καί in 1045 (so Schroeder).

φιλεῖ δὲ [τᾷ] δυστρόπῳ γυναικῶν ἁρμονίᾳ      × E ×‿∪∪‿⏌∪‿

κακὰ δύστανος ἀμηχανία συνοικεῖν,           ×‿∪∪‿∪∪‿∪‿

ὠδίνων τε καὶ ἀφροσύνας.                −×      D

δι' ἐμᾶς ἦξέν ποτε νηδύος ἅδ' αὔρα,          ∪∪−×     D    ×−

τὰν δ' εὔλοχον οὐρανίαν τόξων μεδέουσαν ἀύτευν Ἄρτεμιν

                             × D     ×     D    ×−∪−

καί μοι πολυζήλωτος αἰεὶ

          σὺν θεοῖσι φοιτᾷ      × E ×|                 Eˆ

Cf., at the beginning of the same ode:

τειρομέναν νοσερᾷ κοίτᾳ δέμας ἔντος ἔχειν οἴκων,    D       ×      D    ×−

λέπτα δὲ φάρη ξάνθαν κεφαλὰν σκιάζειν   ×ᵛ∪−×−∪∪−∪−×

                                       (131–34 = 121–24)

Of these demarcations, terminal ×−| is less rare than the others and mer-
its fuller discussion (best put off until something has been said of the
dochmiac character of the passages in which it most often appears). The
association of aeolic and prosodiac can be documented from those passages as well, but enough evidence has been offered already to show why
it would have been natural, by the end of the fifth century, to hear prosodiac and heptadic aeolic as closely related versions of a common *rhythmos
kat'enoplion* (above, 11).

It would not always have been so. Heptadic aeolic is first attested in a
context (Alcaic and Sapphic lyric) where there is no clear trace of prosodiac at all; and even in the early fifth century—to judge from Pindar—its
affinities were more with octadic aeolic than with prosodiac. Plausible reasons for the change can be suggested, but they belong less to the history
of heptadic aeolic than they do to that of its better attested octadic counterpart (see below, 96–97).

# CHAPTER FOUR: OCTADIC AEOLIC

The presence of varying patterns of internal demarcation rarely obscures the basic rhythmic identity of passages composed in octadic aeolic. All colometrists will regard ×× – ᴗ ᴗ – ᴗ – | ×× – ᴗ ᴗ – ‾ and ×× – ᴗ ᴗ – ᴗ – × | × – ᴗ ᴗ – ‾ as homogeneous pieces of aeolic very similar to each other: glyconic and pherecratean separated by diaeresis in the first case and, in the second, either the same combination with caesura instead of diaeresis, or "hipponacteum" separated by diaeresis from a "reizianum." The equivalence of certain aeolic cola to each other also admits of orthodox colometric presentation, even though the interchangeability of $\overline{\underline{\phantom{-}} \, ᴗ \, \underset{A}{ᴗ} \, \overline{\phantom{-}} \, ᴗ \, \overline{\phantom{-}}}$ and $\overline{\underline{\phantom{-}} \, \underset{B}{×} \, \overline{\phantom{-}} \, ᴗ \, ᴗ \, \overline{\phantom{-}}}$ segments which underlies it operates independently of the pattern of demarcation in the equivalent or responding passages:

| | | |
|---|---|---|
| ∣×× – ᴗ ᴗ – ᴗ – ∣ | = ∣×× – × – ᴗ ᴗ – ∣ | (S. *Ph.* 1102 = 1082) |
| ∣ × – ᴗ ᴗ – ᴗ – ∣ | = ∣ × – × – ᴗ ᴗ – ∣ | (E. *HF* 791 = 808) |
| ∣ × – ᴗ ᴗ – ᴗ – × ∣ | = ∣ × – × – ᴗ ᴗ – × ∣ | (S. *Ph.* 1147 = 1124) |
| ∣ – ᴗ ᴗ – ᴗ ᵛˣ ∣ | = | ∣ – × – ᴗ ᴗ ᵛˣ ∣ | (E. *Ion* 1083 = 1099 |
| | | [δείκνυσι <ν> γὰρ ὁ Διὸς ἐκ]) |

It is largely in connection with unusual initial and terminal demarcation, or certain characteristic types of syncopation and modulation, that the notion of epiploke provides a substantially different and, I believe, truer guide to aeolic structure than does colometry.

Initial $\overline{\underline{\phantom{-}} \, ᴗ \, \underset{A}{ᴗ} \, \overline{\phantom{-}} \, ᴗ \, \overline{\phantom{-}}}$ or $\overline{\underline{\phantom{-}} \, \underset{B}{×} \, \overline{\phantom{-}} \, ᴗ \, ᴗ \, \overline{\phantom{-}}}$ causes no problem when, as often, internal demarcation immediately follows:

εἰ γὰρ ὑπ᾽ Ἰλίῳ

πρός τινος Λυκίων, πάτερ   $\overline{\underline{\phantom{-}} \, ᴗ \, \underset{A}{ᴗ} \, \overline{\phantom{-}} \, ᴗ \, \overline{\phantom{-}}}$ ∣×× – ᴗ ᴗ – ᴗ –

—A. *Ch.* 345–46 = 363–64

βακχεύων ἐπέπνει

ῥιπαῖς ἐχθίστων ἀνέμων   $\overline{\underline{\phantom{-}} \, \underset{B}{×} \, \overline{\phantom{-}} \, ᴗ \, ᴗ \, \overline{\phantom{-}}}$ ∣×× – × – ᴗ ᴗ –

—S. *Ant.* 136–37 = 150–51

It merely results in the addition of new names ("dodrans A " [$\overline{\underline{\phantom{-}} \, ᴗ \, \underset{A}{ᴗ} \, \overline{\phantom{-}} \, ᴗ \, \overline{\phantom{-}}}$] and "dodrans B" [$\overline{\underline{\phantom{-}} \, \underset{B}{×} \, \overline{\phantom{-}} \, ᴗ \, ᴗ \, \overline{\phantom{-}}}$] or the like) to the repertory of colometrist terminology.[72] When a different demarcation follows, the consequences can be more serious. At E. *Hipp.* 70–71:

χαῖρέ μοι, ὦ καλλίστα,
καλλίστα τῶν κατ᾽ Ὄλυμπον  $- \cup \cup -\times-\times|\times-\times\underset{B}{-}\cup\cup-\times$

the first colon is probably $\underset{A}{- \cup \cup -\times-\times}$ (above, 69, 74). It is easily taken, however, as some variant on a catalectic $- \cup \cup - \cup -^{-}$, thus obscuring the way the dicolon is an abbreviated echo, rhythmically and verbally, of the preceding

| | |
|---|---|
| χαῖρε, χαῖρέ μοι ὦ κόρα | $\times\times-\cup\cup-\cup-$ |
| Λατοῦς Ἄρτεμι καὶ Διός, | $\times\times-\cup\cup-\cup-$ |
| καλλίστα πολὺ παρθένων | $\times\times-\cup\cup-\cup-$ |
| ἃ μέγαν κατ᾽ οὐρανὸν | $E\,|\times\times\underset{A}{-\cup\cup}-\cup-\times\,|\times\underset{A}{-\cup\cup}-\cup-\times$ + |

ναίεις εὐπατέρειαν αὐλάν, Ζηνὸς πολύχρυσον οἶκον

$$\underset{}{\overline{\quad\text{A}\quad}}\quad\overline{\quad\text{B}\quad}$$
$$- \cup \cup -\times-\times|\times-\times-\cup\cup-\times$$

χαῖρέ μοι ὦ καλλίστα καλλίστα τῶν κατ᾽ Ὄλυμπον        (64–71)

In conjunction with the demarcation $\times\times|$ such initial nuclei can also suggest the existence of the dubiously attested $- \cup \cup -\times-\times-$ as an aeolic "unit" of the same type as $\times\times-\cup\cup-\cup-$ or $\times\times-\times-\cup\cup-$.[73]

A completely non-aeolic analysis may result when movements begin or end within rather than immediately before a nucleus. Such rhythms are largely excluded from drama,[74] but probably occur in non-dramatic lyric:

---

[72] The latter is often assumed to show a form $(\times--\cup\cup-)$ not compatible with the analysis here offered. But the form is a very dubious one in aeolic contexts: imported into *Ion* 118 = 134 by conjecture; created by an unusual scansion (ὑλᾷεντα) designed to bring strophe into line with a corrupt antistrophe at E. *Hel.* 1303 = 1321; requiring extensive emendation of the antistrophe at E. *Sup.* 960 = 968; and at E. *El.* 436–37 = 446–47 easily removed by Triclinius's πρῴραις κυανεμβόλοις[ιν] | <εἰ>ειλισσόμενος (i.e., $\times-\cup\cup-\cup-$ $|-\times-\cup\cup-...$), whether this is an actual reading or a conjecture. (Ar. *Ran.* 1314–18 has ειειειειλίσσετε with initial trill and, probably, polysyllabic scansion of ειειειει in conjunction with a quotation of *El.* 436 in the form πρῴραις κυανεμβόλοις; cf. P. Pucci, "Aristofane ed Euripide," *MemLincei* X.8ᵃ [1961] 390). For iono-choriambic $\cup--\cup\cup-$, see text, 104.

[73] Often posited in the analyses of E. *Hec.* 469 = 478ff. (below, n. 84).

[74] A possible instance at E. *Ion* 112ff. = 128 $(\times-\underset{B}{\times}\underline{-\cup\cup-}\ |\times\times\underset{A}{-\cup\cup}-\cup-\times|\times-\times-$
$\cup\cup- + \underset{B}{\underline{\times-\cup\cup-}}\ \times|\times-\times-\cup\cup-|\times\times-\times-\cup\cup- + -\times-\cup\cup-|\times\times-\cup\cup-^{-})$, the grouping of cola suggested being favored by the parallel openings καλόν γε τὸν πόνον ὦ $(\times-\times-\cup\cup-|)$, κλεινὸς δ᾽ ὁ πόνος μοι $(\underset{B}{\times}-\underset{}{\times}\cup-\times|)$ and εὐφάμους δὲ πόνους $(-\times-$
$\cup\cup-|)$. Cf., in heptadic aeolic, S. *Tr.* 637 = 644 (above, 74).

$$\cup \ \underset{\overline{\phantom{x}\hat{A}\phantom{x}}}{\cup - \cup -} \times \times \underset{\overline{\phantom{x}A\phantom{x}}}{- \cup \cup - \cup} - \times \times \underset{\overline{\phantom{x}A\phantom{x}}}{- \cup \cup - \cup} -$$

θεὸς ἂν μόνος τοῦτ' ἔχοι γέρας, ἄνδρα δ'οὐκ ἔστι μὴ οὐ κακὸν ἔμμεναι

ὃν ἀμήχανος συμφορὰ καθέλῃ     $\cup \cup - \cup - \times \times - \cup \cup -$
$\underset{\overline{A^{\curvearrowright}}}{}$

$-PMG$ 542.15 – 16 (Simonides)[75]

(The last five and the first four quantities of A are designated by, respectively, ^A and A^⌐). The largest accumulation of possible examples is in Pindar, where final $- \cup -$ and $- \cup - \cup -$ following $- \underset{\overline{A}}{\cup \cup - \cup} -$ or $- \times - \cup \cup -$[76] $\underset{\overline{B}}{}$ are most naturally taken as, respectively, the first three ($\bar{\times}$ $\bar{\times} -$) and the first five ($\bar{\times} \bar{\times} - \bar{\times} -$ or $\bar{\times} \bar{\times} - \cup ^{-}$) quantities which would be encountered were the octadic aeolic epiploke continuing on regularly into $\times \times - \cup \cup - \cup -$ or $\times \times - \times - \cup \cup -$. The fifth quantity in $\times \times - \cup \cup - \cup -$ must be replaced by long or anceps when it becomes terminal—hence the notation $\times \times - \cup ^{-}$, as in the parallel case (above, 12) of $- \underset{\overline{A}}{\cup} \bar{\vee} - ^{-}$. A similar $- \cup ^{-}$ as a terminal shortening and modification of the sequence $- \cup \cup -$ is also found in the familiar Eupolidean of comedy: $\times \times - \times - \cup \cup - \times \times \underset{\overline{B^{\curvearrowright}}}{- \times - \cup} ^{-}$.[77] Outside the Eupolidean, $\times \times - \cup \bar{\vee} - ^{-}$ is the $\underset{\overline{A}}{}$ normal clausular sequel to $- \times - \cup \cup -$ and $\times \times - \times - \cup ^{-}$ is rarely $\underset{\overline{B}}{}$ encountered,[78] perhaps because of the ease with which $\bar{\times} \bar{\times} - \bar{\times} - \cup ^{-}$ would suggest iambo-trochaic. Like $\times \times -$ and $\times \times - \cup ^{-}$, however, it

[75] Cf. Pind. O13s5 ($\cup \underset{\overline{A}}{\bar{\vee} - \cup} - \times \times - \underset{\overline{A}}{\cup \bar{\vee} -} ^{-}$), P6s3-4 ($- \cup \cup - \cup - \times \times - \times \underset{\overline{B}}{- \cup \cup} -$ pre-ceded by what seems to be a similar sequence beginning with the fourth quantity of $- \times - \cup \cup -$: $\cup \cup - \times \times - \times \underset{\overline{B}}{- \cup \cup} -$) and N7s5: ($\times - \underset{\overline{A}}{\bar{\vee} \cup} - \times \times - \underset{\overline{B}}{\times \bar{\cup}} ^{-}$).

[76] Cf. O1e1, 5 and 6; N7s1, 2 and 7, P11e3, in every instance following $- \underset{\overline{A}}{\cup \cup - \cup} -$ or $- \times - \cup \cup -$; and for what may be the same shortening of $\times \times - \times - \cup \cup -$ (in its Plautine $\underset{\overline{B}}{}$ form ⟨$\bar{\times} \times$⟩$- \times - \cup \cup -$), the $- $⟨$\times$⟩$- $⟨$\times$⟩$-$ that concludes aeolic or choriambic at *Bacch*. 633, 635a, 636, 638a; *Cas*. 954, 956; *Curc*. 155, 156, 157, *Men*. 586 and *Rud*. 953 and 955. The more frequently encountered Pindaric close $- \cup -$ could be an instance of the admixture of iambo-trochaic with octadic aeolic discussed in the text (82–84); but the extreme rarity of final $\bar{\cdot} \times \bar{\cup} \bar{\cup} - \cup -$ outside Pindar, even in contexts where this admixture is frequent (see text, 82) suggests that we have to do with a more peculiarly Pindaric piece of aeolic technique.

[77] For this analysis of the Eupolidean, see White 508 (following Heph 29.7–15) where $- \cup ^{-}$ is posited as the catalectic form of $- \cup \cup -$ with the citation of what are, presumably, post-Classical examples (*PMG* 975). $- \times - \cup ^{-}$ may also occur in the much rarer Cratinean ($- \cup \cup - \times - \cup - \times \times - \times - \cup ^{-}$; cf. White 540), but there the relation of the close to what pre-cedes is less clear, and analysis complicated by the problematic character of the variants attested, whether rightly or wrongly in Heph 54.20–55.6 ($- \cup \cup - \times - \times - \times \times - \times - \cup ^{-}$ and $- \cup \cup - \times - \cup - - \cup \cup - \cup - ^{-}$). Pherecrates fr. 13 and 96 Kock contain what is in effect a Eupolidean preceded by one or more instances of the sequence $\times \times - \times - \cup \cup -$.

[78] S. *Ant*. 336–37 = 346–47 and 1116–17 = 1127–28 may contain isolated instances—respectively, $\times - \underset{\overline{B}}{\times \bar{\cup} \cup} - \times | \times - \underset{\overline{B^{\curvearrowright}}}{\bar{\times} - \cup} ^{-}$ and a heptadic $- \cup - \times - \underset{\overline{A}}{\cup \cup - \times} - | \times - \underset{\overline{B^{\curvearrowright}}}{\times \bar{\cup}} ^{-}$.

occurs sporadically, usually in the form ⏓⏓–⏓–⏑⁻, in choral lyric.[79] Transition to or from iambo-trochaic by iambic modulation may also fail to be recognized in octadic aeolic, particularly when the iambo-trochaic insertions are brief (more often the case here than in heptadic aeolic), and when their syllabic pattern is distorted by syncopation. Syncopated .–⁻ usually causes no problem in the common cola |××–⏑⏑–⏑–.–⁻ and ××–×–⏑⏑–.–⁻ (the glyconic or choriambic dimeter + spondee of colometrist analysis) but the equally common |×–⏑⏑–⏑–.–⁻ is sometimes given a totally different analysis. Terminal .–⏑– following aeolic (cf. E. *HF* 791 = 808) is much rarer than .–⁻ and so even more easily taken for something else. Thus in E. *Hel.* 515–19:

ἤκουσα τᾶς θεσπιῳδοῦ κόρας          ×–⏑–.–⁻⏑–.–⏑–
ἅ χρήζουσ' ἐφάνη τυράννοις δόμοις    ××–⏑⏑–⏑–.–⏑– +
  ὡς Μενέλαος οὔπω                   –⏑⏑–⏑–×
μελαμφαὲς οἴχεται                    ×–⏑⏑–⏑–
δι' ἔρεβος χθονὶ κρυφθείς            ××–⏑⏑–⁻

the second and third lines are usually taken as two "hipponactea" (×× –⏑⏑–⏑–× + ××–⏑⏑–⏑–×), even though this places the principal rhythmical break between an adjective and its governing noun and ignores the possible parallel with syncopated .–⏑– at the end of the first line.

Contrasting demarcation in the first and fourth lines can cause the same sort of problem in E. *Med.* 155–59 = 180–83:

εἰ δὲ σὸς πόσις καινὰ λέχη σεβίζει   –⏑–××|–⏑⏑–⏑–×
κείνου τόδε· μὴ χαράσσου·            × –⏑⏑–⏑–×
Ζεύς σοι τάδε συνδικήσει·            × –⏑⏑–⏑–×
μὴ λίαν τάκου δυρομένα σον εὐνάταν.  –⏑–××|–⏑⏑–⏑–.–⁻

Any other scansions of the passage will obscure the close parallel with Sappho 96 (–⏑–××–⏑⏑–⏑–××–⏑⏑–⏑–××–⏑⏑–⏑–⏑–⁻) and S. *Phil.* 152–55 = 137–40:

---

[79] Cf. Bacchylides 18s7 and 12, Pind. *N*7s3, 5 and 6, *P*8s6 (××–×–⏑⁻ following –⏑⏑–⏑– or –×–⏑⏑–, and with analysis as iambo-trochaic –⏑–×–⏑– excluded, in the first and last examples, by the sequence –⏓–⏑–⏑–). Paean 2s2 (. . .–×–×–⏑–) and *O* 1s3,3; e2 (text, 162–63) are probably identical, though the context is less indicative. *I*7s6 and *P*8s7 show the same close in heptadic aeolic (. . .×–⏑⏑–⏑–×–×–⏑⏑– |×–×–⏑⁻ in the former passage, ×–⏑–×–×–⏑⁻ in the latter).

νῦν δέ μοι λέγ᾽ αὐλὰς ποίας ἔνεδρος     $- \cup - \times\times \underline{-\times -}_{B} \cup\cup -$
ναίει καὶ χώραν τίν᾽ ἔχει.     $\times\times -\times - \cup\cup -$
τὸ γάρ μοι μαθεῖν οὐκ ἀποκαίριον     $\times - . \ -\times\times - \cup\ \cup - \cup -$

The same insertion of a penultimate cycle of iambo-trochaic (with or without retention of clausular ($\cup$–¯) that distinguished the Euripidean and Sophoclean passages from Sappho 96 appears, along with further syncopation, in *Ion* 498–501:

συρίγγων ὑπ᾽ αἰόλας ἰαχᾶς     $-. -\times\times \underline{-\times -}_{B} \cup\ \cup -.$
ὕμνων ὅτ᾽ ἀναλίοις     $\times - \cup \underline{\cup - \cup}_{A} -.$
συρίζεις, ὦ Πάν, τοῖς σοῖσιν ἐν ἄντροις,     $-. -\times\times \underline{-\times -}_{B} \cup\cup - \times$

τοῖς σοῖσιν Hartung: τοῖσι σοῖς

and, with additional iambo-trochaic insertions, in the lines which immediately follow:

ἵνα τεκοῦσά τις, παρθένος, ὦ μελέα, βρέφος Φοίβῳ     $^{\smile\smile} \cup -\times\times \underline{- \cup\ \cup}_{A} - \cup - \times -. -\times$
πτανοῖς ἐξώρισε θοίναν     $\times - \times \underline{- \cup \cup}_{B} - \times$
θηρσί τε φονίαν δαῖτα πικρῶν γάμων ὕβριν     $- \cup^{\smile\smile}\times\times \underline{- \cup\ \cup}_{A} - \cup -. -\ ^{-}$

Taken together, the two tricola offer a progressively "iambo-trochaicized" version of the two tricola found in the preceding stanza pair:

ὦ Πανὸς θακήματα καὶ     $\times\times \underline{-\times -}_{B} \cup\ \cup -.$
παραυλίζουσα πέτρα     $\times - \times - \cup\ \cup -.$
μυχώδεσι Μακραῖς     $\times \underline{- \cup \times}_{A} - ^{-} +$
ἵνα χοροὺς στείβουσι ποδοῖν     $\times\times \underline{-\times -}_{B} \cup\ \cup -$
'Αγλαύρου κόραι τρίγονοι     $\times\times -\times - \cup\ \cup -$
στάδια χλοερὰ πρὸ Παλλάδος ναῶν     $\times\times^{\smile\smile} \cup\ \cup \underline{- \cup -}_{A} . -^{-};$

and the content shows the same repetition—with the addition of variations and dissonances—as does the rhythm:

(Oh, abode of Pan,     in the spot where

            Aglauros's    celebrate

            daughters    by Athena's temple),

xx-x-∪∪-.|x-x-∪∪-.|  x-∪∪-¯ +  xx-x-∪∪- |x x-x-∪∪-| xx-∪∪-∪-.-¯

-.-xx-x-∪∪-.|x-∪∪-∪-.|-.-xx-x-∪∪-x|˜˜∪-xx-∪∪-∪-x-.-x|x-x-∪∪-x|

(when Pan's pipings resound          -∪˜˜ xx-∪∪-∪-.-¯

through his cave        in the spot where

            a wretched girl   once exposed her child

                     by Apollo).

Two further versions of the tricolon seem to have provided Timotheus with an ending for his *sphragis*:

Μίλητος δὲ πόλις νιν ἁ θρέψασ᾽     xx-∪∪-∪-.-.-
ἁ δυωδεκατειχέος        xx-∪∪-∪-
λαοῦ †πρωτέος ἐξ ᾽Αχαιῶν     xx-∪∪-∪-x

                       -*PMG* 791.234-36

followed, after an invocatory x̄x̄x̄- ∪ ∪ - ∪ - ‖ (ἀλλ᾽ ἑκατάβολε Πύθιε) by

ἁγνὰν ἔλθοις τάνδε πόλιν σὺν ὄλβῳ   -.-xx-∪∪-∪-x
 πέμπων ἀπήμονι λαῷ τῷδ᾽     x-x-∪∪-.-.-.
εἰρήναν θάλλουσαν εὐνομίᾳ     -.-xx-x-∪∪-

                       -*ibid.*, 237-40

At *Cyclops* 656ff. iambo-trochaic is confined to movement opening, and the aeolic sequences are shortened:

ἰὼ ἰώ, γενναιότατ᾽ ὠθεῖτε.      ˜˜∪-.|x-∪∪-x- +
σπεύδετ<ε>, ἐκκαίετε τὰν ὀφρὺν
    θηρὸς τοῦ ξενοδαίτα      -∪-. ‖x-∪∪-∪-|xx-∪∪-¯ +
τυφέτω            -∪-.|
καιέτω, τὸν Αἴτνας μηλονόμον.    -∪-.|x-x-∪∪- +
τόρνευ᾽             -.-.|
ἕλκε, μή σ᾽ ᾽ἐξοδυνηθεὶς
    δράσῃ τι μάταιον       -.-. ‖x-∪∪-¯ + x-∪∪-¯

but there is the same progressive rise in the number of syncopations (here from one per movement to four) and iambo-trochaic cycles (from one to two) as was observed in the paired tricola of the *Ion* and Timotheus passages. The chorus doubles and redoubles its efforts, and the rhythmical sequences it sings, brief as they are, require two inner breaks in the vocal line ( ‖ ) for catching a breath.

Some of the syncopations in the passages just considered involve the iambo-trochaic segment – ◡ –. More often, however, the syncopation occurs within, or at the transition to and from, aeolic (– ◡ –.×– ◡ ◡ – ◡ –‚ –×–◡ ◡ –.×– ◡ ◡ – ◡ – etc.), and might seem a less justified assumption here than in prosodiac and heptadic aeolic (above, 70–71). The alternative to positing syncopation there was to accept the existence of rare collocations of nuclei (D D, A A etc.); here it is transition between iambo-trochaic or octadic aeolic and heptadic aeolic (– ◡ –×– ◡ ◡ – ◡ –‚ ××– ◡ ◡ – ◡ –×– ◡ ◡ – ◡ – etc.). The former is well-attested throughout Greek lyric; and the latter is common enough in Pindar, especially in the line or line close ×× –×– ◡ ◡ –×– ◡ ◡ – – (O9s3, 4, 5, 6; N2s3, N4s4, 5, 6; I7e5, Parth. 2s2–3 and e1 and 2). Against this argument, however, is the commonness of such heptadic insertions—if that is what they are—in Euripides. Elsewhere in Euripidean lyric heptadic aeolic is virtually confined to passages where it is closely linked to prosodiac (see Table V). Nor is there any reason why such insertions should show, as they almost always do, demarcation preceding the base quantity.[80] There is no comparable requirement for octadic aeolic itself, nor for heptadic aeolic when it appears by itself or in combination with prosodiac or iambo-trochaic. The distribution of forms in Euripides and the demarcational pattern are both easily explained, however, if one assumes syncopation of the first quantity of the aeolic double base. If supplied by a pause, this quantity would naturally be preceded by word end; and if supplied by protraction of the preceding syllable it would be accompanied by the normal demarcation . |× rather than by the rarer . × |, which might have produced too marked a rhythmical irregularity. Demarcation at the transition

[80] Of the possible exceptions, only E. Ion 455–56 = 475–76 (××–×–◡ ◡ – ×–×–◡ ◡ – [see text, 208]) is fairly certain. The scansion ××– ◡ ◡ – ◡ –.|×– ◡ ◡ – ◡ –×| –×–◡ ◡ –×|×– ◡ ◡ – – at Hyps. I.ii = I.iii.27–30 depends on restorations in ii.28, iii.28 and iii.29; the irregular ××– ◡ ◡ – ◡ –×|–×–◡ ◡ –××–×–◡ ◡ – – ◡ ◡ – – of Ar. Eccl. 921–23 becomes with Scaliger's ὑφαρπάσαις, ××– ◡ ◡ – ◡ –|××– ◡ ◡ – ◡ –|××– ◡ ◡ – – ◡ ◡ – – and responsion with 916–18—if exact responsion is present—can be obtained by σαυτῆς <ἂν> (Hermann) in 917 and κάλεσον (: κάλει τὸν) in 916; E. Hcld. 894–97 = 903–6 may be two separate movements: ××– ◡ ◡ – ◡ –× (or, with Madvig's ἡδεῖα, ×–×–◡ ◡ – ◡ – –) + ×–◡ ◡ – ◡ –×|– ◡ ◡ – ◡ –×|– ◡ ◡ – ◡ –×; and Bac. 872–76 = 892–96 (along with, perhaps, Hipp. 553–54 = 563–64 [below, n. 244]) has an iambo-trochaic sequence between its octadic aeolic and a concluding, undemarcated ×– ◡ ◡ – –. E. Med. 649–51 = 660–62 is probably – ◡ –×– ◡ ◡ – ◡ – ××– ◡ ◡ – ◡ – – ◡ ◡ – ◡ – – (below, n. 247) though a different, homogeneously octadic analysis is often accepted, e.g., by Page ad loc.

between aeolic and iambo-trochaic is similarly regulated when syncopation occurs (as $- \smile -.\, | \times$ $-\underline{\times}-\smile\smile\underline{-}$ or $-\underline{\times}-\smile\smile\underline{-}.\, | - \smile -$) perhaps for the same reason.[81]

An analogous explanation may account for the regularity with which consecutive aeolic nuclei are separated by demarcation.[82] Syncopation of both base quantities ( . |. ) would inevitably produce this demarcation, whether the syncopation took the form of a pause equivalent in length to two quantities or protraction followed by a pause equivalent to a single quantity. The hypothesis is supported by the structure of specific passages, e.g. S. *Ant.* 100–105 = 117–22:

ἀκτὶς ἀελίου     × × $\underline{- \smile \smile -}$ | $\smile - \times × - \smile \smile - \smile - × ×$ | $- \smile \smile - \smile -$
                A
    τὸ κάλλιστον ἑπταπύλῳ φανὲν Θήβᾳ
                    τῶν προτέρων φάος
ἐφάνθης ποτ᾽ ὦ χρυσέας     × × $\underline{- × -}$ $\smile \smile -$ . |. $- × - \smile \smile -$ | × × $\underline{- × -}$ $\smile \smile - \smile -$ $^{- 83}$
                  B                                        B
        ἀμέρας βλέφαρον
    Διρκαίων ὑπὲρ ῥεέθρων μολοῦσα

where the second tricolon repeats the rhythm of the first with more regular demarcation, substitution of $- × - \smile \smile -$ for $- \smile \smile - \smile -$, and the addition of clausular $\smile -^-$; or E. *Med.* 852–55 = 861–65, which is unlikely to be anything but a syncopated version ($× - \smile \smile - \smile - × | × - \smile \smile - \smile -$
          A
$× | × - \smile \smile - \smile -.\, |.\, \underline{- \smile \times} -$) of 151–54 and the identical 435–38 =
              A

---

[81] E. *Hipp.* 531–32 = 541–42 ($× - × \underline{- \smile \smile} -.\, | \smile - × - \smile -.\, | × \; -\smile \underline{\times}-^-$, a syncopated
                              B                                    A
parallel to the preceding $- × - \underline{\smile \smile} - | × - \smile - × - \smile -$ is exceptional, as are *Hel.* 516 (text, 82)
                            B
and S. *Ant.* 336–37 = 346–47 ($× - × \underline{- \smile} \smile -.\, - | \smile - × - \smile -$ if the alternative scansion sug-
                                    B
gested above [n. 78] is not accepted).

[82] E. *IT* 423–24 = 440–41 is the most likely exception (outside the clausular forms noted in the text, 83–84): $\bar{\times} - \smile \smile - \smile - | \times \underline{- \smile} \smile -$ in the text of the antistrophe. The strophe,
                                          A                B
however, shows $- - - \smile \smile \smile - - | × \underline{- \smile} \smile -$, and no convincing way of bringing it into line
                                          B
with the antistrophe has been found. If both are to be emended, the rhythm may well be
$- × \underline{- \smile} \smile - | \bar{\times} \bar{\times} - × - \smile \smile -$ (see the suggestions of Diggle *ad loc.*) or $× - \smile^{\smile\smile} | \bar{\times} \bar{\times} - × \underline{- \smile} \smile -$
      B                                                                            B
(with Triclinius's Φινείδας in the strophe and δι᾽ ἅλα or the like for Ἑλένα in the antistrophe).

[83] Usually analyzed as $× × - × - \smile \smile - | × × \underline{- \smile} \smile - | × - \; × × - \smile \underline{\smile} - \smile - ×$. But elsewhere
                                            A                        A
in Sophocles the only demarcations allowed with $- \smile \underline{\smile} - × -$ are $- \smile \smile - × - |$
                                                              A
and $- \smile \underline{\smile} - × | - \bar{\times} | . . .$ Cf., for the latter, *Ant.* 844 = 862 (text, 182), *Ph.* 710–11 =
          A
721–22 ($× × - \smile \smile - - \smile \underline{\smile} - × | - \bar{\times} | × - \smile \underline{\smile} - \smile - \smile - -$), *OC* 1247–48 ($\underline{- \smile \smile} - × | - \bar{\times} |$
                              A                    A                                          A
$× - \smile \smile - \smile - . - -$) and 517–18 = 529–30 (text, 203). Euripides seems to have been more
      A
permissive; cf. *Hipp.* 68–71 (text, 80).

442–45 (above, 13).[84]

The instances are not, however, sufficiently numerous to make this suggestion more than a tentative one; and analysis is complicated by two further factors. One cannot be certain when a succession of nuclei marks the beginning of a new movement rather than a continuation, following syncopation, of one already in progress;[85] and there exists a tendency in certain forms of aeolic to use a six-quantity cycle based on the sequences found in the nucleus:

χρήματα καὶ βίαν Κλειταγόρᾳ τε κἀμοὶ μετὰ Θετταλῶν

$$-\cup-\cup-|-\cup\cup-\cup--\cup-\cup-$$
— *PMG* 912b

ἰήιε Παιάν, ἰήιε· Παιὰν δὲ μήποτε λείποι

$$\times-\underset{B}{\underline{\text{v}}}\cup- -|\times-\underset{B}{\underline{\cup}}\cup- -\times-\underset{B}{\underline{\phantom{x}}}\cup\cup--^{86}$$
—Pind. *Pae* 2e9

ὅτε τὸν τύραννον κτανέτην
ἰσονόμους τ' Ἀθήνας ἐποιησάτην

$$\cup\underset{A}{\underline{\text{v}}}-\cup--\underset{A}{\underline{\cup}}\text{v}-$$
$$-\cup\cup-\cup- -\cup\cup-\cup-$$
— *PMG* 893.3–4

κῶμον, Ἰσθμιάδος τε νίκας ἄποινα καὶ Νεμέᾳ
ἀέθλων ὅτι κράτος ἐξεῦρε· τῷ καὶ ἐγώ, καίπερ ἀχνύμενος

$$\times\times-\cup\underset{A}{\underline{\cup}}-\cup-\times\times-\underset{B}{\underline{\times}}\cup\cup-$$

θυμόν, αἰτέομαι χρυσέαν καλέσαι
Μοῖσαν, ἐκ μεγάλων δὲ πενθέων λυθέντες
μήτ' ἐν ὀρφανίᾳ πέσωμεν στεφάνων

$$\times\times-\underset{B}{\underline{\times}}\cup\cup- -\underset{B}{\underline{\times}}\cup\cup--\underset{B}{\underline{\times}}\cup\cup-$$
$$-\times-\cup\cup--\times-\cup\cup-$$
$$-\times\underset{A}{\overline{\underline{\phantom{x}}\underset{}{\cup}\cup-\cup}}-\times\times-^{-}$$
$$\times\times-\cup\cup-\cup- -\cup\underset{A}{\underline{\text{v}}}-$$
—Pindar *I* 8s4–8

(The notation $-\times\overset{\text{B}}{\underset{A}{\underline{\text{v}\cup\underline{\text{v}}}}}-\cup-$ in the last passage indicates the way the sequence $-\times-\cup\cup-$ is heard: first as a continuation of the preceding

---

[84] Cf., also, E. *IA* 753–61 = 764–71, where parallelism between two syntactically and rhythmically isolated tetracola $(\times\times-\times\underset{B}{\underline{\phantom{x}}}\cup\cup-| \ \times\times-\times-\cup\cup-.|.-\underset{A}{\underline{\cup\cup}}-\cup-\times|\times-\times-$ $\underset{B}{\underline{\text{v}}}\cup-$ and $\times-\underset{B}{\underline{\times}}\cup\cup- \ \times|\times-\times-\cup\cup-|\times\times-\cup\cup-\cup-|\times\times-\underset{A}{\underline{\cup}}\cup-\cup-$ preceded by $\times\times-\cup\cup-\cup-|\times\times-\cup\cup-^{-}$ and followed by $-\cup\cup-\times-\cup-\times$, is in favor of the syncopations indicated, as is that between the $\times\times-\cup\cup-\cup-|\times\times-\cup\cup-\cup-|\times\times-\cup\cup-\cup-$ $|\times\times-\cup\cup-\cup-|\times\times-\cup\cup-^{-}$ of *El.* 115–19 = 130–34 and the immediately following $\times-$ $\cup\cup-\cup-.|. \ -\cup\cup-\cup-|\times\times-\cup\cup-\cup-|\times\times-\cup\cup-\cup-\times\times-\cup\cup-^{-}$. Cf., also, the highly regular demarcation of *IT* 428–33 = 444–49 into segments which will be, with syncopation, all of the form $\overset{(\text{v})}{\underline{\phantom{x}}}-\times\underset{B}{\underline{\phantom{x}}}\cup\cup-\overset{(\text{v})}{\underline{\phantom{x}}} : \times-\times-\cup\cup-.|\times-\times-\cup\cup-.| \ \times-\times-\cup\cup-.|\times-$ $\times-\cup\cup-\times|\times-\times-\cup\cup-.| \ .-\times-\cup\cup-|\times-\times-\cup\cup-.$

[85] Cf. E. *Hec.* 466 = 475ff., perhaps three separate movements, perhaps a continuous $\times-\cup\underset{A}{\underline{\cup}}-\cup-.|\times-\cup\cup-\cup-{}_{,}\times\times^{|}-\cup\cup-\cup-.|.-\cup\cup-\cup-\times\times|-\cup\cup-\cup-{}_{,}\times\times^{|}-\cup\cup-\cup$ $-\times|\times\underset{B}{\underline{\times}}-\cup\cup-.| \ .-\times-\cup\cup-|\times\times-\times-\cup\cup-$ and S. *OC* 127–28 = 159–60 (text, 183–84).

[86] Cf., in the same poem, s4–5, e2, 5–6.

hexadic rhythm and then as a part of an octadic ××– ∪ ∪ – ∪ – that starts to be repeated with the ensuing ××–⁻).

Such rhythms are not common anywhere, and secure instances in drama are just as rare as those of initial demarcation within a nucleus. A number of possible ones, however, are provided by clausular ××
– ∪ ∪ – ∪ – – ∪ ∪ – ∪ – ⁻. Terminal – ∪ ∪ – ∪ – ⁻ in this alternative (cf.
  ‾A‾
*LMGD* 134) to the more common ××– ∪ ∪ – ∪ –××– ∪ ∪ – ⁻ may be iono-choriambic; but it is just as easily analyzed as an aeolic – ∪ ∪ – ∪ – ⁻
  ‾‾‾‾‾‾‾A‾‾‾
following directly on another A without an intervening base. The normal clausular rhythms in the other type of octadic aeolic and in iono-choriambic might both be analyzed in a similar way:

$$
\begin{array}{cc}
A & A \\
\overline{× × - \cup \cup - \cup -} & \overline{- \cup \cup - \cup -} \; -
\end{array}
$$

$$
\begin{array}{cc}
B & B \\
\overline{× × - × - \cup \cup -} & \overline{- × - \cup \cup -} \; -
\end{array}
$$

$$
- \cup \qquad \overline{\cup -} \qquad \overline{\cup -} \; -
$$

In all three instances there is a terminal reduction of the cycle of recurrence by two quantities: from eight to six or four to two. The movement ends seven or three quantities after the end of the next to last nucleus, just as it would if there were the terminal shortening of a nucleus found in – ∪ ∪ – ⁻, – ×– ∪ ⁻ and the rarely attested – ∪ ⁻ (i.e., – ∪ ∪ –
  ‾A‾  ‾B‾
modified by loss of final –);[87] but reducing the length of the cycle preserves the characteristic nuclear pattern from the distortion which those forms exhibit.[88] The "distorted" form is regular, though not universal, in one type of aeolic; confined to choral lyric (and the Eupolidean: above, 81) in the other; and hardly used at all in iono-choriambic.

The "un-distorted" forms are all ambiguous: aeolic  – ∪ ∪ – ∪ –  or
  ‾‾‾‾A‾‾‾‾
iono-choriambic – ∪ ∪ – ∪ – ⁻, aeolic – ×– ∪ ∪ – ⁻ or ×× – ∪ ∪ – ⁻ , and
  ‾‾‾B‾‾‾   ‾‾A‾‾
iono-choriambic or iambo-trochaic ∪ – ⁻. In the case of – ∪ ∪ – ∪ – ⁻
context may have determined how the rhythm was heard: as

---

[87] Identified by Hephaestion (29.7–15) as the catalectic form of the choriamb, with the citation of (presumably) Hellenistic examples ( = *PMG* 975).

[88] Also in favor of the analysis – ∪ ∪ – ∪ – ⁻ is the occasional presence of the characteristic
  ‾‾A‾‾
aeolic modulation into dactylic: S. *OC* 1211–14 = 1224–27 (××– ∪ ∪ – ∪ –××– ∪ ∪ – ∪ –
|××– ∪ ∪ – ∪ – –| ∪ ∪ – ∪ ∪ – ∪ – ⁻ and 1243–44 (××– ∪ ∪ –×|– –| ∪ ∪ – ∪ ∪ – ∪ – ⁻;
  ‾‾‾A‾‾        ‾‾‾A‾‾
*PMG* 738.1 (×– ∪ –×– ∪ –.– ∪ –×|×– ∪ ∪ – ∪ –|– ∪ ∪ – ∪ ∪ – ∪ – ⁻ and Ibycus
                  ‾‾‾A‾‾
40/321.3–4 (××– ∪ ∪ –×–|– ∪ ∪ – ∪ ∪ – ∪ –⁻)
           ‾‾A‾‾

$-\cup\cup-\cup-^-$ rather than $-\cup\underset{A}{\underline{\cup\cup}}-\cup-^-$ when found alongside one or more of the numerous unambiguous instances of iono-choriambic linked to aeolic via iambic modulation that appear in drama. Usually this linkage is readily recognized, both when demarcation immediately follows the transitional segment and when (less frequently) it occurs one quantity later:

παιᾶνας δ' ἐπὶ σοῖς μελάθροις     $\times\times-\cup\underset{A}{\underline{\cup}-}\cup--$

κύκνος ὡς γέρων ἀοιδός     $\cup\cup-\times-\cup--$

πολιᾶν ἐκ γενύων     $\cup\cup--\cup\cup-.$

κελαδήσω, τὸ γὰρ εὖ     $\cup\cup--\cup\cup-$

τοῖς ὕμνοισιν ὑπάρχει     $\times\times-\cup\cup-^{-89}$

$-$E. *HF* 689–94 = 677–80

or (sporadically) at some other point:

ὁπόσαι δ' ἐξαπατῶσιν παραβαίνουσί τε τοὺς ὅρκους

$\cup\cup--\cup\cup--\cup\cup--\cup\cup-\times\times|-\cup\cup-\cup-$

τοὺς νενομισμένους

κερδῶν οὕνεκ' ἐπὶ βλάβῃ     $\times\times-\cup\cup-\cup-$

$-$Ar. *Th.* 355–56

The possibility of syncopating a base quantity is not affected by this modulation:

[89] Cf., later in the same play, 785–89 = 803–6 $(\times\times-\cup\underset{}{\underline{\cup}}-\cup-^{'}-_{,}\cup\cup--\cup\cup--\cup\cup-$ $\times|-\times\underset{B}{\underline{\cup}}\cup\cup-$ $|\times\times-\cup\cup-^-$ if the antistrophe's οὐκ ἐπ' ἐλπίδι is replaced with, e.g., εὐέλπιδι), S. *Ant.* 781–84 = 791–94 $(\times-\cup--\cup\cup-|\times-\cup--\cup\cup-\times|\times\underset{A}{\underline{-\cup\cup-}}\cup-\times|\times-$ $\cup\cup-\cup-\times)$, *OC* 510–12 = 521–22 and 176–78 = 192–94 (text, 203); *Ph.* 208–9 = 217–18 $(\times-\times-\cup\cup--\widetilde{\cup\cup}-|\cup\cup-\times-\cup-$ [or $|\cup\cup-\times-.-^-$: cf. Dale 20–21]), E. *El.* 727–28 = 737–38 $(\cup\cup-.^{\smile}\cup-\times|\times-\cup\underset{A}{\underline{\cup}}-\cup-$ [identical to *IT* 1132–33 = 1147–48 if the reading of the strophe in the latter passage is correct]), *Cresphontes* fr. 71.8–9 Austin $(\times$ $-\cup\cup-\cup--|\cup\cup-^{\smile}\cup-$ [or $|\cup\cup-\times^{\smile}\cup-$]), *Hipp.* 749–52 = 739–41 $(\times-\cup\underset{A}{\underline{\cup}}-\cup--$ $|\underset{A}{\underline{\cup\cup}}-\times|\times-\cup\underset{A}{\underline{\cup}}-\cup-$ and *Alc.* 461–62 = 471–72 $(\cup\cup-\times|\times-\cup\underset{A}{\underline{\cup}}-\cup-\cup-^-)$. The last two passages are unusual in including only a single cycle of iono-choriambic, as is E. *Bac.* 569–73, which passes from pure iono-choriambic into aeolic via a single cycle of iambo-trochaic $(\cup\cup--\cup\cup--\cup\cup--\cup\cup-\times|-\cup-\times|\times-\underset{B}{\underline{\times-\cup\cup}}-|\times$ $\times-\cup\cup-\cup^{\simeq})$. The stanza concludes with what is evidently a repeat $(\times\times\underset{B}{\underline{-\cup\cup}}-|\times\times-\cup\underset{}{\underline{\cup}}-^-)$ of the aeolic $\times|\times-\times-\cup\cup-|\times\times-\cup\cup-\cup-$ heard earlier, though the intervening τε τὸν ἔκλυον (574) is textually and rhythmically difficult: perhaps, with both Bothe's deletion of τε and prosodic demarcation, $\times-\cup-\|$, a similar repeat of the preceding iambo-trochaic $\times|-\cup-$.

βροντᾷ γὰρ ἀμφιπύρῳ                    x – x – ‿ ‿ –
                                                    ‾‾‾B‾‾‾
τοκάδα τὰν διγόνοιο Βάκχου             x x – ‿ ‿ – ‿ – x
                                                      ‾‾A‾‾‾
νυμφευσαμένα πότμῳ                     x – ‿ ‿ – ‿ –.

        φονίῳ κατηύνασεν                     ‿ ‿ – x –.‿ – – [90]

                                        —E. Hipp. 559–62 = 549–50


ὁρῶ δίκωπον,                           x – ‿ – x ‖ [91]
    ὁρῶ σκάφος ἐν λίμνᾳ.               x – ‿ ‿ – ‿ –.
        νεκύων δὲ πορθμεύς . . .              ‿ ‿ – ‿ – ‾. . . .
σὺ κατείργεις. τάδε τοί              ‿ ‿ – – ‿ ‿ –.| x – ‿ ‿ – ‿ – x
    με σπερχόμενος ταχύνει

                                        —E. Alc. 252–57 = 259–63


When single cycles of aeolic and double cycles of iono-choriambic
succeed each other frequently, or occupy parallel positions in larger structures, the effect is an assimilation of the two genres reminiscent of what
occurs in mixed prosodiac (above, 71–75). Though such rhythms are
more characteristic of comedy than of tragedy, they appear in tragedy as
well. Cf. S. *Aj.* 1185–91 = 1192–98:


τίς ἄρα νέατος, ἐς πότε λήξει        x x – x – ‿ ‿ – – | ‿ ‿ – – ‿ ‿ – ‿ – ‾
                                                       ‾B‾
        πολυπλάγκτων ἐτέων ἀριθμός,
τὰν ἄπαυστον αἰὲν ἐμοὶ              x x – x – ‿ ‿ – | x – ‿ – x | x – x – ‿ ‿ –
                                                                          ‾‾‾B‾‾‾
        δορυσσοήτων
        μόχθων ἄταν ἐπάγων
τάνδ' ἀν' εὐρυεδῆ Τροίαν,           x x – ‿ ‿ – ‿ –. | x – ‿ ‿ – ‿ –. – ‾
                                              ‾‾A‾‾          ‾‾A‾‾
        δύστανον ὄνειδος Ἑλλάνων


Here the third line is in effect a syncopated version of the first (with
medial – ‿ ‿ – – ‿ ‿ – replaced by . | x – ‿ ‿ – ‿ –), and the second an
acatalectic version of the first and third (with internal x – ‿ – for final
(‿) – ‾). Earlier in the same play the summoning of Apollo at 702 =
713ff. is a shorter, iono-choriambic version of the summoning of Pan at
695 = 708ff.:


[90] If the strophe is emended into responsion by, e.g., Barrett's φονίοισι νυμφείοις. Cf. A.
*Ag.* 1494–95 (x x – ‿ ‿ – – ‿ –. | ‿ ‿ – x – ‿ –, continuing into the prosodiac close .| D ‿ – ‾
in the manner of *PV* 132 = 47 and *Sept.* 726 = 733 [Table IV] or, with Enger's addition of
*damartos*, into a clausular ‿ – ‾); and, probably, S. *Aj.* 702 = 715 (text, 91).

[91] The two anceps quantities may belong to different movements, or to an aeolic base
divided by internal prosodic demarcation of the sort discussed in the text, 129–33.

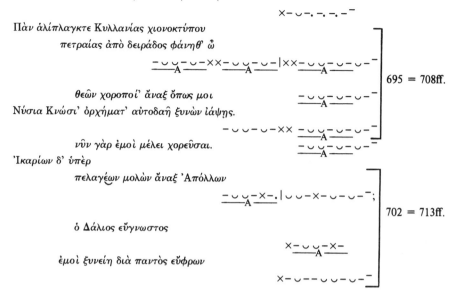

The approximate 3–1–2 ratio between the lengths of the components (17, 7 and 11 quantities for Apollo; 25, 9 and 17 for Pan) remains constant, but there is initial and/or terminal shortening of each component and substitution of iono-choriambic .| ⏑ ⏑ – × – ⏑ – or × – ⏑ – – ⏑ ⏑ – for aeolic × × – ⏑ ⏑ – ⏑ –. As in prosodiac, the character of such structures provides an argument for the assimilation of octadic cycles to double tetradic ones that supplements the argument from strophic responsion between the two rhythms (above, 11).[92]

Responsion and overall structure help explain the use of the single term *bakkheios* (*ibid.*) to designate both aeolic and iono-choriambic. But the links between the two genres are achieved by other means as well, and in ways which are less clearly reflected in demarcational patterns. "Choriambic" modulation of the sort found in prosodiac and heptadic aeolic has its octadic counterparts:

[92] Two of these occasionally responding sequences, iambo-choriambic × – ⏑ – – ⏑ ⏑ – and aeolic × × – × – ⏑ ⏑ – are often assumed to be equivalent versions of a single "polyschematist" dimeter: ⁝×⁝×⁝×⁝ – ⏑ ⏑ –. But their frequent association is more likely to be an instance of the free transition between choriambic and aeolic discussed in the text (88–90). Actual responsion of the two forms is no more frequent than that between × × – × – ⏑ ⏑ – and other iono-choriambic sequences, and the posited × – × – – ⏑ ⏑ – is not attested at all.

τὰν δ᾽ ἔγω τάδ᾽ ἀμειβόμαν

$$\times\times-\cup\cup-\cup-\underbrace{\phantom{xxx}}_{A}$$

χαίροισ᾽ ἔρχεο κἄμεθεν

$$\times\times-\cup\cup-\cup-$$

μέμναισ᾽, οἶσθα γὰρ ὥς σε πεδήπομεν
aeolic

$$\times\times-\underline{\cup\cup-\cup\cup-}\cup-$$
dactylo-anapestic
aeolic

—Sappho 94.6–8

πρὶν σὰν προσιδεῖν χαρίεσσαν ὥραν

$$\times-\cup\cup-\cup\cup-\cup-\times$$

καὶ καλλιχόρους ἀοιδὰς

$$\times-\cup\cup-\cup-\times$$

φιλοστεφάνους τε κώμους

$$\times-\cup\cup-\cup-\times$$

—E. Chresph. 453.6–9 (71 Austin)[93]

μαινομένα κραδία διδύμους ὁρίσασα πόντου

$$-\cup\cup-\cup\cup-\cup\cup-\underbrace{\cup\cup}_{A}-\times$$
πέτρας· ἐπὶ δὲ ξένᾳ

$$\times\quad-\cup\cup-\cup-.$$
ναίεις χθονί, τᾶς ἀνάνδρου

$$\times\quad-\cup\cup-\cup-\times$$
κοίτας ὀλέσασα λέκτρον

$$\times\quad-\cup\cup-\cup-\times$$
τάλαινα, φυγὰς δὲ χώρας

$$\times\quad-\cup\cup-\overline{\phantom{x}}$$
ἄτιμος ἐλαύνᾳ                    —E. Med. 432–38 = 440–45

ματρὸς ἀμφότεροι, διείργει δὲ πᾶσα κεκριμένα

$$\times\times-\underbrace{\cup\cup-\cup-}_{A}\cup-\times\times-\underbrace{\times-}_{B}\cup\cup-$$
δύναμις ὡς τὸ μὲν οὐδέν, ὁ δὲ χάλκεος ἀσφαλὲς αἰὲν ἔδος
μένει οὐρανός . . .

$$\underbrace{\overset{\vee\vee}{\times}-\cup\cup-}_{B}\overset{\vee\vee}{\times}-\underbrace{\cup\cup-}_{B}\cup\cup-\cup\cup-\mid\cup\cup-\cup\cup,$$

—Pind. N6s2–4

but far less often in connection with dactylo-anapestic than with iono-choriambic. The greater and lesser asclepiadeans are the most familiar

---

[93] With Austin's transposition of προσιδεῖν and χαρίεσσαν.

instances:

aeolic     aeolic
××– ∪ ∪ – – ∪ ∪ – ∪ –
iono-choriambic
aeolic         aeolic
××– ∪ ∪ – – ∪ ∪ – – ∪ ∪ – ∪ –
iono-choriambic

Such choriambic modulations are not only more frequent: they show much greater variety than those involving dactylo-anapestic. The iono-choriambic sequences linked with aeolic may be mixed as well as pure, and besides leading into or out of aeolic they may take the form of insertions which extend beyond the confines of a single colon:

βασιλεῦ τᾶν ἱερᾶν ᾿Αθανᾶν     ∪ ∪ – – ∪ ∪ – ∪ – × | × – ∪ ∪ – ∪ – ∪ – ‾
τῶν ἀβροβίων ἄναξ ᾿Ιώνων

–Bacch. 18.1–2

ἵν᾿ ὁ ποντομέδων πορφυρέας λίμνας    ∪ ∪ – . ∪ ∪ – – ∪ ∪ – × – | × × – ∪ ∪ – ∪ – [94]
ναύταις οὐκέθ᾿ ὁδὸν νέμει

–E. Hipp. 743–46 = 733–36

γαμετᾶς οὐρανόνικον·    ∪ ∪ – – ∪ ∪ – – | ∪ ∪ – ∪ – – ∪ ∪ – ∪ – [95]
χαλεποῦ γὰρ ἐκ πνεύματος εἰσι χειμών

–A. Sup. 165–67

(ionic leading into aeolic);

---

[94] Responsion with the θεὸς ἐν ποταναῖς ἀγέλαις θείη of the strophe may be achieved by, e.g., the transpositions printed in Murray's text. Maas's πορφυρέας ποντομέδων is textually easier (see Barrett ad loc.) but posits an unparalleled series of syncopations in ionic: ∪ ∪ – × –.–.∪ ∪ – .– ‾.

[95] For the clausular – ∪ ∪ – ∪ – – ∪ ∪ – ∪ – ‾ see the discussion in the text, 88–89. E. HF 640–41 = 659–60 may be similar, but with iono-choriambic echoed from the end of a preceding movement (text, 47) rather than continued from earlier in the same movement:

ᵛᵛ∪ ∪ – – ∪ ∪ – . | ∪ ∪ – ∪ – ‾ +
∪ × – ∪ – ‾ | ∪ ∪ – ∪ – ‾

The penultimate ∪ ∪ – ∪ – ‾ will be heard both as clausular iono-choriambic and as part of the continuous sequence ˆA A ‾.

$$\times- \cup -- \cup \cup -- \underline{\cup \cup}_{A} - \times- |\times\times- \cup \cup -- \cup \cup -^{-96}$$

φοιτᾷς δ' ὑπερπόντιος ἔν τ' ἀγρονόμοις αὐλαῖς
καὶ σ' οὔτ' ἀθανάτων φύξιμος οὐδείς

−S. Ant. 785−88 = 795−98

(mixed choriambic leading into aeolic);

$$\times\times- \cup \cup -- \cup \cup -- \cup \cup -|- \cup \cup -- \cup \cup -|\times \text{ E }^{97}$$

ξυντίθησι δὲ παιδὸς μόρον ὡς αὐτοφόνως
ὤλετο πρὸς χειρὸς ἔθεν
δυσμάτορος κότου τυχών     −A. Sup. 65−68 = 60−63

(aeolic passing into iono-choriambic and iambo-trochaic);

εἰ μὴ 'γὼ παράφρων μάντις ἔφυν        $\times\times- \cup \cup -- \cup \cup -|- \overline{\underline{\cup \cup}}-- \cup \cup - \cup -^{98}$
καὶ γνώμας λειπομένα σοφᾶς        −S. El. 472−74 = $\underset{A}{487}$−89

(passage from aeolic into iono-choriambic, followed by return to aeolic);

καί σ' ἐν ἀφύκτοισι χερῶν εἷλε θεὰ δεσμοῖς     $- \cup \cup -- \cup \cup -- \underline{\cup \cup}_{A} - \times-$
τόλμα δ'· οὐ γὰρ ἀνάξεις ποτ' ἔνερθεν     $\times\times- \cup \cup -- \cup \cup --| \overline{\underline{\cup \cup}}-- \underline{\cup \cup}_{A} - \cup -$
κλαίων τοὺς φθιμένους ἄνω     −E. Alc. 984−86 = 995−97

(the same, preceded by choriambic passing into aeolic).

In some of these passages the ambiguous transitional segment may have included more than $- \cup \cup -$: $- \cup \cup - \cup --$ in the first example (choriambic $- \cup \cup - \cup -^-$ or aeolic $- \cup \cup - \cup - \times$), $- \cup \cup - \times-$ in the second and fourth ($\underline{- \cup \cup - \times-}_{A}$ or $- \cup \cup - \times-$, an iono-choriambic

[96] E. Ion 1233 probably contains an extended version of the initial iono-choriambic sequence found here: $^{\smile\smile} \cup - \times^{\smile\smile} \cup --| \overline{\underline{\cup \cup}}-- \cup \cup -- \cup \cup -| \times- \cup -- \cup \cup -$ (θοᾶς ἐχίδνας σταγόσι<ν>)| $\underline{- \cup \cup - \cup -}_{A}| \times\times- \cup \cup - \cup -|\times\times- \cup \cup - \cup -|\times\times- \underline{\cup \cup - \cup}_{A} - \times-^-$, the aeolic sequence ending in what seems to be a unique variant on $\cup -^-$.

[97] For an analogue, with dactylo-anapestic replacing iono-choriambic, cf. Pind. I8s11 ($\times\times- \cup \cup - \cup \cup -$) and the identical O10e2, with the more regular aeolic line closes that precede and follow:

O10 s3:   ... $\times\times- \cup \cup - \cup \cup -$
   6:   ... $\times\times \quad \underline{- \cup \cup - \cup}_{A} -$
   e2:   ·   $\times\times- \cup \cup - \cup \cup -^-$
   3,8:   ...   $- \cup \cup -- \cup \cup -$
   4−5:   ... $\times|\times \quad - \cup \cup -- \cup -$
   9:   ... $\times\times- \cup \cup -$

[98] Cf., later in the same play, 1082−84 = 1090−92, where iambo-trochaic replaces iono-choriambic: $\times\times- \cup \cup -. |- \cup - \times- \cup -|- \cup \cup - \cup -.$

segment with demarcation after the first quantity in the iambo-trochaic nucleus), and initial and medial − − − ◡ ◡ − in the last two ($\overline{\smile\smile}$− − ◡ ◡ − or $\overline{×}\,\overline{×}$ − ◡ ◡ −). On occasion, such ambiguity extends to a whole rhythmical context. Thus S. *Aj.* 632–34 = 643–45 may be either aeolic ××− ◡ ◡ −⁻ + ××−◡ ◡−⁻ + ××−◡ ◡−◡−◡−⁻ or ionic $\overline{\smile\smile}$−− ◡ ◡− −| $\overline{\smile\smile}$−− ◡ ◡ − −| $\overline{\smile\smile}$−− ◡ ◡−×−◡−⁻

θρηνήσει, χερόπλακτοι δ'        − − − ◡ ◡ − −
ἐν στέρνοισι πεσοῦνται        − − − ◡ ◡ − −
δοῦποι καὶ πολιᾶς ἄμυγμα χαίτας        − − − ◡ ◡ − ◡ − ◡ − ⁻⁹⁹

The result was probably a highly distinctive rhythm, though it is difficult to suggest a reason for its use without a consideration of the (mainly Sophoclean) contexts in which it appears (see below, 185–92).

Iono-choriambic linked in this fashion to heptadic aeolic occurs in Sappho (128) but rarely thereafter, the one Sophoclean example (*OT* 868–70 = 879–80):

×− ◡ ◡ − ◡ −|×− ◡ ◡ − ◡ −|×− ◡ −×− ◡ ◡ − − ◡ ◡−×−
πατὴρ μόνος, οὐδέ νιν
θνατὰ φύσις ἀνέρων
ἔτικτεν, οὐδὲ μήποτε λάθα κατακοιμάσῃ

being sufficiently close to a (presumably) Sapphic or Alcaic form in Horace (*C* 1.7):

− ◡ ◡ − ◡ −×|− ◡ −×− ◡ ◡ − − ◡ ◡ − ◡ −×
Lydia dic per omnes
te deos oro Sybarin cur properes amando

to suggest use of a specific model. This distribution of iono-choriambic between the two types of aeolic is just the opposite of that of dactylo-anapestic, which appears more commonly in conjunction with heptadic than octadic (above, 91). The same holds true for dactylo-anapestic when it is linked by modulation to both aeolic and iono-choriambic:

⁹⁹ See, on such aeolo-ionic passages in general, *LMGD* 144.

εἴθε λύρα καλὰ γενοίμαν ἐλεφαντίνη,        – ◡ ◡ – × – ◡ –        – ◡ ◡ – ◡ –
                                                                          ‾‾‾A‾‾
καί με καλοὶ παῖδες φέροιεν Διονύσιον ἐς χορόν   – ◡ ◡ – × – ◡ – – ◡ ◡   – ◡ ◡ – ◡ –
                                                                          ‾‾‾A‾‾
                                                            – PMG 900

ἄνθρωπος ἐὼν μή ποτε φάσῃς ὅτι γίνεται αὔριον   × – ◡ ◡ – – ◡ ◡ – – ◡ ◡ – ◡ ◡ – ◡ –
                                                                          ‾‾‾A‾‾
μηδ᾽ ἄνδρα ἰδὼν ὄλβιον ὅσσον χρόνον ἔσσεται   × – ◡ ◡ – – ◡ ◡ –        – ◡ ◡ – ◡ –
                                                                          ‾‾‾A‾‾
                                                      –Simonides 16/521.1–2

In both of these passages a line which contains normal choriambic transition between iono-choriambic and aeolic is juxtaposed to one in which
transition is accompanied by passage into dactylo-anapestic. And Pindar
*N*6e3–4 contains two such transitions:

aeolic        iono-choriambic                    aeolic
× – ◡ ◡ – ◡ ◡ – ◡ ◡ – – ◡ ◡ – | – ◡ ◡ – ◡ ◡ – ◡ ◡ – ◡ –
      dactylo-anapestic                    dactylo-anapestic
κεῖνος γαρ ᾿Ολυμπιόνικος ἐὼν Αἰακίδαις ἔρνεα πρῶτος ἔνεικεν ἀπ᾽ ᾿Αλφεοῦ

Such double linkages are largely confined to the heptadic aeolic of
choral lyric. There they appear in conjunction with the linkings of aeolic
to dactylo-anapestic discussed in the preceding chapter (above, 67–69) as
well as with the hexadic rhythms and unusual forms of catalexis considered earlier in this chapter (above, 78, and 87). The resulting combination of techniques is fundamental to the complex structure of Pindar's
aeolic odes.

   It is, by contrast, modulation into iono-choriambic and the rhythmical
ambiguities which result that are fundamental for one other highly complex form of aeolic, the octadic type found in Sophocles and, to a lesser
degree, Euripides. What such contrasts suggest about octadic aeolic in its
dramatic form is the presence of a tetradic character even more pronounced than that possessed by prosodiac. Hence the restricted role
played by admixture with hexadic, heptadic (above, 85–88) and—through
choriambic modulation into dactylo-anapestic—triadic cycles. Evolution of
dramatic lyric along these lines is probably to some degree responsible for
the shifting affinities of heptadic aeolic (above, 78): as octadic aeolic
becomes more intolerant of non-tetradic groupings of quantities, the two
forms come to be felt as incompatible. The features heptadic aeolic shares
with prosodiac—single base and choriambic modulation into dactylo-
anapestic—thereby become more significant in determining its generic
affinities, and subject to more extensive development. For prosodiac and
and octadic aeolic remain, throughout the history of Greek verse, the
prime instance of lyric opposites. They are almost never connected to

each other by direct modulation;[100] they are rarely found as portions of the same rhythmical movement;[101] and they are only occasionally included in the same poem or practiced with equal variety and resourcefulness by the same poet—unless he happens to be Pindar.[102] The only thing more monotonous than the aeolic of Euripides (once he stops imitating Sophocles) is the prosodiac of Sophocles (who never learns to imitate Euripides).

Within aeolic, antipathies and affinities are, by contrast, a matter of frequencies and fashions, not absolute laws and permanent tendencies. Some techniques are present from the very start in both types of aeolic: pure and mixed composition, choriambic modulation into dactylo-anapestic and iono-choriambic, clausular extension of a nucleus by $\cup - ^-$ and the use of the catalexis $- \cup \underset{A}{\underline{\vee}} - ^-$. Others, like syncopation, hexadic cycles and iambic modulation into iono-choriambic make a belated and sometimes brief appearance. Syncopation is typical of dramatic verse in general; iambic modulation is a function of the progressive tetradization of the octadic type; and composition in hexadic cycles seems to have been a Pindaric and Bacchylidean experiment. But in every instance the character and relative frequency of the techniques used in combination with each other varies from author to author and poem to poem.

---

[100] E. *IA* 1042–44 = 1064–66 (D ×|D |××– ∪ ∪–⁻) is the most likely instance, but problematic because of the unusual double contraction in the second D (– ⌣⌣– ⌣⌣–). Other passages (e.g., *IA* 585–86, *IT* 1267–69 = 1242–44, E. *El.* 482–86, *Cycl.* 52–54) are either corrupt (cf., for the last mentioned, Diggle, *CQ* 65 [1971] 42–43) or lend themselves to other analyses. Occasionally (e.g., at A. *Pers.* 584–90 = 591–97; see below, n. 220) the sequence – – – ∪ ∪–× seems to be heard first as D × then, on a second occurrence, as x̄ x̄ – ∪ ∪–⁻. But the reinterpretation regularly follows the end of one rhythmical movement and the beginning of another. The related modulation (cf. Snell 49) within a single movement at A. *Suppl.* 69–72 = 79–81 is quite exceptional: x̄ x̄ – ∪ ∪–|– ∪ ∪–∪–×‖× – ∪ ∪–∪–×.

[101] S. *Phil.* 855–57 is a possible example (–×– ∪ ∪–×|×–×– ∪ ∪–×– ∪–×| D , but the first colon might be better isolated as a separate movement: ××– ∪ ∪–⁻. E. *Med.* 209–12 is clearer: ×– ∪–×D ×|D |×E |××– ∪ ∪–⁻.

[102] Or Simonides? 50/555 and 26/531 contain what may be prosodiac sequences in close conjunction with others which are octadic aeolic. But division into rhythmical movements is uncertain, as is the degree to which the text should be regularized into straight prosodiac by emendation. And analysis is complicated by the ambiguity of – – – ∪ ∪– (D, –x̄– ∪ ∪–, or x̄ x̄– ∪ ∪–). 76/581.3 for example: ἀελίου τε φλογὶ χρυσέας τε σελάνας (– ∪ ∪– ∪ ∪– |– ∪– ∪ ∪–⁻) allows at least five scansions: D.| –×– ∪ ∪–× or D |××– ∪ ∪–⁻; or (with the synizesis χρυσέας) – ∪ ∪– ∪ ∪–| ⌣⌣– ∪ ∪– ⌣⌣ or D | ×– ∪ ∪–⁻; or (with the regularizing emendation χρυσέας τε μήνας) D |×– ∪–×.

# CHAPTER FIVE:
## ANTISPASTIC, DOCHMIAC, BACCHIO-CRETIC

Aeolo-ionic |‒‒‒◡◡‒-... (i.e., a sequence which may be either
|⤬⤬‒◡◡‒-... or |‒‒‒‒◡◡‒-...: above, 95) has an "aeolo-antispastic" counterpart in |◡‒‒◡◡‒-... (i.e., either aeolic |⤬⤬‒◡◡‒-... or the beginning of an "antispastically" demarcated segment of iono-choriambic: ‒◡|◡‒‒◡◡‒‒◡|◡‒‒-...). Like "major" ionic, the term antispast (above, 17) is a Hellenistic coinage frequently applied in an arbitrary way to the analysis of sequences which are not part of iono-choriambic rhythm at all. But Classical verse probably does contain pure and mixed iono-choriambic sequences demarcated in major ionic fashion (above, 37), and the same is true of antispastic. One may retain the ancient designation for convenience, and consider such sequences alongside certain analogues to them found in other genres (notably, iambo-trochaic and prosodiac). There, too, demarcation may appear, as in the antispast, following the first quantity of a nucleus (×‒◡‒×‒|..., ‒◡◡‒◡◡‒×‒|...) or immediately preceding the final two (|◡‒×‒ ◡‒...).

The rhythm is clearest in a group of sequences which open with what context identifies fairly clearly as antispastic |◡‒‒◡◡‒-... (rather than aeolic |⤬⤬‒◡◡‒-...) or iambo-trochaic |◡‒.‒◡‒-... (rather than dochmiac |⤬‒‒⤬‒-...). Thus at S. *Aj.* 227–32 = 251–56:

οἴμοι, φοβοῦμαι τὸ προσέρπον, περίφαντος ἀνήρ    ×‒◡‒‒◡◡‒‒◡◡‒      ◡‒‒

θανεῖται περιπλάγκτῳ χερὶ συγκατακτάς      ◡‒‒◡◡‒‒◡◡‒       ◡‒‒

κελαινοῖς ξίφεσιν βοτὰ καὶ βοτῆρας ἱππονώμας      ◡‒‒◡◡‒. ◡◡‒|×‒◡‒◡‒‒

it is hard to see the second and third lines as anything but echoes of the first, minus two initial quantities and with, in the third, syncopation and an added cycle of iambo-trochaic. And this relationship is exactly that which exists between mixed iambo-choriambic and mixed antispastic within iono-choriambic epiploke, whether one chooses to call the opening of the second and third lines antispastic or, as is more normal with this and several similar sequences, "headless" ionic (cf. *GV* 295, with the passages cited there: Ar. *Ran.* 324; E. *Ph.* 1539–42 [two instances], *IA* 171–75 [two instances], *Hyps.* I.iv.2).

Syncopation seems to appear in both members of a pair of similarly related dicola at Timotheus 15/791.84–85. The first opens with iambic, the second with antispastic:

φάτ’ ἄσθματι στρευγόμενος　　　　×– ⌣ – – ⌣ ⌣ –.
　βλοσυρὰν δ’ ἐξέβαλλεν ἄχναν　　⌣ ⌣ –.– ⌣ – ⌣ – ̄ +
ἐπαναρευγόμενος　　　　　　　⌣ ⌣̆ – ⌣ ⌣ –.
　στόματι βρύχιον ἄλμαν　　　　⌣̆ ⌣ ⌣̆ ⌣ – ̄ [104]

The sequence ⌣ – – ⌣ – is identifiable as the syncopated iambo-trochaic counterpart ( ⌣ –.– ⌣ –) to ⌣ – – ⌣ ⌣ – at Ar. *Th.* 1016–18, where it opens a foreshortened version of the preceding line:

πῶς ἂν ἐπέλθοιμι καὶ τὸν Σκύθην λάθοιμι　　– ⌣ ⌣ –.– ⌣ –.– ⌣ – ⌣ – ̄
κλύεις; ὦ προσαυδῶ σε τὰν ἐν ἄντροις　　　⌣ –.– ⌣ –.– ⌣ – ⌣ – ̄

and it is similarly identifiable by the way it is lengthened into succeeding ionic at E. *Bac.* 148ff.[105]

δρόμῳ και χοροῖς　　⌣ –.– ⌣ –.
ἐρεθίζων πλανάτας　　⌣ ⌣ –.– ⌣ – –

It also seems to parallel antispastic ⌣ – – ⌣ ⌣ – at the beginnings of the two long, largely iono-choriambic sequences at E. *Ph.* 1508–14 and 1515–18:

---

[104] 26/802 may be similar ( ⌣ ⌣̆ ×– ⌣ – ⌣̆ [μακάριος ἦσθα Τιμόθε’] | ⌣ ⌣ –×– ⌣ –×|– ⌣ – ×– ⌣ –.| – ⌣ – – ⌣ ⌣ – ⌣ – ̄ ), but there is no guarantee that the citation opens with the beginning of a colon.

[105] Cf. Ar. *Ran.* 1346–47, where the initial ἐγὼ δ’ ἁ τάλαινα, prosodically demarcated like the rhythmically related Ἴακχ’ ὦ Ἴακχε of 325 = 341 from the succeeding ionic ( ⌣ ⌣ –×⌣̆ ⌣ – –|), is probably ⌣ –.– ⌣ – –, a foreshortened version of the – ⌣ ⌣ –.– ⌣ – found (1345) at the close of the preceding movement. A pure iono-choriambic counterpart ( ⌣ –.⌣ ⌣ –) to ⌣ –.– ⌣ – may appear at S. *Ph.* 1179, echoing the rhythm and initial repetitions of the immediately preceding line, and perhaps opening an "antispastic" counterpart to its ionic rhythm:

⌣ ⌣ –.⌣ ⌣ –.⌣ ⌣ – – ⌣ ⌣ –.⌣ ⌣ – – (1178–79)
⌣ –.⌣ ⌣ –.⌣ < ⌣ – >– ⌣ ⌣ –.– ⌣ – – (1179–80)
φίλα μοι φίλα ταῦτα παρήγγειλας ἑκόντι τε πράσσειν
ἴωμεν　ἴωμεν　< ⌣ – > ναὸς ἵν’ ἡμῖν τέτακται).

Cf., for further possibilities, *OC* 117 = 150 ( ⌣ –.| ⌣ ⌣ –.| – ⌣ – [ποῦ ναίει] and the Lesbian mill song (*PMG* 869: ⌣ –.⌣ ⌣ –.| ⌣̄ ⌣̄ – – ⌣ ⌣ – –| ⌣ ⌣ –.⌣ ⌣ – – ⌣ ⌣ – –).

ἰώ μοι, πάτερ,                          ∪ −.− ∪ −
      τίς Ἑλλὰς ἢ βάρβαρος ἤ ...        × − ∪ − − ∪ ∪ −. ...

                                                        1508−9
τάλαιν', ὡς ἐλελίζει·                   ∪ − − ∪ ∪ − −
      τίς ἄρ' ὄρνις ...                ∪ ∪ − ×. ..[106]

                                                        1514−15

The variant ἰώ μοί μοι in 1508 would yield the unsyncopated ∪ − × − ∪ −,
which is found alongside ∪ −.− ∪ − at the beginnings of the two almost
identical movements that comprise A. *PV* 901 − 7:[107]

ἐμοὶ δ᾽ ὅτε μὲν ὁμαλὸς ὁ γάμος ἄφοβος        ∪ −. ˘˘ ∪ ˘˘ × ˘˘ ∪ ˘˘ ×
[οὐ δέδια][108] μηδὲ κρεισσόνων θεῶν          − ∪ − × − ∪ −
ἔρως ἄφυκτον ὄμμα προσδράκοι με.            ✳ ∪ − × − ∪ − ∪ − ‾ +
ἀπόλεμος ὅδε γ᾽ ὁ πόλεμος, ἄπορα πόριμος      ∪ ˘˘ × ˘˘ ∪ ˘˘ × ˘˘ ∪ ˘˘ ×
οὐδ᾽ ἔχω τις ἂν γενοίμαν·                    − ∪ − × − ∪ − ×
τὰν Διὸς γὰρ οὐχ ὁρῶ                         − ∪ − × − ∪ −
μῆτιν ὅπα φύγοιμ᾽ ἄν.                        − ∪ ∪ − ∪ − ‾

The commonest of such sequences are ∪ − − ∪ ∪ − ∪ − ‾ and ∪ −.−
∪ − ∪ − ‾, the two labeled *choephorika* by Wilamowitz (cf. *GV* 248−49)
because of the similar way in which they are used, in the *Choephoroe* and
elsewhere, by Aeschylus. They tend to have a clausular or pre-clausular
position in a stanza, and to be heard either as foreshortened versions of a
preceding trimeter (× − ∪ − × − ∪ − ∪ − ‾ at *Ag.* 1487−88 = 1511−12 and
× − ∪ −.− ∪ −.− ∪ − at *Supp.* 96−99 = 103−6) or forelengthened versions of a preceding − ∪ ∪ − ∪ − ‾ (*Pers.* 574−75 = 582−83; *Ch.* 382−85

---

[106] The transmitted text is hard to construe, but corruption, if present, need not affect the
metre. Perhaps one should read ἐλελίζω (Brunck, Porson and Grégoire – Méridier, following
certain *recentiores*).

[107] Alternate scansions require emendation *metri gratia* so extensive (see T. C. W. Stinton,
"Notes on Greek Tragedy," *JHS* 96 [1976] 123−4) that it disturbs the clear parallelism of
the opening dicola of the two sections. Cf., for what may be a similar parallelism, E. *HF*
383−87 = 397−401:

                ∪ − × − ∪˘˘ × |− ∪ − × |− ∪ − × |− ∪ − × +
                ∪ −.− ∪ − × − ∪ − .|˘˘ ∪ − ∪ − ‾ +
                × −.− .− ∪ − ∪ − ‾

[108] Less likely as a gloss on ἄφοβος than, e.g., οὐ φοβοῦμαι (see Stinton [above, n. 107]
124) but, as Stinton himself points out (*ibid.*), paralleled in the scholion to *Pers.* 700
(p. 479.23 Dindorf).

= 397–99, 467–70 = 472–75).[109] A more complex but related pattern appears in E. *Alc.* 455 = 466ff. A terminal dicolon in the Aeschylean manner:

ἦ μάλ᾽ ἂν ἔμοιγ᾽ ἂν εἴη          ⤬˘˘ – ˘ – ˘ – ¯

στυγηθεὶς τέκνοις τε τοῖς σοῖς      ˘ –.– ˘ – ˘ – ¯

echoes a longer, choriambic version of itself heard at the beginning of the stanza:[110]

εἴθ᾽ ἐπ᾽ ἐμοὶ μὲν εἴη                    – ˘ ˘ – ˘ – ¯

δυναίμαν δέ σε πέμψαι          ˘ – – ˘ ˘ – – | ˘ ˘ –.  ˘ ˘ – ˘ – ¯

φάος ἐξ ᾽Αΐδα τεράμνων

$$(455–57 = 466–68)$$

This lengthened version of the rhythm is itself followed immediately by a closer anticipation of the concluding ˘ –.– ˘ – ˘ – ¯:[111]

ποταμίᾳ νερτέρᾳ τε κώπᾳ      ˘˘ ˘ –.– ˘ – ˘ – ¯          (458 = 469)

In one Aeschylean passage the presence of a preceding – ˘ ˘ – ˘ – $\overline{\phantom{A}}$ᴀ$\overline{\phantom{A}}$ – ˘ ˘ – ˘ – ¯ (above, 83–84) favors aeolic analysis for – ˘ ˘ – ˘ – ¯ $\overline{\phantom{A}}$ᴀ$\overline{\phantom{A}}$ and perhaps ˘ – – ˘ ˘ – ˘ – ¯ as well:

---

[109] Cf., also, E. *Alc.* 877 = 894 (a foreshortened version, in the text of the antistrophe, of the ⤬– ˘ –.– ˘ – ˘ – ¯ with which the stanza opens); *Suppl.* 804 = 817 (the same ˘ –.– ˘ – ˘ – ¯ in the same relationship to ⤬– ˘ –.– ˘ – ˘ – ¯ at the end of its own stanza and the stanza preceding); fr. 118.1 (parodied by Aristophanes in the ˘ –.– ˘ –.– ˘ – ˘ – ¯ quoted in the text) and, from the same passage in the *Andromeda*, 117 and (probably) 119. Context is less indicative when ˘ –.– ˘ – ˘ – ¯ is clausular for dactylic systems (E. *Or.* 1012 and *Med.* 137 [in the colometry of *GV* 250]).

[110] The recall is present in the antistrophe as well: ἦ γὰρ ἂν ἔμοιγ᾽ ἄλυπος.

[111] Or – ˘˘ – – ˘ ˘ – ⤬ |˘˘ ˘ –.– ˘ – ˘ – ¯ if the colon καὶ Κωκυτοῖο ῥεέθρων, to which there is no responding passage in the antistrophe, is retained in the text. With the rhythm of the whole passage, compare Ar. *Th.* 995–98 and 990–993:

(– ˘ ˘ – ˘ – ¯)

˘ – – ˘ ˘ – ¯

˘ – – ˘ ˘ – – ˘ ˘ – – ˘ ˘ – ˘ – ¯ (or ˘ – – ˘ ˘ – – ˘ ˘ – ⤬ ˘ –.– ˘ – ⤬)

ὦ πόνος ἐγγενὴς καὶ παράμουσος ἄτας     $-\cup\cup - \cup - - \cup\cup - \cup -^{-}$
                                           $\overline{\quad A\quad}\quad\overline{\quad A\quad}$

αἱματόεσσα πλαγά.                        $-\cup\cup - \cup -^{-}$
                                           $\overline{\quad A\quad}$

ἰὼ δύστον᾽ ἄφερτα κήδη         $\breve{\times}\bar{\times} - \cup\cup - \cup - \times$

ἰὼ δυσκατάπαυστον ἄλγος     $\breve{\times}\bar{\times} - \cup\cup - \cup - \times$

                                         $-$ *Ch.* 466–70 = 471–75

But the general absence of unambiguous aeolic from the contexts under discussion, the total absence of any instances of the usual $-\times$ form of aeolic base in $\cup - - \cup\cup - \cup -^{-}$, and the parallel with the clearly non-aeolic $\cup - - \cup - \cup -^{-}$ all suggest that such aeolic associations as the rhythm had were secondary.

Medial $\mid \cup -$ in iono-choriambic and iambo-trochaic is much rarer than initial, and at times such an anomaly in its context that one suspects it is being used for special effect. Thus at A. *Ag.* 198 = 210:

τρίβῳ κατέξαινον ἄνθος ᾽Αργείων     $\times - \cup -. - \cup - \times -. -. -$
       ἐπεὶ δὲ καὶ πικροῦ                $\cup - \times - \cup -$
       χείματος ἄλλο μῆχαρ            $- \cup\cup - \cup -^{-}$

the placing of demarcation sets the long attrition of the wait at Aulis in sharper contrast to the brutal abruptness of the remedy. It makes the colon introducing the new phase in the action very brief (ἐπεὶ δὲ καὶ πικροῦ) and in so doing prolongs the preceding colon beyond the point where analogy with the earlier portion of the stanzas (the trimeters and tetrameters, all ending in $- \cup - \cup -^{-}$, cited above, 45) led one to expect clausular rhythm and the beginning of a new piece of epiploke. At A. *Ch.* 46 = 57, on the other hand, it is the briefness of what precedes $\mid \cup -$ rather than of what follows that, combined with postponement of the subject, projects Clytemnestra onto the scene with special vehemence:

ἰὼ γαῖα μαῖα, μωμένα μ᾽ἰάλλει     $\times -. - \times - \cup - \times - \cup - \times$
       δύσθεος γυνά.                   $- \cup - \times -$
    φοβοῦμαι δ᾽ ἔπος τόδ᾽ ἐκβαλεῖν     $\cup -. - \cup - \times - \cup -$

The rhythm, and the fear inspired, are echoed exactly in the antistrophe:

νῦν ἀφίσταται.                 $- \cup - \times -$
    φοβεῖται δέ τις. τὸ δ᾽ εὐτυχεῖν     $\cup -. - \cup - \times - \cup -$

Were this type of demarcation entirely confined to contexts such as these one might be inclined to regard it as a peculiar type of caesura within iambic or trochaic, here given unusual semantic prominence. But

initial | ⏑ –.– ⏑ – is so well attested in situations where there is no reason
to label it a "headless" trochaic (–) ⏑ –.– ⏑ – or iambic (×–) ⏑ –.– ⏑ –
that internal . . .– | ⏑ –.– ⏑ – is better regarded as differing only in fre-
quency, not in basic character, from the normal . . .– | ×– ⏑ –.– ⏑ – or
. . .–× | – ⏑ –.– ⏑ –. And even this frequency is subject to fluctuations.
At A. *Sept.* 900 = 887ff. the demarcation | ⏑ –, whether initial or inter-
nal, seems to pervade an entire movement:

| | |
|---|---|
| διήκει δὲ καὶ πόλιν στόνος | ⏑ –.– ⏑ –×– ⏑ – |
| στένουσι πύργοι, | ×– ⏑ –.– |
| στένει πέδον φίλανδρον. | ⏑ –×– ⏑ –.– |
| μένει κτέανα τ'ἐπιγόνοις | ⏑ –.˘˘⏑˘˘×–[112] |
| δι' ὧν αἰνομόροις | ⏑ – – ⏑ ⏑ – + |
| δι' ὧν νεῖκος ἔβα καὶ θανάτου τέλος. | ⏑ – – ⏑ ⏑ – – ⏑ ⏑ –×– |

(The second ⏑ – – ⏑ ⏑ – is preceded by a break in the continuity of the
epiploke, with rhythm, like sense, beginning over again in a repetition of
what appeared six quantities earlier).[113]

Sporadic echoes of the rhythm are heard throughout the more conven-
tionally demarcated sequences that precede and follow. The parallels may
be set forth as follows, with ᴇ designating an undemarcated – ⏑ –.– ⏑ –:

```
                 xE͘
          x– ⏑ – xE
   x– ⏑ –.–| ⏑ –. E˄
                                          875–78 = 881–85
        ⏑ –. E|   x– ⏑ –.–| ⏑ –×– ⏑ –.–| ⏑ –.˘˘⏑˘˘×–| ⏑ – – – ⏑ ⏑ – +
                                   ⏑ – – ⏑ ⏑ –|– ⏑ ⏑ – ⏑ – ̄
                                          887–94 = 900–905
          x–.–.  E   .
                  E|  x–.–.– ⏑ –| x–.  –.–.– ⏑ –|
                                          – ⏑ ⏑ ˘˘×–
                                          895–99 = 906–10
      x– ⏑ –. E˄ +
      x– ⏑ –. E˄ +x      E͘  |x      E͘
                                          911–14 = 921–25
```

---

[112] Text and colometry uncertain. τ' is omitted in two codices, and demarcation in the
lacunose antistrophe may occur two quantities later than in the strophe. For a possible paral-
lel to the whole passage cf. Ar. *Th.* 352–56: ⏑ –.˘˘⏑˘˘×– ⏑ –| x˘˘ ⏑ –.–| ⏑ –.˘˘ ⏑ – –
| ⏑ ⏑ –×– ⏑ – –| ⏑͡ ⏑͡ – ⏑ – ̄

[113] S. *Aj.* 605–8 = 617–20 may be similar:

```
          ⏑ – – ⏑ ⏑ – +
          ⏑ – – ⏑ ⏑ –.
     ˘˘ ⏑ ˘˘×–| ⏑͡ ˘˘˘˘ ⏑ ⏑ – ⏑ – ̄
```

x-. -. - ∪-x-| ∪-. - ∪-[114]          -| ∪ ∪ -- ∪ ∪- ∪-¯ +
                                       - ∪ ∪ -- ∪ ∪ --
                                       ∪ ∪ -- ∪ ∪ -- ∪ ∪ -- ∪ ∪ -- ∪ ∪-
                                       - ∪ ∪- ∪-¯
                                       915-21 = 926-31
x- ∪-. E        .|    Ė +              ∪˘˘- ∪ ∪-|- ∪ ∪- ∪-¯
                                       932-36 = 947-50

x- .-. Ê +           ∪-.˘˘∪-|
x- .-. Ê +      ×     E    |
x- ∪-. E        |
x- ∪-. E        |×    Ė    |
x- ∪-. Ê

                                       937-46 = 951-60


The terminal – ∪ ∪ – x – | twice attested here is rare except in passages where transition to another rhythm is involved. A number of these passages have already been considered in the preceding chapter: those involving an ambiguous – ∪ ∪ – x – or – ∪ ∪ – ∪ – that could function as part of either aeolic or iono-choriambic. A further set of passages involves both iono-choriambic – ∪ ∪ – x – and iambo-trochaic x – ∪ – x – in contexts where dochmiac rhythms are either present and recalled by those sequences, or actually linked to them through modulation.

As was noted earlier (above, 22) dochmiac ( = do in the notation used here) is a rhythm which does not, by and large, admit of epiploke. In this respect it is like the anapest, in conjunction with which it often appears[115] and with one form of which ( ∪ ∪ ˘˘ ∪ ∪ (˘) = ×͞×͞×(˘)) it is actually identical. It shows a single pattern of demarcation isolating |x – – x – | or some multiple of it as a fixed unit of composition.[116] When combined with another rhythm dochmiac further resembles dipodic anapests in that it always begins and ends at a single point. The ubiquitous iamb + dochmiac is always just that: never a trochaic – ∪ – x followed by – – x – x (or vice versa). The anapestic analogy is not, however, exact at every point. Demarcation within dochmiac series occurs at rarer and less regular

[114] Text and scansion for the corrupt 915 = 926 are as suggested in Schroeder.

[115] E.g., at E. *Hec.* 1056–84. Polymestor's second monody resolves itself into a series of movements composed of paired dochmiacs or anapestic metra (|an|), grouped into pairs of "dimeters," each pair followed by a clausular variation, and the last preceded by an an˄. (The analysis requires L's ποίαν ταύταν ἤ in 1059–60: the transposition Ἅλιε τυφλόν [Conomis 44] at 1068; and, at 1081, πείσμασι[ν], and [ὅπ]ως [Nauck] or ἅτε [Weill]). Cf., in general, *GV* 406–7 and *LMGD* 50.

[116] A. *Sept.* 698–701 (seven dochmiacs, all but the sixth demarcated after the first syllable and ending in a hypercatalectic ¯; cf. Parker 11) is an isolated exception, not even paralleled in the responding 705–7.

intervals, producing now monometers and dimeters, now longer lengths—not the regular succession of dimeters subdivided into monometers that is characteristic of anapests. Moreover, other rhythms may stand in verbal synapheia (see Introductory Note) with dochmiac, as they cannot with anapests. And there even exist, atypically, contexts in which the dochmiac seems to be felt as containing a sequence of quantities identical or similar to one which appears in an adjoining piece of epiploke and is susceptible to different types of articulation.

The clearest examples involve dochmiacs of the form ⏓⏑̆–⏓–, which on occasion allow the same choriambic modulation into dactylo-anapestic or iono-choriambic that is permitted with the externally identical aeolic –⏑⏑–⏑–:

| | dochmiac |
|---|---|
| κἀκ χαλεπᾶς δύας ὕπερθ' ὀμμάτων | ⏓– –⏓–\| ⏓– –⏓– \| –⏑⏑–⏑⏑–⏓– |
| κριμναμενᾶν νεφελᾶν ὀρθοῖ | dactylo-anapestic |
| | do |
| | —A. Sept. 228–29 = 221–22[117] |
| λυκοδίωκτον ὡς δάμαλιν ἄμ' πέτραις | do\|do |
| | do\| do |
| | – ⏑⏑–⏓– ⏑– – ⏑⏑– ⏑–¯ |
| ἠλιβάτοις ἵν' ἀλκᾷ πίσυνος μέμυκε φράζουσα βοτῆρι μόχθους | |
| | —A. Supp. 351–53 = 362–64[118] |

Neither modulation is frequent, but the – ⏑⏑–⏑–¯ often used by Aeschylus to close a dochmiac series was probably felt both as a "hyperca-

---

[117] Cf., A. Suppl. 659–62 = 670–73 (below, n. 216). E. Or. 1391–93 (dochmiacs concluded by – ⏑⏑– ⏑⏑– – ⏑⏑– ⏑⏑\|– ⏑⏑ do), Timotheus 15/791.66–69 (– ⏑⏑ do\|⏑̆⏑̆⏑– do\|⏑̆⏑̆⏑– do\|⏑̆⏑̆⏓– if the passage is dochmiac), and S. Aj. 881–87 = 927–31 (– ⏑⏑ do\| – ⏑–\|–⏑⏑ do\|⏓ E\|do in the reading of the strophe. (The antistrophe's text is – ⏑⏑ do\| – ⏑–\|D \|⏓ E \|do, a more unusual sequence to which the nearest parallels are do do\|D ⏓\|D ⏑–¯ at A. Sept. 483–85 = 523–25 and [⏑––\|⏑––]⏑––\|⏑̆⏑̆–⏑⏑–[⏑⏑– ⏑⏑–]⏓– ⏑– at E. Ion 1446–48 and 1465–66).

[118] Concluding a movement that may be introduced by the same iono-choriambic rhythm: ⏑– –⏑⏑–\|do\|... (cf. the ⏑– –⏑⏑– + ⏑– –⏑⏑–\|–⏑⏑–⏓– of Sept. 891–94 = 904–6 [text, 104]). Here, as in Ar. Av. 430 (a quadruple ⏑– –⏑⏑–\|⏑̆–\|) there is no need to assume an anomalous dochmiac with resolved anceps (⏓––⏓̆–). For similar transitions, cf., later in the same play, 630–31 = 644–45 (identical, except for syncopation: do\| – ⏑⏑–⏓– .– –⏑⏑–⏑– –¯); – ⏑⏑–⏓– ⏑–⏑̣–⏑̣– following do at S. Aj. 889–90 = 935–36, E. HF 1024 and, possibly, Rhes. 457 = 824 and 466 = 832; do¯⏑–⏓– ⏑– – ⏑⏑–⏓\|⏑̆⏑̆⏑– –⏓– following do do\|do do\| at E. Ph. 177–78; and, in general, LMGD 106–7.

talectic" do‾ and the common iono-choriambic close – ∪ ∪ – ∪ – ‾.[119]

In such passages the dochmiac contains the same sequence of quantities as one and a half metra of iono-choriambic; and the standard pairing of dochmiac dimeters with iambic trimeters or, less frequently, of single dochmiacs with the sequence ×– ∪ – ∪ – (*LMGD* 115–16, Conomis 28–31) suggests that the rhythm was capable of functioning in certain contexts as a kind of "sesquiamb," two of which would add up to the same succession of (relatively) long and short syllables as three syncopated iambs:

dochmiac (sesquiambic) dimeter:   ×– –×–×̆– –×̆–
iambic trimeter:   ×–.–×– ∪ –.– ∪ –

The relationship is obviously one of approximation rather than identity, but even approximation requires that the concluding ×– of the dochmiac be capable of suggesting the ×– of iambo-trochaic, just as its opening ×̆– would have to suggest iambo-trochaic ∪ –. Both suggestions are probably present, not only when trimeters are paired with dochmiac dimeters, but also when ×– ∪ –×– concludes longer iambo-trochaic sequences in dochmiac contexts (Table VII, A), or a separate colon with a tendency to appear, exactly as the dochmiac does: in pairs, alongside – ∪ ∪ – – – and – – – – – (whether felt as dochmiac ×̄⁽∪̆⁾–×̄– or iono-choriambic – ⌣⌣⁾–×̄–), in conjunction with dipodic anapests, and with the addition of a single hypercatalectic quantity or one or more cycles of bacchio-cretic (see below, 112–14). These cola (see Table VII, B and Appendix V) are sometimes called *dochmiaci Kaibeliani*, after the scholar who first analyzed their character in his commentary to S. *El.* 504–13.

In other passages it is the ×– of prosodiac and dochmiac rather than that of iambo-trochaic or iono-choriambic and dochmiac that forms a transitional segment, either by itself:

---

[119] Were the sequence simply a hypercatalectic dochmiac it would be hard to explain the rarity of clausular ×– –×–‾ (only at E. *HF* 879) and ×̄ᵛ–×̄–‾ (only at S. *OC* 1456 = 1471 and *Ph.* 828 = 844), or the two clausular instances (A. *Ag.* 1411 = 1430, 1449 = 1469) of a sequence (×× – ∪ ∪̆ –‾ or –×– ∪ ∪ –×) on which – ∪ ∪ – ∪ –‾ is a variant in aeolic contexts (text, 83–84).

# TABLE VII: "DOCHMELEGI," "SESQUIAMBI" AND RELATED FORMS

| A: Terminal ×–◡–×– in iambo-trochaic in dochmiac contexts | B: Dochmiaci Kaibeliani | C: prosodiac ‾◡◡◡◡–×–\|×–‾×– dochmiac | D: dochmiac ×–◡‾×–‾◡◡‾ prosodiac | E: Prosodiac with ×–\| demarcation in dochmiac contexts |
|---|---|---|---|---|
| s. *OT* 1331–32 = 1351–52 | *El.* 504–13 | | *OC*1561–64 = 1572–75 ‾‾–\|do\| ◡◡–◡◡–\|do\| –◡–\|×D×–³ | *Andr.* 830–31 = 826–27: ×D×\|D×– |
| *Ph.* 857–62: do\|do‖ –◡◡–◡◡–‾◡‾\| –◡◡–◡◡–◡◡\|+ ×–◡‾.◡–×– | *Ph.* 827 = 843ff. (see Appendix V) | | | *HF* 1028–33: ×D×\|D×– + ×D×\|D×– |
| E. | | *Andr.* 863–65 (?).¹ ◡‾◡◡◡◡◡–◡◡◡◡D×–\|do 841–44: ×D×–‖do do do HF1055–56 and 1069–70:² ×–◡◡◡◡D×–‖do | *HF*1016–18.⁴ do do\| ◡◡–◡◡◡◡◡◡◡–×\|D×– 1205–6: do\|do\|◡◡◡◡D×– | 1185–88: ×–◡–×\|D×– + ×–◡–×\|D×– + ×–◡–×\|D×D×–◡– |
| | | *Tr.* 272–76: ×–◡‾.\|D×D×–◡\|‾◡–◡– + ×–◡–×–×‾◡‾‾+ ×–◡‾.\|D ×–\|do\|do 250–51: ×D ×–\|do | *HF*1078–80: do\|do\|do\|do\| ◡◡–◡◡◡–×‾–◡–× | *Tr.* 256–58: D×D×D×– 266–67: ×D×D×– 269–70: ×‾‾◡–.‖ D×– |
| *Ion*782–83 | 148–50, 894–96 (see *LMGD*59–60) | | *Ion*1474–75: do\|do\|◡◡◡◡– 715–18: do do\|◡◡◡◡D×– + ×–◡–×\|D×– | 1441–42: ×–◡–×\|D\|◡◡–◡◡D×– 1508–9: ◡◡–◡◡◡◡◡◡\|D×\|–◡–×– |

¹ Reading ἐπέρασ[εν] ἀκτάς.

² With Hermann's ἐξ<αν>εγειρόμενος in 1069.

³ Following the text of the antistrophe and scanning φύλακα ‾◡◡‾ παρ᾽ Ἀΐδᾳ in 1572.

⁴ If ἄριστος is correctly emended to ἄπιστος in 1017.

*El.* 1147–49 = 1155–57
do|do|do|⏑⏑–×–|
⏑⏑–×⏑⏑–×–

*Ph.* 1293–95 = 1303–6
×–⏑–×–⏑–|
×–⏑–×–⏑|
⏑×⏑⏑×⏑⏑–×–

*IT* 886–90
⏑⏑–⏑⏑D×|
D×D×|–⏑–×–|
  829–30        do do
×–⏑–×|—D—⏑⏑˘×˘|do(?)

*Ph.* 185–86:
×–⏑–|D×–|do
135–37:
–⏑⏑–⏑⏑–⏑⏑–⏑⏑–⏑⏑
|D×–|do
163:
⏑⏑–⏑⏑–⏑⏑–⏑⏑–
–⏑⏑|D×–|do do

*Hyps.* 64.76–81:
⏑⏑–⏑⏑–⏑⏑–×–|do…×–⏑–do|
⏑⏑–⏑⏑–⏑⏑–×–|do

*Ar.*
*Ran.* 1351:
⏑⏑–⏑⏑–⏑⏑–⏑⏑D×–
|do|˘⏑–

*El.* 585–91:
do|do|⏑⏑–⏑⏑–×–⏑–|
do|do|⏑⏑–⏑⏑–×–⏑–|
do|⏑⏑–⏑⏑–⏑⏑–⏑⏑–
|do
929–30

*Hel.* 639–40
do|do|⏑⏑D×–

*Ph.* 182–84:
do|do|do|do|
⏑⏑–D×–
103–5:
do|do|do|
⏑⏑–⏑⏑–×–

*Phaeth.* 275–76
do|⏑⏑–⏑⏑–×–⏑–|do

*Hel.* 686–87:
×–⏑–×|D|⏑⏑–⏑⏑D×–

*Ph.* 190–92:
–⏑⏑–⏑⏑–––⏑⏑
–⏑⏑–⏑⏑–⏑⏑–⏑⏑
D×–

*Or.* 1256–57 = 1276–77
do do|×D×D×–
×–⏑–×–|⏑⏑–⏑⏑–×–
×–⏑–|⏑⏑–⏑⏑–×–⏑–×–

*Phaeth.* 270–74:
×–⏑–×D×–
×–⏑–.D×–⏑–×–

do|

ὄρεγε νῦν ὄρεγε            do| do

     γεραιὰν νέα          x̄ˇˇ-x-| ∪ ∪ - ∪ ∪ -x-

     χεῖρ' ἀπὸ κλιμάκων        prosodiac

     ποδὸς ἴχνος ἐπαντέλλων

                         —E. *Ph.* 103–5

or as part of − ∪ ∪ −x−:

ἐγὼ δὲ τῷ πρόσπολος ἁ τριτοβάμονος    x− ∪ −. D   x−⌐∪∪−∪∪−x−|x−−x−

     χερὶ δενομένα βάκτρου                do        do

     γεραιῷ κάρᾳ;

                         —E. *Tr.* 274–76

The   x−−x−|   ∪∪−∪∪−   of the former passage is a kind of "dochmelegus," identical to an iambelegus whose first six quantities (x− ∪−x−) have been replaced by a dochmiac, and related to that standard prosodiac sequence in much the same way as dochmiac "dimeter" is to iambic trimeter. (Cf., from the same passage in the *Phoenissae* just quoted, 119–21:

         τίς οὗτος ὁ λευκολόφας           xD.

πρόπαρ ὃς ἀγεῖται στρατοῦ          E |x− ∪ −x D x−

         πάγχαλκον ἀσπίδ'

         ἀμφὶ βραχίονι κουφίζων;

Here the terminal − ∪ ∪ − ∪ ∪ −x− from the earlier passage is echoed, but in a context that combines prosodiac with the more usual iambo-trochaic rather than dochmiac). When a "dochmelegus" is prolonged into the colon close ∪ ∪ − ∪ ∪ −x−| there may be a further suggestion of dochmiac, which in fact follows as part of the same movement at E. *Hyps.* 64.76–77 and 80–81 (respectively,

         do     do         do

         x−−x−| ∪ ∪ − ∪ ∪ − ∪ ∪ −x−| do

               ⌐D

and the same with initial do replaced by x− ∪ − [Wilamowitz's τέκνον is read in 77]).

In such passages (Table VII, CDE) the poet (almost always Euripides) makes use of a demarcation which appears occasionally in prosodiac, even when no hint of dochmiac is present:

μεταμώνια θηρεύων ἀκράντοις ἐλπίσιν

⏑ x⏟‒ ⏑ ⏑‒x‒ ⏑‒x‒ ⏑‒
      D

—Pind. *P*3e9

σὺ δ' ὦ Διός,          ⏑‒x‒| ⏑⏑‒⏑⏑‒x D x‒|⏑⏑‒⏑⏑‒x‒⏑‒
διπύρους ἀνέχουσα λαμπάδας ὀξυτάτας χεροῖν
Ἑκάτα παράφηνον ἐς Γλύκης

—A. *Ran.* 1361–66[120]

Dochmiac itself contained no alternative possibility of demarcation; otherwise one might have found, alongside x‒‒x‒| ⏑⏑‒⏑⏑‒ and ‒⏑⏑‒⏑⏑‒x‒| x‒‒x‒, in which prosodiac takes on a grouping of syllables into cola reminiscent of dochmiac, a transitional x‒ᵈᵒ|x‒⏑⏑‒⏑⏑‒, ‒ᴰ‒⏑⏑‒x|‒x‒‒x‒ or the like, in which the reverse occurred. It is, naturally, epiploke which adapts itself to the demarcational canons of the metric form which it is combined, not vice versa.

This summary of rhythmical usage may have exaggerated to some extent the non-metric character of transitional passages in dochmiac contexts. x‒⏑‒x‒ and ⏑⏑‒⏑⏑‒, in particular, could have been felt on occasion as variants on the dochmiac itself rather than segments of different rhythms in partial epiploke with it. Yet the analysis is probably right in a sufficiently large number of instances to provide further testimony to the importance of epiploke, even in a rhythmical environment largely shaped by other principles.[121] And it can be supported by an additional group of passages in which dochmiac stands in even closer relationship to another one of the epiplokai presented and discussed in Chapter One.

[120] Cf. E. *Hec.* 649–50 (x‒⏑‒x‒|⏑⏑‒⏑⏑‒x‒ + x‒⏑‒x|D x‒), *Rhes.* 459–63 = 825–29 (ᴰ x‒⏑‒ + ‒⏑‒x‒⏑‒xD x‒ + x‒|⏑⏑‒⏑⏑‒x‒⏑‒x), Ar. *Av.* 1337–38 (|⏑‒xD x‒⏑‒xD if the line, quoted from Sophocles, is the beginning of a colon), E. *Med.* 206 (⏑‒xD x, continuous with a preceding ⏑⏑‒⏑⏑‒x‒⏑‒x‒|⏑˘˘x˘˘⏑˘˘x‒ if one reads and scans ἰαχὰν ἄιον in the first line of the stanza), and the passages from the *Hippolytus* and the *IT* discussed in the text (78 and 207).

[121] The principles are least in evidence when transitions from dochmiac into prosodiac are involved. There the "dochmelegic" modulation through epiploke is more common than a strictly "metric" do | x D... (only at E. *Or.* 1255–57 = 1275–77 [do do|x D x Dx‒] and, perhaps, 180–83 [do|do|x‒⏑⏑‒⏑⏑‒⏑⏑ ‒⏑⏟‒‒ x D]. Other possible instances are in passages where the dochmiac itself is ambiguous with prosodiac [S. *Aj.* 903 = 946 ‒⏑⏟ᵈᵒ‒‒ |x D] or bacchio-cretic [E. *Tr.* 587–89 = 591–93: ⏑‒‒|⏑‒‒| ⏑‒‒|⏑‒xD; cf., for the ambiguity, text 112–14]).

The dochmiac, in the form ⏑ − − ⏑ − which accounts for well over two-thirds of its attested occurrences (cf. Conomis 23), is externally identical with a bacchio-cretic ⏑ − − ⏑ −. The two rhythms often appear in the same context and share, up to a point, the same pattern of resolution. There is no prohibition in either against the sequence ⏑⏓− (contrast iambo-trochaic, where this would involve resolution preceding syncopation), even though the longer runs of short syllables characteristic of dochmiac are excluded from pre-Hellenistic bacchio-cretic. It is possible therefore that where metrist or colometrist analysis hesitates between positing dochmiac preceded by one or more bacchiacs and dochmiac followed by one or more cretics, the alternative analyses are simply different ways of articulating a single piece of epiploke:

| ba | | ba | | do | |
|----|----|----|----|----|----|

⏑ − − ⏑ − − ⏑ − − ⏑ −

| | do | | cr | | cr |
|----|----|----|----|----|----|

| ba | | do | | cr |
|----|----|----|----|----|

Thus A. *Sept.* 168 = 176 would be heard both as a headless version of the mixed bacchio-cretic which precedes, and as a dochmio-cretic introduction to the pure dochmiac that follows:

ἰὼ παναλκεῖς θεοί,                    × − ⏑ − − ⏑ − [122]

ἰὼ τέλειοι τέλειαι τε γᾶς           × − ⏑ − − ⏑ − − ⏑ − | − ⏑ − ⏓ ⏑ −

τᾶσδε πυργοφύλακες

πόλιν δορίπονον μὴ προδῶθ'

ἑτεροφώνῳ στρατῷ                    ⏑ − ⏓ ⏑ − − ⏑ − | ⏓ ⏑ − − ⏑ −   168 = 176
                                       ‾do‾

κλύετε παρθένων, κλύετε πανδίκως χειροτόνους λιτάς   ⏑ ⏓ − ⏑ − | do | do [123]
                                                          ‾do‾

At times the transitional segment conforms exactly to the patterns of both rhythms, at times to that of only one of them. Thus at E. *Ph.* 320–31:

ἦ ποθεινὸς φίλοις          − ⏑ − − ⏑ −

---

[122] Cf. E. *HF* 735 = 753 (× − | ⏑ − − ⏑ − between dochmiacs).

[123] Similar ambiguities can arise between dochmio-iambic and mixed bacchio-cretic:

(iambo-bacchiac + mixed bacchiac)

A. *PV* 694–95: × − ⏑ − − ⏑ − − ‖ ⏑ − − ⏑ − × − ⏑ − ‾

(iambo-bacchiac + do + iambo-trochaic)

(mixed bacchiac + ba + dochmiac)

E. *Ph.* 298–300: ⏑ − − ⏑ − × − ⏑ − − | ⏑ − − ⏑ − ⏓ ⏑ ⏓ × − | ⏑ − − ⏑ − − ⏑ −

(do + iambo-trochaic + 3 do + cretic)

ἢ ποθεινὸς Θήβαις     $- \cup -- \times -$     + 9 dochmiacs
                      ――do――

the final $- \times -$ is likely to suggest a continuation of the preceding cretic movement, even though $- \times -$ is not a form allowed in pure bacchio-cretic contexts. Such a form does appear sporadically when bacchio-cretic is linked to dochmiac,[124] presumably because of the cretic character imparted to the final three quantities of the dochmiac $\times -- \times -$ in passages such as this. It is found, for example, in the mixed bacchio-cretic of Ar. *Ran.* 1352–55:

ἐμοὶ δ᾽ ἄχε᾽ ἄχεα κατέλιπε<ν>     $\cup - \overset{\smile\smile}{\phantom{x}} \cup \overset{\smile\smile}{\phantom{x}} \overset{\smile\smile}{\phantom{x}}\underset{do}{} \cup -$
δάκρυα δάκρυα δ᾽ ἀπ᾽ ὀμμάτων     $\times \overset{\smile\smile}{\phantom{x}} \cup \overset{\smile\smile}{\phantom{x}} \times - \cup -$
ἔβαλον ἔβαλον ἀ τλάμων     $\times \overset{\smile\smile}{\phantom{x}} \cup \overset{\smile\smile}{\phantom{x}} - \times -$
                      ――do――

where the final $- \times -$ completes a more characteristically dochmiac version of the bacchio-cretic $\cup \overset{\smile\smile}{\phantom{x}} \overset{\smile\smile}{\phantom{x}} \cup -$ found in the first line.[125]

The most extensive piece of evidence in favor of this analysis comes from the *Agamemnon*, where $( \cup -- ) \cup -- \cup -- \cup -$ serves both as an introduction ([ba]|ba|do) and conclusion (do|cr|[cr]) to some of the pure dochmiac sequences in the great amoibaion of 1072 = 1076ff. Cassandra begins the passage with what is probably a series of bacchiacs, prosodically demarcated:

ὀτοτοτοῖ, πόποι δᾶ     $\cup \overset{\smile\smile}{\phantom{x}} - \| \cup -- \|$
Ἄπολλον, Ἄπολλον     $\cup -- \| \cup -- \|$ [126]

the rhythm being extended, in her next set of lines, to a cretic close:

Ἄπολλον, Ἄπολλον     $\cup -- \| \cup -- \|$
ἀγυιᾶτ᾽, ἀπόλλων ἐμός     $\cup -- | \cup -- \cup -$     1080–81 = 1085–86

which prepares the way for the unambiguous dochmiac that appears for

---

[124] Cf. the instances of $---$ in responsion with $- \cup -$ cited at *LMGD* 102 and 118, to which one should perhaps add E. *Or.* 170–73 = 191–94 ($- \cup - \times - \cup -$ do $- \times -$|do). $\overline{- \cup -}$ also seems to acquire, when in dochmiac contexts, some of the latter's tolerance for sequences of five shorts: cf. the examples cited in *LMGD* 109–10, to which should be added E. *HF* 888 (below, n. 127).

[125] With the last two lines compare E. *Or.* 1305–10: $\times \overset{\smile\smile}{\phantom{x}} \cup \overset{\smile\smile}{\phantom{x}} \times \overset{\smile\smile}{\phantom{x}} \cup -- \times -$ |do|$\times \overset{\smile\smile}{\phantom{x}} \cup \overset{\smile\smile}{\phantom{x}} \times \overset{\smile\smile}{\phantom{x}} \cup -$ .|$\overset{\smile\smile}{\phantom{x}} \cup \overset{\smile\smile}{\phantom{x}} \times \overset{\smile\smile}{\phantom{x}} \cup \overset{\smile\smile}{\phantom{x}}$ (reading δάκρυσιν ἔπεσε) |$\times - \cup - \times \overset{\smile\smile}{\phantom{x}} \cup - \times - \cup -- \times -$, and *Ph.* 178 (above, n. 118).

[126] The parallel with the subsequent 1080–81 = 1085–86 is against the readings ὀτοτοτοῖ and ὤπολλον; cf. on the latter, Fraenkel *ad loc.*

the first time—and in a form ($\bar{\times}^{\smile\smile}-\smile-$) not compatible with bacchio-cretic—at the beginning of the following stanza.

$\smile--\smile-.\ldots-\smile-$ is next heard (1102–3 = 1110–11) at the end of Cassandra's portion of the same stanza, concluding with a return to the $\smile^{\smile\smile}-\smile-$ (1100 = 1107) with which she began:

ἰὼ πόποι, τί ποτε μήδεται        ×– ⌣ – | ×˘˘ – ⌣ –
. . . . .
1100 = 1107

ἄφερτον φίλοισιν,
δυσίατον· ἀλκα δ' ἑκας ἀποστατεῖ        ⌣ – – | ⌣ – – | ⌣ – – ⌣ – –   ⌣˘˘ – ⌣ –
do
1102–3 = 1110–11

The earlier instance of resolved $\smile^{\smile\smile}-\smile-$ was a clear dochmiac and its recurrence was probably heard in the same way.[127] Resolution helps give a different demarcation to $\smile--\smile-.\ldots-\smile-$ when it appears in the next stanza (1118 = 1129) leading away from a preceding dochmiac of the form $\overset{\smile}{\times}^{\smile\smile}-\smile-$ into a cretic close:

φόνου· στάσις δ' ἀκόρετος γένει        ×– ⌣ – | $\overset{\displaystyle\times^{\smile\smile}-\times-}{\text{do}}$
κατολολυξάτω θύματος λευσίμου        ⌣˘˘ – ⌣ – – ⌣ – | – ⌣ –

The same rhythm appears at 1143 = 1153:

ἀκόρετος βοᾶς, φεῦ, ταλαίνας φρεσίν        ⌣˘˘ – ⌣ – | – ⌣ – – ⌣ –

which echoes, in abbreviated form, the immediately preceding:

φρενομανής τις εἶ θεοφόρητος, ἀμφὶ δ' αὐτᾶς θροεῖς
νόμον ἄνομον. οἷά τις ξουθά        do | do $\overline{\smile-\overset{do}{-}\smile-}$ | ˘˘ ⌣˘˘ | – ⌣ – – $^-$

(Final – $^-$ is probably the catalectic shortening of cretic – ⌣ –, with the necessary replacement of ⌣ by long or anceps, that appears in the earliest cretics attested [Alcman 58] and sporadically thereafter).

---

[127] For further instances, from dochmiac contexts, of the sequence $\smile--\smile-.\ldots-\smile-$ with initial bacchius or bacchii isolated by demarcation, cf. A. *Eum.* 788–90, *Sept.* 104–5, E. *HF* 888 (⌣ – – | ⌣ –˘˘ | ⌣˘˘ – ⌣ – ‖), *Or.* 316–18 = 332–34 (if the antistrophe's text is correct) and 1437–42 (if 1441–42 are scanned, with transposition of παλαιᾶς and ἕδραν, ⌣˘˘ ˘˘ ⌣ – | ⌣ – – ⌣ – – ⌣ –), *Bac.* 1177–78 = 1193–94, 1181–82 = 1196–97 (if Murray's colometry is accepted) and 1019 (identical with the first eleven quantities of 1014–16 and with 1021 [⌣ – – ⌣ – – | ⌣˘˘ – ⌣ – if one scans γελῶντι προσώπῳ περίβαλε βρόχον]); and *Rhes.* 695–96 = 713–14.

Whenever, as at 1123–24 = 1134–35, the sequence – ◡ – do occurs:

ξυνανύτει βίου δύντος αὐγαῖς·         ◡⏝⏑̄◡ – – ◡ – – | ◡ – ◡ – – ◡ –[128]
        ταχεῖα δ' ἄτα πέλει

the rhythm could be regarded as having passed, via an ambiguous ◡ – – ◡ –, from a three-quantity cyclical movement into a five-quantity one:

triadic

◡ ⏝ – ◡ – – ◡ – – | ◡ – ◡ – – ◡ –

pentadic

Traces of such pentadic movement may appear amid the pure or mixed bacchio-cretic of archaic lyric:

Κρόνου παῖδ' ἐς ἀφνεαν ἱκομένους     ◡ – – ◡ – ◡ – ⏝ ◡ –
μάκαιραν Ἱέρωνος ἐστίαν            × – ◡⏝ – ◡ – ◡ –

—Pind. O1s10–11

γεγωνητέον ὅπι δίκαιον ξένων ἔρεισμ' Ἀκράγαντος     ◡ – – ◡⏝ – ◡ – – ◡ – ◡ – – ◡ –‾

—Pind. O2s6

linked occasionally with a hexadic sequence (× – ◡ – ◡ – × that stands in the same relationship to × – ◡ – × as – ◡ – ◡ – – to – ◡ – –:

δίνασεν ὄμμα, καρδίαν τε οἱ σχέτλιον ἄμυξεν ἄλγος     × – ◡ – ◡ – × – ◡ – – ◡⏝ – ◡ –‾

—Bacch. 17s18–19[129]

It is conceivable, therefore, that one of the ancestors of dramatic dochmiac was such a rhythm, a theory of origins which would help account for the existence of another version of this pentadic cycle, the "hypodochmiac" (– ◡ – ◡ –) as what seems an occasional variant on the dochmiac itself (*LMGD* 114–15, Conomis 31–34). If, for example, O1s10 were to become, with metric reinterpretation, a pair of dochmiacs, it would be natural to take the following × – ◡⏝ – ◡ – ◡ – as an iambic metron

---

[128] Cf. E. *Ph.* 186–88: do do do – | ◡ – – | ◡ – – – ◡ – | do and *Bac.* 1014–16 (◡ – – ◡ – – | ◡ – – | ◡⏝ ⏝ ◡⏝ do | do).

[129] The analyses of this and the preceding two passages are essentially those in Dale (65 and 77–78, where, however, × – ◡ – and × – ◡ – ◡ – are regarded, not as epiploke segments, but as the units – ◡ – and – ◡ – ◡ – preceded by "link" anceps). See, further, text, 152–55 and Appendix II.

followed by a five-quantity dochmiac equivalent. The process of reinterpretation may still be going on in the earliest (or one of the two earliest) passages in which consecutive dochmiacs are attested (Aeschylus fr.
278 = 343 Mette), probably from the satyr play produced (in 472 B.C.)
along with the *Persae*.[130] There a concluding ∪−−∪−|−∪∪−∪− is
almost certainly a pair of dochmiacs, but what precedes is better described
as mixed bacchio-cretic.[131] The "dochmiac" demarcation |∪−−∪−|
occurs, as well as several pentadic cycles, but neither with sufficient regularity to establish the cycle in the form ∪−−∪− as a basic unit of movement.

   The provenance of this proto-dochmiac suggests that in the 470's the
rhythm still lacked, not only the metric character, but even the tragic
associations it would acquire later in the century. It is only in the *Septem*
(467) that both are clearly in evidence; and from then on the development seems to have been irreversible.[132] Why "metricization" of the
rhythm should have taken the form it did, with substitution of anceps for
short, is impossible to say—perhaps through assimilation of the beginning
and end of the dochmiac to those of its "sesquiambic" analogue (×−∪−
×−). But that metricization should occur in one fashion or another
should cause no surprise. For fifth-century dochmiac, in which ×−∪−
∪−, −∪∪−×− and −∪−∪− come eventually to appear, not as parts of
a simple or compound epiploke along with ∪−−∪−, but as equivalent
versions of a single polymorphous metrical unit, stands in somewhat the
same relationship to the mixed bacchio-cretic interspersed with pentadic
cycles of *Olympian* 2 and Bacchylides 17 as does Hellenistic ionic (above,
32–40) to that of the fifth century. And Hellenistic bacchio-cretic is similarly related to its fifth-century prototype. In the latter, cretic, bacchiac
and "palimbacchiac" are segments of a single epiploke:

---

[130] Of the possible instances of dochmiacs in the *Persae* itself (cf. Webster 115 and 118)
only two (976 and 1076) show a form (x̄ ⌣ ⌣ ∪ −) incompatible with bacchio-cretic, and neither of these is adjacent to another dochmiac.

[131] ∪−−∪−∪−−∪−×−∪−∪−|∪−−∪−|∪−−∪−|×−∪−∪−−∪−−|∪−×−∪−∪
−−∪− if editors are right in assuming strophic responsion between 1–5 and 10–14 in the
papyrus fragments; cf., however, Lloyd-Jones *ad loc.*

[132] *Sept* 565–66 = 628–29 may show pentadic rhythm without regular dochmiac demarca-
tion: ⌣∪⌣−∪−∪−−‖∪⌣—∪− |−∪−∪−; but textual difficulties and the unusual prosodic
demarcation make the passage problematic.

$$- \cup - - - \cup -$$

cretic
bacchiac
palimbacchiac

In Hellenistic times they become equivalent versions of a single unit capable of exhibiting any "pentaseme" combination of syllables—i.e., any combination whose total time value is equivalent to that of five shorts:

$$\underline{12} \ \underset{\cup}{3} \ \underline{45}$$
$$\underline{1} \ \underline{23} \ \underline{45}$$
$$\underset{\cup}{12} \ \underline{34} \ 5^{133}$$
$$- - \cup$$

The parallel relationships suggest that a similar process of metricization was carried through in different areas at different times. The dochmiac is the product of a fairly early stage in a process which was eventually to become all pervasive. Not, probably, the first stage, but rather one which, as the largely Euripidean instances of partial epiploke with iambo-trochaic and prosodiac indicate, was still not complete in the late fifth century. Once again (cf. above, 105) the parallel, and contrast, with the anapest is instructive. For there metricization was completed much earlier—as soon as it was decided (c. 600 B.C. [?], by Lycurgus or Tyrtaeus or whoever) that Spartan hoplites on the march should always lead off with the same foot and that this foot should always be raised and set down to the double short of dactylo-anapestic. Poets responded by detaching the Πηληϊάδεω Ἀχιλῆος colon from its original hexameter context and using it—transformed into a repeatable

$$\overline{\cup\cup} \ - \ \cup\cup \ - \ \cup\cup \ - \ \overline{\cup\cup} \ \overset{..}{-}$$

left-right-left-right-left-right-left(right)—

as the nucleus for a new rhythm from which the epic freedom to articulate dactylo-anapestic movement in different ways had been strictly eliminated:

---

[133] Of the possible combinations, only $\cup--$ fails to appear in Mesomedes 2 (cf. Maas 33.5). The existence of bacchius, palimbacchius and cretic as versions of a single metric unit probably explains the ancient contention that the forms are not linked by epiploke. Cf. Heph 110.18–19 and 150.27–151.7, which contrast the homogeneous (*homoeides*) forms generated from cretic by transfer of a long from initial to final position with the *antipathounta metra* generated in similar fashion from iambs and dactyls.

οὐ γὰρ πάτριον τᾷ Σπάρτᾳ          an|an⌢

—PMG 856.6

The wider implications of this suggestion for *Versgeschichte* will be considered at greater length in Part Two.

# CHAPTER SIX: PRELIMINARY CONCLUSIONS

The evidence offered in the last four chapters has complicated to some degree the system of types and sub-types set forth in Chapter One, but has not, I think, affected its underlying order and consistency. The list of mixed forms presented there has been expanded to include combinations of iono-choriambic or dactylo-anapestic with aeolic and prosodiac, as well as various linkings between dochmiac and other rhythms; and the "iambic" modulation considered originally has turned out, on more thorough examination, to be one among a number of possible ways of joining two rhythms. The other, more specialized types, are "trochaic" modulation between iono-choriambic and iambo-trochaic or prosodiac (54–58), "choriambic" modulation between dactylo-anapestic or iono-choriambic and aeolic (67–69, 91–94), and the "sesquiambic" (106–110) and "paeonic" (112–14) modulations involving dochmiac.

The standard positions for demarcation (immediately following a nucleus, or one quantity thereafter) are not affected by such modulations. Other demarcations are possible, but only one has more than sporadic importance: that which occurs two quantities after the nucleus in most pure or mixed forms where the cycle of recurrence is four quantities or more. Hence iambo-trochaic $\times - | \cup -$, prosodiac $\times - |$ and aeolic $| - \cup \cup - \cup -$.

Initial demarcation shows the same variety and placement as internal; terminal demarcation may also occur following a clausular modification which either shortens a nucleus by one quantity (hence aeolic $- \cup \cup - \cup -$ $\times \times - \cup \cup -^-$ iambo-trochaic $- \cup - \cup -^-$ and paeonic $- \cup - -^-$ [above, 114]) or introduces iambo-trochaic $\cup -^-$ immediately after the nucleus of another rhythm. The former procedure tends to be avoided when the result would be terminal demarcation at a point where, in a non-terminal sequence, the first or second member of a double short would appear. Aeolic $- \times - \cup \cup - \times \times - \times - \cup^-$ is accordingly rare, and $- \times - \cup \cup - \cup -^-$ or $- \times - \cup \cup - - \times - \cup \cup -^-$ (however analyzed: see above, 88) is the preferred alternative; iono-choriambic $- \cup \cup - - \cup^-$ is rejected in favor of $- \cup \cup - \cup -^-$; and there is no trace of a clausular prosodiac $- \cup \cup - \cup \cup - \times - \cup \cup - \cup^-$ (i.e., D × D^, with terminal shortening of the second nucleus) alongside D × D $\cup -^-$.

The sequence ∪ ∪ is subject to contraction, frequently in dactylo-anapestic, sporadically elsewhere; the quantity following a nucleus ending in ∪– to syncopation. Bacchio-cretic may be an exception to the latter rule,[134] but it allows, like iambo-trochaic, the syncopated nuclear sequence ∪̆ –:

ὃς φεύγων γάμον ἀφίκετ' ἐς ἐρημίαν     –.– – ∪ᵛᵛ– ∪ᵛᵛ– ∪ –

—Ar. *Lys.* 786–87 = 810–11

Iambo-trochaic is distinguished by the frequency with which it appears in partial epiploke with all genres except dactylo-anapestic. The association with iono-choriambic is close enough to make cycles of one rhythm interchangeable with cycles of the other in certain contexts (30–33); and some double cycles of mixed iono-choriambic are similarly interchangeable with single cycles of prosodiac (64–65) and octadic aeolic (91). The blurring of genre distinctions which allows for, or results from, this, as well as that which stems from the close structural similarity and frequent association of prosodiac and heptadic aeolic have already been discussed (above, 11, 71–75, 90–91).

The most striking irregularity presented by the system is the special position of dactylo-anapestic. Except when linked choriambically to aeolic or prosodiac, dactylo-anapestic in a heterogeneous context is always separated from the other ingredients by word end; and the position of word end is always fixed in such a way that only one demarcation of a sequence is possible:

solvitur acris hiems grata  vice veris et Favoni     – ∪ ∪ – ∪ ∪ – ⌢⌢ ∪ ∪  + E ˆ

Dactylo-anapestic and iambo-trochaic are here rhythmically disjunct or, to use the ancient term, asynartete.[135] Verbal demarcation coincides with the single point at which one rhythm breaks off and the other starts up. Epiploke is excluded here, just as it is excluded, even in rhythmically homogeneous passages, from movements so short that they consist of a single colon.

---

[134] Cf., however, the sequences – ∪ – ∪ – and ∪ – ∪ – –, often analyzed as syncopated cretic (– ∪ –. ∪ –) and bacchiac (∪ –. ∪ – –) dimeters when they appear in Plautus. Ar. *Ran.* 1359 (– ∪ – ∪ – in the midst of a cretic series) may be an isolated surviving example in Greek.

[135] For description and enumeration of examples, see Korzeniewski, 123–28 and L. E. Rossi, "Asynarteta from the Archaic to the Alexandrian Poets," *Arethusa* 9 (1976) 223–29.

On a larger scale, many of the internally continuous sequences examined in the preceding chapters are juxtaposed in the same asynartete manner with other structures when they constitute the major subdivisions of stanzas and poems. Sometimes these subdivisions are rhythmically identical: the repeated stanzas of a monostrophic ode, for example, or the repeated lines of a poem constructed *kata stichon*. At other times they are different: the principal movements or "periods" found within a strophe or an astrophic monody or kommos. The scope of this rhythmical mode—the length of the disjunct movements it contains as well as their internal analysis—is something which needs closer investigation if one is to come to a final evaluation, not simply of the number and diversity of the structures produced by epiploke, but their relative importance in the total lyric repertory.

It is in the nature of such asynartete compositions that they resist systematic treatment. The shorter ones tend, when any but the simplest of overall patterns are involved, to be felt as rhythmical because of the character and identity of their separate parts. They lend themselves perfectly to the process of isolating and identifying individual units separated by diaeresis that is one of the forms colometrist analysis can take (above, 26). The larger structures are often astrophic, created expressly for a single literary moment and deriving their unity more from content than rhythmical consistency and coherence.

The character and frequency of both types, however, varies less within a given period than it does over the whole range of Greek lyric. A historical treatment is in order here, and a fairly extensive one. For asynartete composition antedated in all probability the earliest efforts to create a coherent system of versification based on epiploke, competed with epiploke throughout its history, and was eventually to supplant it almost completely in verse composed for reading and recitation.

# PART TWO: EPIPLOKE IN THE
# HISTORY OF GREEK VERSE

# CHAPTER SEVEN: THE BEGINNINGS
## (ALCMAN, STESICHORUS, SAPPHO AND ALCAEUS)

Six of the seven forms of epiploke discussed in Part One are already clearly attested in the initial phases of the Lesbian, Western and Peloponnesian lyric traditions. Heptadic and octadic aeolic as well as, less abundantly, iono-choriambic and dactylo-anapesstic appear in Sappho and Alcaeus; dactylo-anapestic and prosodiac in Stesichorus; iambo-trochaic,[136] aeolic and dactylo-anapestic in Alcman. Of the traditions they represent, the Lesbian is by far the most abundantly documented in its earlier stages, hence provides the best starting point for estimating the extent to which, at given periods and in the work of given poets or groups of poets, composition in lyric metre involved composition in epiploke. The evidence, presented in Table VIII, is remarkably consistent and clear-cut. The identifiably aeolic sequences attested in Sappho, Alcaeus and their Latin imitator Horace all seem to come, with very few exceptions, from poems consisting either of a single piece of continuous epiploke, or two or more exact repetitions of such a sequence. The aeolic epiploke involved may be either heptadic or octadic, pure or mixed, and choriambically modulated into either dactylo-anapest or pure iono-choriambic—all, however, subject to certain restrictions. There are no sure instances of both heptadic and octadic within a single poem;[137] modulation into dactylo-anapestic or iono-choriambic must always be followed, within the same colon, by return to aeolic; and in the case of dactylo-anapestic this colon is never pre-terminal in a stanza. Demarcation is located in one or the other of two ways: (1) initially before a base and

---

[136] Cf. 16.1–3 (× E ×|E ×|E), the use of clausular ∪−⁻ in both trochaic (E ×|E ×|E ^ [60]) and iambic (×−∪−×−∪−∪−⁻ [59a1–2], and what may be demarcation before the final quantity of a nucleus in the second member of an asynartete ×−∪−× + −×−∪−⁻ (14). The Stesichorean −−−∪−⁻ may be identical (i.e., −x̄−∪−×: cf. West 49–50). It appears in the *Eriphyla* (*SLG* 176.8) and the Lille fragment (text in P. Parsons *ZPE* 26 [1977] 14–19), both times concluding, like −×−∪−× in Alcman, a largely dactylo-anapestic stanza. Alcman's line is preserved, along with what may be a related ∪−×−∪−× from Simonides (28/533) as an instance of iambic with "spondaic" substitution in the second half of a metron (Heliodorus *ap. GL* 3.428).

[137] C-14 (×−∪∪−⁻−∪∪⁻−∪−×|−∪−××−∪∪⁻−∪−) and the alternating ××−∪∪−...
           A           A
and ×−∪∪−... of B11/43, H4/143 and H40.179 (see D. L. Page, *Sappho and Alcaeus* [1955] 324) are possible instances, but in all four passages the sequence which precedes |×−∪∪−... is missing and so could have ended in a first base quantity, yielding the rhythm ×|×−∪∪−.... attested in the last two lines of A-9 (××−∪∪−∪−×|×−∪∪−−∪∪−∪−).

125

## TABLE VIII: LESBIAN AEOLIC

| A: Internally demarcated sequences repeated to form an entire poem. | B: Undemarcated sequences repeated to form a poem (sometimes grouped by ancient editors into two-line stanzas) | C: Sequences whose context is unknown |
|---|---|---|
| **I:** *Pure aeolic* | 1. Z34\|357: ××A××Ax×A×−∪− | 1. 133: ×−∪∪−∪−∪−∪− |
| | 2. 96: −∪−××A××Ax××A ∪− | 2. 112: A×A A×‖ |
| | | A×A×‖ |
| | 3. 43−52: ××−∪∪−∪∪A | 3. 154: ×A∪−− |
| | 4. P1\|296: ××−∪∪−∪∪−∪A^ | ×A∪−−2 |
| | | 4. (*ap.* Heph 32.18) |
| | | ××A× |
| | | 5. Z61\|384 |
| | | 6. *Inc. auc.* 17 and 21 ×−∪−×A× |
| | | 7. *Inc. auc.* 22 ×−∪−×A×−∪− |
| | | ×A×−∪−× |
| **II:** *Mixed aeolic* | | 8. 123: −∪−××A× |
| 1. −∪−×A×‖ | | 9. 102: ×−∪−××A∪−− |
| −∪−×A×‖ | | ×−∪−××A∪−−3 |
| −∪−×A×(\|)A^ | | |
| (sapphic stanza) | | 10. 110a: ××−∪∪A^ |
| 2. ×A\|×A×−∪− | | ××−∪∪A^ |
| (99 col i beginning) | | ××−∪∪A^ |
| 3. ?\|...×A\|×E | | 11. 115: ××−∪∪−∪∪A^ |
| (99 col i, end) | | ××−∪∪−∪∪A^ |
| 4. 98 | | |
| ××A\|××A + −∪−××A | | |
| ×A×\|×A ×−∪−× | | |
| 4a. (306Ab Voigt [Alcaeus]) 1 | | |
| **III:** *Modulations into dactylo-anapestic* | | |
| 5. 94 | | |
| ××A\|××A\|××−∪∪A | | |

---

1 See R. Führer, *ZPE* 54 (1984) 40.

2 129 probably begins with the last eight quantities of A ∪− (ἔμεθεν δ'ἔχησθα λάθαν) but the following ἤ τιν' ἄλλον ἀνθρώπων ἔμεθεν φίλησθα is obscure.

3 Cf. Bacch. 2: ×−∪−×̆×̄−\|∪−−∪− + −∪∪−∪∪−××−\|×̆−∪−−×\|E‖×̆×̄ −\|A∪−−××−\|×̆∪−−∪−∪−−∪− where consistent word end following the first quantity of an aeolic nucleus is against taking the initial line as ×E^ + ∪∪−×−∪− .

IV: *Modulations into iono-choriambic*
6. ××A‖××–⌣⌣–A
   Horace C.1.3

5. F3|117b top: ××–⌣⌣–A

7. A5|5,D9|67:
   ××–⌣⌣–A‖××–⌣⌣–A|
   ××–⌣⌣–A|×× A

6. 53–57: ××–⌣⌣––⌣⌣–A
7. 58–91: ×–⌣⌣––⌣⌣–A×

8. G2|130:
   ××–⌣⌣–A|××–⌣⌣–A‖
   ×× A ×|×–⌣⌣–A‖

9. ××–⌣⌣–A‖××–⌣⌣–A‖
   ×× A⁺+×× A
   Horace C.1.5

V: *Mixed aeolic with modulations into dactylo-anapestic*
10. ×–⌣–×A×‖×–⌣–×A‖×–⌣–×–⌣–×(ı̊)–⌣⌣A× (alcaic stanza)

VI: *Mixed aeolic with modulations into iono-choriambic*
11. D12|70: ×–⌣–××A|××–⌣⌣–A|
12. Horace C.1.7 A×‖–⌣–×–⌣⌣–A×

12. *Inc. auc.* 16: ×–⌣⌣–A×

13. 128: –⌣⌣––⌣⌣–A×[4]
14. 140: ××–⌣⌣––⌣⌣–A·[5]
15. *GL* 6.264.4: (?)
    ××–⌣ ⌣–⌣⌣–Å
    –⌣⌣––⌣⌣––⌣⌣–A×

16. 150: ×–⌣⌣–A×|–⌣–××A[6]

[4] Choriambic ...–⌣⌣–⌣⌣–⌣⌣– is less likely here, given the absence from Lesbian poetry of any unambiguous choriambic cola, and the parallel with C-2 and A-12.
[5] Cf., also, 113 (οὐ γὰρ <ἔστ> ἀτέρα νῦν πάϊς ὢ γάμβρε τεαύτα [*suppl.* Hoffmann]) –rhythmically equivalent (cf. DH 6 p.127.21–128.13) to a phrase in Demosthenes 23.1: μήτε μικρὸν ὀρῶιτά τι καὶ φλαῦρον ἁμάρτημα ἐ– (–⌣–⌣⌣– ⌣⌣––⌣⌣–⌣⌣).
[6] Emending to δόμοισιν rather than the usual δόμωι in the transmitted οὐ γὰρ θέμις ἐν μονσστόλωι οἰκίᾳ makes the lines a differently demarcated version of A-11 and removes an anomalous break in rhythmical continuity.

thereafter immediately following a nucleus (full or catalectically shortened); (2) one quantity further on in the epiploke. Ordinarily only one way is used in a given poem.[138] Anomalous demarcation is confined to C-1. This line forms, together with C-7 and the final twelve quantities of B-1, a triad of sequences analyzable as twelve-quantity segments of the same rhythm, beginning, respectively, one quantity before, immediately before and within a double base:

$$
\begin{array}{ll}
\text{C-1:} & \times\ +\ -\ \cup\ -\ \cup\ \cup\ -\ \cup\ -\ \cup\ -\ ^{-} \\
\text{B-1:} & \times\ \times\ -\ \cup\ \cup\ -\ \cup\ -\ \times\ -\ \cup\ - \\
\text{C-7:} & \times\ -\ \cup\ \cup\ -\ \cup\ -\ \times\ -\ \cup\ -\ \times
\end{array}
$$

Two other aeolic forms, the lesser asclepiad (B-5) and C-11, form a similar triad with a line attested in Alcman:

$$
\begin{array}{ll}
\text{Alcman 50:} & \times\ +\ -\ \cup\ -\ \cup\ \cup\ -\ -\ \cup\ \cup\ -\ ^{-} \\
\text{the asclepiad:} & \diagup\ \ \times\ \times\ -\ \cup\ \cup\ -\ -\ \cup\ \cup\ -\ \cup\ - \\
\text{C-11:} & \times\ -\ \cup\ \cup\ -\ -\ \cup\ \cup\ -\ \cup\ -\ \times
\end{array}
$$

The first quantity in C-1 and Alcman 50 is anceps and so cannot be taken in the most natural way as the final one in a preceding nucleus. It must be, rather, a prefixed or procephalic element of the sort which may appear occasionally in later lyric.[139] The ensuing double base appears in the form $-\cup$, perhaps to supply the initial anceps with the sequel of syllable lengths which it always has elsewhere in aeolic. In similar fashion, the clausular modification of $\times -\ \cup$ that appears in C-1 has, here as always in Greek verse, the form $\cup -^{-}$ that avoids the anomalous four long syllables of $\ldots -\bar{\times}-^{-}$.

Breaches of the prevailing rhythmic continuity are as rare as breaches of the pattern of demarcation. A-4 is the surest example. For there to be continuity between its second and third cola there must be syncopation of a kind unattested elsewhere in Lesbian poetry: $\times\times-\cup\cup-\cup-|\times\times-\cup\cup-\cup-.|-\cup-\times\times-\cup\cup-\cup-$. Somewhat less certain is A-9. The Lesbian model—if there was one— for this Horatian stanza had a penulti-

---

[138] Exceptions occur in the sapphic and alcaic stanzas, C-4-5, B-2, A-8 and C-16. They are more frequent if C-7-8, C-12 and B-7 contain heptadic aeolic, but these sequences are more naturally taken as octadic, differing only in demarcation from the parallel ones found in, respectively, B1-2, B-5 and B-6.

[139] Cf. *PMG* 542.12 (text, 159), S. *Ant.* 1140 = 1149 (below, Appendix VI), *Phil.* 141 = 156, E. *Or.* 816 = 828 and *Bac.* 897.

mate colon ending in the aeolic catalexis $- \cup \underset{A}{\cup} - -$.[140] Other possibilities are fairly unlikely ones: 141 (κῆ δ' ἀμβροσίας μέν), where there is too much uncertainty about lacunae and responsion in the surviving citations to determine the rhythm (cf. Dale 90); 111 (ἴψοι δὴ τὸ μέλαθρον. . .), which is probably a dactylic hexameter interrupted *kata triton trochaion* by the refrain ὑμήναον and followed by another hexameter or two dactylo-anapestic cola; and 132, sometimes regarded as aeolic but preserved at Heph 53.16–18 as an example of iambo-trochaic asynartetes. If Hephaestion is wrong, the poem might be given aeolic shape along the following lines:

$$- \cup - \times - \cup - \times - \cup - \times \mid - \cup - \times - \cup - \times \underset{A}{- \cup \cup - \cup -} \times$$
ἔστι μοι κάλα πάις χρυσ[ιοισιν]ανθέμοισιν
ἐμφέρην ἔχοισα<τὰν> [141]μόρφαν Κλέϊς ἀγαπάτα
$$- \cup - \times - \cup - \times - \cup - \times \mid - \cup - \times < - \cup - \times \underset{A}{- \cup \cup - \cup -} \times >$$
ἀντὶ τᾶς ἐγωὐδὲ Λυδίαν<κε>παῖσαν
οὐδ' ἐράνναν <ἀνταμειβοίμαν 'Ασίας ἄρουραν>

(or, with transposition, ἐράνναν οὐδὲ παῖσαν; cf., for a syncopated version of the same rhythm, Ar. *Eccl.* 903–5 [Table V]: $- \cup - \times - \cup -.- \cup - \times \mid - \cup - \times - \cup - \times \mid - \cup \cup - \cup - \times$). However Hephaestion's testimony is interpreted, rhythmical disjunction within repeated aeolic sequences of Lesbian poetry seems to have been a very occasional license—one way (modulation into dactylo-anapestic was another) of setting off a final colon from its predecessors as a clausula.

Disjunction is, of course, much more frequent if, as is often assumed, the prosodic demarcation which occurs within many of these sequences (e.g., in the sapphic and alcaic stanzas) is accompanied by the end of one rhythmical movement and the beginning of another. The assumption is supported by the fact that such demarcation is often detectable in Greek poetry of all kinds at the end of what are fairly certain, on other grounds, to be complete, distinct rhythmical movements; and by the fact that, unlike verbal demarcation, it never occurs, except by way of clear rhythmical license, within one member of a pair of responding sequences at a

---

[140] I 1/322: λάταγες ποτέονται | κυλίχναν ἀπὺ Τηΐαν seem to be the final lines of such a stanza, though the identical ××- ∪ ∪-¯ + ××- ∪ ∪- ∪- sometimes given as a scansion for 121.1–2 is dubious. The lines are just as easily taken as ××- ∪ ∪-- ∪ ∪-- ∪ ∪- ∪- (see P. Maas, *Kleine Schriften* [Munich 1973] 3).

[141] Hephaestion's own analysis of the line as E × + × E^ requires the addition of a syllable after μόρφαν (<ἀ>Κλῆϊς or the like), but the supplement <τὰν> has the advantage of restoring normal Lesbian usage with nouns qualified by a predicate adjective (see E. Lobel, ΑΛΚΑΙΟΥ ΜΕΛΗ [Oxford 1925] xci-xcii).

point that falls inside a word in the other member. It has accordingly been standard practice, ever since Boeckh's edition of Pindar, to regard the segments of a lyric stanza which intervene between two prosodic demarcations as rhythmical "periods," units analogous to the periods of rhetorical prose in that they are felt to possess a certain "roundness" or "completeness" (*LMGD* 11) and to create, as they end, the feeling that a natural stopping point, or rhythmical "closure" has been reached.

The phenomenon of continuity just observed[142] is against the validity of this assumption for Lesbian lyric in general. If prosodic demarcation always meant rhythmical break or closure, one would expect to find more than one certain and one probable example, within stanzas, of disjunct sequences such as $- \cup \underset{A}{\times} - ^- + \times \times - \cup \cup - \cup -$ and $\times \times - \cup \cup - \cup - +$ $- \cup - \times \times - \cup \cup - \cup -$. And against making the assumption valid for all of Greek lyric is the difficulty, both in Lesbian poetry and elsewhere, of seeing just what it is that gives many segments labeled periods their "completeness." Hexameters and trimeters, which can constitute whole poetic utterances or be repeated stichically to form whole poems, certainly deserve the label; as do sequences ending in cola used frequently at the close of poems and stanzas (e.g., the $- \cup \cup - ^-$ and $\times - \cup \cup - ^-$ found in the refrains ὦ τὸν Ἄδωνιν and ἰήιε Παιάν). But the correlation between such sequences and those which appear prosodically demarcated within stanzas is far from absolute. There are, moreover, fairly clear examples of well-defined rhythmical forms which contain internal prosodic demarcation in some of their occurrences but not in others. The continuous dactylic and anapestic "systems" of drama are usually demarcated after every fourth dactyl or every other anapestic metron, ending when their movement is modified through catalexis or modulation into a different rhythm. The demarcation is regularly verbal, but occasionally prosodic as well— usually when it coincides with the end of a vocative phrase, change of speaker or syntactic pause[143]—but occasionally even when none of these are present.[144] And it is unlikely that in any of these instances prosodic

[142] The "smooth carry-over" from one line to the next "even when there is hiatus or brevis in longo" which is noted as characteristic of Lesbian verse by Dale (96).

[143] Cf., in anapests, A. *Ag.* 1537, S. *OC* 188, Ar. *Vesp.* 1010, *Th.* 776, 1065 (vocatives); S. *Ant.* 932, *OC* 139, 143, 170, 1757, E. *Alc.* 78, *Med.* 1396, Ar. *Pax* 469, *Nub.* 892 (change of speaker); E. *Hipp.* 1372, *Hec.* 83,147 and 159, *Ion* 167, *Tro.* 98 and 171, *IT* 231, Ar. *Th.* 777 (syntactic pause), with the general discussion in Diggle (above, n. 36) 95–97. At S. *El.* 242 and E. *Phaeth.* 81 one must recognize further examples or admit anomalous acatalectic period closes (cf. Page *ad* E. *Med.* 166–67). A number of additional examples are usually removed by emendation, perhaps unnecessarily: cf. A. *Pers.* 18, *Sept.* 824, *Ag.* 794, *Eum.* 314.

[144] Cf. Ar. *Pax* 114–15 with Platnauer *ad loc.*, E. *Ph.* 191 and 1497 (αἵματι δεινῷ ‖ αἵματι λυγρῷ), *Hcld.* 608–9 = 619–20, and A. *Ag.* 154 and 158, where Dale (190) rightly insists on the unlikelihood of any break in the long run of dactyls, but rather than allow prosodic

demarcation was sufficient in itself to mark the end of rhythmical movement.

The existence of such passages has led some metricians to reject the general view that prosodic demarcation is always a sign of period end.[145] Others draw a distinction between periods and "verses," or between "major" periods and "minor periods."[146] A period or "major" period is a self-sufficient rhythmical whole analogous to the period of prose. A "minor" period or verse is a segment bounded by prosodic demarcation.

Partially as a result of such efforts at greater precision, the term "period" has become so ambiguous that there are good reasons for using it sparingly when referring to units other than the stanza or the repeated line of stichic verse. These are unquestionably rhythmical sequences with the self-sufficiency and wholeness that the word period suggests. But what internal prosodic demarcation, or overall structure, identifies as the main component parts of a stanza are much harder to classify. Some of them may be potentially independent periods capable of standing alone in other contexts; some seem to be discontinuous movement segments: disjunct but not autonomous; still others need be no more than the principal subdivisions in epiploke or homogeneous metron series. The three parts of the rhythm $\times\times - \cup \cup - \bar{} + \times\times - \cup \cup - \bar{} + \times\times - \cup \cup - \cup - \times\times - \cup \cup - \bar{}$ used in the ephymnia of several tragic choruses (A. *Supp.* 640ff., *Ag.* 367ff., E. *HF* 348ff.) belong, fairly clearly, to the first category. The sequence $- \cup \cup - \bar{}$ frequently closes stanzas and poems and is always immediately followed in aeolic contexts by demarcation. It brings the inner movement of each part to a definite end; and if the stanza holds together, it is only because of a larger, secondary (a)(a)(b) structure into which the parts enter as separate entities. The sapphic stanza shows a comparable (a)(a)(b) structure, in which (b)$(- \cup - \times - \cup \cup - \cup - \times$ (|) $- \cup \cup - \bar{}$ is a prolonged version of (a)$(- \cup - \times - \cup \cup - \cup -)$ rather than, as in the ephymnion, a forelengthened one. But in Sappho's rhythm there is an additional formal ingredient absent from the ephymnion: the continuous back and forth between single base and alternating aeolic or iambo-trochaic nucleus that is only broken to create the clausular $- \cup \cup - \cup - \times - \cup \cup - \bar{}$. And the practice of Alcaeus and Sappho is well enough documented to suggest that this additional ingredient, which makes the

---

demarcation to be compatible with rhythmical continuity chooses the more violent expedient of positing two "dactylic" cola ending in anceps: . . . $- \cup \cup - \cup \cup - \times | - \cup \cup - \cup \cup -$. . . .

[145] Cf. Kraus 26 and 146[2], followed by Pohlsander *ad OC* 1215 = 1228 and *OT* 1190 = 1199.

[146] Cf. *LMGD* 11–12 ("major" and "minor" period) and L. E. Rossi, "Verskunst," *Der kleine Pauly* 5 (Stuttgart 1976) 1211 ("Vers" and "Periode").

three parts of the (a)(a)(b) pattern subdivisions of a single rhythmical flow, was felt to be essential.

Internal prosodic demarcation is found in the Aeschylean instances of the ephymnion rhythm. But rhythmical discontinuity does not always require prosodic demarcation. The two cola of the elegiac pentameter are never, except by a very rare license, so separated, even though the purely verbal demarcation between them coincides with interruption of the dactylic rhythm[147] just as it is purely verbal demarcation that indicates the end of one rhythm and the beginning of another in asynartete compounds of dactylic $-\cup\cup-\cup\cup-\cup\cup-\cup\cup$ and iambo-trochaic (Maas 35). Prosodic demarcation ($\|$) and rhythmical discontinuity ($+$) should probably be regarded as separate phenomena, usually but not always found in conjunction with each other. Demarcation and the phenomena which indicate its presence (normally short syllables scanned long, contiguous vowels in apparent hiatus) are a natural result of any major pause in delivery such as *might* follow the end of one rhythmical movement and the beginning of another. But the pentameter shows that such discontinuity *need* not have been accompanied by a pause. Conversely, a pause that has the effect of lengthening a syllable or preventing the coalescing of vowels need not be so long that it interrupts the continuity of the rhythm. It could easily be no longer than whatever time it takes to close off the preceding flow of sound—a sort of glottal stop.

This "consonantal" explanation of pause is implicit in Dionysius of Halicarnassus's use (*De Demosth.* 38) of the same terms ("interval" [*diastasis*], "intervening time" [*metaxy chronos*]) for the disjunction between syllables created by hiatus and that caused by an accumulation or harsh collocation of consonants. Since such accumulation and collocation can occur within a verse, the analysis suggests that the temporal "distance" between syllables separated by hiatus need not be any greater than that between certain syllables in synapheia with each other. When prosodic closure has the effect of preventing the coalescing of vowels or lengthening an otherwise short syllable, this distance is partially filled by a glottal stop or by a momentary pause no longer in duration than the one or two consonants which would have to be added to produce the same effect. Closure of this sort is the cause, not the result of pause, though doubtless more noticeable than the closure which separates consonants or a long vowel and a consonant. Some such analysis is almost necessary to explain

---

[147] Syncopation could, of course, have made the line continuously dactylic ($-\cup\cup-\cup\cup-$ $|\stackrel{\smile}{\phantom{.}}\stackrel{\smile}{\phantom{.}}|-\cup\cup-\cup\cup-$) but would be anomalous in the archaic context where the pentameter first appears and is excluded, for the Hellenistic period at any rate, by the designation *pentametron* (Hermesianax 7.36 p. 99 Powell).

why tragic poets are reluctant to divide a syntactic unit by hiatus at the end of a trimeter[148] and why Aristoxenus (*ap. GL* 6.63.5–10) notes the sharper division between verses that occurs when a final long is supplied by a syllable normally scanned short. Neither division would have been felt as special if verses were always, even in the absence of hiatus or lengthening, followed by full stop or extended pause.

Such stops and pauses must have been normal in some verse forms; elsewhere, even in the absence of hiatus or final lengthening, the minimal prosodic demarcation created by a momentary shutting off and resumption of the flow of sound probably created a sharper separation than mere verbal demarcation—just as, conversely, mere prosodic synapheia created a weaker link than verbal synapheia. But the exact degree to which prosodic demarcation was compatible with rhythmic continuity—and rhythmical discontinuity with prosodic synapheia—may well have been determined by the taste of a particular poet or particular epoch. Euripides, unlike Aeschylus, seems to have excluded prosodic demarcation from the ephymnion rhythm;[149] and the Cologne Archilochus papyrus (*SLG* 478) shows both prosodic demarcation and rhythmical discontinuity in the sequence $- \cup \cup - \cup \cup - \| \times - \cup - \times - \cup -$, though the dramatists only allow verbal demarcation in such asynartete combinations of dactylic and iambo-trochaic.[150] Similarly, the sequence $\times - \cup \cup - \cup - \times$ E ($\hat{}$), which regularly shows purely verbal demarcation (before or after anceps: see Table V) in drama, appears as $\times - \cup \cup - \cup - \times \| $E in Alcman's Partheneion.

The Partheneion rhythm, though it is not the work of a Lesbian poet, is probably the single most important piece of evidence in favor of the argument for rhythmical continuity within the aeolic stanza that is being offered here. For it shows the same regular alternation of single base with aeolic or iambo-trochaic nucleus as is found in the sapphic and alcaic stanzas; and, seen as epiploke, it is simply a variant on the alcaic, considerably expanded and with a different set of internal, largely prosodic demarcations:[151]

Alcaeus: (a)   $\times - \cup - \times - \cup \cup - \cup - \|$

(a)   $\times - \cup - \times - \cup \cup - \cup - \|$

(b)   $\times - \cup - \times - \cup - \times( \mid )$   $- \cup \cup - \cup \cup - \cup - \times$

[148] See, most recently, T. C. W. Stinton, *CQ* 71 (1977) 67–72.

[149] The presence of thirty-two purely verbal demarcations within the rhythm at it appears in *HF* 348–441, and *Bac.* 402–5 = 417–20, and within the related forms of *Alc.* 962 = 973ff. (below, Appendix VI) is not likely to be accidental.

[150] See Rossi (above, n. 135) 216–19.

[151] The similarity was first pointed out, to my knowledge, by G. Thomson, *Studies in Ancient Greek Society*[3] (New York 1961) 470–71.

Alcman: (a)   $-\cup-\times-\cup-\|\times-\cup\underset{A}{\cup}-\cup-\times\|$
(a)   $-\cup-\times-\cup-\|\times-\cup\cup-\cup-\times\|$
(a)   $-\cup-\times-\cup-\|\times-\cup\cup-\cup-\times\|$
(a)   $-\cup-\times-\cup-\|\times-\cup\cup-\cup-\times\|$
(b)                    $-\cup-\times-\cup-\times-\cup\overset{(\smile)}{\smile}\times\|$ [152]
$-\cup-\times-\cup-\times-\cup-\times\|$
$-\cup-\times-\cup-\times\,|$
$-\cup-\times-\cup\overset{(\smile)}{\smile}\times\,|$
$-\cup\cup-\cup\cup-\cup\cup-\cup\cup\,|$
$-\cup\cup-\underset{A}{\cup\cup}-\cup\overset{\smile}{\smile}\times$

Corresponding to the two (a)'s in Alcaeus are four, each one with an added cycle of iambo-trochaic; eight extra cycles are added to (b) together with four additional dactylo-anapestic ones. The dactylic character given to the close of the stanza is thus far more pronounced than in Alcaeus and is reflected in the puzzling responsion, attested here and only here in Greek poetry, between $-\cup\cup-\cup\cup-\cup-\times$ and $-\cup\cup-\cup\cup-\cup\cup-$. Alcman has perhaps assimilated the two sequences as different versions of $-\cup\cup-\cup\cup-\cup\times + {}^-$, i.e., a concluding "hypercatalectic" quantity preceded by a terminally modified dactylic segment that has several possible parallels elsewhere in archaic lyric (see Appendix I). With long anceps the sequence shows the same succession of syllables as aeolic $-\cup\cup-\underset{A}{\cup\cup}-\cup-\times$, with short anceps the same as dactylo-anapestic $-\cup\cup-\cup\cup-\cup\cup-$.

Whether or not one accepts this theory of a "dactylized" aeolic $-\cup\cup-\cup\cup-\cup-\times$, the overall resemblance between Alcaeus and Alcman is too close to be coincidental. One stanzaic form must derive from the other, or both from a common prototype. Alcaeus's stanza is the simpler and, as will be argued later (138), more "primitive." Moreover, though we are told of Alcman's Sardian origin and the activity of Terpander of Lesbos in establishing the first "school" (*katastasis*) of lyric composition at Sparta a generation or two before Alcman (Hellanicus, *FGrHist* 4F85), there is no tradition of comparable activity on the part of Peloponnesian poets in Lesbos and Asia Minor. It is thus likely that the Alcaic form was, if not Alcman's model, more similar to a common prototype than the Alcmannic one was. For our present purposes, however, it

[152] Resolution here and at the same penultimate position four cola later (lines 2 and 32 in the fragment of the poem that survives) provides further reason for not taking either sequence as an independent period. On the rarity of such penultimate resolution, see Maas 37.

is sufficient to emphasize that the Partheneion (and, possibly, the one other extended piece of mixed aeolic that appears in Alcman)[153] seems to make the same use of continuous epiploke with internal prosodic demarcation as can be seen in Sappho and Alcaeus, and in connection with the same type of aeolic rhythm. The sharpest contrast to this mode of composition found in the purely lyric forms of the early archaic period is provided by the surviving dactylo-anapestic poems of Stesichorus (the *Geryoneis* [*SLG* 7–87], *Syotherae* s5–7, e7, *PMG* 243, *GL* 1.512.23–25; cf. Haslam 11–12). Discontinuous series containing from two to fourteen cycles each are juxtaposed to create stanzas. Within each series, division into cola, where it is detectable, does not affect rhythmic continuity; but there is no comparable continuity between one series and the next. In so far as the still meagre evidence allows us to judge, Stesichorean prosodiac was intermediate in character between aeolic and dactylo-anapestic: continuous alternation of base and nucleus (often passing into dactylo-anapestic) through the bulk of what survives, but varied occasionally by the presence of fairly short sequences rhythmically disjunct from their surroundings.[154]

The explanation for the more restricted role which epiploke plays in early non-aeolic poems may lie in the history, or pre-history, of the two rhythms involved. Both derive, in all probability, from forms in which the compass of epiploke was even more limited—Stesichorean dactylo-anapestic via expansion from the epic hexameter, where rhythmic break occurs every six cycles and demarcation is always, except at the central caesura of the line, dactylic; mixed prosodiac from asynartete combinations of single dactylic or prosodiac cola with iambo-trochaic (cf. Alcaeus Z60/383 [– ⏑ ⏑ – ⏑ ⏑ – + ×– ⏑–×] and Archilochus 168–71 [×– ⏑ ⏑– ⏑ ⏑–× + ᴇ‸], both combinations, apparently, repeated *kata*

---

[153] 3.2–6: ᴇ ×‖ᴇ ×|ᴇ |×– ⏑ ⏑–⏑–×–⏑–‖×–⏑– (or …|×– ⏑ ⏑–⏑–×–⏑ ⏑–⏑– ×|) between dactylic tetrameters. 64 (…–⏑ ⏑–⏑–×–⏑–×|–⏑–×–⏑ ⏑–…) may have been similar. Other aeolic passages are too short to allow generalizations about rhythmic structure, though catalexis seems to have been more frequent than in the Lesbians (125: – ⏑–×–⏑ ⏑–‾; 45: ×–⏑–×–⏑ ⏑–‾ + ×–⏑–…; 59b: –⏑–×–⏑–⏑–‾ + × ᴇ |××–⏑ ⏑–⏑–; 38: × ᴇ |××–⏑ ⏑–‾ + –⏑–⏑…).

[154] There are no sure instances of discontinuity in the two Stesichorean (or possibly Stesichorean) stanzas that lack modulation into dactylo-anapestic (from the *Nostoi* and *POxy* 2735; cf. Haslam 46–49), or (except in the …–$\overline{(\overline{\smile\overline{\smile}})}$–$\underset{D}{\smile\smile}$–⏑ ⏑–×–⏑– + D × D × –⏑–× of *Iliou persis* s5–8 [*ibid.*, 24]) within the pure or mixed prosodiac sections of other stanzas. *Iliou persis* e7–10 (D |×–⏑–×–⏑–×–⏑–× + ––⏑ ⏑–⏑ ⏑–– + ⏑ ⏑–⏑ ⏑– ⏑ ⏑––) looks like a return to the dactylo-anapestic with which the strophe begins; 15/192.1–3 (× D ×|–⏑–×–⏑–×– + ––⏑ ⏑–⏑ ⏑–– if correctly transmitted) may be from a similar context; and ×–⏑–× in s6 of the Lille fragment follows on the prosodiac "hexameter" discussed in the text (136, with n. 156).

*stichon*).[155] Pure prosodiac epiploke, of which there is no trace in Alcaeus, Sappho or Alcman, may be another derivative from the hexameter, which seems to be interchangeable with D × D × in the Lille fragment of Stesichorus.[156]

Aeolic, by contrast, is separated by a much longer development from any such prototype. The prototype, if it existed, belongs to the pre-history of Greek lyric, and its character can only be a matter of more or less plausible inference from the parallels between Aeolic and Vedic versification. The parallels involve identical prosodic systems, isosyllabic rhythmical patterns based on a partially regulated sequence of longs and shorts, preference for stanzaic construction in lines of eleven, twelve or eight syllables, and, on occasion, resemblances between specific verse forms (e.g., the Sapphic hendecasyllable and ×−×−× ∪ ∪ − ∪ − ¯, one of the most common varieties of the Vedic triṣṭubh).[157] If, as a number of scholars have argued,[158] these parallels are sufficient to establish a common Indo-European origin for Vedic and Lesbian rhythm, the development which led to the latter can be most plausibly reconstructed by positing as its starting point stichic and stanzaic forms in which each line is an independent rhythmical entity. This method of composition is still to be found in the Vedas, where the regulation of syllable quantities becomes more strict as each line moves toward its close. Line end thereby becomes a clearly marked rhythmic cadence. In Lesbian aeolic, on the other hand, a regularization of the succession of quantities through all, or most, of each line has made possible, throughout the stanza, a partial homogenization of the movement of octosyllables with that of hendecasyllables or dodecasyllables. The short line becomes a single octadic, or double tetradic cycle; and it is the linking of one of these cycles with a single tetrad that forms a dodecasyllable. Hendecasyllables become abbreviated dodecasyllables (e.g., ××− ∪ ∪ − ∪ −×− ∪ − shortened into ××− ∪ ∪ − ∪ − ∪ − ¯, ×− ∪ −××− ∪ ∪ − ∪ − into − ∪ −××− ∪ ∪ − ∪ − etc.); or else heptads (×− ∪ ∪ − ∪ −×) combined with tetrads (×− ∪ −×) and octads combined with triads (e.g., ××− ∪ ∪ − ∪ − passing internally into dactylo-anapestic).

---

[155] So Snell 51–52. Cf. M. L. West's similar remarks ("Greek Poetry 2000–700 B.C.," *CQ* 67 [1973] 180) on the probable antecedents of Alcman's dactylic and trochaic series.

[156] For the development posited here (a dactylic − ∪ ∪ − ∪ ∪ − ⏕ − ∪ ∪ − ∪ ∪ − ⏕ reinterpreted as − ∪ ∪ − ∪ ∪ −×− ∪ ∪ − ∪ ∪ −×) see M. S. Haslam, "The Versification of the New Stesichorus," *GRBS* 19 (1978) 40–41 and 56–57.

[157] Cf., in general, R. Schmitt, *Dichtung und Dichtersprache in indo-germanischer Zeit* (Wiesbaden 1967) 307–13.

[158] See, most recently, M. L. West, "Indo-European Metre," *Glotta* 51 (1973) 161–70 and above (n. 155) 179–81; and Nagy 27–36.

If Vedic practice is a valid guide to the character of the parent forms, the original line cadence was usually – ᴗ – or ᴗ – ¯. This tendency may persist even in later Greek, where preferred demarcation in all forms of epiploke allows an alternation between ᴗ – | and ᴗ – ¯ |, whether ᴗ – – | (octadic aeolic, iono-choriambic, bacchio-cretic), ᴗ – x̄ | (prosodiac, heptadic aeolic, iambo-trochaic) or ᴗ – ᴗᴗ| (dactylo-anapestic). Greek epiploke also allows the cadence ᴗ ᴗ – |, not favored in Vedic, but none of the forms which exhibit it belong to the earliest stratum of lyric. Anapestic ᴗ ᴗ – | is first extensively attested in Stesichorus, aeolic – x – ᴗ ᴗ – | in Pindar, and choriambic – ᴗ ᴗ – | in Anacreon. (Ionic ᴗ ᴗ – – |, on the other hand, is already to be found in Alcaeus, perhaps deriving from an exclusively tetradic organization of the rhythm of octasyllables and dodecasyllables ending in ᴗ – ¯).[159] Vedic usage also suggests an original unwillingness to include hendecasyllables and dodecasyllables in the same stanza, and this too may be reflected in the repertory of aeolic forms. The combination of heptadic and octadic rhythms which such inclusion would favor is not attested in any poem of Sappho or Alcaeus.

The process of homogenization and regularization has not been carried through with uniform thoroughness, for the varying degrees of consistency and sharpness with which demarcation appears within the stichic or stanzaic periods of Lesbian aeolic are perhaps best explained as reflections of the different degrees to which epiploke has taken its place alongside the inherited pattern of line lengths as a major source of formal unity.[160] At one extreme are the – ᴗ – x x – ᴗ ᴗ – ᴗ – x x – ᴗ ᴗ – ᴗ – x x ¯ ᴗ ᴗ – ᴗ – ᴗ – ¯ of B–2 and the x x – ᴗ ᴗ – ᴗ – x x – ᴗ ᴗ – ᴗ – x – ᴗ – of B–1, descendants, perhaps, of stanzas with an 11–8–11 and 8–12 disposition

---

[159] The existence of mixed ionic along with pure ionic in Sappho and Alcman is suggested by a comparison of Sappho 134 and 100 with Alcman 47:

ᴗ ᴗ – ᴗ – ᴗ – – ᴗ ᴗ – ¯    134
– ᴗ – – ᴗ ᴗ – – ᴗ ᴗ – ¯    100
– ᴗ – – ᴗ ᴗ – ᴗ – ᴗ . . .    47

But 134, cited by Hephaestion, is the only line of which we can be fairly certain that we possess its exact metrical shape. If the other two are incorrectly transmitted or analyzed, its existence need indicate no more than that, for whatever reason, there was one stereotyped variant on the better attested ᴗ ᴗ – – ᴗ ᴗ – – ᴗ ᴗ – –.

[160] For a listing of Vedic forms, see E. V. Arnold, *Vedic Metre* (London 1905) 243–49. The 8–12, 8–8–11, 11–11–8–11, 11–11–8–8 and 8–8–12–12 arrangements of syllables into lines mentioned in the text are, respectively, Nrs. 2, 10, 40, 39 and 27 in his catalogue. There is no exact parallel to the 11–8–11 form posited, but cf. Nrs. 13 (11–7–11) and 39 (11–11–8–11).

of syllables into lines.[161] Here the prevailing octadic movement created by the regularization of quantity series is sufficiently pronounced to allow the poet to dispense with internal demarcative patterns altogether. In the ××–∪∪–∪–|××–∪∪–∪– + –∪–××–∪∪–∪– and ××–∪∪– ∪–|××–∪∪–∪–|××–∪∪–∪∪–∪– of A-4 and 5, on the other hand, one can see different outgrowths of an 8-8-11 pattern. Original demarcation is maintained and the final sequence set off by modulation or rhythmic break from what precedes. Intermediate in character is the alcaic stanza, in which the final two lines of an 11-11-8-11 pattern seem to have been replaced by a single one in which demarcation appears regularly, but not always, one quantity beyond the position it occupied originally.[162] In similar fashion the sapphic stanza may recover an earlier 11–11–8–8 arrangement in which the final two lines have become a single one, with internal demarcation (usually) and quantitative pattern (always) regulated to make its opening recall the initial two lines. The same process applied to the initial two lines of an 8–8–12–12 pattern would yield, with consistent "ionization," the ∪∪––∪∪––∪∪––∪∪––|∪∪– –∪∪––∪∪––|∪∪––∪∪––∪∪–– of Alcaeus A10/10.[163]

The predominance of epiploke is still more striking in those poems in which it has permitted a discarding of the external as well as internal boundaries of the inherited system, producing, through catalexis and new combinations of rhythmic cycles, demarcated sequences of 7, 10, 14 and 15 syllables for which no parallels can be cited in Vedic (e.g., the ××– ∪∪–⁻ of A9, the ××–∪∪–∪∪–⁻ of C-9, the –∪∪–∪–× –∪∪–∪–× of C-2, and the –∪–×–∪∪––∪∪–∪–× of A-12).

---

[161] Cf. A-6 (*sic te diva potens Cypri/sic fratres Helenae lucida sidera*) where an original division into two separate lines may be preserved.

[162] The ××–∪∪––∪∪–∪–‖××–∪∪––∪∪–∪–‖ ××–∪∪–∪–×| ×–∪∪– –∪∪–∪– of A-8 may derive in similar fashion from a stanza ending 12–8–12 (cf. Nrs. 17 and 45 in Arnold's listing [above, n. 160]), though not enough instances of the rhythm survive for us to know whether, as in the alcaic stanza, the third internal demarcation was merely usual rather than obligatory. The same 12–8–12 pattern may lie behind the concluding 11–9–12 of the Attic skolion rhythm (*PMG* 884ff.); and a 12–12–12–12–11 could yield the 12–13–10–13 (τούτῳ πατέω...)–11 of *PMG* 909 (the song of Hybrias the Cretan)—though the absence of any instances of verbal synapheia between the members of the 11–9 sequence makes the suggestion much more hypothetical. (Cf., on such shifts of colon boundary in general, the suggestive discussion in Nagy 279–302).

[163] For the colometry, see Fuehrer (254–57), who notes that the 4–4–2 or 3–3–4 distribution of metra into cola adopted by some editors would require internal prosodic demarcation. Synapheia, however, is found throughout Horace's imitation (cf. *GL* 6.91.9–10 and 387.2065–71), and is implied for Alcaeus by Hephaestion's remarks (65.12–21) on the debate among metricians as to whether the poem should be considered a series of equal ten-metron stanzas or a single hypermeter.

The Partheneion rhythm goes farther along this line than anything in Sappho and Alcaeus—perhaps beyond the confines of aeolic itself in its closing sequence (above, 134),[164] yet only by application of principles also present in the work of the Lesbians. If the development of Aeolic verse is to be reconstructed in some such fashion as this, it is parallel in its character to that suggested earlier for prosodiac and dactylo-anapestic, and parallel in its starting point to one, at any rate, of the probable sources of the mode of early archaic composition which most rigorously excludes epiploke. The epodic distichs and asynartete dicola of Archilochus make considerable use of iambic dimeters and trimeters (full or catalectic), in which it is natural to see descendants of the same octosyllables, dodecasyllables and hendecasyllables that yield, in aeolic, glyconics, asclepiads, and sapphics and alcaics. For the rest of his repertory, Archilochus draws on different sources (dactylic hexameter, trochaic tetrameter, and shorter sequences created by decomposing hexameters and full or catalectic trimeters into the cola most frequently encountered within them);[165] but he combines these forms in the same disjunct fashion attested in the stanzas of the Vedas. Disjunct composition of this sort can also be seen in the Archilochean and Alcaic dicola which are plausibly regarded (above, 135) as the ancestors of mixed prosodiac. The rhythm is too scantily attested in the earliest stages of its development to know at what point or whether other influences had to be brought into play to make the rhythm, in its fully matured form, a close analogue to heptadic aeolic (above, 66–75).[166] The development,

[164] With the much more extensive dactylization evident at the close of the *Partheneion* one may contrast what seems to be an unwillingness, in the Lesbian poets, to allow dactylic modulation in any sequence longer than the ××– ∪ ∪ – ∪ ∪ – ∪ ∪ – ∪ ∪ – ⁻ of B-4. The sequence contains sixteen syllables, suggesting that a combination of two inherited octosyllables is being given an internal dactylic rhythm. But the rhythm is not sufficient, on its own, to generate sequences longer than this—an acatalectic ××– ∪ ∪ – ∪ ∪ – ∪ ∪ – ∪ ∪ – ∪ –, for example, which one might expect to find alongside ××– ∪ ∪ – ∪ ∪ – ∪ ∪ – ∪ ∪ – ⁻, just as one finds acatalectic ××– ∪ ∪ (– ∪ ∪)– ∪ ∪ – ∪ – (B-3, A-5) alongside catalectic ××– ∪ ∪ (– ∪ ∪)– ∪ ∪ – ⁻ (C-10–11).

[165] See Snell 39–41 for this analysis of the dactylic tetrameters, "lecythia," and "ithyphallics" of Archilochus. To his list one should perhaps add × E ˆ, the second colon in the iambic tetrameter (cf. fr. 324: ×E ˆ [τήνελλα καλλίνικε] + E [χαῖρ' ἄναξ 'Ηράκλεες] + trimeter). The tetrameter itself is not attested in our fragments, but may be attributable to Archilochus on the basis of *PDub* 193a (see W. Peek, "Neues von Archilochos," *Philologus* 99 [1955] 49).

[166] It is conceivable, for example, that – ∪ ∪ – ∪ – ×– ∪ –×, an aeolic hendecasyllable, provided the model for the combination of dactylic and iambo-trochaic found in Alcaeus's – ∪ ∪ – ∪ ∪ – + ×– ∪ –× and that Archilochus's combination of "paroemiac" (×– ∪ ∪ – ∪ ∪ –×) and iambo-trochaic was a "dactylized," asynartete version of an aeolic ×– ∪ ∪⎯⎯ – ∪ –×|E ˆ.
⎯A⎯

however, by whatever stages it occurred, may well have been similar to that which turned the disjunct ancestors of aeolic verse into the continuous stanzas of Alcaeus and Sappho. And the dactylic hexameter itself has often been derived in the same way, from some sort of disjunct dicolon.[167]

A tendency toward increasing use of epiploke is thus one of the most striking characteristics of the earliest non-stichic Greek verse of which we are informed, or concerning which we can conjecture (see Table IX). It has progressed further in some genres than in others, but only Archilochus seems to be totally free of its influence. Continuity within lyric stanzas is the rule; and when the rule is infringed, two or three seems to be the maximum number of breaks allowed. Sequences longer than sixteen quantities are rarely without internal demarcation; but the colon groups which result are usually part of a single epiploke. Exceptions only appear later;[168] and when they appear in the work of poets who make extensive use of both disjunct and continuous composition, it is sometimes possible to suggest reasons why one mode was found more appropriate than another on a given occasion. This question cannot be answered for the earlier period, but a more general piece of speculation about the origins of both modes is worth making.

Disjunct composition is an inherited technique. In seeking an explanation for extensions of its use during the seventh century, one need look no further than the rhythmic inventiveness of an Archilochus. Epiploke, on the other hand, seems to be a Greek innovation, and the reasons for its appearance are less clear. One fairly simple explanation suggests itself, however.

In spoken or sung poetry the length of any piece of rhythmical movement is limited—both by the necessity for the performer to catch his breath from time to time, and by the sense pauses in the text he is reciting. Once the singer or speaker is provided with an instrumental accompaniment, however, the length of such movements ceases to be limited by anything but the hearer's capacity for apprehending a long musical line as a single aesthetic whole. Greek lyric was, of course, a form which combined poetic text, melody, instrumental accompaniment and, often, dancing; but the character of the combination was not uniform through the whole history of all its genres. While there may never have been a period when poetry was recited without any musical accompaniment whatsoever,

---

[167] E.g., a combination of headless with full "paroemiac" $- \cup \cup - \cup \cup - \times \; + \; \times - \cup \cup - \cup \cup - \times$.

[168] The Rhodian swallow song (*PMG* 848) is an early exception if, as is usually assumed, its technique is genuinely archaic. But the technique, whatever its date, may belong to a relatively "popular" stratum in Greek poetry to which the generalizations of the text do not apply.

TABLE IX: Derivation of Greek Verse Forms

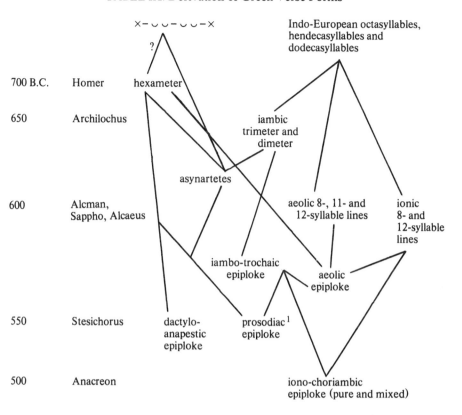

|  |  |  |
|---|---|---|
| | × − ∪ ∪ − ∪ ∪ − × | Indo-European octasyllables, hendecasyllables and dodecasyllables |
| 700 B.C. | Homer — hexameter | |
| 650 | Archilochus | iambic trimeter and dimeter |
| | | asynartetes |
| 600 | Alcman, Sappho, Alcaeus | aeolic 8-, 11- and 12-syllable lines — ionic 8- and 12-syllable lines |
| | | iambo-trochaic epiploke — aeolic epiploke |
| 550 | Stesichorus | dactylo-anapestic epiploke — prosodiac[1] epiploke |
| 500 | Anacreon | iono-choriambic epiploke (pure and mixed) |

---

[1] Mixed prosodiac epiploke may already appear in Alcman, but there are no passages which cannot be equally well explained as asynartete combinations of iambo-trochaic with dactylo-anapestic or single prosodiac cola.

it is fairly clear that accompaniment became progressively more prominent during the course of the archaic and classical periods, that the impulse for this development was provided when Greek settlers in the Eastern Aegean came into contact with an Asiatic musical tradition more sophisticated than what they had known on the mainland, and that the point of most extensive and fruitful contact was the island of Lesbos. What ancient writers tell us about the early history of music is often contradictory and unreliable, but the consistency with which it points to this last conclusion is too great to be entirely misleading. At the head of the Greek musical tradition stands the half-legendary Phrygian *aulistēs* Olympus, teacher of Terpander of Lesbos and inventor, according to one account (ps.-Plut., *De mus.* 29.1141b) of two rhythms, prosodiac and bacchiac (i.e., iono-choriambic or aeolic: above, 10–11). Terpander is regularly credited with inventing a more sophisticated version of the lyre, as well as a new instrument, the *barbitos* (devised, according to Pindar [fr. 125.3], in imitation of the Lydian *pēktis*). He, or Sappho, is said to have introduced the mixo-Lydian mode,[169] as well as, according to one widely accepted view of the nature of the Terpandrian nome, the practice of composing musical settings with a fixed melody. He and his student, the Ionian Polymnestos, appear, presumably, as apostles of the new music, in Sparta (ps.-Plut., *De mus.* 9.1134c, 12.1135c), as does his countryman Arion in Corinth and Magna Graecia.

The effects of Asiatic music on Greek poetry were obviously extensive. One of them may well have been to open up hitherto closed poetic structures, allowing a continuous flow of rhythm through them and ultimately beyond them, into new structures more extensive and more varied than those countenanced by the tradition. And the new rhythms, some of them, perhaps, first used in purely instrumental compositions,[170] would have spread, along with the new music, from the Aeolid to the Peloponnesus, Magna Graecia and other centers of lyric art. The hypothesis is in accord with all the available evidence: the Greeks' own traditions about their musical history and the predominantly Asiatic character of the names borne by their musical instruments; the parallels and contrasts between Lesbian versification and that of the Indo-European prototype which is reconstructible for it; the striking similarities between the Partheneion rhythm and the Alcaic stanza; the tendency of most lyric forms to retain, well into the fifth century, the isosyllabism characteristic of Lesbian

---

[169] Cf. ps.-Plut. *De mus.* 28.1140f (Terpander) and 16.1136d (Sappho).

[170] Olympus, a purely instrumental musician, is credited not only with prosodiac and bacchiac, but also (ps.-Plut. *De mus.* 7.1133f and 10.1134e) with the *kata daktylon eidos* of Stesichorus and the cretic of Thaletas (below, n. 172). The tradition may well be wrong, but there is nothing implausible about it.

poetry; and the failure of genres which, like epic and iambic and their epodic derivatives, made minimal use of musical accompaniment, to develop any analogue to the large lyric stanza.[171] More generally, the hypothesis accords well with the "very high degree of musical conformity from end to end of the Greek world," and the "shortness and richness of the whole 'age of lyric,'" two phenomena suggesting that, within this world, "communication was speedy and effective," and that "the poets whose skill and creativeness could impose themselves with authority were manageably few."[172]

The oriental genie whom Greek poets took into their service in the seventh century proved, as is well known, increasingly difficult to control; and he is usually credited with a major share in the ultimate downfall of the very lyric tradition whose early phases, according to the argument just presented, he did so much to foster (see below, 200–207). There is certainly truth in the usual view, but it should be pointed out that the complaints of unruliness which begin to be heard in the fifth century, coupled with assertions of the proper (and primeval) supremacy of words over accompaniment, tell only half the story. Poets must have realized, almost from the start, that a price had to be paid for the added dimension which strings and woodwinds gave to their art, a price which they paid willingly until, in the fourth century, it finally began to be too high. The same poet who creates for poetic texts the lordly epithet *anaxiforminges* (Pind. *O.* 2.1) also knows that, when the instrument belongs to Apollo and the Muses, it is for the lyre to give commands and poets to follow: πείθονται δ' ἀοιδοὶ σάμασιν.[173]

[171] If the long, internally demarcated continuous series of lyric verse are unavailable to poetry intended for a more rudimentary type of instrumental accompaniment, undemarcated structures such as those of Sappho 96 (B-2) are even more peculiarly the domain of lyric; cf., on the latter, L. E. Rossi, *RFIC* 94 (1966) 196–99.

[172] Dale 177. Unequivocal evidence for the separate Peloponnesian tradition of lyric composition posited by West (above, n. 155) 181–84 is largely lacking. Alcman's divergences from Archilochean and Lesbian practice can almost all be accounted for as purely individual elaborations on a shared repertory of inherited forms: hexameter, trimeter, tetrameter and their derivatives on the one hand and, on the other, "aeolized" versions of Indo-European lines and stanzas. The cretics of fr. 58 are probably a non-Peloponnesian import, as is suggested by the name itself and the traditions linking Thaletas of Gortyn both to the invention of the metre (Strabo 10.4.16 p. 480, ps.-Plut. *De mus.* 10.1134de) and to Spartan musical traditions (*ibid.*, 9.1134bc and Athenaeus 15.22 p. 678c). Even the characteristically Dorian anapests are plausibly derived, like the Archilochean $- \cup \cup - \cup \cup - \cup \cup - \cup \cup$ (above, n. 165), from the hexameter (text, 117–18).

[173] Pindar's text (*P.* 1.3) illustrates the point by following lyre into a double syncopation (π‌είθονται). This particular modification of normal speech rhythm is more characteristic of tragedy than epinician, but Pindaric prosodiac is distinguished throughout by its admission of the less striking $\_\cup\_ . \overset{D}{\_} \overset{\cup}{\_} \overset{-}{\_}$, of which there is little or no trace as yet in Alcman or Stesichorus (text, 146).

# CHAPTER EIGHT: LATE ARCHAIC LYRIC

The poetry of Simonides, Anacreon, Pindar and Bacchylides exhibits roughly the same range of continuous and disjunct forms of composition found in the work of their predecessors in the seventh and early sixth centuries; and the forms continued to be associated, by and large, with the same rhythms. Disjunct composition is still the rule in dactylo-anapestic, whether used for entire stanzas or in combination with other rhythms;[174] whole stanzas continue to be made up of single pieces of aeolic or iono-choriambic epiploke; and both types of composition are attested for prosodiac, sometimes within the compass of a single poem. Only in the aeolic odes of Pindar (below, 155–61) do we find a sharp departure from methods attested earlier. Elsewhere innovation seems to affect the character and variety of the rhythmic sequences used rather than the way they are linked to each other within stanzas.

The line of descent from earlier models is clearest in the aeolic of Anacreon and (if she belongs to this period) Corinna. Except in Anacreon 3/348 and 12/357, there are no sure examples of rhythmical break within a stanza, and expansion of the repertory of forms at certain points is accompanied by a narrowing at others. Longer continuous sequences are attested (e.g., the $\times\times- \cup\cup-\cup-|\times\times-\cup\cup-\cup-|\times\times-\cup\cup-\cup-$ $|\times\times-\cup\cup-\cup-|\times\times-\cup\cup-^-$ of Anacreon 3/348 and 12/357); iono-choriambic may be mixed as well as pure, and the catalexis $-\cup\cup-^-$ is frequent. In Corinna $\underline{-\times-\cup\cup-}_B$ is virtually interchangeable with $\underline{-\cup\cup-\cup-}_A$. On the other hand, heptadic aeolic has disappeared entirely;[175] combination of aeolic with other rhythms, whether dactylic,

---

[174] Cf., for pure dactylo-anapestic, *PMG* 287.1–2, 3–4 (reading ἀπείρ<ον>α), 5 and 7; 317.al, 311.a, 314.1, 303a.1–2 (Ibycus) and 567.1–3 and 571 (Simonides); and, for mixed forms, the "dactylo-aeolic" stanzas discussed in the text, 145–48. Anacreon 86/431 (trimeter + E⌢) is pure iambo-trochaic asynartete combination in the Archilochéan manner, and ⌣⌣)–⌣⌣)– + E⌢ may appear at 433.2 and 434.1–2.

[175] Transposition of εἰδότες to follow κυκλώσεσθε would remove the one possible exception (100/445: $\times\times-\cup\cup-\cup-\times-\cup-\|\times\underline{-\cup\cup-\cup--}_A\cup...$) as well as other anomalies in the fragment, yielding $\times\times-\cup\cup-\cup-|\times\times-\cup\cup-\cup-\times-\cup-$ (cf. Alcaeus Z34/357 [Table VIII, B-1] and Bacchylides fr. 20a5–6). It has been doubted, however, whether Anacreon's wording is preserved in our citation beyond the initial $\times\times-\cup\cup-\cup-$ (see Gentili *ad loc.*, and M. L. West, *CQ* 64 [1970] 210²).

iono-choriambic or iambo-trochaic, is much rarer;[176] and demarcation in aeolic is almost always after a nucleus or before a base. The result is a versification dominated in its aeolic forms by glyconic and, in Corinna, choriambic dimeter. It is natural to see in these cola descendants of Indo-European octosyllables, extensively attested in Vedic, but for some reason used sparingly by the Lesbians.[177] On the other hand, the predominance of $|\times\times- \cup\cup- \cup-|$ and $|\times\times-\times- \cup\cup-|$ can also be interpreted as one result of a much more widespread tendency toward expansion and reinterpretation of inherited forms in terms of tetradic rhythm. Octadic cycles are favored over heptadic ones, perhaps because they can be taken as double tetrads; demarcation occurs at eight-quantity intervals; and iono-choriambic ceases to appear primarily as a rhythmical digression within aeolic cola and becomes, either by itself or in conjunction with the tetrads of iambo-trochaic, the basis for whole stanzas in which demarcation shows the same variations that were once reserved for aeolic. Both tetradic and octadic rhythm (the latter through use of the cycle $\overline{-\cup\cup-}$ $\overline{\times-\cup-\times}$) thereby acquire, for the first time, the full range of possibilities of which they were to be capable in Greek (above, 7–10).

A comparable development can be traced in prosodiac, which is also employed extensively (though less consistently than Anacreontic aeolic and iono-choriambic) as a basis for continuous composition. The two most striking innovations which distinguish the mixed prosodiac of Pindar and Bacchylides from that which survives of Stesichorus are, first, the presence of syncopation and, second, introduction of iono-choriambic through trochaic modulation. The first is probably one of the modifications of inherited poetic technique which music was to make increasingly possible during the archaic and classical periods, just as, at an earlier period, it had facilitated the introduction of a more varied stanzaic structure based on epiploke (above, 130–43). The effect of the second is to create a partial assimilation of the eight-quantity prosodiac cycle and the four-quantity iambo-trochaic one (above, 63–65). Unlike Anacreontic aeolic and iono-choriambic, which develop tetradic or pure octadic rhythms at the expense of the mixture of tetradic and octadic or heptadic

---

[176] Modulation into iambo-trochaic only in 27/372 ($\times\times- \cup\cup- \cup-\|\times$ E) and perhaps 100/445 (see preceding note). Choriambic modulation into iono-choriambic appears in 31/376 ($\times\times- \cup\cup- \cup-|\times\times- \cup\cup-- \cup\cup-- \cup\cup- \cup-\times$), 30/375 and 29/374 (if emended by, e.g., Barnes's εἰκοσίχορδον and Hartung's μαγάδην into $\times\times- \cup\cup- \cup-|\times\times- \cup\cup--$ . . .). There is no trace of the iambic modulation between aeolic and iono-choriambic found in Pindar (text, 159) and Bacchylides 2, 6 (Table VIII, n. 2), and fr. 20a (below, n. 211).

[177] The Sapphic or pseudo-Sapphic *PMG* 976 (δέδυκε μὲν ἁ σελάνα) is the only possible example of an entire Lesbian stanza composed in eight-quantity cola: $\times- \cup\cup- \cup-\times$ repeated four times.

forms found in the Lesbians, prosodiac preserves the inherited mixture of types. But it introduces a modification which serves to underline the commensurability of the two ingredients in the mixture. The commensurability, it should be noted, may involve more than prosodiac sequences of the form – ◡ ◡ – ◡ ◡ –. The longer – ◡ ◡ – ◡ ◡ – ◡ ◡ –, in which the dactylo-anapestic affinities of prosodiac come to the fore, is also used in such a way as to suggest that it is related to the sequence – ◡ ◡ – ◡ ◡ – – ◡ – in the same way as – ◡ ◡ – ◡ ◡ – is to its occasional equivalent – ◡ ◡ – – ◡ – (above, 64). In both instances extension of – ◡ ◡ – (felt as a segment of prosodiac or dactylo-anapestic) into ‾‾D‾‾◡◡–◡◡‾ is equated with a passage from – ◡ ◡ – (felt as ionochoriambic) into iambo-trochaic via trochaic modulation (– ◡ ◡ – – ◡ –) —as if the two procedures were interchangeable sequels to – ◡ ◡ – in mixed prosodiac, whether it was preceded by – ◡ – ×, – ◡ ◡ – ◡ ◡ – × or – ◡ ◡. The parallel between sequences with and without antecedent – ◡ ◡ is suggested by a comparison of, e.g., the beginning and end of the triad in Pind. *P1*. The shorter – ◡ ◡ – – ◡ – occurs in both passages and in contexts identical except for the fact that one contains the longer – ◡ ◡ – ◡ ◡ – – ◡ – as well, the other the corresponding – ◡ ◡ – ◡ ◡ – ◡ ◡ – in which extension rather than modulation occurs. The separate triads of the poem are thus bound together more closely by the way each one after the first begins with an echo of its predecessor:

Σικελία τ' αὐτοῦ πιέζει   ⏑⏑–×–◡–×                                      s7

– ◡ – × – ◡ – × – ◡ ◡ ‾‾D‾‾‖◡◡–×–|[178] ◡ ◡ –⏑⏑◡–×–◡–× +

στέρνα λαχνάεντα· κίων δ' οὐρανία συνέχει

νιφόεσσ'' Αἴτνα | πανέτης χίονος ὀξείας τιθήνα,

– ◡ – × – ◡ – × – ◡ ◡ – ◡ ◡ – ‖ – ◡ – × – |   ◡ ◡ – – ◡ – × Ḍ ×–
τᾶς ἐρεύγονται μὲν ἀπλάτου πυρὸς ἀγνόταται                           e1

ἐκ μυχῶν παγαί·                                                      2

πόταμοι δ' ἀμέραισιν μὲν προχέοντι ρόον κάπνου[179]

ll. 19–22

---

[178] The demarcation and its counterpart in the epode is present everywhere except at the transition between the second and third triads, where it occurs one quantity later in both stanzas (lines 40 and 42). Cf. on such epode/strophe echoes, West 67.

[179] There may be similar echoes between *P4e4–5* and 6–7:

4–5:   – ◡ ◡ – × – ◡ – × – ◡ – ×‾‾D‾‾◡◡–◡◡◡ – ‖ × – ◡ ◡ ‾‾D‾‾◡◡◡ – ◡ ◡ – × – ◡ – ×

6–7:            – ◡ – × – ◡ – × – ◡ ◡ – ‖ – ◡ – × – ◡ ◡ – ◡ ◡ – ‖ – ◡ – × – ◡ – ×

and between the close of strophe and epoke in *I3–4*:

Parallels between general structure and internal demarcation in the four lines of *N*1e point to the existence of the same correspondence:

$$-\cup-x-\cup-x-\cup\cup\overline{-\cup\cup-}|\overline{-\cup-}$$
$$-\cup\overline{-\cup\cup}\overline{-}\overset{D}{\cup}\overline{-|\cup\cup-}|x-\cup-x-\cup-$$
$$-\cup-x-\cup\overset{D}{\cup}\overline{-\cup\cup-\cup\cup-}x-\cup-x-\cup-$$
$$x-\cup-.\qquad\overline{-\cup\cup--\cup-}\quad x-\cup-$$

and in *N*8e the opening of 6 is similar enough to that of 2–3 and 5 to suggest that all three be analyzed as containing the same trochaic modulation and so as leading steadily, through progressively shorter segments of dactylo-anapestic or prosodiac succeeded by this modulation, to the uniform iambo-trochaic of 7:

2–3:  $-\cup-x-\cup\cup-\cup\cup-\|\overline{\cup\cup--\cup}-x$ D $x-\cup-$

5:  $-\cup-x \qquad -\cup\cup\overline{-\cup\cup-}\ \overline{-\cup-}$

6:  $-\cup-x \qquad \overline{-\cup\cup-}\ \overline{-\cup-}x$ D $x$

7:  $-\cup-x \qquad -\cup-x \qquad -\cup-x-\cup-x|$ E[180]

Most strikingly, perhaps, $-\cup\cup-\cup\cup-|\cup\cup-x-\cup-x-\cup-x$ at the end of the fourth epode in Bacchylides 5:

*καί νιν ἀμειβόμενος τάδ' ἔφα· θνατοῖσι μὴ φῦναι φέριστον* (159–60)

responds to $-\cup\cup-\cup\cup-|-\cup-x-\cup-x-\cup-x$ in the other epodes, just as $x-\cup\cup-\cup\cup-x-\cup-x$ in the epode beginnings that immediately precede (151) and follow:

*Βοιωτὸς ἀνὴρ τάδε φών[ησέν* $\cup-x$    (191)

responds to $x-\cup\cup--\cup-x-\cup-x$ elsewhere:

---

str.:    $-\cup-x-\cup-\ x-\cup\cup\overline{-\cup}\overset{D}{\cup}\overline{-\cup\cup}-.-\cup-x\|-\cup-x-\cup-x-\cup-x$

ep.:    $-\cup-x-\cup-x-\cup-\|x-\cup\cup-\cup\cup--\cup-x-\cup-|x-\cup-x-\cup-x-\cup-$

[180] The longest dactylo-anapestic sequence in the series can be regarded as generated by a similar modulation from an even longer one found in the strophe:

str. 3–4:  $-\cup-x-\cup-x-\cup-x-\cup\cup--\cup\cup\overline{-}\overset{D}{\|}\overline{\cup\cup-\cup\cup-}x-\cup-.$D $x$

ep. 2–3:  $-\cup-x-\cup\cup-\ \cup\cup-\|\cup\cup--\cup-$ x D $x-\cup-$

ep. 4 and 5 (beginning)  x–⏑⏑‾ᴰ‾–⏑⏑‾–x–⏑–x;

ep. 1–3 (beginning)  x–⏑⏑‾‾–‾⏑‾–x–⏑–x;

ep. 4 (end)  –⏑⏑‾‾ᴰ‾⏑‾–|⏑⏑‾–x–⏑–x–⏑–;

ep. 1–3, 5 (end)  –⏑⏑‾–⏑⏑‾–|‾⏑⏑‾–x–⏑–x–⏑–

The Bacchylidean example is unique—unless A. *PV* 533–35 = 542–44 is taken in this way rather than as D.|–⏑–... = D.|⏑⏑–... (above, Table IV)—and even in Pindar such modulation, with the iono-choriambic interpretation of the –⏑⏑– in –⏑⏑–⏑⏑– which it involves, is sporadic at best.[181] But the tetradic affinities of prosodiac, particularly in Pindar, are quite clear; and the rhythm as Pindar uses it is linked to the sort of composition that prevails in Anacreon in one important additional way. Whatever its frequency in the prosodiac of Stesichorus may have been (above, 135, with n. 154), continuous composition is the rule in Pindar. This is a natural inference from the extreme rarity of the sequences ..._⏑ᴰ⏑_x ‖ x_ᴰ⏑_... anywhere except at the break between stanzas and triads, a rarity as striking as that of ...–⏑⏑–‾‖xx–⏑⏑–⏑–... and ...–⏑⏑–⏑–‖–⏑–... in Lesbian (above, 130). Similarly, ‖⏑⏑–(⏑⏑–)... is almost always preceded by (–⏑⏑)–⏑⏑–‖, of which it is presumably an extension, part of the same prosodiac or dactylo-anapestic movement.[182] In the few instances where discontinuity does occur, there are reasons for believing that it marks a demarcation that is meant to be more prominent than the others in the stanza. At *P*1s1–3 the lyre begins the musical performance, the dance hearkens to it, and poets follow its lead, in a line that is appropriately set apart from what precedes by rhythmical break, the unusual syncopation –⏑̆– (above, 143, with n. 173) and the unusual demarcation x–|:

τᾶς ἀκούει μὲν βάσις ἀγλαΐας ἀρχά.    ...–⏑–x D x– +

πείθονται δ' ἀοιδοὶ σάμασιν    –.–.–⏑–x–⏑–‖xD x–⏑–.–⏑–xD

ἀγησιχόρων ὁπόταν προοιμίων ἀμβολὰς τεύχῃς ἐλελιζομένα

---

[181] –⏑⏑–⏑⏑––⏑– is, however, somewhat more frequent than one would expect if syncopation (D .–⏑–) were involved in every instance. D .–⏑– exactly parallels –⏑–.D and could be expected to appear roughly as often—not three times as often, as it in fact does (12 occurrences within lines in Pindar as against 4 for –⏑–.D; see the listings in Snell's edition, 2.165–67). One explanation for the discrepancy is that –⏑⏑–⏑⏑––⏑– is sometimes the non-syncopated –⏑⏑–⏑⏑––⏑– and so not analogous to –⏑–.D.

[182] Cf. West 73. At *P*3e8–9 the disjunction may isolate a clausular ‖⏑⏑–⏑⏑–... (–⏑–xD x–⏑–x + ^D xE), but syncopation is also a possibility: x–⏑–.–‖⏑⏑–⏑⏑– x–⏑–x–⏑–. ‖⏑– on its one occurrence (*O*6s6) is fairly clearly a continuation of the Dx– with which the preceding sequence ends (...Dx–‖⏑–...); cf. Snell 54.

In *I*1e a rhythmically disjunct line (16) isolates the beginning of the Castor and Iolaus song:

ἀνία τ' ἀλλοτρίαις οὐ χερσὶ νωμάσαντ' ἐθέλω      D  ×−∪−×−∪∪− +

ἢ Καστορείῳ ἢ 'Ιολάοι' ἐναρμόξαι νιν ὕμνῳ.        ×−∪−×−∪∪−−∪−×−∪−× +

κεῖνοι γὰρ ἡρώων διφρηλάται Λακεδαίμονι καὶ Θήβαις ἐτέκνωθεν κράτιστοι    ×E×D×E×

and the song ends at the same point in the second triad.[183] At *P*9s1−2 the first occurrence of the repeated ∪∪−×D×. . . is isolated as an initial fanfare:

ἐθέλω χαλκάσπιδα Πυθιονίκαν                    ∪∪−×D×|E×− +
    σὺν βαθυζώνοισιν ἀγγέλλων
Τελεσικράτη Χαρίτεσσι γεγωνεῖν                 ∪∪−×D×|D×D×
    ὄλβιον ἄνδρα διωξίππου στεφάνωμα Κυράνας

Only the disjunction at *N*8e4−5 (×−∪−×−∪−×− + −∪−×. . .) occurs for no apparent reason.[184]

The rhythm . . ._ D _ ‖ _ D _. . . is frequent and may indicate rhythmical break. But it is also found within lines and cola, where it is probably the result of syncopation; and there is no need to give it a different explanation when it appears elsewhere. When found accompanied by prosodic demarcation in a context which does not otherwise show syncopation (e.g., *P*9e), it may be a way of setting off line from line more sharply, but not to the point of breaking rhythmic continuity.

Bacchylidean practice is rather different, showing discontinuity at approximately one out of every seven internal prosodic demarcations. About half the examples appear in poem 11, however, whose strophe is a series of disjunct lines built around a central ×D⏓'−∪−:

×D×−∪−×−∪−×      +

---

[183] The line occurs at comparable if less pronounced junctures in the third and fourth triads, marking the return (50) from a gnomic passage to talk of victory and introducing (67) the gnomic generalization with which the whole poem ends.

[184] More formal considerations seem at work in *Hymn* 1, where the disjunction ×‖× is twice linked to breaks in the prevailing alternation of iambo-trochaic and prosodiac nuclei (. . .−∪− × D × −∪− . . .), and perhaps in *O*6s4 as well, where it marks off a chiastically constructed opening tetrad (cf. Korzeniewski 148). In the latter poem, however, ×‖× is accompanied by thematic transitions at 5, 12, 33, 68, 75, 89; and the formal bipartition it creates may have something to do with the often noted double focus of the ode: on Syracuse and Arcadia, Hagesias as victor and Hagesias as seer, Pindar's own Boeotian heritage and his non-Boeotian theme.

$$
\begin{aligned}
&\times\text{D} \, . - \cup - \times - \cup - \times \quad && + \\
&\text{D} \mid \times\text{D} \, . - \cup - \times - \cup\,\cup - \quad && + \\
&\times\text{D}\ \times\text{D}\ \times - \cup - \times \quad && + \\
&\times\text{D}\times\text{D}\times\text{D}\ \times - \cup - \times \quad && + \\
&\times\text{D}\ \times - \cup - \times - \cup - \times
\end{aligned}
$$

(echoed, perhaps, at the beginning of the epode: $\times$D$\mid\times$D$\mid\times-\cup-\times$ + D$\times$D$.-\cup-\times-\cup-\times$ + $\times$D$\times-\cup-\times-\cup-$...). Elsewhere discontinuity isolates the initial salutation in 5s ($\times$D$.-\cup-\times-\cup-\times$ + $\times$D$\times$D$\times$ $-\cup-$),[185] reinforces the parallel structure of the two opening movements in 13s:

$$
\begin{aligned}
&\times\text{D}\times \quad -\cup-\times\mid\text{D}\times-\cup-\times \quad -\cup-\times \; + \\
&\times\text{D}\times\Vert \quad -\cup-\times-\cup-\times\text{D}\ \times \quad -\cup-
\end{aligned}
$$

and separates the two parts of 14s:

$$
\begin{aligned}
&-\cup-\times\text{D}\times-\cup-\times\Vert-\cup-\times-\cup-\times-\cup-\times \; + \\
&\times\text{D}\times-\cup-\times-\cup-\times \quad -\cup-\times-\cup-
\end{aligned}
$$

At 10s2–3 the emphatic repetition of the sequence $\mid\times-\cup-\times-\cup-\times(-\cup-\times)\mid$ which discontinuity creates may have been suggested by the content: the athlete's competition in two events in succession:

$-\cup-]\ οὔροισιν ἐπὶ σταδίου \qquad\qquad -\cup-\times\text{D}\Vert\times-\cup-\times-\cup-\times \; +$

$θερμὰν ἔτι πνέων ἄελλαν$

$ἔστα,\ [βρέχω]ν\ δ'\ ἄιξε\ θατήρων\ ἐλαίῳ \qquad \times-\cup-\times-\cup-\times-\cup-\times \; \Vert$

$φάρε'\ [ἐς -\cup\cup]\ ἐμπίτνων\ ὅμιλον \qquad\qquad \text{D}\ \ \times-\cup-\times$

Bacchylides' more frequent use of disjunction is perhaps to be linked to the character of his stanzaic structures—simple enough that rhythmical break is likely to reinforce their basic articulation rather than interfere

---

[185] The final line of 10s is similarly set off from what precedes, as well as 8.10 ($\times-\cup-\times$D$\times$ between $\times-\cup-\times$D$\times$ and $\times-\cup-\times$D...), which interrupts the summary of the athlete's achievements with an address to Zeus. The two stanzas which mix prosodiac with aeolic are, like Pindar's aeolic odes (text, 156–61) composed in a series of disjunct movements: $\times-\cup-\times-\cup-\cup-^{-}$ + $\times$D$\cup-^{-}$ + $\times-\cup\cup-\cup\cup-\cup-$ $\times-\cup-\times-\cup\cup-\cup-\times$ (3s) and $\times$E$\times\mid$D$\mid\times$D$\times\mid$E$^{\wedge}$ + $\times$D$\times$D$\mid\times$E$^{\wedge}$ + $\overline{\times\text{D}}-\cup\cup-\times-\cup-\times-\cup-^{-}$ + $\times-\cup\cup-\cup-\times-\cup\cup-\cup-\times-\cup-$ + $\times$D$\times-\cup-\times-\cup-$ + ?$\mid$E$^{\wedge}$ + $\times-\cup\cup-\cup-\times\mid$ $-\times-\cup^{-}$ (?) + $-\cup-\cup\cup-\cup-\cup-$ (19s).

with their being heard as rhythmical wholes—perhaps to his preference for long passages of straight narrative, where the influence of the epic manner, with its series of disjunct stichoi, might favor composition in independent sequences of roughly the same length and structure. The latter possibility is strengthened by the existence of a similar contrast between the Pindaric and Bacchylidean manner in mixed bacchio-cretic (above, 13 and 115–16). Break in the bacchio-cretic epiploke in which O2 and Bacchylides 17 are composed is indicated by clausular modulation into prosodiac ×– ◡ ◡ – or ×– ◡ ◡ – ◡ ◡ –×– ◡ – ◡ –, by juxtaposition of base quantities (– ◡ – –|×– ◡ – or – ◡ –×|×– ◡ –) and by the sequence . . .– ◡ –|x̄ – ◡ – (successions of three long syllables being virtually excluded from all passages in the two poems which are shown by the presence of verbal synapheia to be continuous specimens of the rhythm).[186] Both strophe and epode of Baccylides' poem are divided by such breaks into five to eight movements, corresponding for the most part to the articulation of the narrative into its major stages. Thus the first strophe contains the setting of the scene for the ensuing action on the human (1) and divine (2) level, Minos's lust (3: κνίσεν τε . . .), his act (4: θίγεν δέ . . .), Theseus's reaction (5–6: ἴδεν δέ . . . καρδίαν τε . . . ἄμυξεν ἄλγος) and rebuke (7–8: εἶρέν τε . . .):

1) ̈◡–◡––◡–◡––◡̈◡–◡–×–◡–◡––◡–◡–|–◡–×̈◡–[187]

κυανόπρῳρα μὲν ναῦς μενέκτυπον Θησέα δὶς ἑπτά τ’ἀγλαοὺς ἄγουσα κούρους Ἰαόνων
Κρητικὸν τάμνε πέλαγος,

2) ×–◡̈×–◡̈––◡––◡––◡–|×–◡̈×̈◡––

τηλαυγέι γὰρ ἐν φάρεϊ Βορήιαι πίτνον αὖραι κλυτᾶς
ἕκατι πελεμαιγίδος ’Αθάνας

---

[186] See Maas 56a, where a similar prohibition against groupings of more than three shorts is also pointed out. The prohibitions do not exclude internal x̄, but require that it always appear (except, possibly, at O2.10) in the sequences ̈x̄– and –x̄̈. The groupings of long and short syllables may reflect an effort to preserve, in mixed bacchio-cretic, the same syllable combinations found in a pure bacchio-cretic ancestor, where triple longs would not arise and the consecutive resolutions which produce sequences of more than three shorts would have been avoided.

[187] – ◡ –×– ◡ – may respond to a pure bacchio-cretic – ◡ – – ◡ – in the second strophe at this point (cf. the parallel equivalence found occasionally between pure and mixed ionochoriambic sequences, and, for other instances in the transmitted text of this poem, Fuehrer 177ff.). Here, however, analysis is complicated by further divergences from the – ◡ –×– ◡ – pattern in the second antistrophe (see Appendix II).

3) x‒ ∪ ‒ ‒ ∪˘˘‒ ∪ ‒ x‒ ∪ ‒ | ‒ ∪ ∪ ‒ x‒ ∪ ‒ x‒ ∪ ∪ ‒ ∪ ∪ ‒ | x‒ ∪ ‒ ∪ ‒ [188]

κνίσεν τε Μίνωϊ κέαρ ἱμεράμπυκος θεᾶς

      Κύπριδος ἀγνὰ δῶρα, χεῖρα δ' οὐκέτι παρθενικᾶς ἄτερθ' ἐράτυεν

4) x‒ ∪ ‒ ‒ ∪ ‒ x‒ ∪ ‒˘˘ ∪ ‒ x‒ ∪ ‒ ‒ ∪ ‒

θίγεν δὲ λευκᾶν παρηΐδων· βόασέ τ' Ἐρίβοια χαλκοθώρακα Πανδίονος

5) ‒ ∪˘˘‒ ∪ ‒ ‒ ∪ ‒ x‒ ∪ ‒

ἔκγονον, ἴδεν δὲ Θησεύς, μέλαν δ' ὑπ' ὀφρύων

6) x‒ ∪ ‒ ∪ ‒ x‒ ∪ ‒ ‒ ∪˘˘‒ ∪ ‒ ‾

δίνασεν ὄμμα, καρδίαν τε οἱ σχέτλιον ἄμυξεν ἄλγος

7) x‒ ∪˘˘‒ ∪ ‒ ∪ ‒

εἶρέν τε· Διὸς υἱὲ φερτάτου

8) ˘˘∪ ‒˘˘∪ ‒ x‒ ∪ ‒ ‒ ∪ ‒ | ‒ ∪ ‒ ∪˘˘‒ ∪ ‒ ‒ ∪ ‒ [189]

ὅσιον οὐκέτι τεᾶν ἔσω κυβερνᾷς φρενῶν θυμόν, ἴσχε μεγαλοῦχον ἦρως βίαν.

In the epode of the first triad there is the immediate sequel to Theseus's speech (1) and (2–5) the reply to it: the invocation of Zeus (2) Minos's divine birth and a request for a confirming sign (3: [εἴπερ με νύμφα] ... τέκεν ... νῦν πρόπεμπ'), Theseus's divine birth and the requested confirming sign (4: [εἰ δὲ καί σε Τροιζηνία] ... φύτευσεν Αἴθρα ... ἔνεγκε κόσμον) and a concluding invitation to wait for the first of these signs (5: εἴσεαι δ' αἴκ' ἐμᾶς κλύῃ Κρόνιος ...)

1) x‒ ∪˘˘‒ ∪ ‒ ‒ | ∪ ‒ x‒ ∪ ‒ | ‒ ∪˘˘‒ ∪ ‒ | ‒ ∪ ‒ x‒ ∪ ‒ ‒ ∪ ‒ ∪ ‒ ‾

τόσ' εἶπεν ἀρέραιχμος ἥρως·

  τάφον δὲ ναυβάται

  φωτὸς ὑπεράφανον

  θάρσος· ἁλίου τε γάμβρῳ χόλωσεν ἦτορ

2) x‒ ∪˘˘‒ ∪ ‒ | ‒ ∪ ‒ ‒ ∪˘˘‒ ∪ ‒ | ‒ ∪˘˘‒ ∪ ‒ ‒ ∪ ‒ ‾

ὕφαινέ τε ποταινίαν

  μῆτιν, εἶπέν τε· μεγαλοσθενὲς

  Ζεῦ πάτερ, ἄκουσον· εἴπερ με νύμφα

---

[188] For the unusual series of free responses sometimes posited at this point, as well as for other divergences from the metrical scheme printed which are not mentioned in the notes, see Appendix II.

[189] Initial x̄‒ ∪ ‒, marking the beginning of a new period, appears in the second antistrophe (118). On the responsion, see above, n. 187 and Appendix II.

3) ×-ᴗ--ᴗ--ᴗ-‖-ᴗ-×-ᴗ-|×-ᴗ˘˘-ᴗ-ᴗ--ᴗ--ᴗ|-×-ᴗ--ᴗ-   190

Φοίνισσα λευκώλενός σοι τέκεν
    νῦν πρόπεμπ᾽ ἀπ᾽ οὐρανοῦ
    θοὰν πυριέθειραν ἀστραπάν, σᾶμ᾽ ἀρίγνωτον·
    εἰ δὲ καί σε Τροιζηνία

4) ×-ᴗ˘˘-ᴗ--ᴗ--ᴗ-×-ᴗ-‖-ᴗ-ᴗ˘˘-ᴗ-×-ᴗ--ᴗ-|×-ᴗ--ᴗ-×-ᴗ-

σεισίχθονι φύτευσεν Αἴθρα Ποσειδᾶνι τόνδε χρύσεον
    χειρὸς ἀγλαὸν ἔνεγκε κόσμον ἐκ βαθείας ἁλός,
    δίκων θράσει σῶμα πατρὸς ἐς δόμους.

5) -ᴗ--ᴗ-ᴗ-˘˘ᴗ--|ᴗ-ᴗ--ᴗ--ᴗ-

εἴσεαι δ᾽ αἴκ᾽ ἐμᾶς κλύῃ Κρόνιος εὐχᾶς
    ἀναξιβρέντας ὁ πάντων μεδέων

Divergences from "normal" period length (7 to 10 bacchio-cretic cycles) and from the prevailing harmony of rhythmic and syntactic structure only appear as the narrative reaches its highpoints of intensity or excitement (cf. s5–7 and e3–4 above, and the corresponding sections of the other stanzas: Theseus's reiterated command to Minos (ll. 39–42), leap into the sea (81–85), awe-struck view of the Nereids (101–8) and final, triumphant return (120–29).

In the second Olympian, by contrast, the segments isolated by rhythmical break are neither so numerous or so like each other as to create even such a partial analogy to stichic structure. In the strophe a succession of two equal dicola, followed by a longer tricolon and final monocolon, serves to set off the third member of the tetrad (the one in which Theron is introduced) as more important than the surrounding ones:

ἀναξιφόρμιγγες ὕμνοι          ×-ᴗ--ᴗ--‖ᴗ˘˘-ᴗ--ᴗ˘˘  -ᴗ˘˘-ᴗ-
    τίνα θεόν, τίν᾽ ἥρωα τίνα δ᾽ ἄνδρα κελαδήσομεν;

                              ×-ᴗ--ᴗ˘˘-ᴗ˘˘×-ᴗ--ᴗ-‖ -ᴗ-˘˘ᴗ-
ἤτοι Πίσα μεν Διός, Ὀλυμπιάδα δ᾽ ἔστασεν Ἡρακλέης
    ἀκρόθινα πολέμου

Θήρωνα δὲ τετραορίας ἔνεκα νικαφόρου    ×-ᴗ˘˘  -ᴗ-˘˘ᴗ--ᴗ-‖

---

190 Here, and in the next section, a new period should perhaps begin with the prosodic demarcation after the first colon, as it was assumed to do at s5. The analysis in the text is, however, supported by the close parallel between the rhythms of (3) and (4):

3) ×-ᴗ--ᴗ--ᴗ-‖-ᴗ-×-ᴗ-|×-ᴗ˘˘  -ᴗ-ᴗ--ᴗ-    -ᴗ|-×-ᴗ--ᴗ-
4) ×-ᴗ˘˘-ᴗ--ᴗ- -ᴗ-×-ᴗ-‖-ᴗ-ᴗ˘˘ -ᴗ-×-ᴗ--ᴗ-|  ×-ᴗ- -ᴗ-×-ᴗ-

γεγωνητέον ὅπι δίκαιον ξένων          ∪ –   – ∪‸‸– ∪ – – ∪ –
ἔρεισμ᾽ Ἀκράγαντος          ∪ –   – ∪ – –
εὐωνύμων τε πατέρων ἄωτον ὀρθόπολιν          × – ∪ – ∪‸‸– ∪ –     × – ∪ ∪ –

In the epode even rhythmic break before the final dicolon does not prevent it from functioning with the preceding monocolon as a slightly shortened version of the opening tricolon:

× – ∪ – – ∪ – – ∪ – ‖ – ∪ – × – ∪‸‸– ∪ – – ∪ – – ‖ ∪‸‸× – ∪ – × – ∪‸‸× – ∪ –

λοιπῷ γένει· τῶν δὲ πεπραγμένων
ἐν δίκᾳ τε καὶ παρὰ δίκαν ἀποίητον οὐδ᾽ ἂν
χρόνος ὁ πάντων πατὴρ δύναιτο θέμεν ἔργων τέλος.

× – ∪ – – ∪ – ×‸‸∪ – – +

λάθα δὲ πότμῳ σὺν εὐδαίμονι γένοιτ᾽ ἄν·

× – ∪‸‸– ∪ – – ∪ – – ‖ ∪ – × – ∪ – ×

ἐσλῶν γὰρ ὑπὸ χαρμάτων πῆμα θνῄσκει
παλίγκοτον δαμασθέν

One major break thus divides the stanza in approximately the same proportion as Pindar's contrary thoughts on retribution and release, inevitability and hope (παρὰ δίκαν ἀποίητον οὐδ᾽ ἂν χρόνος ... λάθα δὲ πότμῳ σὺν εὐδαίμονι ...) divide the entire poem.

The mixed bacchio-cretic of Pindar and Bacchylides may stand in somewhat the same historical relationship to the catalectic cretic hexameters used stichically by Alcman (58) as do the dactylo-anapestic sequences of Stesichorus to the epic hexameter (above, 135). The internal movement of a disjunct stichos has been made the basis for a series of longer and more varied lengths which continue to be combined with each other in the same way as were the original hexameters. Pindar uses a more developed version of the rhythm, in which stanzaic movement more nearly approximates the continuity found in his prosodiac.[191]

A similar process of evolution may lie behind the one remaining group of late archaic rhythms to be considered, the aeolic stanzas of Pindar. These stanzas occupy an unusual position in the versification of the period (above, 145), but foreshadowings of their technique appear earlier, in at least two of the three Ibycean stanzas whose structure survives complete.

---

[191] Mixed bacchio-cretic, along with the occasional pentadic cycles found in Pindar and Bacchylides, as well as modulations into prosodiac, appears already in Simonides (36/541; see B. Gentili, *Maia* 16 [1964] 302–3; West, *ZPE* 37 [1980] 142–43), who may have been the immediate model for both poets. The one surviving fragment does not, however, allow conclusions as to Simonidean stanzaic structure.

All three show initial repetition of a dactylic or aeolic sequence followed by an "epodic" element in which this sequence is expanded. Composition may be continuous in the $-\cup\cup-\cup\cup-\cup\cup-\cup\cup|-\cup\cup-\cup\cup-$ $\cup\cup-\cup\times|-\cup\cup-\cup\cup-|\cup\cup-\underset{A}{\underline{\cup\cup}}-\cup-\times$ of 1/282s, but is almost certainly disjunct in 5/286.1–7 and 1/282e:

$$\cup\cup-\cup\cup-\cup\cup-\overline{\cup\cup}$$
$$-\cup\cup-\underset{A}{\underline{\cup\cup}}-\cup-\ +\qquad\qquad \cup\cup-\cup\cup-\cup\cup-\overline{\cup\cup}\ +$$
$$-\cup\cup-\cup\cup-\cup-\ +\qquad\qquad \cup\cup-\cup\cup-\cup\cup-\overline{\cup\cup}\ +$$
$$-\cup\cup-\cup\cup-\cup-\ +\qquad \times\times-\ \cup\cup-\cup\cup-\underset{A}{\underline{\cup\upsilon}}-^{-}\ +$$
$$-\cup\cup-\cup\cup-\cup\cup-\cup\cup\qquad\qquad\qquad -\cup\cup-^{-}|\underset{A}{\underline{\cup\upsilon}}-\cup-$$
$$-\cup\cup-\cup\cup-\cup\cup-\cup\cup$$
$$-\cup\cup-\cup\cup-\cup\cup-\cup\cup|-\cup\cup-\underset{A}{\underline{\cup\upsilon}}-\cup-\times\ (5/286.1-7)^{192}\qquad\qquad (1/282e)$$

(In the second example, the epodic element is the fourth line, which incorporates the repeated dactylo-anapestic movement that precedes into an aeolic $\times\times-\cup\cup-\cup\cup-\underset{A}{\underline{\cup\upsilon}}-^{-}$. What follows is a kind of coda: iono-choriambic moving into aeolic, but so demarcated that its five initial quantities recall the closing $-\cup\cup-^{-}$ of the preceding four lines.) The "dactylo-aeolic" sequences which predominate here have analogues in Sappho, Alcaeus and Alcman, but there they are always (as in 1/282s) followed by the end of a stichic or stanzaic period. In the more clearly innovative of his stanzas, Ibycus seems to have combined a series of clausular rhythms so that they form the disjunct parts of a single whole. Continuity within the stanza ceases to exist and overall structure becomes the main unifying element, as in the ephymnion rhythm discussed above (131).

There are clear analogues in several Pindaric stanzas, though the dactylo-aeolic sequences are less uniform and may be introduced by iambo-trochaic (via either the iambic modulation $-\cup-\times\times-\underset{A}{\underline{\cup\cup}}-\cup-$ or the choriambic modulation $-\cup--\underset{A}{\underline{\cup\cup}}-\cup-$); cf. *Paean* 9s:

192 Verbal synapheia between two of the $-\cup\cup-\cup\cup-\cup-$ sequences and so, presumably, rhythmical continuity has been suggested by West (above, n. 65) in order to make lines 8ff. of the fragment respond to 1ff. as the beginning of an antistrophe. But verbal synapheia between two instances of the sequence $-\cup\cup-\cup\cup-\cup-$ is not elsewhere attested in Greek poetry. For the rhythm of 1/282s see Appendix I.

ἀκτὶς ἀελίου τί πολύσκοπε μήσεαι      × × – ◡ ◡ – ◡ ◡ – ◡ ◡ – ◡ –

ὦ μᾶτερ ὀμμάτων, ἄστρον ὑπέρτατον      × – ◡ – × ×    – ◡ ◡ – ◡ –

ἐν ἀμέρᾳ κλεπτόμενον; <τί δ'>ἔθηκας ἀμάχανον   × – ◡ –    – ◡ ◡ – ◡ ◡ – ◡ ◡ – ◡ –

ἰσχὺν ἀνδράσι καὶ σοφίας ὁδόν,      × ×    – ◡ ◡ – ◡ ◡ – ◡ –

ἐπίσκοπον ἀτραπὸν ἐσσυμένα;      ◡ – ◡ ◡ – ◡ ◡ – ◡ ◡ –¹⁹³

ἐλαύνεις τί νεώτερον ἢ πάρος;      × ×    – ◡ ◡ – ◡ ◡ – ◡ –

ἀλλά σε πρὸς Διός, ἱπποσόα θοάς      – ◡ ◡ – ◡ ◡ – ◡ ◡ – ◡ –

ἱκετεύω ἀπήμονα,      ◡ ◡ – ◡ ◡ – ◡ –

εἰς ὄλβον τινὰ τράποιο Θήβαις      – – – ◡ ◡ ◡ – ◡ –

ὦ πότνια πάγκοινον τέρας.      ×    – ◡ ◡ – ◡◡ – ◡ –

The scansion of the last two lines is uncertain, but the clausular effect of the epodic variation on the prevailing pattern which they contain is clear.

Lines may begin or end in dactylo-anapestic in these pieces of Pindaric aeolic, and the most characteristic form of modulation from dactylo-anapestic to another metre is via the sequence ◡ – into bacchio-cretic (pure or mixed):

dactylo-anapestic
————————————
. . . ◡ ◡ – ◡ ◡ – ◡ ◡ – ◡ ◡ – (◡̆) ◡ – – ◡ –. . .
                       bacchio-cretic¹⁹⁴

Frequency of resolution at the point indicated suggests that the transitional segment was not simply ◡ –, but ◡ – ◡̆ ◡̆, heard both as a dactylo-anapestic ◡ – (◡◡) and a bacchio-cretic ◡ – (◡̆).¹⁹⁵ The rhythm's most extensive use within a single poem is in O10, where it is heard at the opening of the strophe:

---

¹⁹³ Initial ◡̆ is ambiguous. The short syllable may supply either the second quantity of a dactylo-anapestic ◡ ◡ or one quantity in an aeolic base.

¹⁹⁴ Cf. O5s2 and e2, O14s9, P2s3 (text, 163), N6s (text, 167) and e (Appendix III, B3), Pae9e1, Parth1e1–2 and s3, Pae4e1, fr. 169s (Appendix III, A2), and Pae6s8 (Appendix III, C).

¹⁹⁵ Less likely to be . . . – ◡ ◡ ◡̄ – ◡ ◡ –. – ◡ –, given the absence, except in the doubtfully authentic O5e1, of any unambiguous Pindaric example of the unsyncopated counterpart (D × – ◡ –). Both sequences were characteristic of dactylo-epitritic and so, perhaps, excluded from the poet's compositions in octadic aeolic (see text, 96). Similar considerations may explain why the triple longs characteristic of dactylo-epitritic are avoided in the mixed bacchio-cretic sequences found in aeolic stanzas, just as they are in the mixed bacchio-cretic of O2 and Bacchylides 17 (text, 152 with n. 186).

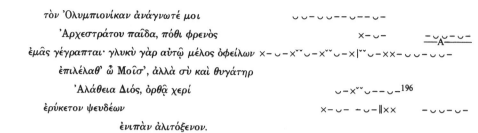

τὸν Ὀλυμπιονίκαν ἀνάγνωτέ μοι          ⏑⏑−⏑⏑−−⏑−−⏑−

Ἀρχεστράτου παῖδα, πόθι φρενὸς          ×−⏑−          −⏑⏑⏑−⏑−

ἐμᾶς γέγραπται· γλυκὺ γὰρ αὐτῷ μέλος ὀφείλων ×−⏑−×⏑−×⏑−×|⏑−×−×⏑−−⏑⏑−⏑⏑−

ἐπιλέλαθ᾽ ὦ Μοῖσ᾽, ἀλλὰ σὺ καὶ θυγάτηρ

Ἀλάθεια Διός, ὀρθᾷ χερί          ⏑−×⏑−−⏑−196

ἐρύκετον ψευδέων          ×−⏑−  −⏑−‖××    −⏑⏑−⏑−

ἐνιπὰν ἀλιτόξενον.

and throughout the more complicated epode, with its repeated transitions from dactylo-anapestic or aeolic into bacchio-cretic and then back to aeolic:

$$
\begin{array}{ll}
××−×\overline{\text{B}}⏑⏑−|⏑⏑−\,⏑−\,‖××−⏑⏑−⏑⏑− & 1 \\
\quad\quad (⏑⏑)−\,⏑−\,⏑−\quad −⏑⏑−⏑−^{197} & 2 \\
\overline{\text{B}} \quad ×−⏑⏑−−⏑⏑−\,⏑−×|× \quad −⏑⏑−⏑−^{198} & 3 \\
\quad\quad ×−⏑−⏑−^{199} & 4 \\
\quad\quad ⏑⏑−⏑⏑− & 5 \\
\quad\quad ×−⏑⏑−⏑⏑−⏑⏑−⏑− & 6 \\
\overline{\text{B}} \quad ×−⏑⏑−⏑⏑−|⏑−  ××−⏑⏑− & 7
\end{array}
$$

Lines 4–6 contain analogues to the three rhythmical elements of 1–3 and 7 (dactylo-anapestic, bacchio-cretic and aeolic), but separately and in a different order. Taken together they constitute a pre-terminal variation which, in conjunction with the return (in 7) to the prevailing pattern, gives a loose epodic structure to the whole stanza.[200] The pattern of 1–3 and 7 is sufficiently uniform to suggest that the prosodic demarcation within 1 (and perhaps the similarly located one before the final ××−

[196] The close is ambiguous, perhaps a cretic −⏑−, perhaps an echo of the opening of the aeolic ××−⏑⏑−⏑⏑− that has just preceded.

[197] Perhaps identical in its first ten quantities to the penultimate −−−⏑⏑⏑−⏑−− of Pae9s (text, 157).

[198] Iono-choriambic appears in the initial section of the line at the point where the others show dactylo-anapestic; for similar linkings of the two rhythms in aeolic contexts, see Appendix III, B.

[199] On this sequence, presumably an iambo-trochaic counterpart to bacchio-cretic −⏑−⏑−, see text, 115. It is confined to the beginning or end of periods, followed by −⏑− at O14s10 and I8s12, by transition to aeolic at P11e5 (text, 165) and Pae2s1, and by further iambo-trochaic at O13s3–4.

[200] Cf., in Bacch. 16s7–12 (below, Appendix III, B2), the two short penultimate sequences which contain separately the dactylic (or dactylo-aeolic) and iambo-trochaic that are combined in both the surrounding lines.

⏑ ⏑ – ⏑ – of the strophe) does not mark a rhythmical break. In general, however, prosodic demarcation in Pindar's dactylo-aeolic is accompanied by clear rhythmical break so often that demarcation itself involves some presumption in favor of discontinuity, even when a break is not evident in the actual sequence of quantities. The manner first seen in Ibycus has undergone much elaboration in detail, but it remains the same in essentials (see, for further examples, Appendix III, A).

A somewhat similar ancestry is traceable for the other type of sequence which, along with the heavily dactylic ones just considered, figures most prominently in Pindaric aeolic. The undemarcated alternation between double base and nucleus (with or without initial or concluding iambo-trochaic) that constitutes whole stanzas in Alcaeus and Sappho (× × – ⏑ ⏑ – ⏑ – × × – ⏑ ⏑ – ⏑ – × – ⏑ – in Z34/357, – ⏑ – × × – ⏑ ⏑ – ⏑ – × × – ⏑ ⏑ – ⏑ – × × – ⏑ ⏑ – ⏑ – ⏑ – ⁻ in 96; cf. B-1 and B-2 in Table VIII) [—A— under the last nucleus] reappears, with a variety of initial and terminal demarcations, as the basic repeated movement in the stanzas of Simonides' skolion on *aretē* (*PMG* 542):

| | |
|---|---|
| οὐδέ μοι ἐμμελέως τὸ Πιττάκειον νέμεται, | – ⏑ ⏑ – ⏑ ⏑ – ⏑ – × × – ⏑ ⏑ –<br>—A— –A^^— |
| | ⁻ × × – ⏑ ⏑ – ⏑ – × × – ⏑ ⏑ – ⏑ – × – ⏑ –<br>—A— |
| καίτοι σοφοῦ παρὰ φωτὸς εἰρημένον· χαλεπὸν φάτ' ἐσθλὸν ἔμμεναι. | |
| | ⏑ ⏑ – ⏑ – × × – ⏑ ⏑ – ⏑ – × × – ⏑ ⏑ – ⏑ –<br>—^A— |
| θεὸς ἂν μόνος τοῦτ' ἔχοι γέρας, ἄνδρα δ' οὐκ ἔστι μὴ οὐ κακὸν ἔμμεναι | |
| ὃν ἀμήχανος συμφορὰ καθέλῃ. . . | ⏑ ⏑ – ⏑ – × × – ⏑ ⏑ –<br>—^A— –A^^ |
| πάντας δ' ἐπαίνημι καὶ φιλέω, ἑκὼν ὅστις ἔρδῃ | ⏑⏑ – ⏑ – × × – ⏑ ⏑ – ⏑ – × × – ⁻ |
| | (or × – ⏑ – × × – ⏑ ⏑ – + ⏑ – – ⏑ – ⁻)<br>–A^^— |
| μηδὲν αἰσχρόν· ἀνάγκᾳ δ' οὐδὲ θεοὶ μάχονται | – × – ⏑ ⏑ – × \| E^<br>—B— |

The basic pattern is varied at the end, creating the same roughly epodic structure observable in Pindar's dactylo-aeolic.

More regular analogues to Simonides' stanza appear in Bacchylides (Appendix III, D), less regular ones in Pindar. Pindaric variations include admixtures of heptadic aeolic (above, 85); modulations to and from dactylo-anapestic, iono-choriambic, iambo-trochaic or mixed bacchio-cretic; and occasional excursions into hexadic rhythm (above, 87). All of these procedures, attested sporadically elsewhere, are sometimes found alongside a more peculiarly Pindaric use of what seems to be dyadic rhythm: alternating longs and shorts leading into or away from an aeolic nucleus with initial – ⏑ or terminal ⏑ –, and distinguished from iambo-trochaic by the absence of long anceps or other indications of the presence of tetradic rhythm:

φύονται δὲ καὶ νέοις ἐν ἀνδράσιν πολιαί

θαμάκι παρὰ τὸν ἀλικίας ἐοικότα χρόνον

— O4e8-9

Here subdivision of the alternating sequences would be arbitrary and would obscure the way they expand a normal ‿‿‿‿‿‿ into equivalent lengths of twelve quantities each. (Cf., for further instances, O1s6-7 and e3 [below, 151-52], P2s1, 5-6 and 8 [below, 162-63]).

When dyadic rhythm is present, the sequence − ‿ − ‿ ‿ − ‿ − can be taken as an extension of either − ‿ ‿ − ‿ − or − ‿ − ‿ ‿ −:

Καφισίων ὑδάτων λαχοῖσαν αἴτε ναίετε καλλίπωλον ἕδραν       1

ὦ λιπαρᾶς ἀοίδιμοι βασίλειαι       2

·Χάριτες Ἐρχομενοῦ παλαιγόνων Μινυᾶν ἐπίσκοποι,       3

κλῦτ' ἐπεὶ εὔχομαι, σὺν γὰρ ὕμμιν τά τε τερπνὰ καὶ       4

τὰ γλυκέ' ἄνεται πάντα βροτοῖς       5

O14s[201]

Here the movement of the first line suggests both the "A" rhythm of 2 and the "B" rhythm of 3, and the former does not establish itself as basic to the stanza until the contrasting section that begins in 4 (prayer is succeeded by justification for prayer at this point in both strophe and antistrophe, with σὺν γάρ responding to Λυ]δῷ γάρ).

At P8s5 − ‿ − ‿ ‿ − ‿ − both recalls the "A" and "B" rhythms that have preceded:

φιλόφρον Ἡσυχία Δίκας       1

ὦ μεγιστόπολι θύγατερ       2

βουλᾶν τε καὶ πολέμων       3

ἔχοισα κλαῖδας ὑπερτάτας,       4

Πυθιόνικον τιμὰν Ἀριστομένει δέκευ.       5

τὺ γὰρ τὸ μαλθακὸν ἔρξαι τε καὶ παθεῖν ὁμῶς

ἐπίστασαι καιρῷ σὺν ἀτρεκεῖ

and looks forward to the extended piece of dyadic alternation that appears, after an interlude of almost regular octadic movement, at the close of the

---

[201] Pae6e may be similar, with dactylo-anapestic expansions; see Appendix IIIC.

epode:

| | | |
|---|---|---|
| βία δὲ καὶ μεγάλαυχον ἔσφαλεν ἐν χρόνῳ. | ⏓–⏓–⏑⏑–⏓⏓–⏑–⏑‾ | e1 |
| Τυφὼς Κίλιξ ἑκατόγκρανος οὔ νιν ἄλυξεν | ⏓–⏓–⏑⏑–⏓⏓–⏑⏑–‾ | 2 |
| οὐδὲ μὰν βασιλεὺς Γιγάντων· δμᾶθεν δὲ κεραυνῷ | ⏓⏓–⏑⏑–⏑–⏓⏓–⏑⏑–‾ | 3 |
| τόξοισι τ᾽ Ἀπόλλωνος ὃς εὐμενεῖ νόῳ | ⏓–⏑⏑––⏑⏑–⏑–⏑– | 4 |
| Ξενάρκειον ἔδεκτο Κίρραθεν ἐστεφανωμένον | ⏓⏓–⏑⏑–⏑–⏓⏓–⏑⏑–⏑– | 5 |
| υἱὸν ποίᾳ Παρνασσίδι Δωριεῖ τε κώμῳ | ‾⏓⏓–⏓–⏑⏑–⏑–⏑–‾ | 6 |

Utilization of all the possible variants in this sort of composition would obviously create rhythmical chaos. Often, however, a single pattern dominates (e.g., that which emerges in *P*8s6 and prevails throughout the epode, or the even more conspicuous ones in *O*9s, *N*2, *N*4 and *I*7s [see Appendix III, D]). The lines of the stanza—almost always disjunct—form a set of variations on a single rhythmical theme—both in the poems under consideration now and in the less numerous dactylo-aeolic ones examined earlier. As variations become more elaborate—sometimes to the point of obscuring the theme under a layer of ornamentation—and as contrasting motifs are introduced in greater profusion, the rhythm acquires a flexibility and range that has no parallel in any of the lyric forms considered thus far. The sharpest contrast is with the sustained evenness and equilibrium imparted to Pindar's own dactylo-epitritic by continuous internal rhythm, frequent demarcation at intervals of 8, 12 or 16 quantities, and use of cyclical patterns fewer in number and, for the most part, commensurate with each other. The contrast is, I believe, reflected in the subjects treated in the epinicians; and the desire for a more versatile, expressive rhythmical instrument may have contributed to the development of the striking idiosyncracies which Pindaric aeolic displays.

In dactylo-epitritic the poet distances himself more consistently from the complexities of his subject—in the direction of general festive exuberance, for example, or sustained development of a single theme or narrative. Aeolic, on the other hand, is characterized by immediacy, tension, variety and contrast. Of the four Hieron odes, the two in aeolic are the ones that have most impressed readers for the brilliance of their images of power and violence (*O*1) or the obscurity of what is often taken for local and topical reference (*P*2). Dactylo-epitritic, on the other hand, is reserved for the ceremonial splendors of *P*1 and the studied consolation of *P*3. It is difficult to conceive a dactylo-epitritic rendering of the opening of *O*1, with its striking initial juxtapositions, its abrupt expansion of focus to embrace the sun of Olympic contests, and—at the end—the turn to the picture of poets celebrating at the court of Hieron:

ἄριστον μὲν ὕδωρ ὁ δὲ χρυσὸς αἰθόμενον πῦρ          ⅩⅩ‒∪∪‒∪‒ⅩⅩ‒∪∪‒¯   1

ἄτε διαπρέπει νυκτὶ μεγάνορος ἔξοχα πλούτου.     ∪¨‒∪‒ ‒∪∪‒∪∪   ‒∪∪‒¯   2
                                                                                        ──Ａ──
εἰ δ' ἄεθλα γαρύειν                                              ⅩⅩ‒∪‒∪¯   3
                                                                                ──Ｂ──
ἔλδεαι, φίλον ἦτορ,                                              ⅩⅩ‒∪∪‒∪¯   4
                                                                                ──Ａ──
μηκέθ' ἀλίου σκόπει                                              ⅩⅩ‒∪∪‒∪¯   5
                                                                                ──Ｂ──
ἄλλο θαλπνότερον ἐν ἁμέρᾳ φαεννὸν ἄστρον ἐρήμας δι' αἰθέρος

                          ‒∪‒∪¨∪‒∪‒∪‒∪∪∪∪‒ⅩⅩ‒∪¯   6
                                                      ──Ｂ──
μηδ' Ὀλυμπίας ἀγῶνα φέρτερον αὐδάσομεν.     ‒∪‒∪‒ ∪‒∪∪∪‒ⅩⅩ‒   7
                                                                                      ──Ｂ──
ὅθεν ὁ πολύφατος ὕμνος ἀμφιβάλλεται

                          Ⅹ¨∪¨Ⅹ‒∪‒Ⅹ‒∪‒   8

σοφῶν μητίεσσι κελαδεῖν                                  ∪‒ ‒∪‒¨∪‒   9

Κρόνου παῖδ' ἐς ἀφνεὰν ἱκομένους             ∪‒‒∪‒∪‒¨∪‒   10

μάκαιραν Ἱέρωνος ἑστίαν.                             Ⅹ‒∪¨‒∪‒∪‒   11

Aeolic (1‒2), bacchio-cretic (2, with perhaps a hint at the start of 1) and dactylo-anapestic (3) cluster together in the opening lines, mirroring the cluster of images; then they sort themselves out into aeolic (cresting in the dyadically expanded 6‒7) followed (9‒11) by bacchio-cretic. The iambo-trochaic of 8, with its single longs and single shorts in alternation, strikes a transitional balance between the single longs and double and single shorts of the preceding aeolic and the single shorts and double and single longs of the following bacchio-cretic.

After these pyrotechnics some sort of regularization and steadying seems to have been required, and so in the epode the contrasts of the strophe have largely disappeared. Dactylo-anapestic is eliminated; the one dyadic sequence is sharply curtailed; and the bacchio-cretic and aeolic which, after a brief hint in s1‒2, appeared separately, now combine to provide a basic repeated pattern: bacchio-cretic of varying lengths (Ⅹ‒ ∪‒‒∪‒, ∪‒‒∪‒, ∪‒) leading into ‒∪∪‒∪‒, ‒Ⅹ‒∪∪‒ or ──Ａ──   ──Ｂ── ‒∪∪‒, followed by an aeolic clausular sequence: Ⅹ‒∪∪‒¯, ‒∪∪‒ ∪‒¯ or a shortened version of ⅩⅩ‒Ⅹ‒∪∪‒∪‒.[202]

Συρακόσιον ἱπποχάρμαν βασιλῆα· λάμπει δὲ οἱ κλέος   Ⅹ‒∪¨‒∪‒‒∪∪‒∪‒ⅩⅩ‒∪¯   1
                                                                                                ──Ａ──
ἐν εὐάνορι Λυδοῦ Πέλοπος ἀποικίᾳ                         ∪‒‒∪∪‒  ⅩⅩ¨∪‒∪¯   2
                                                                                            ──Ｂ──
τοῦ μεγασθενὴς ἐράσσατο Γαιάοχος             ‒∪‒∪‒∪∪∪‒ⅩⅩ‒   3

Ποσειδάν, ἐπεί νιν καθαροῦ λέβητος ἔξελε Κλωθώ,   ∪‒‒∪‒‒∪∪‒∪‒Ⅹ ‒∪∪‒¯   4
                                                                                                  ──Ａ──
ἐλέφαντι φαίδιμον ὦμον κεκαδμένον.             ∪∪[203]‒Ⅹ‒∪∪‒ⅩⅩ‒∪¯   5
                                                                                   ──Ａ──

[202] For similar parallels between the orderings of rhythmical types within the individual lines of a stanza, see Appendix III, E.

ἢ θαυματὰ πολλὰ καὶ πού τι καὶ βροτῶν        ‾ – ∪ ‿ – ∪ – ××– ∪ ‾        6

φάτιν ὑπὲρ τὸν ἀληθῆ λόγον        ∪‾‾– ∪ ∪ –    ××–        7

δεδαιδαλμένοι ψεύδεσι ποικίλοις ἐξαπατῶντι μῦθοι        ∪ – – ∪ – – ∪ ‿ – ∪ – – ∪ ∪ – ∪ – ‾        8

In *P*2s two inner sections (3–4 and 5–6) dominated by, respectively, dactylo-aeolic and dyadic expansion, are framed by the more varied combinations of dyadic rhythm with normal aeolic sequences that open and close the stanza:

μεγαλοπόλιες ὦ Συράκοσαι βαθυπολέμου

   ‾‾ ∪ ‾‾ ∪ – ∪ – ∪ – ∪‾‾ ∪ – 204        1

τέμενος Ἄρεος ἀνδρῶν ἵππων τε σιδαροχαρμᾶν δαιμόνιαι τροφοί,

   ‾‾ ∪ – ∪ ∪ –××– ∪ ∪ – ∪ –×– ∪ ∪ – ∪ –        2

ὕμμιν τόδε τᾶν λιπαρᾶν ἀπὸ Θηβᾶν φέρων

   ‿‾ ∪ – ∪ ∪ – ∪ ∪ – ∪ ∪ – – ∪ –        3

μέλος ἔρχομαι ἀγγελίαν τετραορίας ἐλελίχθονος

   ∪ ∪ – ∪ ∪ – ∪ ∪ –        ×– ∪ ∪ – ∪ ∪ – ∪ –        4

εὐάρματος Ἱέρων ἐν ᾇ κρατέων

   ×– ∪‾‾ ∪ – ‿ – ∪ ∪ –        5

τηλαυγέσιν ἀνέδησεν Ὀρτυγίαν στεφάνοις

   ×– ∪‾‾ ∪ – ∪ ‾ ∪ ∪ – ∪ ∪ –        6

ποταμίας ἔδος Ἀρτέμιδας ᾆς οὐκ ἄτερ

   ‾‾ ∪ – ∪ ∪ – ‾‾ ∪ – – ∪ –        7

κείνας ἀγαναῖσιν ἐν χερσὶ ποικιλανίους ἐδάμασσε πώλους

   ×– ∪ ∪ ‿ – ∪ – – ∪ – ∪ – ‿ ‾‾ ∪ ∪ – ∪ – ‾        8

Syracuse as nurse of men and horses (1–2), the Theban poet's mission (3–4) Hieron's victory (5–6) and then (7–8) Syracuse once again (cf. the recall of τέμενός Ἄρεός ἀν- in ποταμίας ἔδος Ἀρ-) together with Artemis's patronage of horsemanship, are four different aspects of the theme which the rhythm seeks to differentiate rather than unify.

---

203 Initial ∪ ∪ and, in the following line, initial ‾ are ambiguous: perhaps felt as the final quantities (‾‾ or –) of the introductory bacchio-cretic that elsewhere appears as ×– ∪ – – ∪ –, ∪ – – ∪ – or ∪ –. ∪ ∪ –×– ∪ ∪ – is equally difficult at *O*4s1: ∪ ∪ –×– ∪ ∪ – – ∪ ∪ – ∪ ∪ –⊻⊼– ∪ – ‾: perhaps the final seven quantities of the (–)×– ∪ ∪ – –×– ∪ ∪ – that opens s7 and s8–9 in the same poem.

204 Perhaps felt as dyadic rhythm leading into the first three quantities of – ∪ ‾ ∪ ∪ – (appearing here, just as they do in 2 and 7, in the resolved form ‾‾ ∪ –).

Thematic unity does come later, as three of the four triads end by criticizing the ungrateful man who withholds praise in the face of merits such as Hieron's. But this unity only emerges indirectly, by way of parable, or through implicit association of the vice of ingratitude with the contrary one of adulation. The octadic aeolic in which the triads culminate (. . . – ∪ – ∪ ∪ – ∪ – × × – ∪ ∪ – ∪ – ×) emerges in like fashion, after a pair of curtailed approximations (≃∪ – ∪ ∪ – ∪ – – ∪ – and × × – ∪ ∪ – ∪ – – ∪ – in e5–6) and through unification of the . . .– ∪ – ∪ ∪ – and ∪ –. . . . which have been separated, through most of the stanza, by disjunction (or, if the rhythm of e1–4 and 8–9 is continuous, prosodic demarcation (. . . – ∪ ≃ ∪ ∪ – ‖ ∪ –. . . .):

ἱερέα κτίλον 'Αφοδίτας· ἄγει δὲ χάρις    (or                              )    e1

φίλων ποίνιμος ἀντὶ ἔργων ὀπιζομένα·                                         2

σὲ δ', ὦ Δεινομένειε παῖ, Ζεφυρία πρὸ δόμων
                                                                            3

Λοκρὶς παρθένος ἀπύει, πολεμίων καμάτων ἐξ ἀμαχάνων
                                                                            4

διὰ τεὰν δύναμιν δρακεῖσ' ἀσφαλές.
                                                                            5

θεῶν δ'ἐφετμαῖς 'Ιξίονα φαντὶ ταῦτα βροτοῖς
                                                                            6

λέγειν ἐν πτερόεντι τροχῷ                                                     7

παντᾷ κυλινδόμενον·                                                          8

τὸν εὐεργέταν ἀγαναῖς ἀμοιβαῖς ἐποιχομένους τίνεσθαι
                                                                            9

(Initial ‾ in 8, like initial ∪ – in 2–4 and 9 is probably ambiguous: either an aeolic base or the close of a nucleus; and the whole pattern is varied by what seems to be a digression into tetradic rhythm in 7).[205] Hieron's less

[205] The resulting mixture of hexadic (– ∪ ∪ – ∪ – – ∪ – ∪ ∪ –  – × ≃ ∪ ‾), octadic and tetradic forms is a less orderly version of the progressively lengthening cycles of N7e:

formidable fellow dynast is hymned in dactylo-epitritic (*O3*) or the even more regular bacchio-cretic (*O2*—probably the most striking instance of an ode devoted exclusively to the development of a single theme). The Aiginetan odes use dactylo-epitritic when they concentrate on the whole history of the Aeacids (*N8*) or the first two generations of the family (*O8, N5, I6*) or recent achievement (*I5*). Aeolic is for the ultimately tragic careers of Ajax, Achilles and Neoptolemus (*I8, N3, N7*), or, passing to another royal house, Clytemnestra:

νηλὴς γυνά· πότερόν νιν ἄρ’ Ἰφιγένει’ ἐπ’ Εὐρίπῳ
$$\times - \underbrace{\smile - \smile \smile}_{B} - \smile \smile - \smile \underbrace{\smile}_{A} - \smile - -$$  il

σφαχθεῖσα τῆλε πάτρας
$$\times - \underbrace{\smile}_{B} - \smile \smile -$$  2

ἔκνισεν βαρυπάλαμον ὄρσαι χόλον;  $$- \underbrace{\smile - \smile \smile}_{B} \underbrace{\smile}_{A} - $$  $$- \smile -$$  3

ἢ ἑτέρῳ λέχει δαμαζομέναν  $$- \smile - \times - \underbrace{\smile - \smile \smile}_{B} -$$  4

ἔννυχοι πάραγον κοῖται; τὸ δὲ νέαις ἀλόχοις
$$- \underbrace{\smile - \smile \smile}_{B} - \times \times$$  $$\underbrace{\smile - \smile \smile}_{B} - 5$$

ἔχθιστον ἀμπλάκιον καλύψαι τ’ἀμάχανον  $$\times - \underbrace{\smile \smile}_{B} - \smile -$$  $$- \underbrace{\smile}_{B^?} - 6$$

ἀλλοτρίαισι γλώσσαις·  $$- \smile \smile - \smile -$$  $$-$$  e1

κακολόγοι δὲ πολῖται.  $$\underbrace{\smile - \smile \smile}_{A} -$$  2

ἴσχει τε γὰρ ὄλβος οὐ μείονα φθόνον·  $$\underbrace{- \smile \smile - \smile}_{A} -$$  $$- \underbrace{\smile}_{B^?} - 3$$

ὁ δὲ χαμηλὰ πνέων ἄφαντον βρέμει.  $$\underbrace{\smile - \smile \smile}_{A} - \smile -$$  $$- \smile - 4$$

θάνεν μὲν αὐτὸς ἥρως Ἀτρεΐδας  $$\times - \smile - \smile - \times^{\smile} \smile -$$  5

ἵκων χρόνῳ κλειταῖς ἐν Ἀμύκλαις  $$\times - \smile - \times \underbrace{- \smile \smile}_{A} -$$  6

P11.22–32

Here all the lines except s1 and 5 and e6 can be analyzed as segments of the sequence $\times - \smile - \smile - \times - \underbrace{\smile \smile}_{B} \underbrace{\smile}_{A} \smile - - - \smile \underbrace{\smile}_{B} \smile -$ (and s1 may be such a segment with dactylo-anapestic expansion). The rhythm, with its avoidance of any of the aeolic norms of repetition is a suitable matrix from which to generate the story of enormity of a different sort. Shifting initial and terminal demarcation create sequences in which various regular patterns are hinted at but never (except in s5 and e6) actually present.

Aeolic is also the rhythm for poems in which Pindar is concerned to make apologies or amends, whether real or conventional (*N7, O10*); and in the poems for Arcesilas of Cyrene it is the rhythm for the present or the recent past: the tangle of chariots at Delphi out of which the driver Carrhotus emerged victorious, or the local sights along the route of the victory procession (*P5*). Dactylo-epitritic, on the other hand, recounts the remote tale of the Argonauts (*P4*), with its elaborate, larger-than-life paradigms for the reconciliation which the poem is to achieve or memorialize in Cyrene.

Athletic defeat is touched on fleetingly in dactylo-epitritic, in three rigidly parallel adjective-noun pairs:

> ἐν τέτρασιν παίδων ἀπεθήκατο γυίοις        x– ᵕ –xDx
>
> νόστον ἔχθιστον καὶ ἀτιμοτέραν γλῶσσαν καὶ ἐπίκρυφον οἶμον     – ᵕ –xD x  D   x
>
> O8.68–69

Aeolic develops the triad at greater length, allowing the hearer to savor first the sweetness of victory lost, then, in more insistent detail, as a more regular movement emerges (above, 160) the discomfiture of the defeated:

> τέτρασι δ'ἔμπετες ὑψόθεν                    ᵛᵛᵕ–ᵕ ᵕ–ᵕ–
>
> σωμάτεσσι κακὰ φρονέων                      –ᵕ–ᵕ ᵕᵛᵛᵕ–
>
> τοῖς οὔτε νόστος ὁμῶς                        x–ᵕ²̲ ̄ᴮ̲ ̲ᵕᵕ–
>
> ἔπαλπνος ἐν Πυθιάδι κρίθη.      x–ᵕ–       –ᵕᵕ–ᵕ–
>
> οὔτε μολόντων πὰρ ματέρ' ἀμφὶ γέλως γλυκὺς   –ᵕᵕ–x|x–ᵕ²̲ ̄ᴮ̲ ̲ ᴬ̲ –ᵕ–
>
> ὦρσεν χάριν· κατὰ λαύρας δ' ἐχθρῶν ἀπάοροι   x–x²̲ ̄ᴮ̲ ̲ᵕᵕ–x|x–ᵕ²̲ ̄ ̲ ̲ ̄ᴬ̲ ̲̂ –
>
> πτώσσοντι, συμφορᾷ δεδαγμένοι.    x–ᵕ–   x–ᵕ–ᵕ⁻
>
> P8.81–87

In similar fashion, the elaborate aeolic priamel of *O1* (above, 162) becomes in the dactylo-epitritic of *O3.42* a straightforward εἰ δ'ἀριστεύει μὲν ὕδωρ κτεάνων δὲ χρυσὸς αἰδοιέστατος (x– ᵕ –xD x– ᵕ –x– ᵕ –). Equally suggestive are the contrasts between *P2.83–85* and *I4.52* (on hurting one's enemies), *N7.77–79* and *N8.15* (the poem as an exotic necklace or headband) and *N6.7–11* and *N11.37–43* (human vicissitudes likened to the alternation of fertile and fallow in the life of a field). The first member of each pair is aeolic, the second dactylo-epitritic.

The brevity and insignificance of human life when seen against the context of divine eternity is a returning theme in the epinicians, but it is probably no accident that its most memorable statement comes at the opening of the aeolic *N6*, in a stanza which refers to man's origins (ἓν ἀνδρῶν [γένος]), capacities (ἢ μέγαν [νόον]) and destiny (ἄμμε πότμος) in disjunct or partially disjunct phrases so compressed that they seem hardly more than punctuations in the encompassing flow of dactylo-aeolic:

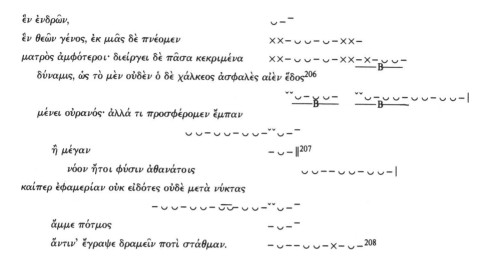

ἐν ἐνδρῶν,

ἐν θεῶν γένος, ἐκ μιᾶς δὲ πνέομεν

ματρὸς ἀμφότεροι· διείργει δὲ πᾶσα κεκριμένα

δύναμις, ὡς τὸ μὲν οὐδὲν ὁ δὲ χάλκεος ἀσφαλὲς αἰὲν ἕδος[206]

μένει οὐρανός· ἀλλά τι προσφέρομεν ἔμπαν

ἦ μέγαν

νόον ἤτοι φύσιν ἀθανάτοις

καίπερ ἐφαμερίαν οὐκ εἰδότες οὐδὲ μετὰ νύκτας

ἄμμε πότμος

ἄντιν' ἔγραψε δραμεῖν ποτὶ στάθμαν.

Even the simple crescendo used for the past glories of Thebes at the opening of *I.* 7:

τίνι τῶν πάρος, ὦ μάκαιρα Θήβα,

καλῶν ἐπιχωρίων μάλιστα θυμὸν τεὸν

εὔφρανας; ἦρα χαλκοκρότου πάρεδρον

Δαμάτερος ἀνίκ' εὐρυχαίταν

ἄντειλας Διόνυσον, ἦ χρυσῷ μεσονύκτιον νείφοντα δεξαμένα τὸν φέρτατον θεῶν;

is rather different in its effect from a series of lengthening lines in dactylo-epitritic. For there lines are less distinctly separated than in aeolic, hence less easily compared with each other as discrete wholes; and they tend to decompose themselves, regardless of length, into their lowest common denominator—the underlying approximation to a tetradic rhythm to which there is no counterpart in a mixture of heptadic and octadic aeolic forms—making the whole stanza not simply a succession of lines,

[206] For hexadic rhythm linked, as here, with bacchio-cretic and expansion into dactylo-aeolic, see Bacchylides 16e (Appendix III, B2).

[207] Either paeonic or iambo-trochaic, like the opening – ◡ – of the final lines, or perhaps heard with the following ◡ ◡ – as – ◡ – ‖ ◡ ◡ –, which would make the parallel with the earlier dactylo-aeolic even closer.

[208] Text and response in the final line are uncertain. The analysis suggested here requires no more emendation than other possibilities (× – ◡ ◡ – ◡ ◡ – × – ◡ – for example) and has the advantage of not introducing a unique example of the sequence . . . ◡ ◡ – ◡ ◡ – × – ◡ – (above, n. 195) into Pindaric aeolic. If it is right, χρυσαλακάτου in 36 and ἄμμορος in 14 must be emended (e.g., by Hermann's χρυσοπλοκάμου and ἄμορος).

but a continuous whole built up through the multiplication of such tetrads.

It is not possible—nor should one expect—to find a clear reason for choice of rhythm in every Pindaric epinician. We are obviously not dealing with a definite rhythmical ethos comparable to that possessed by the dochmiacs and (on occasion, at any rate) ionics of drama. What is involved seems to be, rather, a potentiality for certain kinds of effect of which the poet might or might not avail himself. There is an ethos to aeolic or dactylo-epitritic only to the extent that there can be said to be an ethos for the major or minor scale. Dactylo-epitritic is Pindar's epinician major, aeolic his epinician minor. That the different possibilities of the two forms—intimately linked to the different roles played by epiploke in stanza construction—could be utilized in many instances does not mean that they were used in all instances, or that there were not some poetic commissions where either rhythm would have done for Pindar's purpose. [209]

Of the two forms, aeolic strikes one as, by and large, the more "expressive." Yet it lacks certain resources available to the other: not simply a capacity for spun-out legato, but the ritards and emphases created by syncopation, and the sustained intensifying power of short, regularly recurring rhythmical cycles. Regularity and irregularity, continuity and disjunction, commensurability and non-commensurability of basic rhythmic patterns tend to appear separately in late archaic lyric, helping thereby to establish the identity of mutually exclusive genres. The full range of expressive possibilities which the techniques of the period contained was only brought into play in a different lyric context and for the radically different needs of Attic drama.

---

[209] A purely formal use of rhythmic contrast within the single genus of aeolic can be seen in *O*14s and *O*9e. In both stanzas return to heptadic aeolic rounds off the composition, after an intervening section in which dactylo-aeolic (*O*9e3–6) or a heterogeneous combination of bacchio-cretic, dactylo-anapestic and hexadic rhythms (*O*14s5–11) has been dominant.

# CHAPTER NINE: AESCHYLUS

Most of the recurrent features which distinguish the lyric versification of Aeschylus from that of his predecessors and contemporaries are those characteristic of dramatic lyric in general: anapestic systems (presumably part of the Doric heritage of tragedy, descended from the march rhythm [above, 117] first attested in Spartan *embatēria*), dochmiacs used in quasi-metric fashion rather than as isolated sequences in the midst of paeonic; long runs of iambo-trochaic with frequent syncopation of both anceps and short (the former attested moderately well, the latter very sparsely in non-dramatic lyric);[210] and polymetric stanzas composed of internally homogeneous passages in contrasting rhythms.[211] In one respect, however, Aeschylus is as unlike Sophocles and Euripides as he is unlike Pindar, Bacchylides and their predecessors. Disjunct composition, both in homo-geneous and polymetric contexts, is used to an unparalleled extent—so pervasively that only iono-choriambic among non-metric forms is largely free of its influence.[212] Its presence, in conjunction with a somewhat less strict counterpart to Anacreon's preference for recurring octadic cycles regularly demarcated (above, 146) is responsible for much of what is specifically Aeschylean in lyric versification.

Pindar provides a partial parallel here, for both authors are reluctant to use long sequences of pure aeolic. *Ag.* 717–19 = 727–29 (××– ∪ ∪– ∪–×|×– ∪ ∪– ∪–×|×– ∪ ∪– ‾) is the only such sequence in Aeschylean tragedy[213] to contain as many as three nuclei, and *I*7s5

---

[210] Principally in the iambo-trochaic lines or line beginnings which sporadically vary the pre-vailing pattern in Pindaric aeolic; cf. *P*5s11 (Appendix III, E2), *P*6s7 (×–.–×– ∪–×– ∪–) and *P*7e3 (×–.–.– ∪–×– ∪ ∪̲–̲ ∪–).

[211] Polymetry in archaic lyric normally takes the form of brief (usually clausular or pre-clausular) digressions into a contrasting pattern, or a consistent mixing of two or more types (iambo-trochaic and prosodiac; iambo-trochaic, aeolic and dactylo-anapestic, etc.) through the whole rhythmical fabric. For an atypical instance of composition in the manner common in drama, see Bacchylides fr. 20a:

∪ ∪–– ∪ ∪––– ∪ ∪–×– ∪–– ∪ ∪––– ∪ ∪–|××– ∪ ∪̲–̲ ∪–×– ∪–|
 ××– ∪ ∪– ∪–×× ∪ ∪– ∪–×– ∪–.

[212] Not entirely. Cf. the succession of disjunct sequence ending in – ∪ ∪– ∪– ‾ at *Ag.* 198–204 = 212–17, 768–71 = 776–81 and the passages cited in the text, 101–3.

[213] From satyr drama there is the ××– ∪ ∪– ∪–|××– ∪ ∪– ∪–|××– ∪ ∪– ∪– |××– ∪ ∪– ‾ of *Dictyulci* 806–9 ( = 815–18).

169

(above, 156) the only Pindaric example with as many as four. In Aeschylus, however, the restriction extends to other genres, and there are fewer corresponding restrictions on minimum length. Iambic or choriambic linking of aeolic into the same movement with tetradic rhythm is less frequent than in the other dramatists,[214] and there is a corresponding use, rare in the other dramatists,[215] of ionic . . .⏑⏑−−| or trochaic . . .−⏑−×| succeeded by a brief (usually clausular) piece of disjunct aeolic:

| | |
|---|---|
| ××−⏑⏑−¯ | *Pers.* 640 = 646 |
| ××−⏑⏑−⏑− | *Sept.* 321−23 = 333−35 |
| ××−⏑⏑−⏑−× | *Ch.* 330−31 = 361−62 |
| ××−⏑⏑−⏑−\|−⏑⏑−⏑−¯ | *Ag.* 695−97 = 713−15 |
| | *PV* 418−19 = 423−24 |
| ××−⏑⏑−⏑−××−⏑⏑−⏑− | *Pers.* 634−36 = 641−43 |

Even the briefest of these aeolic sequences appears on a number of occasions as a separate movement[216] and there are several parallel instances[217] of full or syncopated (×−⏑−)×−⏑−⏑−¯ as the main ingredient in

---

[214] Iambic modulation appears only at *Sept.* 328−29 = 340−41 (⏑⏑−−⏑⏑−|××−⏑⏑− ⏑−) and 754−55 = 761−62 (×−⏑−×−⏑−|××−⏑⏑−⏑−), *Suppl.* 90 = 95 (−⏑−×−.− ×|×−⏑⏑−⏑−×), 576−77 = 584−85 (×E|××−⏑⏑−¯) and 867−68 = 877−78 (××− ⏑⏑−⏑−‖⏑⏑−.⏑⏑−−), *Ch.* 52−53 = 64−65 (×−⏑−−⏑⏑−|××−⏑⏑−¯), 332−33 = 315−16 (−⏑⏑−⏑⏑−⏑−.|E ʾ), 324−26 = 354−56 (×−⏑−×−⏑−×−⏑−×|×−⏑⏑− ⏑−|××−⏑⏑−¯) and 345−46 = 363−64 (−⏑⏑−⏑−|××−⏑⏑−⏑−|×−.−.−⏑−⏑−¯) along with the *Agamemnon* passages cited in the text (163−64). Choriambic modulation is even rarer: *Sept.* 324−25 = 336−37 (×−⏑⏑−−⏑⏑−−⏑⏑‿−⏑−×) and *Suppl.* 60−63 = 65−68 and 165−67 (text, 88−89).

[215] Only at E. *Bac.* 902−6 (××−⏑⏑−⏑−×|Ex + ××−⏑⏑−⏑−×|Ex + ××−⏑⏑− ⏑−×) and, perhaps, *Ion* 1240−42 (⏑⏑−−⏑⏑−−|⏑⏑−−⏑⏑−− + ×× −×−⏑⏑−|××−⏑⏑−¯ if the transmitted text is correct).

[216] Cf., in addition to the ephymnion rhythm (text, 122) the six consecutive instances at *Sept.* 295−300 = 312−17, the shorter series at *Pers.* 1022−24 = 1034−36 and *Dictyulci* 802−3 and 809−11 ( = 812−13 and 818−20), and the single ××−⏑⏑−¯ (whether following ×−⏑−.−⏑−×, −⏑⏑−⏑−× or ××−⏑⏑−¯) at *Pers.* 557 = 567 *Ag.* 697 = 716 and *Suppl.* 558 = 567. *Suppl.* 659−62 = 670−73 might be an aeolic variant (−⏑⏑‿−⏑−× + −⏑⏑−⏑−× + −⏑⏑−×−⏑−|−⏑⏑−⏑⏑‿−⏑−×) on the ephymnion that immediately follows, but is more likely to have been heard in relation to the dochmiacs of the following stanza as do¯ + do¯ + −⏑⏑−−×−⏑−|−⏑⏑do¯ (cf., for the sequences involved, text, 100).

[217] E.g., *Suppl.* 590 = 595ff., 698 = 704ff., *Ag.* 192 = 205ff., 218 = 228ff., 367 = 385ff., and *Ch.* 434 = 439ff. The disjunct . . .−⏑−× + ×−⏑−. . . is, however, exceedingly rare, as everywhere in drama (see *LMGD* 75).

iambo-trochaic passages, or of (x)D ∪ −⁻ or xD ⩛'E ^ in prosodiac.[218]
Moreover, though long passages of continuous iambo-trochaic are well
attested, prosodiac, whether pure or mixed, is subject to restrictions on
maximum length almost as strict as those which operate in aeolic. *Suppl.*
49–51 = 39–43 (D .│D .│Ex−∪∪−−∪∪−∪∪−∪∪−⁻) and 72–76
= 82–85 (xE .│D −∪∪−.−∪∪−∪∪−.│E) are the only fairly certain
instances, outside the *PV*, of continuous mixed sequences with more than
one modulation; and though DD and D xD are well attested, they are
almost always demarcated—again with the exception of the *PV*—into
exactly responding D│xD, D│xD or D│D. (The − ⌣⌣D −│⌣⌣−∪∪│−
− ⌣⌣−∪∪−x of *Suppl.* 86–88 = 91–93 is anomalous enough to require
a different analysis, perhaps as a dactylo-anapestic − ⌣⌣−∪∪−∪∪−⌣⌣
+ ∪∪−∪∪ + ⌣⌣−⌣⌣−∪∪−⌣⌣). The regularity suggests that in at
least some of these passages demarcation coincides with rhythmical break.
At *Pers.* 568–75 = 576–83 the inference is virtually guaranteed by the
intervening exclamations and the assimilation (through transitional −−−
∪∪−⁻) of prosodiac −∪∪−∪∪−x to a disjunct aeolic xx−∪∪−⁻:

| | | |
|---|---|---|
| τοὶ δ' ἄρα πρωτομόροιο | −∪∪−∪∪−x | |
| φεῦ | D            x | *extra metrum* |
| ληφθέντες πρὸς ἀνάγκας | −−−∪∪−⁻ + | |
| ἠέ | xx A^ | *extra metrum* |
| ἀκτὰς ἀμφὶ Κυχρείας | −−−∪∪−⁻ | |
| ὀᾶ | | *extra metrum* |
| ἔρρανται· στένε καὶ δακνάζου | | |
| βαρὺ δ' ἀμβόασον | xx−∪∪−∪−−│∪∪−∪−⁻‖ + | |
| οὐράνι' ἄχη, | x⌣∪− | |
| ὀᾶ, | | *extra metrum* |
| τεῖνε δὲ δυσβάυκτον | −∪∪−∪−⁻²¹⁹ + | |
| βοᾶτιν τάλαιναν αὐδάν. | ∪−. −∪−∪−⁻ | |

---

[218] Cf., for the former, *Ag.* 1547–49 (−∪∪D∪−⁻ + −∪∪−∪−⁻ + x−. −. −∪−∪−⁻) and
the passages discussed in the text (172, 177–78); for the latter, *Sept.* 752 = 760, 756–57 =
764–65, 770–71 = 776–77 and 781–84 = 788–91 (D│−∪∪−x− + D│−∪∪−.−∪−.−⁻)│.
[219] Probably heard both as an echo of the earlier −│∪∪−∪−⁻ and as an anticipation of
the following catalectic sequence in iambo-trochaic. Cf. the closely parallel *Ch.* 466 = 471ff.
(above, 102–3).

The evidence is not always as consistent or conclusive as here.[220] *Suppl.*
524–26 = 531–33 is almost certainly a continuous ×–ᴗ––ᴗᴗ–
×D ×D ᴗ–⁻ (above, 58) and the mixture of the cola D and D × at *Ch.*
809–10 and *Eu.* 963–65 = 983–85 suggests similar analyses (respectively, D ×| D. | D ᴗ–⁻ and D .|D .|D ×|D ×). On the other hand, the
D |(D |)D |D ᴗ–⁻ of *Ag.* 1005–7 = 1022–24 and *Su.* 854–57 = 843–46
recalls with its simple epodic structure the ××–ᴗᴗ–⁻ + ××–ᴗᴗ–⁻
+ ××–ᴗᴗ–ᴗ–××–ᴗᴗ–⁻ cited earlier as a typical example of disjunct form at its simplest and clearest.

There is a similar uncertainty (cf. *LMGD* 44) with the –ᴗᴗ–...
–ᴗᴗ–ᴗᴗ–⁻|E ⁽^⁾ found at *Pers.* 881–888, 870 = 878, 881 = 890, *Ag.*
166 = 175, 1017 = 1034, and *Eu.* 366 and 388 = 396: either dactyloanapestic passing into prosodiac D ×|E ⁽^⁾[221] or an asynartete ...–ᴗᴗ–
ᴗᴗ–ᴗᴗ– �= + E ⁽^⁾.[222] The latter type of analysis is, however, the one
which best accounts for what was, for Aristophanes, at any rate, a quintessentially Aeschylean rhythm, the ×–ᴗ––|ᴗᴗ–ᴗᴗ–ᴗᴗ–⁻ parodied at *Ran.* 1264ff.:

Φθιῶτ' 'Αχιλλεῦ, τί ποτ' ἀνδροδαίκτον ἀκούων     ×–ᴗ–× + ᴗᴗ–ᴗᴗ–ᴗᴗ– ⏗⏗

The dicolon is a kind of "iambepos" (see Appendix IV) beginning with
what precedes the penthemimeral caesura in a trimeter and ending with
what follows the same caesura in the hexameter. As such it is a perfect
rhythmical emblem for the characteristically Aeschylean wedding of epic
grandeur to the *lektikon* of iambic, and a perfect counterpart to the Euripidean rhythm Aristophanes sets up against it: the same penthemimer
extended into a full trimeter by a phrase (ληκύθιον ἀπώλεσεν) in which

---

[220] Cf., in addition to the passages cited in the text, the stanza which immediately follows
the one quoted: D ×| D ×|D ×|D ×| ---ᴗᴗ–×|---ᴗᴗ–×|–ᴗᴗ–ᴗ–⁻ (584–90 =
591–97), where syntax and prosodic break after the second D × suggest the analysis D ×|D ×
+ D ×|D × + ⎺⎺D⎺ᴗᴗ–ˣ⎽ₓₓA^ + ××–ᴗᴗ–⁻ + ⎽–ᴗᴗ–ᴗ–⁻⎽A⎽, a repetition of the opening
four movements of the preceding stanza, but with doubling into (continuous D ×| D×) of
each of the first two and interruption of the fourth through loss of the central quantity in the
sequence ××–ᴗᴗ–ᴗ––|ᴗᴗ–ᴗ–⁻.

[221] Cf., for less ambiguous instances of this rhythm, *Pers.* 904–6 (–ᴗᴗ–ᴗᴗ–ᴗᴗ–
ᴗᴗ–ᴗᴗ– ⏗⏗| –ᴗᴗ–ᴗᴗ–|×E ^) 885 = 895 (–ᴗᴗ–ᴗᴗ–ᴗᴗ–ᴗᴗ–|ᴗᴗ–ᴗᴗ–
|ᴗᴗ–ᴗᴗ –⏗⏗⎽D⎽ᴗᴗ–, ×'E ^) and 856 = 862 (– ⏗⏗–ᴗᴗ–ᴗᴗ–ᴗᴗ–ᴗᴗ–|×E^ if one
scans ἰσόθεος.

[222] Clearly disjunct are *Ag.* 119–20 = 136–37 (–ᴗᴗ–ᴗᴗ–ᴗᴗ–ᴗᴗ–ᴗᴗ– ⏗⏗ +
×E), *Eum.* 370–71 = 379–80 (–ᴗᴗ–ᴗᴗ–ᴗᴗ–ᴗᴗ + –.–.–ᴗ–ᴗ–⁻) and *Pers.* 854
= 860 (...–ᴗᴗ–ᴗᴗ–ᴗᴗ–ᴗᴗ + –ᴗ–.–⁻ if one accepts a text that gives final –ᴗ–
––).

iambic's potential for the commonplace is fully realized.

Disjunct composition need not, of course, have been confined to passages composed of sequences which end in catalexis or appear rarely in verbal synapheia with each other. Without such indications, however, its presence can be hard to detect. Disjunct analysis is most plausible when, for the sake of terminal variation, a repeated pattern (e.g., the | E | of *Ag.* 1008–13 = 1025–30, or the | x – ⏑̣ – x̣ – ⏑ – x – ⏑ – | of *Su.* 776–78 = 784–86) is lengthened, shortened or replaced by a contrasting rhythm (– ⏑ ⏑ – ⏑ ⏑ – ⏑ ⏑ – ⏑ ⏑ – ⏑ ⏑ – ⏑ ⏑ – ⏑ ⏑ – ⏑̅⏑̅ + E in the first example, x Ė| x E | x – ⏑ – x – ⏑ – x – ⏑ – in the second).[223] Elsewhere it is better to speak of the principal parts or subdivisions of a stanza and dispense with the notations | and + which indicate continuous or disjunct composition.

The possibility that such subdivisions occur within a continuous piece of epiploke must, however, be reckoned with even when they are set apart from each other by modulation. *Ag.* 680ff. is the most striking example, with its transitions, in the first stanza, from iambo-trochaic to iono-choriambic (. . .E | – ⏑ ⏑ – x – ⏑ – . . . [685–86 = 704–5]); in the second, from prosodiac to iambo-trochaic to aeolic (D x |D x |D x ‖E x E ‖x x – ⏑ ⏑ – ⏑ – x x – ⏑ ⏑ – ¯); and, in the third, from iono-choriambic to aeolic to iono-choriambic to aeolic (– ⏑ ⏑ – x – ⏑ – | x x – ⏑ ⏑ – ⏑ – – | ⏑ ⏑ – – ⏑ ⏑ – – ⏑ ⏑ – x – ⏑ – – | ⏑ ⏑ – – ⏑ ⏑ – – | ⏑ ⏑ – – ⏑ ⏑ – x ‖x – x̱ – ⏑ ⏑ – | x x – ⏑ ⏑ – ¯). Prosodic demarcation accompanies some of the modulations and favors disjunct analysis. But the consistency with which, throughout the ode, continuous scansion is possible (only the openings of the second and third stanza pairs and the conclusions of the first and fourth[224] resist this analysis) may be more than coincidental. The subject is Helen and Paris, hybris and the children of hybris, and the way delight slips over insensibly into disaster. The fluidity of the rhythm and the smoothness of the modulations thus have their counterparts in the human events described:

---

[223] Cf. *Ch.* 546 = 461ff., and, perhaps, 66 = 71ff., where, however, corruption in the closing sequence makes analysis uncertain.

[224] Clausular – ⏑ ⏑ – ⏑ – ¯ echoing the end of a preceding movement which passes smoothly from syncopated to non-syncopated to resolved iambo-trochaic, and then, briefly, into ionic:

– ⏑ – . – ⏑ – . – ⏑ – . – ⏑ – . – ⏑ – x – ⏑ –
          x – ⏑ – x |⁓ ⏑ – x – ⏑ – x – ⏑ –
              x ⁓ ⏑ – x⁓ ⏑ – x
                  ⁓ ⏑ – x – ⏑ – –
                        ⏑ ⏑ – ⏑ – ¯

πάραντα δ'ἐλθεῖν ἐς 'Ιλίου πόλιν λέγοιμ' ἄν          ⏓–⏑–.–⏑–⏓–⏑–⏑–‾ +

φρόνημα μὲν νηνέμου γαλάνας                              ⏓–⏑–.        –⏑–⏑–‾ +

ἀκασκαῖον <δ'>ἄγαλμα πλούτου                            ⏓–.–.        –⏑–⏑–‾ +

μάλθακον ὀμμάτων βέλος                                         –⏑⏑–⏓–⏑–|

    δηξίθυμον ἔρωτος ἄνθος.                           ⏓⏓–⏑⏑–⏑––|²²⁵

παρακλίνασ' ἐπέκρανεν δὲ γάμου πικρὰς τελευτάς,

                       ⏑⏑––⏑⏑––⏑⏑–⏓–⏑––|

    δύσεδρος καὶ δυσόμιλος                                  ⏑⏑––⏑⏑––|

    συμένα Πριαμίδαισιν                                        ⏑⏑––⏑⏑–×‖

        πομπᾷ Διὸς ξενίου                                    ⏓–×⏟–⏑⏑–|
                                    B
        νυμφόκλαυτος 'Ερινύς.                                 ⏓×–⏑⏟–‾
                                    A

                            (737–49 = 750–62)

With disjunction and end of period after the fifth and eighth cola, the stanza would be dominated by the balance and contrast between the iambo-aeolic of its opening pentacolon and the iono-aeolic of its closing one. With the analysis suggested above, the structure is more dynamic: symmetry and balance only exist in the three disjunct sequences with which the initial calm is described, and the coda which should round off the triad unfolds unexpectedly and without any break into a long disaster roll.

If such passages are representative of a large number in which the possibility of epiploke exists, *Pers.* 634ff. is much less ambiguous. It provides strong grounds for believing that, on occasion at any rate, Aeschylus was capable of continuing and even developing the techniques of his predecessors in this mode of composition. The three stanza pairs which the ode contains share a common iono-choriambic core, to which different articulations are given:

1) –⏑⏑––⏑⏑––|

  ⏑⏑––⏑⏑–|×⁚⁚⏑–× + ⏓⏓–⏑⏑–⏑–××–⏑⏑–⏑– + ×⁚⁚⏑–.‖–⏑–×      + ⏓⏓–⏑⏑–‾

2) –⏑⏑––⏑⏑––|

  ⏑⏑–×–⏑––‖⏑⏑––                           ⏑⏑–.⏑⏑––|⏑⏑–×|D ⏑–‾

3) –⏑⏑–×–⏑––|

  ⏑⏑––⏑⏑––⏑⏑––|                               ⏑⏑–.–⏑––|⏑⏑–    ⏑–‾

The relationship between 2 and 3 is particularly close, involving practically identical colon structures and identical placing of syncopation. The first

---

²²⁵ The strong syntactic break (following the fifth colon) in both strophe and antistrophe can be paralleled elsewhere in the play within what are fairly generally assumed to be continuous movements: cf. 198 = 211 and 449 = 468.

stanza shows essentially the same rhythm, interrupted by aeolic (above, 170), without consistent ionic demarcation, and broken up, after the initial dicolon, into short units characterized by strong punctuation, resolution and an admixture of iambic demarcation. These units have a parallel in the penultimate ◡ ◡ – × of the second stanza, which consists of a single word ('Αιδωνεύς = θεομήστωρ) that repeats, following punctuation, the initial word of the preceding colon and is immediately followed by modulation into prosodiac. The third stanza begins and ends with a passage in contrasting rhythm (dochmiac or bacchio-cretic), but in its central section there are no brief, sharply demarcated sequences; internal demarcation is homogeneously ionic; and the iono-choriambic epiploke ends with its own catalexis ( ◡ – ¯ ) rather than clausular modulation. The ode becomes gradually more regular, integrating a smoothly flowing ionic epiploke out of the *disiecta membra* presented at the outset; and this transition corresponds to the changing mood of the singers. Prayer for the return of Darius is the recurrent theme throughout, but it is prayer mingled with lamentation and uncertainty in the first stanza:

ἦ ῥ' ἀίει μου μακαρίτας   – ◡ ◡ – – ◡ ◡ – – |
 ἰσοδαίμων βασιλεὺς   ◡ ◡ – – ◡ ◡ – |
βάρβαρα σαφηνῆ     x˘˘◡ – × +
ἰέντος τὰ παναίολ' αἰανῆ δύσθροα βάγματα; xx– ◡ ◡ – ◡ – xx– ◡ ◡ – ◡ – +
παντάλαν' ἄχη
διαβοάσω;       x˘˘◡ –. ‖≈◡ – × +
νέρθεν ἆρα κλύει μου;    xx– ◡ ◡ – ¯

In the second, prayer is fortified by evocation of the past glories of the monarch:

ἦ φίλος ἀνήρ, φίλος ὄχθος  – ◡ ◡ – – ◡ ◡ – –
φίλα γὰρ κέκευθεν ἤθη.  ◡ ◡ – × – ◡ – – ‖
'Αιδωνεὺς δ'ἀναπομπὸς ἀνείης, ◡ ◡ – – ◡ ◡ –. ◡ ◡ – – |
'Αιδωνεύς,      ◡ ◡ – × |
  οἷον ἀνάκτορα Δαριᾶνα   D ◡ – ¯
   ἠέ        *extra metrum*

In the third prayer is still more confident and insistent, a virtual heralding of the coming epiphany amid the destruction caused by Darius' successor:

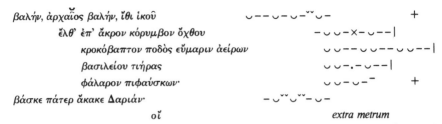

The epode shifts the rhythm to what seems to be a mixture of dactylo-anapestic and iambo-trochaic, though in the second line τί τάδε, δυνάστα, δυνάστα (675) there may be an echo (×˘˘∪−. ∪∪−⁻) of the ×˘˘∪−. ‖−∪−× of the first stanza.

The ode exhibits a more gradual and elaborate version of what is probably the single most common movement within Aeschylean stanzas: disjunct opening succeeded eventually by a more continuously sustained closing run; and the prevalence of the pattern may tell us something about the reasons for the extended use of rhythmical disjunction throughout Aeschylean lyric. Disjunct combination of sequences which contrast in length or rhythmic character is one obvious way of adapting the resources of Greek lyric to the needs of drama. Transition, reversals, a shifting succession of mood and emotions are more accurately reflected in such a mode of composition than they would be in a disjunct series of homogeneous lines or a composition which effected modulations without a rhythmical break. And a departure from this mode—in the direction of a more continuous, even rhythm whose formal properties are thereby revealed more clearly is one way of achieving a sense of finality at the end of the stanza. The poet distances himself emotionally from the action before ceasing to comment upon it.

Disjunct linking of similar sequences is, for different reasons, equally suited to the dramatist's purpose. The artistic considerations here are probably akin to those which helped to determine the rhythms developed specifically for drama or first extensively used there (above, 165). All of those involve, in various ways, a tightening and, on a certain level, regularization of lyric form. Dochmiac, anapestic and iambo-trochaic are composed of continuous repetition of a single, short rhythmical cycle to which dactylo-anapestic alone among forms used frequently in non-dramatic lyric offers a parallel. And as if to avoid the danger of monotony created by this regularization, certain types of variation are permitted on a hitherto unprecedented scale: resolution (dochmiac and anapest), contraction (anapest) and syncopation (iambo-trochaic). The variations, however, are all ones which it is possible (perhaps through the use of an increasingly versatile musical accompaniment) to introduce without affecting exact rhythmical equivalence.

The repeated disjunct units used by Aeschylus are rarely as short as single dochmiacs or anapestic metra; but they do produce a much more regular, insistent pattern than do recurrent cycles within a continuous rhythm capable of more than one type of articulation, or longer disjunct sequences such as those of Pindaric aeolic. The result is a capacity for intensification which, no less than contrast and variety, makes Aeschylean lyric a rich source of dramatic effect. The dramatic chorus tends to be directly involved in the mighty events of which it sings. The non-dramatic chorus, by contrast, has its immediate concerns circumscribed by place and present occasion, so that heroic action is seen at several removes, both spatially and temporally. It chronicles or celebrates what the dramatic chorus acts and suffers. The immersion in a given mood or situation required of the latter is more complete and overwhelming, and requires a corresponding concentration of rhythmical effect:

Ξέρξης μὲν ἄγαγεν,                         – .– × – ◡ –

   ποποῖ.                                  *extra metrum*

Ξέρξης δ᾽ἀπώλεσεν,                         – .– × – ◡ –

   τοτοῖ.                                  *extra metrum*

Ξέρξης δὲ πάντ᾽ ἐπέσπε δυσφρόνως           – .– × – ◡ – × – ◡ – . |

   βαρίδεσσι ποντίαις                      E

                                          — *Pers.* 550 – 54 = 560 – 64

The tight rhythmic grip in which its song is held is ultimately that of the strap of necessity which holds all the participants in the action, protagonists and chorus alike.

Variations and abrupt modulation may underline a dramatic shift or reversal, but they rarely suggest the free play of fancy allowed the non-dramatic singer amid the related atmosphere of symposium or celebration. More often they reflect some sort of tension: a struggle, not always successful, to break free from the master mood or line of reflection imposed by the situation:

οὐδ᾽ ὅστις πάροιθεν ἦν μέγας παμμάχῳ θράσει βρύων     – .– .– ◡ – × – ◡ – .– ◡ – × – ◡ – .|E

   οὐδὲ λέξεται πρὶν ὤν.

ὃς δ᾽ἔπειτ᾽ ἔφυ, τριάκτηρος οἴχεται τυχών.            – ◡ – × – ◡ – .– ◡ – × – ◡ –

Ζῆνα δέ τις προφρόνως ἐπινίκια κλάζων                 – ◡ ◡ – ◡ ◡ – ◡ ◡ – ◡ ◡ – ⁻

   τεύξεται φρενῶν τὸ πᾶν.                            E

                                        *Ag.* 167 – 75 = 160 – 66

There need be no leap to a new subject matter—merely passing to a new level of intensity in evoking the old:

ἰάπτει δ''Ασίδος δι' αἴας                        ⏓–.–.–⏑–⏑–‾ +

μηλοβότου Φρυγίας διαμπάξ,                 D ⏑–‾ +

περᾷ δὲ Τεύθραντος ἄστυ Μυσὸν      ⏓–⏑–.–⏑–⏑–‾+

Λύδιά τ'ἀν' γύαλα                                    D ‖²²⁶

καὶ δι' ὀρῶν Κιλίκων                               D

Παμφύλων τε διορνυμένα                        – ꠸D |

        πὰρ ποταμούς τ'ἀενάους               – ⏑ ⏑––⏑ ⏑–|

καὶ βαθύπλουτον χθόνα καὶ τὰν 'Αφροδίτας πολύπυρον αἶαν.

                – ⏑ ⏑––⏑ ⏑––⏑ ⏑––⏑ ⏑–⏑–‾

                                    —Su. 547–55 = 538–46

Here the increasing duration of the wanderings and the increasing variety
of their geographical settings are heard in prosodiac cola lengthening into
iono-choriambic. Simultaneously, however, there is a feeling of inevitability and sameness, as the second main section comes round (after a long
digression in which the respite that modulation coupled with rhythmical
break would bring does not materialize) to finishing its repetition of the
pattern of the first:

1) ⏓–.–.–⏑–⏑–‾ +     D                                 ⏑–‾
2) ⏓–⏑–.–⏑–⏑–‾ +     D ‖
                              D
                    – ꠸D|–⏑ ⏑––⏑ ⏑–|–⏑ ⏑––⏑ ⏑––⏑ ⏑–‾

The prominence of continuous composition in mixed prosodiac in the
lyrics of the *PV* (above, 171) may be, as more than one scholar has
suggested,[227] a sign of non-Aeschylean authorship. On the other hand,
one might argue that an uncharacteristic rhythm is only to be expected in
a play where, uncharacteristically for Aeschylus, the chorus is neither protagonist itself nor inevitably involved in the protagonist's fate.

There can be little doubt that Aeschylean lyric is, by contrast with that
of most of its predecessors, a popular art form—perhaps even, by Pindaric
standards, a little vulgar in some of its rhythmical effects. Whether
greater popular appeal means a form more immediately rooted in popular
traditions is uncertain. One readily feels in Aeschylean versification, as in
the outlines of Aeschylean tragedy itself, a simplicity and power to which
it is easy to attach the adjective primitive. But the antecedents of both, if

---

[226] D + D + – ꠸D if disjunct; D . ‖D . |–꠸D if continuous; cf., for the ambiguity,
text, 171–72.

[227] Cf., most recently, M. Griffith, *The Authenticity of the Prometheus Bound* (Cambridge
1976) 39–40.

they exist, are submerged parts of a tradition that only surfaces with Aeschylus himself. The Rhodian swallow song (ten repetitions of $\cup\cup$)– $\cup\,\cup-^-$ ‖ followed by some sort of clausula)[228] together with a sprinkling of skolia[229] and verse inscriptions[230] are the most likely remnants of such a tradition; and few of them are demonstrably pre-Aeschylean.[231] The genealogy is, of course, plausible enough in itself and has parallels elsewhere in the history of music. Most strikingly, one might compare the way a combination of greater expressivity with greater formal simplicity, the latter stemming in part from the use of popular dance rhythms, helps set Viennese classicism apart from its late baroque antecedents.[232] Ultimately, however, historical reconstructions tell us less about the actual effect of Aeschylean versification than a comparison with the extant non-dramatic work of Aeschylus's contemporaries. The material for such a comparison is fairly abundant and was surveyed in the last chapter. The gap it reveals, in power, expressivity, and formal clarity, is not likely to have been filled to any significant degree by Thespis, Phrynichus,[233] or such popular models as they, or Aeschylus himself, might have followed.

[228] Perhaps $-\cup\,\cup-\times\,|-\cup-\times-$, recalling in its initial $-\cup\,\cup-\bar{\times}$ the dactylo-anapestic which precedes (compare the relationship of the initial five quantities in final $-\cup\,\cup--|\cup\,\underset{A}{\cup}-\cup-$ to the preceding line ends in Ibycus 1.282e (text, 156). For this "brachycatalectic" trimeter, cf. the immediately following πότερ᾽ ἀπίωμες ἢ λαβώμεθα; ($^-\cup\,\cup-\times\,|-\cup-\times-$) and, separated by four regular trimeters, ἂν δὴ φέρῃς τι μέγα τι δὴ φέροις (δή τι codd.). The form is mentioned at Heph 13.18–14.3, ascribed to Alcaeus at GL 6.143.21 and called an *alcmanicum* at GL 6.521.2.

[229] Cf. PMG 892 ($\times-\cup\,\cup-\cup-\ +\ \times-\cup\,\cup-\cup-\ +\ \times\times-\cup\,\cup-\cup-\times\,|\times-\cup\,\cup-\cup-$), 899–901 (text, 96), 909.1–5 (above, n. 162) and the Attic skolion rhythm. PMG 869 may belong here as well ($\times-\cup\,\cup-\ +\ \times\times-\cup\,\cup-^-\ +\ \times\times-\cup\,\cup--\cup\,\cup-^-$ if the rhythm is aeolic [so Webster 61]), but problems of dating are complicated by problems of scansion. Analysis as a continuous piece of ionic (above, n. 105) is at least as likely as the one just suggested.

[230] E.g., the dedication of Echembrotus quoted in Pausanias (ii. p. 62 West): a hexameter between what may be two instances of $\times-\cup\,\cup-^-\ +\ (\overset{\smile}{-})\cup-\times-$ (θῆκε τῷ Ἡρακλεῖ and μέλεα καὶ ἐλέγους.

[231] Comedy too offers parallels (cf. Appendix V) which may be *volkstümlich*. But the method of composition is atypical, at least of Aristophanic comedy, where even the repeated $\times\times-\cup\,\cup-^-\ +\ \times\times-\cup\,\cup-^-$ ... found in Pherecrates 79, Crates 33 and Eupolis 162 (cf. White 547) is only paralleled in the suspect Ran. 1258–60.

[232] Further parallels are offered by developments in the plastic arts—notably the loss, in Classical sculpture, of the "Zierlichkeit und . . . reichen Schmuch . . . der für die Mädchenstatuen der Burg charakteristisch ist" (noted by Wilamowitz [GV 110] in his comparison of Aeschylus and pre-Aeschylean lyric).

[233] The scanty remains of pre-Aeschylean dramatic lyric show an incidence of continuous modes of composition considerably higher than what one would expect to find in a comparable sampling from Aeschylus. Cf. TGrF 3 (Phrynichus) F 9 and 13 (prosodiac), 14 (ionic) and 6 (. . .$-\cup\,\cup-\cup-|\times\times-\cup\,\cup--\cup\,\cup--\cup\,\cup-\cup-\|\times\times-\cup\,\cup--\cup\,\cup-\cup-$).

# CHAPTER TEN: SOPHOCLES AND EARLY EURIPIDES

The lyrics of Sophocles provide the earliest surviving examples of a manner which continues to be important down to the end of the century, in Euripides as well as Sophocles, and in comedy as well as tragedy. It is also the prevalent manner in the earliest plays of Euripides, the poet's more characteristic lyric techniques only beginning to appear, sporadically, in the *Hcld.* and *Andr.* and extensively in the *HF.* Hence the decision to treat the lyrics of the *Alc., Med.* and *Hipp.* along with those of Sophocles in a chapter devoted to what was probably the dominant manner in drama during the third quarter of the fifth century.

The manner, by contrast with Aeschylus's, makes fuller use of the rhythmical resources of the whole choral and monodic tradition. Dactylo-epitritic is part of the Sophoclean repertory from the beginning, as are heptadic aeolic,[234] extended pieces of continuous octadic aeolic, and frequent passage, via both iambic and choriambic modulation, between aeolic and iono-choriambic. All four of these non-Aeschylean usages involve epiploke, and in passages where they appear there is a corresponding decline in the frequency of the asynartete composition favored by Aeschylus. The latter is now largely confined to *kommoi*, where the frequent shift of speaker and mood favors its use, and to astrophic passages, where the mimetic possibilities it offers can be exploited free from the constraint imposed by response. (For choral passages composed, atypically, in the Aeschylean manner, see Appendix V.)

Symptomatic of the new technique is the way brief sequences isolated by rhythmical break from their surroundings are used, not as the basic building blocks of a stanza, but as adjuncts to them—sometimes terminally (composing a "double clausula" or clausula plus coda),[235]

---

[234] Only four possible instances in Aeschylus: see Table V.

[235] Cf. *El.* 135 = 152, *OT* 472 = 482, 1096–97 = 1108–9, *OC* 1084 = 1095 and *Ant.* 140 = 154 (unless scanned . . .– ∪ ∪–×|−∪∪−⁻ cf. above, n. 59), with the discussion in Dale 10–16. To the passages collected and analyzed there one should perhaps add *OT* 881–82 = 871–72 (∪ ∪–×–∪– + –∪–∪–⁻) and *Ph.* 1213–17 (××–×–∪∪–| –∪–×–∪–×– ∪–|××–×– ∪ ∪–×| ×–×–∪∪–∪–⁻ + ×–∪–× if one accepts Gleditsch's ὦ πόλις [ὦ] πόλις or a solitary Sophoclean instance of the Euripidean x̄ ×̆ in the first colon and emends the third to ὅς γε σὰν λιπὼν ἱερὰν λίβ[αδ]'). The concluding . . .|×–∪∪–⁻ + E ˆ of *OT* 472 = 482 recurs at *Hipp.* 1142ff. (×–∪––∪∪–|×˘˘∪–×|–∪∪–⁻ + E ˆ, followed either by the nearly identical ×˘˘∪∪–⁻ + *extra metrum* + E ˆ or by ×˘˘∪∪–∪–.|E ˆ).

181

sometimes medially:

οἴμοι γελῶμαι. τί με πρὸς θεῶν πατρῴων

×– ᴗ – – ᴗ ᴗ – × – ᴗ – ×

οὐκ οἰχομέναν ὑβρίζεις,    ×‒ᴗ͞A͞ᴗ‒ᴗ‒× +

ἀλλ’ ἐπίφαντον;    – ᴗ ᴗ –͞ +

ὦ πόλις, ὦ πόλεως

πολυκτήμονες ἄνδρες· ἰώ,    – ᴗ ᴗ – ᴗ – | × × ‒͞A͞ᴗ͞ᴗ – ᴗ |‒ ×

Διρκαῖαι κρῆναι, Θήβας τ’    × – ͞ᴗ͞ᴗ – × | – × [236]

εὐαρμάτου ἄλσος, ἔμπας    × – ᴗ ᴗ – ᴗ | – ×

ξυμμάρτυρας ὕμμ’ ἐπικτῶμαι.    × – ᴗ ᴗ – ᴗ – . –͞

—S. Ant. 839–46 = 857–65

sometimes initially, to be immediately repeated as the beginnings of longer pieces of continuous movement

ἐρώτων δ’,    ᴗ – – +

ἐρώτων ἀπέπαυσεν, ὤμοι,    ⚹ ⚹ – | ᴗ ᴗ – ᴗ – × [237]
⎯A⎯

κεῖμαι δ’ ἀμέριμνος οὕτως    × – ᴗ ᴗ – ᴗ – ×

---

[236] For the contracted aeolic nucleus, cf. in the same play 1137–38 = 1146–47 (× – ᴗ – ͞ᴗ͞ᴗ– | × – ᴗ – ᴗ ᴗ –) and with the rhythm of the whole stanza compare the closely similar 806 = 823ff. that immediately precedes:

839 = 857ff.

× – ᴗ – – ᴗ ᴗ – × – ᴗ – × | × – ᴗ ᴗ – ᴗ – ×    + – ᴗ ᴗ – ͞ +    – ᴗ ᴗ – ᴗ –

× × – ᴗ ᴗ – ᴗ | – ×

× – ͞ᴗ͞ᴗ – × | – × | × – ᴗ ᴗ – ᴗ | – × | × – ᴗ ᴗ – ᴗ – . –͞
⎯A⎯

806 = 823ff.

× – ᴗ – – ᴗ ᴗ – ᴗ – ͞ + – ᴗ ᴗ – ᴗ –

× × – ᴗ ᴗ – ᴗ – ×

× – × – ᴗ ᴗ –

× × – × – ᴗ ᴗ – × × – × – ᴗ ᴗ – + – ᴗ ᴗ – ͞ +    × × – ᴗ ᴗ – ͞ +

× – × – ᴗ ᴗ – × × | – ᴗ ᴗ – ᴗ – ×ᵢ x' – ᴗ ᴗ – ᴗ – . –͞

[237] For this and the related sequences in the OC, see Kraus 169. Other possible instances are:

ᴗ – – ‖ +    (E. Alc. 255–56 = 262–63 [retaining the μέθες

ᴗ – – | ᴗ ᴗ – – ᴗ ᴗ –. . . .    με omitted in L P]

ᴗ – × ‖ +

ᴗ – × | – ᴗ – . ᴗ ᴗ –. . . .    (Ar. Ran. 325–26 = 340–41)

ᴗ – – +

ᴗ – – + ⚹ ⚹ – ᴗ ᴗ – ᴗ (–)    (E. Tr. 321 = 337, Suppl. 990–91 = 1012–13
and, perhaps, 1002–3 = 1025–26)

× –. – ᴗ – ͞ + × – ᴗ ᴗ – ᴗ –. . . .    (E. Ion 190–91 = 201–2)

| | |
|---|---|
| ἀεὶ πυκιναῖς δρόσοις | ×‒⏑⏑‒⏑‒. (or ×‒⏑⏑‒⏑‒ + ‒⏑⏑‒⏑‒) |
| τεγγόμενος κόμας, | .‒⏑⏑‒⏑‒ |
| λυγρᾶς μνήματα Τροίας | ××‒⏑⏑‒¯ |

—*Aj.* 1205–10 = 1217–22

| | |
|---|---|
| ἔρως, | ×‒ + |
| ἔρως, ὃ κατ' ὀμμάτων | ×‒⌊⏑⏑‒⏑‒.  (A) |
| στάζεις πόθον εἰσάγων γλυκεῖαν | ×‒ ⏑⏑‒⏑‒⏑‒¯ |

—*Hipp.* 525–26 = 535–36

*OC* 119 = 151ff. is unique in the number and positioning of such repeated phrases:

| | |
|---|---|
| ἐκτόπιος συθείς, | ‒⏑⏑‒⏑‒ |
| ὁ πάντων | ⏑‒‒ + |
| ὁ πάντων ἀκορέστατος. . . | ⚨⊼‒⌊⏑⏑‒⏑‒ · · · |
| πλανάτας | ⏑‒‒⌊ + |
| πλανάτας τις ὁ πρέσβυς, οὐδ' ἔγχωρος· προσέβα γὰρ οὐκ | ⚨⊼‒⌊⏑⏑‒⏑‒××‒⏑⏑‒⏑‒ |
| ἄν ποτ' ἀστιβὲς ἄλσος ἐς τἀνδ' ἀμαιμακετᾶν κορᾶν, | ××‒ ⏑⏑‒⏑‒××‒⏑⏑‒⏑‒ [238] |
| ἃς τρέμομεν λέγειν | ‒⏑⏑‒⏑‒ + |
| καὶ παραμειβόμεσθ' | ‒⏑⏑‒⏑‒ |

---

××‒⏑⏑‒¯ + (×)×‒⏑⏑‒⏑‒. . .

(E. *Hec.* 444 = 455ff. and *Ion* 1080 = 1096 [unless taken as ⏑‒‒⏑⏑‒×⌊×‒×‒⏑⏑‒; cf. A. *Vesp.* 316–18: ⏑‒.‒⏑‒×⌊×‒⏑⏑‒⏑‒ .⌊×‒⏑⏑‒¯])

⏑‒‒⏑⏑‒ +
⏑‒‒⏑⏑‒.⌊⏑̆⏑̆̆×‒⌊⏑̆⏑̆̆ ⏑⏑‒⏑‒¯    (S. *Aj.* 605–8 = 617–20 [above, n. 113])

[238] A new movement may begin here, and following the prosodic demarcation four cola later. But as in the stanza from the *Ajax* just quoted, continuous scansion (with syncopation) is also possible; and it would make this group of cola an even closer anticipation of what follows:

⏑‒‒ +
⚨⊼‒⌊⏑⏑‒⏑‒××‒⏑⏑‒⏑‒⌊
××‒ ⏑⏑‒⏑‒××‒⏑⏑‒⏑‒ . ⌊.‒⏑⏑‒⏑‒    + ‒⏑⏑‒⏑‒ (A)
⏑‒‒ +
⚨⊼‒⌊⏑⏑‒⏑‒××‒⏑⏑‒⏑‒‖××‒⌊⏑⏑‒⏑‒¯‖ + ⏑⏑‒⏑‒‒⌊⏑⏑‒×‒ (A) (A)

However analyzed, the recall of ‒⏑⏑‒⏑‒⌊‒⏑⏑‒⏑‒ by the later ‒⌊⏑⏑‒⏑‒‒ ‖⏑⏑‒⏑‒‒ is an argument against the reading ἄγεις in the antistrophe which, with emendation of the strophe (λόγος οὐδὲν ἄγονθ' = λόγον εἴ τιν' ἄγεις), would substitute ⏑⏑‒ ⏑⏑‒ for ⏑⏑‒⏑‒‒ in the penultimate colon.

ἀδέρκτως                                                      ∪ − − +

ἀφώνως, ἀλόγως τὸ τᾶς εὐφάμου στόμα φροντίδος    ⨯ ⨯̄ −| ∪ ∪ − ∪ − ⨯⨯ − ∪ ∪ − ∪ − ‖

ἱέντες· τὰ δὲ νῦν τιν' ἥκειν                           ⨯ ⨯̄ −| ∪ ∪̣ − ∪ − ⁻  +

λόγος οὐδὲν ἄζονθ',                                    $\underline{\phantom{xxx}{}^A\phantom{xxx}}$   239
                                                      ∪ ∪ − ∪ − −|∪̌ ∪̌ − ⨯ −

ὃν ἐγὼ λεύσσων

περὶ πᾶν οὔπω δύναμαι τέμενος              an an |

γνῶναι ποῦ μοί ποτε ναίει.                  an an⁀

Their repetitive character, however, is such as to create in every instance more an echo of the segment of epiploke that has immediately preceded than the inauguration of a new movement.

In spite of this extensive use of continuous composition, whole stanzas consisting of a single piece of epiploke in the manner of early lyric are fairly rare.[240] Continuity is more often confined to the interior of the main subdivisions in a stanza. These subdivisions, usually three (more rarely, two or four) in number, are, of all the non-stichic, non-stanzaic units in Greek verse, the ones which best deserve the label "period" in the full sense of the term. They are, in effect, miniature stanzas which, to a far greater degree than the colon groupings within a typical Aeschylean stanza, display both the internal unity and sharp internal demarcation that make them complete, unified rhythmical statements. And like the major subdivisions in a multi-stanzaed Aeschylean ode they may be in contrasting rhythms—sometimes as many as three or four, all of them equally prominent. In the single Aeschylean stanza, by contrast, there are rarely more than two (whether in pure or mixed form), and one of these is often the dominant one, with the other providing counterpoint or structural variation.[241]

Dactylo-anapestic and iambo-trochaic continue, as in early lyric, to resist combination into continuous wholes (except in prosodiac contexts); but even here the characteristic Sophoclean concern for blocking into a small number of distinct though formally interrelated periods is evident:

---

[239] Presumably a modification of the common clausular sequence − ∪ ∪ − ∪ − −| ∪ ∪ − ∪ −⁻ designed to create a transition to the succeeding anapest via an ambiguous ∪ ∪ − − − ($\overset{\frown}{\phantom{x}}{}^A$ ∪ ∪ − ⨯ − or an).

[240] *Tr.* 94–130 and the initial stanzas of the first three choral odes in the *Medea* are exceptional: dactylo-epitritic in the Pindaric manner with only prosodic demarcation to create internal division. *El.* 823 = 837ff., *OT* 483 = 498ff. and *OC* 510 = 521ff. are probably made up each of a single piece of epiploke but rely for continuity on musical means to which there is no clear parallel in non-dramatic lyric (text, pp. 193–95 and 203–4).

[241] The stanzas in the ode beginning at *Ag.* 681 are the most striking exception, perhaps for good reason; see text, 173–74.

Χο.  θάρσει μοι, θάρσει                     – ‿‿– ‿‿– + E (?)
     τέκνον, ἔτι μέγας οὐρανῷ

     Ζεύς, ὃς ἐφορᾷ πάντα καὶ κρατύνει          x‥‿–.–‿–‿–‾ +
     ᾧ τὸν ὑπεραλγῆ χόλον σέμουσα               x‥‿–.–‿–‿–‾ +
     μήθ᾽ οἷς ἐχθαίρεις ὑπεράχθεο μήτ᾽ ἐπιλάθου  – ‿‿– ‿‿– ‿‿– ‿‿– ‿‿– ‿‿‖ +
     χρόνος γὰρ εὐμαρὴς θεός.                    x E ˆ

     οὔτε γὰρ ὁ τὰν Κρίσᾳ                    x‥‿–.–‾ (or x‥‿–x–) +
     βούνομον ἔχων ἀκτὰν                     x‥‿–.–‾ (or x‥‿–x–) +
     παῖς ᾽Αγαμεμνονίδας ἀπερίτροπος            – ‿‿– ‿‿– ‿‿– ‿‿ +
     οὔθ᾽ ὁ παρὰ τὸν ᾽Αχέροντα θεὸς ἀνάσσων.    x‥‿‥x– ‿‥‿–‾

Ηλ.  ἀλλ᾽ ἐμὲ μὲν ὁ πολὺς ἀπολέλοιπεν ἤδη      x‥‿‥x‥‿–‿–‾ +
     βίοτος ἀνέλπιστος, οὐδ᾽ ἔτ᾽ ἀρκῶ·         x‥‿–.–‿–‿–‾ +
     ἅτις ἄνευ τοκέων κατατάκομαι               – ‿‿– ‿‿– ‿‿–‿‿ |
     ᾆς φίλος οὔτις ἀνὴρ ὑπερίσταται,          – ‿‿– ‿‿– ‿‿–‿‿ |
     ἀλλ᾽ ἀπερεί τις ἔποικος ἀναξία            – ‿‿– ‿‿– ‿‿–‿‿ |
     οἰκονομῶ θαλάμους πατρός, ὧδε μὲν           – ‿‿– ‿‿– ‿‿–‿‿ +
          ἀεικεῖ σὺν στολᾷ                    x–.–.–‿–|
          κεναῖς δ᾽ ἀμφίσταμαι τραπέζαις.     x–.–.–‿–‿–‾
                                            —El. 173–92≈153–72

Here the succession of two catalectic iambic cola followed by a clausular combination of dactylic and iambic constitutes a thrice repeated pattern, considerably expanded on its final appearance to provide a terminal variation, and prefaced by a brief introduction in which (if correctly analyzed above) dactylo-anapestic and iambo-trochaic are both present, but not in the form they will subsequently assume.

The Sophoclean manner may be described, and perhaps arose, as a compromise between the smooth lyric flow found in certain parts of the archaic tradition and the more broken, abrupt style of Aeschylus, with its frequent and at times sharp and obtrusive articulations. A similar compromise may be seen in the guarded use Sophocles and Euripides make of some of the variations on normal aeolic movement found in archaic choral lyric. Hexadic rhythm largely disappears, as well as combinations of single and double-base aeolic in a single continuous sequence (above, 85–86). Modulation between aeolic and iono-choriambic is frequent, but subject to certain restrictions. The "choriambic" transitions $\underline{\phantom{}}$‿‿$\underline{\phantom{}}$ $\underline{\underline{\phantom{-}}}$‿‿$\underline{\phantom{}}$ and (x)x–‿‿– $\underline{\underline{x-}}$‿$\underline{\phantom{}}$ seem to occur freely only when the iono-choriambic sequence contains at least three nuclei within a single colon. Shorter sequences, except in the stereotyped asclepiad, only appear when so demarcated as to produce a colon close capable of a double analysis:

$$\ldots \underline{- \cup \underset{A}{\cup - \cup} - } \times \qquad \text{or} \qquad \ldots - \cup \cup - \cup -^{-} \qquad \text{(iono-choriambic)}$$

$$\ldots \underline{- \cup \underset{A}{\cup - \cup} - }^{(\cdot)} - \qquad \text{or} \qquad \ldots - \cup \cup - \times - ^{(\cdot)} - \times$$

$$\ldots - \cup \cup - - \underset{A}{\cup} \underset{\times}{\cup} -^{-} \qquad \text{or} \qquad \ldots - \cup \cup - - \cup \cup -^{\times}_{-}$$

The first two are the more common:

| | |
|---|---|
| ὦ κλεινὰ Σαλαμίς, σὺ μέν που | $\times \times - \cup \cup - \cup - \times$ |
| ναίεις ἁλίπλακτος εὐδαίμων | $\times - \cup \cup - \underset{}{\times} - . - \overline{\times}$ |
| | (i.e., $\times \underline{- \cup \underset{A}{\cup} - \cup -} . -^{-}$ or $\times - \cup \cup - \times - . - \times$) |
| πᾶσιν περίφαντος αἰεί. | $\times - \cup \cup - \cup - \times$ |

$$-Aj.\ 596-98 \approx 608-11$$

| | |
|---|---|
| ξύνοιδε Πηνειὸς ὁ καλλιδίνας | $\times - \cup - - \cup \cup - \cup -^{-} +$ |
| μακραί τ' ἄρουραι πεδίων ἄκαρποι | $\times - \cup - \underline{- \cup \underset{A}{\cup} - \underset{\times}{\cup} -}^{-} \parallel$ |
| καὶ Πηλιάδες θεράπναι | $\times - \cup \cup - \cup - \times\ ^{242}$ |

$$-H.\ F.\ 368-70 \approx 352-55$$

The clausular $(\cdot) -^{-}$ in the second line of each passage may indicate, as often, end of a rhythmical movement; but the ensuing sequence created by positing such a closure (rather than a continuous $\ldots \times - (\cdot) - \times | \times - \cup \cup - \cup - \times$. or $\ldots - \cup \cup - \cup - \times | \times - \cup \cup - \cup - \times$) is distinctly peculiar. An aeolic $\times - \cup \cup - \cup - \times$ serving as coda to a clausular $\underline{- \cup \underset{A}{\cup} - \cup - (\cdot)} -^{-}$ or $- \cup \cup - \cup -^{-}$ might be expected to occur rather less often than $\times \times - \cup \cup - \cup - \times$, which shows the more frequent type of aeolic demarcation. The latter, however, is not securely attested at all.[243] It is more likely that in passages such as these the poet is attempting to minimize the effect of the departure from octadic or tetradic movement produced by choriambic modulation within epiploke. He achieves this by introducing the departure in such a way that it seems to contain the familiar clausular extension of a

---

[242] Cf. *Hcld.* 892–94 = 901–3 ($\times - \cup - \times - \cup - \times - \cup - |\underline{- \cup \underset{A}{\cup} - \cup -}^{-}_{\times} |\times - \underset{}{\times} \cup \cup - \cup -^{-}$
(with Madvig's ἡδεῖα: cf. above, n. 80).
[243] The closest parallels all involve the coda $\times \times - \cup \underset{A}{\cup} - \cup - (\cdot) -^{-}$ or $\times \times - \cup \cup -^{-}$: E. *Alc.*
575–78 = 585–87 ($\times \times - \cup \cup - \cup - . | \times - \cup \cup - \cup - . -^{-} + \times \times - \cup \cup -^{-}$) *Ion* 1059–60 =
1072–73 ($\ldots - | \cup \cup - \cup -^{-} + \times \times - \cup \cup - \cup - . -^{-}$) and *Hcld.* 758 = 769 (Table VI).

four- or eight-quantity cycle. In similar fashion, the $-\cup\overline{\underset{A}{\overset{B}{-}}\cup\cup}-\cup-$
encountered in Pindar (above, 159–60) is introduced in such a way as to
suggest clausular . . . $-\times\underset{B}{\overset{}{-}}\cup\cup-\cup-\bar{}$:

τέγγουσα, θερμᾶς δ᾽ ἐπὶ νῶτα πέτρας          $\times-\cup--\underset{A}{\overset{}{\cup\cup}}-\cup-\bar{}$  $\times$

εὐαλίου κατέβαλλ᾽ ὅθεν μοι          $\times-\cup\underset{A}{\overset{B}{-}}\cup\cup-\cup-\times$ (or × B $\cup-\bar{}$)

πρῶτα φάτις ἦλθε δεσποίνας          $\times-\cup\cup-\cup-.-\bar{}$

$-$Hipp. 128–30 = 138–40[244]

An alternative possibility is that reinterpretation of $-\cup\cup-\cup-\bar{}$ or
$-\cup\cup-\cup-\underset{A}{\overset{}{(\cup)}}-\bar{}$ as $-\cup\cup-\cup-\times$ or $-\cup\cup-\times-(\cup)-\times$ allows an ordinarily clausular sequence to function as part of a continuous piece of epi-
ploke. In either case what is essential is a colon which, if heard only with
what precedes or only with what follows, forms part of a regular, continuous piece of octadic or tetradic rhythm. The possibility of hearing it this
way makes the effect of internal clausula or departure from octadic and
tetradic movement less jarring.

As to why the effect should have been sought at all, one can only offer
suggestions based on specific passages. At *Hipp.* 525 = 535ff. the use of
$\times-\cup\underset{A}{\overset{}{\cup}}-\cup-\cup-\bar{}$ within movements (526, 528) weakens its clausular
force at what is marked by punctuation (527 = 537) and prosodic break
(537) as movement end. The movement so concluded (525–27) thereby
acquires the character of a sub-movement within a larger one that extends
from 525 to the unambiguously clausular $-\cup\underset{A}{\overset{\wedge}{\cup}}-\bar{}$ of 529:

ἔρως ὁ κατ᾽ ὀμμάτων          $\times-\cup\underset{A}{\overset{}{\cup}}-\cup-.$

στάζεις πόθον εἰσάγων γλυκεῖαν          $\times-\cup\cup-\underset{\times}{\overset{}{\cup}}-\cup-\bar{\times}$          526

ψυχᾷ χάριν οὓς ἐπιστρατεύσῃ,          $\times-\cup\underset{A}{\overset{}{\cup}}-\cup-\cup-\bar{}$ +          527

μή μοί ποτε σὺν κακῷ φανείης          $\times-\cup\cup-\underset{\times}{\overset{}{\cup}}-\cup-\bar{\times}$          528

μηδ᾽ ἄρρυθμος ἔλθοις          $\times-\cup\underset{A}{\overset{}{\cup\times}}-\bar{}$

[244] Cf., later in the play, 546–52 = 556–62 and the immediately following sequence
(perhaps an abbreviated version of the same rhythm):

546–52:
$\times\times-\times\underset{A}{\overset{B}{-}}\cup\cup-\cup-\bar{}$ $-\times|\times-\times-\underset{B}{\overset{}{\cup}}\cup-|\times\times-\cup\cup-\cup\cup-\times|\times-\cup\underset{A}{\overset{}{\cup}}-\cup-.|\cup\cup-\times-.-\bar{}$

553–54:
$\times\times-\times\underset{A}{\overset{B}{-}}\cup\cup-\cup-\bar{\times}|$          $-.--\cup\cup-\bar{}$

The latter sequence may, however, be $\times\times-\times\underset{B}{\overset{}{-}}\cup\cup-\times-\cup|-\times-\cup\cup-\bar{}$ (above, n. 80).

At *OC* 678-80 = 691-93 demarcation counterpoints the prevailing aeolic by first suggesting ( ⏑ ⏑ − ⏑ − x̄ x̄ − | ) then actually producing an ionic | ⏑ ⏑ − x̆ − ⏑ − − |, with its Bacchic associations:

χειμώνων ἵν' ὁ Βακχιώτας αἰεὶ         ×× − | ⏑ ⏑ − ⏑ − x̄ x̄ − ⎡⏑̆⏑ ⏑ − x̆ − ⏑ − x̄

        Διόνυσος ἐμβατεύει,         × − ⏑ ⏑ − ⏑ − × [245]

θε[ι]αῖς ἀμφιπολῶν τιθήναις

At *Alc.* 442-44 = 452-54, as at *HF* 368-70 (above, 186) a preceding clausular − ⏑ ⏑ − ⏑ − ⏑ − ⎺ is echoed from within a continuous movement (here aeolic passing into iono-choriambic):

πολὺ δή, πολὺ δὴ γυναῖκ' ἀρίσταν         ⏑ ⏑ − ⏑ ⏑ − ⏑ − ⏑ − ⎺ +

λίμναν 'Αχεροντίαν πορεύσας         x̄ − ⏑ ⏑ − x̆ − ⏑ − −| ⏑ ⏑ − ⏑ − −

        ἐλάτᾳ δικώπῳ

(Cf., later in the same ode, the partial echo of ⏑ ⏑ − ⏑ ⏑ − ⏑ − ⏑ − ⎺ by x̄ − ⏑ ⏑ − ⏑ − ⏑ − ⎺, this time from within a reverse movement [iono-choriambic to aeolic]:

σὺ γὰρ ὦ μόνα, ὦ φίλα γυναικῶν         ⏑ ⏑ − ⏑ ⏑ − ⏑ − ⏑ − ⎺ +

σὺ τὸν αὐτᾶς         ⏑ ⏑ − x̄ | x̄ − ⏑ ⏑ − ⏑ − ⏑ − ⎺

        ἔτλας πόσιν ἀντὶ σᾶς ἀμεῖψαι

                                                     −460-62 = 470-72)

A prosodiac and heptadic aeolic counterpart ( ⏑ ⏑ − ⏑ ⏑ − ⏑ ⏑ − ⏑ − ⎺ ) echoed from within x̄ − ⏑ ⏑ − ⏑ ⏑ − ⏑ − ⎺ − | ⏑ ⏑ − ⏑ − ⎺ ) may appear later in the play:

[245] Rhythmically preferable to the unparalleled (text, 186 with n. 243) . . .− ⏑ ⏑ − ⏑ − ⏑ − ⎺ + ×× − ⏑ ⏑ − ⏑ − × obtained by emending the antistrophe's οὐδ' αὖ | (or οὐδ' ἅ | ) χρυσάνιος 'Αφροδίτα at this point.

δώμασιν ἀρτιθανῆ·                    $- \cup \cup - \cup \cup - | \cup \cup - \underline{\cup \cup} - \cup \cup - -$

τὸ γὰρ εὐγενὲς ἐκφέρεται πρὸς αἰδῶ.

ἐν τοῖς ἀγαθοῖσι δὲ πάντ' ἔνεστιν          $\times$ $= \cup \cup \underline{\overset{D}{\cup} - \cup \cup} - \cup - \overline{\underset{A}{}} - | \underset{A}{\cup \cup - \cup} -$

σοφίας ἄγασθαι.

$-600 - 603 = 591 - 94$

ἄγασθαι : ἄγαμαι codd.

if one removes asyndeton by the emendation suggested.[246] (The corrupt strophe can be accommodated equally well to either reading). $\times - \cup \cup$ $- \cup \underline{\cup - \cup} - \times (|)$ echoes a preceding $\times - \underline{\overset{D}{\cup \cup} - \cup \cup} - \cup - -$ in the same way at Bacch. 13e2–3:

1 $\times - \cup - \times^{\cdot \cdot} \cup - \cup - -$

2 $\times - \cup \cup - \cup \cup - \cup - -$

3 $\times - \cup \cup \underline{- \cup \underset{A}{\cup} - \cup} - \times (|) - \cup - \times \underline{- \cup \underset{A}{\cup} - \cup} - \times$

Elsewhere in the Alcestis it is the possibility of hearing aeolic . . . $- \cup \cup - \cup - (\overset{\cup}{\cdot}) - -$ as part of prosodiac D $\times - (\overset{\cup}{\cdot}) - \times$ rather than iono-choriambic $- \cup \cup - \times - (\overset{\cup}{\cdot}) - \times$ that allows the sequence to be continuous with what follows:

ἀνόνατ' ἀνόνατ' ἐνύμφευσας          $\cup \underset{D}{\times} \underline{\overset{A}{- \cup \cup} - \cup} -. - \overline{\phantom{x}}$
$\phantom{xxxxxxxxxxxxxxxxxxxxxxxxxx} - \times \phantom{x} \times$

οὐδὲ γήρως ἔβας τέλος σὺν τᾷδ'          $- \cup -. - \cup - \times -. - \times$

ἔφθιτο γὰρ πάρος.

οἰχομένοας δὲ σοῦ, μᾶτερ, ὅλωλεν οἶκος          $\underline{- \cup \underset{A}{\cup} - \cup} - | \underline{- \cup \underset{A}{\cup} - \cup} - -$
$\phantom{xxxxxxxxxxxxxxxxxxxxxxxxxxxxxxxx} 412 - 15 = 400 - 403 \phantom{x}^{247}$

At Aj. 628 = 640ff. the aeolo-ionic

---

[246] The Stesichorean ὅτε ἦρος ὥρᾳ | κελαδῇ χελιδών (34/211) may be the conclusion of a similar dicolon. Cf., for initial $\cup \cup - \cup \cup - \cup \cup - \cup - -$, the Stesichorean "archebulean": $\cup \cup - \cup \cup - \cup \cup - \cup \cup - \cup - -$ (Table VI).

[247] Emending the corrupt strophe to, e.g., ἀντιάζω <σ'> ἐγώ σ' ἐγὼ μᾶτερ πρός σε καλούμενος, σὸς . . . (: καλοῦμαι σ' ὁ σὸς codd.) ποτὶ σοῖσι πίτνων στόμασιν νεοσσός. (Cf. Med. 645–47 = 655–57: $\cup \underset{D}{\times} \underline{\overset{A}{- \cup \cup} - \cup - \times} | - \underset{\times - \cup}{} - \cup -| \phantom{x}_D$ (or $| - \cup \cup - \cup -$) and 648–51 = 659–62: $\underline{\cup \underset{\overset{\wedge}{D}}{\cup - \cup \cup - \cup} - \underset{\times}{} } \cup - \underset{\times}{} | - \cup - \times - \cup \underline{\cup - \cup} - \times \times - \cup \cup - \cup - - | \cup \cup - \cup - -$ where the ambiguities of initial $\cup \cup - \cup \cup - \cup - \cup - -$ may have helped prepare the way for the highly unusual (text, 85–86 with n. 80) transition to octadic aeolic at the end.

οὐδ᾽ οἰκτρᾶς γόον ὄρνιθος ἀηδοῦς     x̄ x̄ - ◡ ◡ | -⌢-◡ ◡ ◡ - ⁻

ἤσει δύσμορος ἀλλ᾽ ὀξυτόνους μὲν ᾠδάς     - | ⏖ - - ◡ ◡ | - ⌢ - ◡ ◡ - ◡ - ⁻

is so demarcated ( | --- ◡ ◡ | in alternation with | -- ◡ ◡ -- | or | --
◡ ◡ - ◡ - ⁻ | ) as to recall the | x̄ - ◡ - x̄ | in alternation with | -- ◡ ◡ -
◡ - | or | x̄ - ◡ ◡ - ◡ - x | of the mixed aeolic with which the stanza
began:

ἦ που παλαιᾷ μὲν σύντροφος ἀμέρᾳ     x̄ - ◡ - x̄ | x̄ - ◡ ◡ - ◡ - |

                                          x̄ - ◡ - x̄ | x̄ - ◡ ◡ - ◡ - x | E
λευκῷ δὲ γήρᾳ μάτηρ νιν ὅταν νοσοῦντα
                  φρενομόρως ἀκούσῃ

The echo, heard more distantly in the aeolo-ionic --- ◡ ◡ -- | ---
◡ ◡ -- | --- ◡ ◡ - ◡ - ◡ - ⁻ (above, 95) with which the stanza closes,
helps to preserve rhythmical unity through the sharp transitions of the
poet's text: from the feeble, wasting grief of a mother's old age (παλαιᾷ
... ἀμέρᾳ, λευκῷ ... γήρᾳ) to the violent lamentations that follow
(ὀξυτόνους μὲν ᾠδάς and [in the passage quoted on p.95] δοῦποι και
πολιᾶς ἄμυγμα χαίτας). The antistrophe moves in similar fashion from
paternal pride (ὃς ἐκ πατρῴας ἥκων γενεᾶς ἄριστος [x̄ - ◡ - x̄ | x̄ -
◡ ◡ - ◡ - x]) to paternal grief (ὦ τλᾶμον πάτερ, οἵαν σε μένει πυθέσθαι
[--- ◡ ◡ | -- ◡ ◡ - ◡ - ⁻] ... ἄταν). The rhythmical—and musical—
realization of these transitions must have been one of the main sources of
the stanza's effectiveness.

The most complicated use of the rhythms under discussion begins at
*Ant.* 604 = 615ff.:

| | | | |
|---|---|---|---|
| τεάν, Ζεῦ, δύνασιν τίς ἀνδρῶν | ×× | - ◡ ◡ - ◡ - × | 1 |
| ὑπερβασίᾳ κατάσχοι, | × | - ◡ ◡ - ◡ - × | 2 |
| τὰν οὔθ᾽ ὕπνος αἱρεῖ ποθ᾽ ὁ †παντογήρως | | | |
| | × - ◡ ◡ - | - ◡ ◡ - ◡ - × | 3 |
| οὔτ᾽ ἀκάματοι θεῶν μῆνες | × - ◡ ◡ - x̆ -.-- |²⁴⁸ ◡ ◡ - | - ◡ ◡ - ◡ -- | 4 |
| < ◡ >αγήρως δὲ χρόνῳ δυνάστας | | | |

²⁴⁸ Responsion with the antistrophe is most simply achieved at this point by assuming that
each has lost a syllable:

str.:  ×  - ◡ ◡ - ◡ ---- | < ◡ > ◡ -- ◡ ◡ - ◡ - ×
ant.: < × > - ◡ ◡ - ◡ --- |  ◡  ◡ -- ◡ ◡ - ◡ - ×

(e.g., σὺν ἀγήρῳ δὲ or < παν > αγήρως [echoing what may have been a παντο-compound in
the preceding line] and < εὖ > or < σάφ᾽ > εἰδότι in the antistrophe). Against the usual
emendation of one line to conform with the other are the absence of non-metrical reasons

κατέχεις 'Ολύμπου                         ∪ ∪ – × – . – |              – ∪ ∪̲ – ∪ – –   5
                                                                           A
μαρμαρόεσσαν αἴγλαν·
τό τ' ἔπειτα καὶ τὸ μέλλον               ∪ ∪ – × – ∪ –                              × 6
καὶ τὸ πρὶν ἐπαρκέσει νόμος ὅδ'· οὐδὲν ἔρπει   × – ∪ ∪ – ×̆ – . ̈× – ∪ –             × 7
θνατῶν βιότῳ πάμπολύ γ' ἐκτὸς ἄτας.      × – ∪ ∪ –              – ∪ ∪̲ – ∪ – ×   8
                                                                           A

where the demarcation in 4, 5 and 7 creates four apparent catalexes:

4: ×̄ – ∪ ∪̄̆ – ×̆ – . – –̄ |̲ ∪ ∪ – – ∪ ∪̲ – ∪ – –̄
                              A

5:   ∪ ∪ – × – . – |        – ∪ ∪̲ – ∪ – –̄
                                   A

7: × – ∪ ∪ – ∪̆ – . | ̈∪̆ – ∪ –         ×̄     (i.e., × A . | E ^ or × – ∪ ∪ – × – . ̈× – ∪ – ×)

Here immediate context is probably a less important consideration than the desire to establish a rhythmical leitmotif—easily recognizable because of its unusual character—which is to reappear through much of the rest of the play. The echo, verbal as well as rhythmical, is most striking at 785 = 795ff.:

φοιτᾷς δ' ὑπερπόντιος ἐν τ' ἀγρονόμοις αὐλαῖς       × – ∪ – – ∪ ∪ – – ∪ ∪̲ – × –
                                                                        A ^      A
καὶ σ' οὔτ' ἀθανάτων φύξιμος οὐδείς,          × × – ∪ ∪ – – ∪ ∪ – ×̄
                                                             A
οὔθ' ἀμερίων σέ γ' ἀνθρώπων,       × – ∪ ∪ – ×̆ – . – –̄
                                                        – |̲ ∪ ∪ – ∪ – –249
                ὁ δ' ἔχων μέμηνεν

                (cf. in 606: οὔτ' ἀκάματοι θεῶν μῆνες)

It is still audible, though less distinct, at 944 = 955ff.:

_____

for suspecting either text, and the presence elsewhere in the stanza of rhythmical parallels both to the – ∪ ∪ – ∪ – × | × – ∪ ∪ – . . . demarcation with which the first colon begins in the strophe and the . . . – ∪ ∪ – ∪ – – – | ∪ ∪ – – with which it ends in the antistrophe.

249 The clear syntactical and rhythmical parallel between × – ∪ ∪ – – ∪ ∪ – –̄ and × – ∪ ∪ – ∪ – . – –̄ in this passage gives some support to the transmitted text of El. 121 = 137ff., where the two actually respond to each other (as part of × × – × – ∪ ∪ – × × – ∪ ∪ – ∪ – . – –̄
                                                                           B
= × × B × × – ∪ ∪ – – ∪ ∪ – –̄. The iono-choriambic affinities of . . . – ∪ ∪ – ∪ – . – –̄ and – ∪ ∪ – – ∪ ∪ – –̄ could have justified the responsion, by which a pure – ∪ ∪ – – ∪ ∪ – –̄ becomes equivalent to a mixed, syncopated – ∪ ∪ – × – . – –̄. Cf. E. Hipp. 552, where the minimal emendation φονίοισ<ιν> θ' ὑμεναίοις will produce the same responsion with 562. Exact correspondence can be obtained fairly easily there (above, n. 90) but no convincing emendation has been suggested in the other passage.

$$\overline{\phantom{xx}}\text{A}\hat{\phantom{x}}\overline{\phantom{xx}}$$
ἔτλα καὶ Δανάας οὐράνιον φῶς      × × − ∪ ∪ − − ∪ ∪ − ̄
                                        − | σ̄ῡ− − ∪ ∪ − − ∪ ∪ − × −
ἀλλάξαι δέμας ἐν χαλκοδέτοις αὐλαῖς                    —̄A—̄

κρυπτομένα δ' ἐν

τυμβήρει θαλάμῳ κατεζεύχθη          − ∪ ∪ − − | σ̄ῡ− − ∪ ∪ ∪− ∪ −.− ̄
                                                    —̄A—̄

and much fainter in the succeeding 949–51 = 960–62:

κ̀αὶ Ζηνὸς ταμιεύεσκε γονὰς χρυσορύτους     × × − ∪ ∪ − − ∪ ∪ − − ∪ ∪ −
ἀλλ' ἁ μοιριδία τις δύνασις δεινά          × × − ∪ ∪ −      − ∪ ∪ − × −
                                                            —̄A—̄

where the demarcative pattern of the earlier passages in absent. Finally, it disappears altogether, as modulation into iono-choriambic is replaced by modulation into dactylo-anapestic, first followed by return to aeolic and then by passage into mixed prosodiac ("an elegiambus set on an aeolic base" [Dale 197]):

κατὰ δὲ τακόμενοι μέλεοι μελέαν πάθαν      × × − ∪ ∪ − ∪ ∪ − ∪ ∪ − ∪ −
                                                            —̄A—̄
κλαῖον ματρὸς ἔχοντες ἀνύμφευτον γονάν      × × − ∪ ∪ − ∪ ∪ − × − ∪ −
                                          −977–80 = 966–67

This is part of the *Antigone* music, a note first sounded once the jubiliation of the parodos and the ambiguous anthropology of the first stasimon have given way to more sombre thoughts, and echoed until these are replaced by the false hopes of the final ode (1115 = 1126ff.). Like the Ajax passage just discussed, it is probably a good example of the πικρὸν καὶ κατά-τεχνον of early Sophoclean style.

Combination of rhythmical continuity with sharp demarcation in a way not found in non-dramatic choral lyric is characteristic of the "aeolo-ionic" just examined, and it is also central to the second of the primarily Sophoclean adaptations of epiploke to be considered in some detail in this chapter.[250] It was noted earlier (37) that "major" ionic demarcation is attested in tragedy. Most of the instances are Sophoclean, and they are sufficiently numerous that the restrictions on their use may be significant. They never open stanzas, and they are always preceded by other

[250] Outside of Sophocles and early Euripides the basic form of modulation involved in all of the passages just considered is quite rare, confined to the Bacchylidean (text, 189), and Euripidean (text, 186; above, n. 242) passages cited, A. *Ag.* 1483–84 = 1507–8 (× − ∪ ∪ − ∪̆ − .−× | × − ∪ ∪ − ∪ ̄), E. *Ion* 219–21 (text, 204) and, possibly, *Or.* 816–18 = 828–30: × − ×̲−̲∪̲ ∪̲−̲ ∪ − × | × − ∪ ∪ − ∪ − × | × − ∪ ∪ − (a means of transition from the "B-type" aeolic with which the stanza begins to the "A-type" with which it ends).

sequences in iono-choriambic or, more rarely, iambo-trochaic.[251] The most natural explanation for this is that major ionic cola are rhythmically continuous with what precedes. The explanation requires assuming in most instances, one or more non-syllabic quantities before the beginning of a colon, but the assumption would be in accord with the general structure of all the contexts in which major ionic appears. The rhythm is best documented in *El.* 823 ≈ 837ff. The stanza's highly symmetrical structure may be set forth as follows:

$$x^{\smile\smile}\,\cup--\cup\,\cup--\cup\,\cup--\cup\,\cup\,|--\cup\,\cup--\,|\qquad\text{(a)}$$

$$--\cup\,\cup--\,|\cup\,\cup--\qquad\text{(b)}$$

$$--\cup\,\cup--\,|-\,|\qquad\text{(c)}$$

$$--\cup\,\cup--\,|\cup\,\cup--\qquad\text{(b')}$$

$$--\cup\,\cup--\cup\,\cup--\cup\,\cup--\cup\,\cup--\cup\,\cup--\cup\,\cup--\,\bar{x}-\ ^{252}\qquad\text{(a')}$$

There is apparent interruption of the iono-choriambic epiploke between all five components of the pattern, except where b' follows c. Here an intervening long (the exclamation φεῦ) creates what could be rhythmical continuity:

$$\ldots-\cup\,\cup--|\,\overline{\cup\cup}|--\cup\,\cup-.\ldots$$

The overall symmetry of the passage is such that the connection between these cola is unlikely to be any different from that between other consecutive members of the abcb'a' pattern. Φεῦ could, of course, be *extra metrum*, which would allow discontinuity at all four breaks; but if so, it is difficult to see why this exclamation should be on a different footing from the ἒ ἔ, αἰαῖ (ἒ ἔ, ἰώ) at the end of b, which is clearly a piece of ionic. The simplest solution to the problem posed by its presence in the text is to assume that the rhythm – | $\overline{\cup\cup}$ | – at this point corresponds to – | .. | – at the other three points of demarcation—i.e., to a sequence in which two quantities are supplied by pause rather than an interjection. The whole

[251] A. *Ch.* 789 may be an exception, but is easily taken as two exclamations *extra metrum* followed by minor ionic (parallel to what appears in the other mesodes: 807 and 827). Ar. *Av.* 1393–94 is probably $--\cup\,\cup-x|-\cup-x-\cup-x|^{\smile\smile}\cup-^{-}$ (εἴδωλα πετεινῶν | αἰθεροδρόμων οἰωνῶν ταναοδείρων) but there is nothing to indicate the relation of the colon to its original rhythmical context. Cinesias is singing dithyrambic snatches, not complete movements.

[252] The conclusion is assumed to be $\bar{x}-$ (rather than $-\overline{\cup\cup}$ or $.-^{-}$) because of the frequency of the colon close x–| in the major ionic contexts discussed subsequently (text, 194–97). Cf., also, in the stanza immediately following, $-\cup-.-\cup-x-$ (849 = 860) and $-\cup\,\cup-x-$ (853 = 864).

stanza thereby becomes a single continuum, brought to a natural stopping point only at the end, where the rhythm . . .– ⌣ ⌣ – x̄ – appears for the first time. The verbal components of the continuum are five cola or colon sets, separated from each other in one instance by the interjection φεῦ, in the other three by a pause of the same length. This pause gives sharper articulation to the formal structure, and in four of its six occurrences is dramatically appropriate as well: after Electra's initial outcry in (b) (the chorus is startled at the interruption and hesitates before proceeding) and before (a′) (Electra takes a breath before beginning the long undemarcated run with which the stanza closes):

Χο. ποῦ ποτε κεραυνοὶ Διός, ἢ ποῦ φαέθων ἅλιος εἰ ταῦτ᾽ ἐφορῶντες
                                          κρύπτουσιν ἕκηλοι,
Ηλ.                                                    ἒ ἒ αἰαῖ.
Χο.                           ὦ παῖ, τί δακρύεις;
Ηλ.                                                    φεῦ
Χο.                           μηδὲν μέγ᾽ ἀύσῃς.
Ηλ.                                                    ἀπολεῖς.
Χο.                                                    πῶς;
Ηλ. εἰ τῶν φανερῶς οἰχομένων εἰς ᾿Αίδαν ἐλπίδ᾽ ὑποίσεις κατ᾽ ἐμοῦ τακομένας μᾶλλον
                                                    ἐπεμβάσει

x˘ ⌣ – – ⌣ ⌣ – – ⌣ ⌣ – – ⌣ ⌣ |– – ⌣ ⌣ – –|..|
                    – – ⌣ ⌣ – –|⌣ ⌣ – –|..|
                    – – ⌣ ⌣ – –|⌣◡|
                    – – ⌣ ⌣ – –|⌣ ⌣ –|–|..|
                    – – ⌣ ⌣ – – ⌣ ⌣ – – ⌣ ⌣ – – ⌣ ⌣ – – ⌣ ⌣ – – ⌣ ⌣ – x̄ –

A similar symmetry, involving simpler elements, suggests the same analysis for *Aj.* 1199–1211ff.:

ἐκεῖνος οὐ στεφάνων        x – ⌣ –. ⌣ ⌣ –|– ⌣ ⌣ – – ⌣ ⌣ –|
οὔτε βαθειᾶν κυλίκων        – ⌣ ⌣ – – ⌣ ⌣ – –|..|– – ⌣ ⌣ – – ⌣ ⌣ –|
νεῖμεν ἐμοὶ τέρψιν ὁμιλεῖν   οὔτε γλυκὺν αὐλῶν ὄτοβον – ⌣ ⌣ – – ⌣ ⌣ –|– ⌣ ⌣ – –
                           δύσμορος, οὔτ᾽ ἐννυχίαν
                           τέρψιν ἰαύειν.

Once again, the quantities which pause must supply if there is to be a single piece of epiploke are the two which precede the major ionic colon opening. [253]

Adding a similar set of quantities in the middle of *O. T.* 483 = 498ff. keeps the regular structure of the stanza (elsewhere demarcated throughout before or after every fourth base quantity). It also

---

[253] For another instance of what may be double syncopation in this ode, see text 183.

emphasizes, by pause, the major syntactic break (antistrophe) or (strophe) the expanded perspective—generational and dynastic—introduced by *Labdakidais*:[254]

δεινὰ μὲν οὖν δεινὰ ταράσσει σοφὸς οἰωνοθέτας          – ⌣ ⌣ – – ⌣ ⌣ – – ⌣ ⌣ – – ⌣ ⌣ –

οὔτε δοκοῦντ' οὔτ' ἀποφάσκονθ'· ὅτι λέξω δ' ἀπορῶ.          – ⌣ ⌣ – – ⌣ ⌣ – – ⌣ ⌣ – – ⌣ ⌣ –.

πέτομαι δ' ἐλπίσιν, οὔτ' ἐνθάδ' ὁρῶν οὔτ' ὀπίσω.          ⌣ ⌣ – – ⌣ ⌣ – – ⌣ ⌣ – – ⌣ ⌣ –.

τί γὰρ ἢ Λαβδακίδαις, ἢ τῷ Πολύβου          ⌣ ⌣ – – ⌣ ⌣ –. | . . | – – ⌣ ⌣ –[255]

νεῖκος ἔκειτ', οὔτε πάροιθέν ποτ' ἔγωγ' οὔτε τανῦν πω          – ⌣ ⌣ – – ⌣ ⌣ – – ⌣ ⌣ – – ⌣ ⌣ – – ‖

ἔμαθον πρὸς ὅτου δὴ βασάνῳ <– ⌣ ⌣ –>          ⌣ ⌣ –. ⌣ ⌣ – – ⌣ ⌣ – – ⌣ ⌣ –.

ἐπὶ τὰν ἐπίδαμον φάτιν εἰμ' Οἰδιπόδα          ⌣ ⌣ –. ⌣ ⌣ – – ⌣ ⌣ – – ⌣ ⌣ –

Λαβδακίδαις ἐπίκουρος ἀδήλων θανάτων.          – ⌣ ⌣ –. ⌣ ⌣ –. ⌣ ⌣ – – ⌣ ⌣ –

The remaining examples of major ionic follow the sequence ×–, whether it forms part of iambo-trochaic (×)– ⌣ –×–, dochmiac ×– –×– or another piece of major ionic (– – ⌣ ⌣ –×–). All these end in "sesquiambic" demarcation (above, 107), and it is tempting to make the major ionic colon continuous with what precedes by positing a single non-syllabic quantity:

ἦ που ὀλοὰ στένει          ×˘˘⌣–×– +

ἦ που ἀδινῶν χλωρὰν          ×˘˘⌣–×–|.|– – ⌣ ⌣–×–|.|– –⌣ ⌣–

τέγγει δακρύων ἄχναν

ἀ δ' ἐρχομένα

μοῖρα προφαίνει δολίαν καὶ μεγάλαν ἄταν.          – ⌣ ⌣ – – ⌣ ⌣ –|– ⌣ ⌣–×–

          —*Trach.* 846–50 = 857–61

---

[254] Cf. Kraus 143, on the "atempause innerhalb des ionischen Presto" created by the substitution of a spondee for a minor ionic metron—i.e., in the analysis suggested here, of .. – – for ⌣ ⌣ – –.

[255] For the triple syncopation posited here, cf. A. *Ch.* 789–93 (perhaps: *extra metrum* [above, n. 251] + ⌣ ⌣ –×– ⌣–. ⌣ ⌣–. |.. |– –| ⌣ ⌣– –⌣ ⌣– – and the puzzling "anapests" of *Pers.* 952–54 = 965–66, which may be a syncopated version, with parallel demarcation, of the ionic that precedes:

          ⌣ ⌣ –. ⌣ ⌣– –‖ ⌣ ⌣–×– ⌣|– –⌣ ⌣– –

Ἰάων γὰρ ἀπηύρα, Ἰάων ναύφαρκτος Ἄρης ἑτεραλκής
νυχίαν πλάκα κερσάμενος          δυσδαίμονά τ' ἀκτάν

          ⌣ ⌣ –. ⌣ ⌣ –.   ⌣ ⌣ –.|..|   – –⌣ ⌣– –

(Cf. the somewhat different ionic analysis [⌣ ⌣ –. ⌣ ⌣ –. ⌣ ⌣ –. ⌣͞͞⌣–. ⌣ ⌣ – –] given by West 125).

ἔλεσθ᾽ ἔλεσθέ μ᾽ οἰκήτορα                    x – ⌣ – do‖

ἔλεσθέ μ᾽ οὔτε γὰρ θεῶν γένος               x – ⌣ – x̄ = ̲d̲ᾱ x̄ – | . | – – ⌣ ⌣ – x – ⌣ –

    οὔθ᾽ ἀμερίων ἔτ᾽ ἄξιος

    βλέπειν τιν᾽ εἰς ὄνασιν ἀνθρώπων.        x – ⌣ – x – ⌣ – x –

                                            – Aj. 396–400 ≈ 414–17

The close of the preceding stanza in the *Tr.* and the immediate sequel
in the *Aj.* are parallel, but substitute - x̆ - ⌣ - for major ionic – – ⌣ ⌣ -. . .:

ἀλλά μ᾽ ἁ Διὸς                              – ⌣ – x – | . | – x – ⌣ – ‖˘̆ ⌣ ⌣ – x –  +

    ἀλκίμα θεὸς

        ὀλέθριον αἰκίζει

ποῖ τις οὖν φύγῃ;                           – ⌣ – x –  +

ποῖ μολὼν μένω;                             – ⌣ – x – | . | – x – ⌣ – x – ⌣ – x – ⌣ –

    εἰ τὰ μὲν φθίνει, φίλοι †τοῖσδ᾽ ὁμοῦ πέλας

        μώραις δ᾽ ἄγραις προσκείμεθα         x – ⌣ – x – ⌣ – ‖

        πᾶς δὲ στρατὸς δίπαλτος ἄν με        x – ⌣ – x – ⌣ – x | – ⌣ ⌣ –¯
                                                          —A^—
            χειρὶ φονεύοι

                                            – Aj. 401–11 = 418–29

πῶς γὰρ ἂν ὁ μὴ λεύσσων                      x˘̆ ⌣ – x – | . | ˘̆ x˘̆ ⌣˘̆ | x E ^

    ἔτι ποτ᾽ ἔτ᾽ ἐπίπονον

        ἔχοι θανὼν λατρείαν;

                                            – Tr. 828–30 = 838–40

Comparable passages from Sophocles and early Euripides are *OT* 1208–11
= 1217–20, *El.* 246–50 and 1273ff., *Alc.* 213 = 226ff. (three
instances),[256] *Med.* 847–49 = 857–59 and *Hipp.* 135–38 = 125–28.
From later tragedy there is *Ph.* 1023–25 = 1047–49, *Or.* 992–94 and
1499ff., and *Rh.* 250–51 = 260–61. In every instance |– x̆ – ⌣ – |
appears preceded by (x)– ⌣ – x –, – ⌣ ⌣ – x – or ⌣ – – ⌣ – (do or x –. –
x̆ –),[257] and with a variety of sequels: (x)– ⌣ –. . ., (–) ⌣ ⌣ –. . . and

---

[256] Assuming that the strophe of 215 = 228 should be emended to correspond with the
antistrophe (e.g., as αἰαῖ, εἰσί τις [Wilamowitz, followed by Murray] or τίς ἔξεισι, τίς;
[257] *Alc.* 234–35 = 222–23 may contain a variant which begins two quantities earlier in the
epiploke and syncopates both sequences: x – ⌣ – x – ⌣ | – x –. – . – | . | – x –. – | x D x
‾ | ⌣ ̲D̲ – ⌣ ⌣ – ⌣ – ¯ (βόασον ὤ, στέναξον, | ὤ Φεραία χθών, | τὰν ἀρίσταν | . . .), but
analysis is complicated by corruption in the responding . . . | καὶ πάρος γὰρ † τοῦδ᾽
ἐφεύρες † καὶ νῦν |.

××– ᴗ ᴗ – ᴗ –. The linking with the preceding colon creates, like the pairing of ordinary dochmiacs (above, 107), what is, in some sense, a trimeter equivalent; but the equivalence suggested here is more exact: a succession of quantities identical to what appears in the syncopated trimeter ⁽×⁾–⁽·⁾– ×–.–×– ᴗ –. It is unlikely that the two types of linking are completely parallel, given the rarity of dochmiacs in the context,[258] the frequency of prosodic demarcation (suggesting the presence of a pause following the first colon), and the existence of passages in which – – ᴗ ᴗ – appears rather than –×̆– ᴗ –. On the other hand, it is equally difficult to reject the dochmiac analogy altogether and make –×̆– ᴗ – and what precedes into independent disjunct sequences. An isolated |– ᴗ – ᴗ –| is very rare in the midst of normal iambo-trochaic or ionochoriambic.[259] It seems to have required an accompanying ⁽×⁾– ᴗ –×– or ᴗ – – ᴗ –, and the most simple explanation for the requirement is that the two sequences were rhythmically continuous.[260]

Further support for making the colon openings – – ᴗ ᴗ – and –×̆– ᴗ – part of a rhythmical continuum with what precedes, as well as a possible link between the Classical and Hellenistic versions of major ionic, is provided by the Dictaean hymn to Zeus, first published in 1908 and usually dated to the fourth or third century B.C.[261] The poem consists of six distichs, in alternation with seven repetitions of an identical refrain. What survives of the first, second, third and fifth distichs is compatible with the scheme:

```
×–      ×–      ×–          ×–      ×–      ×–
–     ᴗ–     ᴗ|–     ᴗ – – ᴗᴗ|–     ᴗ–     ᴗ|–     ᴗ – – ᴗᴗ||
–ᴗ      –ᴗ      –ᴗ          –ᴗ      –ᴗ      –ᴗ
```

i.e., two major ionic tetrameters acatalectic, ending in the – – ᴗᴗ found in the Cleomachean (above, 31). The final distich, however, seems to offer

[258] Dochmiacs are only found in the stanza from the Ajax discussed in the text, and preceding OT 1208 = 1218ff. and El. 247–50.

[259] And only appears where there is some reason for the analysis |–×̆– ᴗ –|: see Appendix VI.

[260] In the three or four instances (E. Or. 992–94, Ph. 1023–24, S. Aj. 404–5 = 421–23, and, possibly, OT 1209–11ff.) where there is a triple rather than double – ᴗ – ᴗ – the first may be a disjunct monocolon anticipating the movement of the following pair, just as the ×– ᴗ –do of Aj. 396 = 414ff. and the ×– ᴗ –×– of Tr. 846 = 857ff. (text, 195) anticipate the opening of the succeeding movement into major ionic. Unlike ×– ᴗ –×–, however, (above 107)ᴵ – ᴗ – ᴗ – is never repeated at greater length as the basis of an entire disjunct composition.

[261] On the hymn, see, most recently, M. L. West, "The Dictaean Hymn to the Kouros," JHS 85 (1965) 149–54.

minor rather than major ionic:

[θόρε κὲς] πόληας ἀμῶν, θόρε κὲς ποντοφόρος νᾶας     ∪∪−×−∪−−|∪∪−−∪∪−−

θόρε κὲς ν[έος πολ]είτας, θόρε κὲς Θέμιν κλ[. . .     ∪∪−×−∪−−|∪∪−×−. . .[262]

—a highly anomalous responsion if, as is likely, all the distichs were sung to the same music. The simplest way to account for the phenomenon is to assume initial and final syncopation, so that major and minor ionic sequences occupy slightly different positions in a single piece of musically continuous epiploke:

Distichs 1–3, 5:     ∪∪|−×̲⁻∪−×̲⁻∪|−×̲⁻∪−−σ̲υ̲|−×̲⁻∪ . . . − σ̲υ̲

Distich 6:     ∪∪ −×−∪−−|∪∪ −×̲⁻∪−−| ∪∪−×−∪ . . .| ∪∪|[263]

A comparison of the text of the final two distichs supports this analysis:

5.2:     [κὲς λάι]α καρπῶν   θόρε, κὲς τελεσ[φόρους οἴκους

         −−∪∪−−|∪∪|−×−∪−−σ̲υ̲

         ∪∪|−×−∪−−|∪∪|−. . .

6.1–2:     θόρε   κὲς] πόληας ἀμῶν, θόρε κὲς . . .

           θόρε   κὲς ν[έος πολ]είτας, θόρε κὲς . . .

Here it is hard to believe that the sequence κὲς λάια καρπῶν in the first line was not intended to be sung to the same stretch of music as κὲς νέους πολείτας in the third; and this would only be possible if the two lines stood in the relationship suggested to a shared quantitative pattern. One is tempted to suppose that the word *thore,* which occupies the same position rhythmically wherever it appears in the poem, was accompanied by a leap that, by itself, could have supplied the syncopated quantities at the beginning of the lines in distichs 1–3 and 5. But, however supplied, the two quantities would occupy the same position in the epiploke as those

---

[262] The remainder is hard to restore. Suggested supplements (e.g., κλ<ηνάν>, κλ<ειτάν>) usually require assumption of the problematic contraction ∪∪−×−.−⁻).

[263] Central rather than initial or terminal syncopation may occur in distich 4, which is only partially preserved, but seems to have consisted of minor followed by major ionic:

∪∪−×]−∪−×−∪−×−∪−−|..|−×̲⁻∪−−σ̲υ̲−×−∪−−σ̲υ̲

(Reconstructing the first line as major ionic −×̲⁻∪]|−∪−−|−∪−∪|−∪−− would result in the metron form −∪−×̄ not otherwise attested in Greek until the second century A.D. (text, 36).

which were assumed to appear in the Sophoclean $- \cup \cup - - | \stackrel{\smile}{\cup} \stackrel{\smile}{\cup} | - -$ $\cup \cup -$ examined earlier.

The opening of the distichs may be continuous with the close ( . . . $\times - \cup - ^-$) of the refrain which precedes each of them.[264] If so, the poem is further linked to Classical practice by the absence of any clear instances of major ionic at the start of a rhythmical movement. If there was rhythmical discontinuity at this point, so that a new movement began with $^(\stackrel{\smile}{\cup} \stackrel{\smile}{\cup})$, the rhythmic technique has moved further in the direction of the Hellenistic Sotadean, which is an independent stichos and so an example of initial rather than internal major ionic. But at whatever point in the development from Sophocles to Sotades our text stands, it is easy to see how the development might have occurred. Regularized internal minor ionic demarcation, followed occasionally by two syncopated quantities, would suggest interpretation as a series of equivalent stichoi, some beginning with $\cup \cup - -$ and some with $\stackrel{\smile}{\cup} \stackrel{\smile}{\cup} - -$, and ultimately a mode of composition in which $\stackrel{\smile}{\cup} \stackrel{\smile}{\cup} - -$ appeared at the beginning of a movement. Cf., for a possible example, *PTeb.* i, p. 3:

ξουθὰ δὲ λιγύφωνα             $.. - ^{\vee\vee} \cup \cup - - \parallel$

ὄρνεα διεφοίτα               $.. - ^{\vee\vee} \cup \cup - - \parallel$

$<ἀ>ν'$ ἐρῆμον δρίος, ἄκροις . . .   $\cup \cup - - \cup \cup - - |$

(p. 185 Powell)

followed by 15 minor ionic dimeters and one trimeter.[265]

When this composition was used in verse intended for recitation rather than singing, the syncopated quantities, like all aspects of the rhythm that depended on music or dance for their realization, would disappear, leaving

---

[264] Part of a line which may also be major ionic (Δίκταν ἐς ἐνιαυτόν) $(- - \cup \cup - \times - \cup - \times - \cup - -)$. The orthography of the stone, however, varies between ἐς and εἰς (which would yield the minor ionic $(σ\overline{σ}) - - \cup \cup - . . .)$ and there is no way of knowing in what fashion the line, however, scanned, was linked to the $\times - \cup - \times - \cup - \times - \cup - \times | - \cup - \times - \cup - \times - \cup - \times - \cup -$ that precedes it in the refrain.

[265] Cf., also, Pl. *Pseud.* 1273ff.—equal tricola (if iambic shortening is legitimate in *ăd hŭnc mḗ modum*), the first with minor, the second with major-ionic opening:

ad hunc me mod(um) intul(i) illis satis facete    $\cup \cup - \times - \cup - \times^{\vee} \cup - -$
nimis ex discipulina                  $\cup \cup - - \cup \cup - -$
quipp(e) ego qui prob(e) Ionica perdidici.    $\overline{σσ}^{\vee} - \cup \cup - ^{\vee\vee} \overline{σσ}^{\vee} -$
    sed palliolat(im) amictŭs sic haec       $.. | - - \cup \cup - \times - \cup - -$
incessi ludibundus.                   $\overline{σσ} - \times - \cup - -$
plaudunt, "párŭm" clamitant mih(i) ut revortar  $\overline{σσ} - ^{\vee\vee} - \cup - \times - \cup - -$

(For the metron sequence $\overline{σσ} - ^{\vee\vee} | - \cup - -$ see text, 32).

the opening $--\cup\cup-$. . . or, in the mixed iono-choriambic of the Sotadean, $-\overset{\times}{\phantom{}}\overset{-}{\phantom{}}\underset{\cup}{\phantom{}}-$. . . If, however, there were ever occasions on which the Sotadean or related forms were sung and danced as well as recited, the syncopated quantities may have been retained or reintroduced (supplied by gestures perhaps: a bit of the obscene mimesis which some ancient testimony associates with major ionic).[266] The hypothesis would help explain why the rhythm itself seems to have been felt as indecent, quite apart from the content, often harmless or even edifying, of the Sotadeans composed in it.

It is easy to understand the Classical reluctance to begin a poem with syncopated quantities, however supplied. To do so would be to tip the always precarious balance between text and musical accompaniment too far in the direction of the latter. It is harder to see why the initial quantity sequences $--\cup\cup$. . . and $-\times-\cup$. . . in themselves were found objectionable. Perhaps, however, both were too ambiguous—too much like anapestic $\overline{\cup\cup}-\cup\cup$. . . or aeolic $\times-\cup\cup$. . . in the one instance, and too much like aeolo-ionic $\overline{\cup\cup}--\cup$. . . . or trochaic $-\cup-\overset{\smile}{\times}$. . . . in the other (compare the reluctance, in Classical ionic, to use the potentially ambiguous opening $\overline{\cup\cup}-\overset{\smile}{\times}-\cup-$. . . above, 40–41]). A concern for rhythmical clarity is something which the Sophoclean lyric manner has in common with the Aeschylean, however much Sophocles may surpass his predecessor in variety, in complexity, and in the virtuosity of his efforts—through fuller use of epiplokai and their ambiguities—to make the lyric stanza a harmony as well as a unity.

---

[266] The ancient writers who refer to Sotades by the generic term *kinaidologos* or *iōnikologos* (Athenaeus 14.13 p. 620e) and derive this type of poetry from earlier lyric that imitated the talk and manner of the *cinaedus* (Strabo 14.1.41 p. 648) do not specify the rhythm involved; and the name "ionic" itself seems to have referred originally to the dialect in which Sotades' *iōnikoi logoi* were written, not their metre (see R. Westphal and A. Rossbach, *Metrik der Griechen*[2] I [Leipzig 1867] 110). But Sotades is not known to have used any other verse form, and it is reasonable to assume that his indebtedness to predecessors, like most such indebtednesses in the history of the Greek lyric, involved imitation of metre as well as content.

# CHAPTER ELEVEN:
## THE LATE FIFTH CENTURY AND AFTER

The late fifth century was, or seemed to contemporary conservatives, a period of intense musical innovation; and Euripides, as the most influential composer of the day, is usually assumed to have been a modernist in rhythmical as well as other matters. Both assumptions are doubtless correct, but they should not lead us to expect unprecedented or unprecedently irregular forms in all the rhythmical genres encountered in Euripidean tragedy. One kind of unprecedented irregularity, it is true, does become almost a regular occurrence: unlike syllable sequences appear more frequently as rhythmical equivalents, through a hitherto unprecedented use of resolution (dochmiac[267] and iambo-trochaic), contraction (anapests), syncopation (iambo-trochaic[268] and aeolic[269]), long anceps (dochmiac[270]) and unusual forms of aeolic base and nucleus ($\bar{\times}\bar{\times}$ and $-\cup\cup-\cup\cup-$ whether taken as $-\bar{\times}-\cup\cup-$ or $-\cup\cup-\bar{\times}-$).[271]

In other ways, however, Euripidean lyric can display a regularity, even monotony, of structure that is un-Sophoclean and has few parallels in

---

[267] The statistics in Conomis (23) show nearly twice as many forms with two or more resolutions in Euripides as in Aeschylus and Sophocles combined.

[268] Less frequent than in Aeschylus and Sophocles, but showing, particularly in trochaic, a greater variety of forms; cf. the *conspectus metrorum* in Schroeder (118–20 [Aeschylus], 84–86 [Sophocles], 193–95 [Euripides]).

[269] Found outside Euripides and Euripidean parody (Ar. *Ran.* 1318–19 and 1348–51) only at S. *Aj.* 1190–91 = 1197–98 (text, 90), *OT* 1196 = 1204, Ar. *Vesp.* 316–18 (above, n. 237), *Av.* 676ff. ($-\cup\cup-\times-.\mid \times-\cup\cup-\cup-\mid\times\times-\cup\cup-\cup-\mid\times\times-\cup\cup-\bar{\phantom{-}}$), and possibly, S. *Aj.* 1209 = 1221 (text, 173), *Ant.* 100 = 117ff. (text, 86) and *OC* 127 = 59 (text, 183). A. *Suppl.* 815–16 = 823–24, often analyzed as $-\cup\cup-\cup-\mid \bar{\times}\bar{\times}-\cup\cup-\cup-.\mid\bar{\times}-\cup\cup-\cup-\times$ is better taken with the instances of syncopated iono-choriambic presented in the text, 51.

[270] Except in the common $\bar{\times}\check{}\check{}-\times-$, Euripidean instances of long anceps are six times as numerous as those from other tragedians: cf. Conomis 23.

[271] Euripidean influence is probably present in all the non-Euripidean passages where these forms appear: Ar. *Th.* 1136ff. (four instances of $\bar{\times}\bar{\times}$, one or two of $-\cup\cup-\cup\cup-$), *Ran.* 1323 ($-\cup\cup-\cup\cup-$), S. *Ph.* 1213 ($\bar{\times}\bar{\times}$ if the line is not emended: above, n. 235), and, possibly, *OC* 237–40 ($\times\times-\times\check{}\check{}\cup-\mid$ [or, without ἀλαόν, $-\times-\cup\cup-\mid\mid$] $\bar{\times}\bar{\times}-\cup\cup-\cup\cup-$ $\mid\times\times-\times-\cup\cup-\cup-\bar{\phantom{-}}$). $\bar{\times}\bar{\times}$ at Ar. *Ran.* 1322 (περίβαλλ' ὦ τέκνον ὠλένας) may also be an instance, but there are no likely parallels in what actually survives of Euripides.

Aeschylus. This is especially true of aeolic, beginning with the *Andromache*. Whole movements can now be constituted by strict alternation of double base and nucleus—occasionally as many as ten times in succession—broken only by the occasional insertion, through iambic modulation, of a double cycle of iambo-trochaic or iono-choriambic.[272] In many shorter aeolic sequences demarcation is regularized before the base;[273] and choriambic modulation is practically eliminated from the genre altogether.[274] The consistent octadic movement which its absence favors has a parallel in many iambo-trochaic and iono-choriambic contexts. There a similar effect is obtained by regular demarcation before or after every other base, syncopation at corresponding points in every other cycle, or regular alternation between single cycles of iambo-trochaic and iono-choriambic.[275]

The length and regularity of such passages are paralleled in the long series of dactylic tetrameters found in Sophocles' last three plays (cf. Dale 207–9);[276] and other aspects of late Sophoclean lyric testify, sporadically, to the popularity and character of the new manner. Its influence can

---

[272] Cf. *Hec.* 466 = 477ff. (above, n. 85), *Suppl.* 973–79, *HF* 643–54 = 661–72 and 673–81 = 687–95 (if scanned with initial ×–⏑––⏑⏑–. |.–×–⏑⏑–×|×–×–⏑⏑–); 792–97 = 809–14, *El.* 150–56, 169–74 = 192–97, 435–41 = 445–51, 701–7 = 715–21, *IT* 427–38 = 444–55, 1096–1105 = 1113–22, *Hel.* 1308–19 = 1326–37, 1487–94 = 1503–11, *Ph.* 232–38, *Cycl.* 41–48 = 55–62, 63–72, *Bac.* 864–75 = 884–95, *IA* 216–24, 546–57 = 561–72, 753–61 = 764–72, and the Euripidean parody of Ar. *Ran.* 1317–28.

[273] Cf. the aeolic portions of *Suppl.* 990 = 1012ff., *El.* 112 = 127ff., *Or.* 832–843, *Bac.* 402 = 416ff., and *IA* 164 = 185ff. A typically Euripidean variant involves the disjunction . . . –⏑⏑–⁻ + (×)×–⏑⏑–⏑_, either setting off a final, one-colon coda (*Hipp.* 737 = 747, *Hel.* 1352, *Ph.* 231, *Bac.* 156, *IA* 215, 775, 783, 790, and, possibly, 211: παρά τε κροκάλαισ<ι> + δρόμον ἔχοντι σὺν ὅπλοις) or concluding a dicolon (××–⏑⏑–⏑–⏑– ××–⏑⏑–⁻) that acts as a disjunct introduction to a longer series (*Suppl.* 971ff. and *Bac.* 403 = 416ff. Cf., also, *Rhesus* 344–47 = 353–56: . . .|××–⏑⏑–⁻ + ××–⏑⏑–⏑–⁻ and ××–⏑⏑–⁻ + ××–×–⏑⏑–⏑–⁻).

[274] Isolated instances at *Ion* 1232 (above, n. 96), *El.* 460–63 = 472–75 (××–⏑⏑– [or ⏑––⏑⏑–] –⏑⏑––⏑⏑––⏑⏑–×–⏑––|⏜⏝ –⏑⏑–⏑–⁻) and *Bac.* 113–14 = 128–29 (××–⏑⏑––⏑⏑––⏑⏑––⏑⏑––⏑⏑–⁻).

[275] Cf. *Suppl.* 44ff. (ionic), 621–25 = 629–33 (iambic), *HF* 411–18 = 427–35 (iambo-trochaic), *Tr.* 522–30 = 542–50 (iambic), 551–67 (iambic), *Hel.* 167–251 (trochaic), *Ph.* 239–45 = 250–56 (trochaic), 638–89 (trochaic), *Or.* 998–1004 and 1457–66 (iambo-trochaic), *Bac.* 64–72, 370–402 and 519–70 (ionic) and Timotheus 15/791.160ff. (iambo-trochaic).

[276] Cf., for Euripidean instances, *Hel.* 375–84, *Ph.* 828–31 and 1502–7, *Or.* 1005–11 and *Hyps.* I.ii.10–14. Comedy also offers parallels (cf. *Pax* 114–18, *Nub.* 282–86 = 305–10, *Eccl.* 1170–76), although here, as often with comic analogues to late Euripidean and Sophoclean technique, it is impossible to know whether we are dealing with a new development or a traditional feature of comic versification introduced into tragedy at a fairly late date.

probably be seen in the *Phil.* (remarkable for a regularity of aeolic demarcation not found in earlier Sophocles),[277] as well as in the *OC.* There the pure octadic aeolic series attains, for the first time, a truly Euripidean length (176–83 = 192–200: $\overline{\cup\cup}$– – $\cup$ $\cup$ – – $\cup$ $\cup$ – – $\cup$ $\cup$ – – $\cup$ $\cup$ –
×|x–$\underset{A}{\underline{\cup\cup–\cup}}$–x|x–$\cup$ $\cup$ – $\cup$ –x|x–$\cup$ $\cup$ – $\cup$ –x|x–$\cup$ $\cup$ – $\cup$ –|   xx–$\cup$ $\cup$ –
$\cup$–xx–$\cup$ $\cup$ – $\cup$–|   xx–$\cup$ $\cup$ – $\cup$–xx$\underset{A}{\underline{–\cup}}$$_{\cup}$–¯); and the similarly constructed *OC* 510 = 521ff., while containing a characteristically Sophoclean choriambic modulation and ambiguous clausular sequence (above, 185–92), may be, in at least one way, more Euripidean than anything attested in Euripides himself:

Χο.  δεινὸν μὲν τὸ πάλαι κείμενον ἤδη κακὸν ὦ ξεῖν' ἐπεγείρειν,

    ὅμως δ' ἔραμαι πυθέσθαι     $\overline{\cup\cup}$– – $\cup$ $\cup$ – – $\cup$ $\cup$ – – $\cup$ $\cup$ – –$\cup$ $\cup$–x|x    $\underset{A}{\underline{–\cup\cup\,{-}\,\cup}}$–x

Οἰ.       τί τοῦτο;            *extra metrum*

Χο.  τᾶς δειλαίας ἀπόρου φανείσας          x$\underline{–x\overset{B}{\underline{–\cup}}\underset{A}{\underline{\cup}}\,{-}\,\cup}$$_{-x}$

    ἀλγηδόνος ᾷ ξυνέστας.           x – $\cup$ $\cup$ – $\cup$ –x

Οἰ.  μὴ πρὸς ξενίας ἀνοίξῃς            x – $\cup$ $\cup$ – $\cup$ –x

    τᾶς σᾶς ἃ πέπονθ' ἀναιδῆ.           x – $\cup$ $\cup$ – $\cup$ –x

Χο.  τό τοι πολὺ καὶ μηδαμὰ λῆγον χρῄζω      x – $\cup$ $\cup$ – – $\underset{A}{\underline{\cup\,\cup}}$–x–x

    ξεῖν' ὀρθὸν ἄκουσμ' ἀκοῦσαι.          x – $\cup$ $\cup$ – $\cup$ –x

Οἰ.       ὤμοι.               *extra metrum*

Χο.  στέρξον, <σ'>[278] ἱκετεύω          x – $\cup$ $\cup$–x

Οἰ.       φεῦ φεῦ               *extra metrum*

Χο.       πείθου.              $\underset{A}{\underline{–}}$  ¯×

    κἀγὼ γὰρ ὅσον σὺ προσχρῄζεις.       x $\underset{A}{\underline{–\cup\cup\,{-}\,\cup}}$–.–¯

Here the failure of the three exclamations *extra metrum* to break the continuity of the epiploke[279] suggests the presence, in extreme form, of an

[277] Cf. 169–79 = 180–90, 1123–29 = 1146–52, 1140–45 = 1163–68 and most of the aeolic sections of the *amoibaia* at 1081ff. and 1169ff.

[278] Bergk's emendation to restore responsion with the παῖδες, δύο . . . of the antistrophe. The alternative is to assume a highly irregular prosodiac demarcation at this point, or to read παῖδε (Elmsley) in the antistrophe. The latter, however, creates the rhythmically problematic – $\cup$ $\cup$ $\cup$ – – and gets no support from Attic usage, which favors plural rather than dual noun forms in conjunction with the numeral δύο (see E. Schwyzer, *Griechische Grammatik* [2] [Munich 1950] 49 with n. 4).

[279] The exclamations are not only *extra metrum* but *extra sensum* to the point of being totally ignored by the party to whom they are addressed. For similar treatment of such interruptions cf. *OC* 199 (ἰὼ μοί μοι between the sixth and seventh cola of the passage mentioned in the text), *El.* 855 = 866 (τί φῄς = παπαῖ), *Alc.* 874 = 891ff. (φεῦ φεῦ and ἰώ μοί μοι in both strophe and antistrophe preceding, respectively, the fourth and the thirteenth quantities in x– $\cup$ |–.– $\cup$ –x– $\cup$ –|x– $\cup$ –. . .). Contrast, in the immediately preceding 872 = 889ff.,

uncharacteristically Sophoclean feeling for the rhythmical sustaining power
of pure aeolic. Euripides provides the nearest parallel; cf. *Ion* 219– 21 =
205 – 7:

| | | |
|---|---|---|
| Χο. | σέ τοι, τὸν παρὰ ναὸν αὐδῶ· | ××–∪ ∪–∪–× |
| | θέμις γυάλων ὑπερβῆναι, | x‾–∪‾∪‾–x‾–·‾–‾x |
| | λευκῷ ποδί γ’ | x–∪∪ |
| Ἰω. | οὐ θέμις, ὦ ξέναι | *extra metrum* |
| Χο. | οὐδόν; | ‾–‾ |
| | | ‾A‾ |

where Ion's dactylo-anapestic interruption is shown to have no effect on
the main rhythmical line by the fact that it, like his five other interposi-
tions in this stanza, has no parallel in the strophe. One wonders whether
such interruptions were not delivered simultaneously with portions of the
other participant's lines, a suggestion which is supported, for the Sophoclean passage, by the demarcation, in both strophe and antistrophe, of
sequences rhythmically identical with the interruptions:

| | | |
|---|---|---|
| Οἰ. | ὤμοι | ×– |
| Χο. | στέρξον <σ’>ἱκετεύω. | ×–\|∪ ∪–×\| |
| Οἰ. | φεῦ φεῦ. | –× |
| Χο. | πείθου. | –× |
| | | –A———— |

(cf., in the antistrophe:

| | |
|---|---|
| Χο. | πῶς φῆς; |
| Οἰ. | παῖδες, δύο δ’ἄτα |
| Χο. | ὦ Ζεῦ |
| Οἰ. | ματρός). |

The operatic effect thus achieved would be yet another instance of the
diversity of verbal realizations which a single quantity sequence might
have in the closing years of the century.

---

the rhythmical treatment of the interjections αἰαῖ and ἒ ἔ, both of which call forth a response
upon being uttered:

| | | |
|---|---|---|
| Ἄδμ. | αἰαῖ. | ×–\|∪–×–∪–·–∪– |
| Χο. | πέπονθας ἄξι αἰαγμάτων. | |
| Ἄδμ. | ἒ ἔ. | ×–·\|˘˘×–∪– |
| Χο. | δι’ ὀδύνας ἔβας | |

If the Euripidean lyric of the period gives, in spite of such passages, the impression of variety, irregularity and even confusion, it is largely through its astrophic sections, particularly monodies and amoibaia. These favor disjunct structure as they did in Sophocles and Aeschylus but now tend to be longer and occupy a larger portion of each play's lyrics.[280] The new uses of epiploke which help to create this diversity are remarkable for the frequency with which they involve dactylo-anapestic in one fashion or another. Even metric anapests take on a more varied periodic structure— not simply a regular succession of full metra or dimeters concluded by catalexis, but disjunct collocations in which the catalectic an an^ or, on occasion, shorter sequences, may constitute the basic repeated unit, with clausular or pre-clausular variation provided by an acatalectic an(an), or disjunct introduction of a contrasting rhythm.[281] Continuous dactylo-anapestic sequences which pass back and forth from one type of demarcation to the other appear in the plays written in the last years of the century as they had not done elsewhere since the *Persae*.[282] Modulation between prosodiac and dactylo-anapestic is more frequent in Euripides than any other dramatist,[283] and the contexts involved are not simply the dochmiac ones discussed above (101–3).[284] Also peculiar to Euripides (and his contemporaries and successors) is the use of the | ∪ ∪ − ∪ ∪ − demarcation characteristic of those dochmiac contexts as an initial rhythm alongside a similarly demarcated prosodiac ^D; cf. Ar. *Av.* 1313 ≈1325ff.:

[280] Outside of Euripides and the author of the *Rhesus* astrophic monodies and amoibaia are found only at A. *PV* 93–100, 114–27, and 561–73; S. *Tr.* 879–95, *Ph.* 1169–1217 and *OC* 208–55.

[281] Cf., for example, *Ion* 144–50 (a repeated an an^ + an to which a quadruple (‿) ∪ ∪ − −− forms a clausula, succeeded by a new grouping: an an^ + an an); 172–78 (a quintuple an an^ followed by an|an an|−−−−−), 897–904 (triple an an^ + ∪ ∪ ∪|∪ ∪ ∪ + an|an an^, followed by an an^ + an an + −−−−−) and the passages cited below, Appendix VIII).

[282] Cf. the passages cited above, n. 23. *Hipp.* 1374–75 (∪ ∪ − ∪ ∪ − ∪ ∪|− ∪ ∪ − ∪ ∪|− ∪ ∪ − ∪ ∪ − ∪ ∪ − may be an earlier example, but hiatus before the concluding − ∪ ∪ − ∪ ∪ − ∪ ∪ − makes the text suspect; see Barrett *ad loc.*

[283] Confined in Aeschylus and Sophocles to the beginning and ends of prosodiac movements (see text, 68 with n. 62). *Ant.* 354–56 = 365–67 (text, 69) is an isolated exception.

[284] Typical instances are:

| | | |
|---|---|---|
| | ×D ∪ ∪ −\| ∪ ∪ − ∪ ∪ −×− ∪ −× | *Alc.* 435–37 = 445–47 |
| D .\|− ∪ − | ×D ×− ∪ −×D \| ∪ ∪ −×D ×\|− ∪ −×\|E\|×D | *Andr.* 789ff. (unless regularized by Stevens' <σ'> ἐπ' in 792) |
| ∪ ∪ − ∪ ∪ −− ∪ −×\|D ×D ∪ ∪ −×−\| ∪ −.− ∪ −.−\| ∪ − ∪ − ͞ | 1014 = 1022ff. |
| ——A | | |
| ×Ex\|E. \|D \| ∪ ∪ − ∪ ∪ −×− ∪ − ∪ − ͞ | *Tr.* 835 = 855ff. |
| ×− ∪ − | ×−\| ∪ ∪ − ∪ ∪ − ∪ ∪ −   ×− ∪ − ∪ − ͞ | *Hel.* 1111 = 1126 |
| | ×D .\|D ∪ ∪ − ∪ ∪ −×− ∪ −× | *Rhes.* 529–30 = 549–50 |

∪ ∪ − ∪ ∪ −∪∪− ∪ ∪ −|×−∪−.−⁻ +
<br>—D—
                 ×    E ^  +

∪ ∪ − ∪ ∪ −∪∪− ∪ ∪ −|×    E ^  +
<br>—D—

∪ × − ∪ ∪ − ×       +
<br>—D—

∪ × − ∪ ∪ − ×       +
<br>—D—

∪ ∪ − ∪ ∪ − ∪ ∪ − ∪ ∪ −|∪ ∪ − ∪ ∪ −∪∪−∪ ∪ − ×    E ^
<br>—D—

and, more elaborately, with iono-choriambic forming a transitional section to concluding iambo-trochaic, 451 ≈ 539ff.:

δολερὸν μὲν ἀεὶ            ^D . | ∪ ∪ −×− ∪ −|×− ∪ −.−⁻ +[285]

κατὰ πάντα δὴ τρόπον

πέφυκεν ἄνθρωπος.

σὺ δ' ὅμως λέγε μοι,          ^D . | ∪ ∪ −×−.−.| − ∪ −.−⁻ +

τάχα γὰρ τύχοις ἂν

χρηστὸν ἐξειπὼν

ὅτι μοι παρορᾷς ἤ          ^ Dx +

δύναμίν τινα μείζω         ^ Dx +

              ∪ ∪ − ∪ ∪ − ∪ ∪ − ∪ ∪ D|×    − ∪ −.−⁻ +

παραλειπομένην ὑπ' ἐμῆς φρενὸς ἀξυνέτου, σὺ δὲ τοῦθ'

                οὐρᾶς λέγ' ἐς κοινόν.

ὃ γὰρ ἂν σὺ τύχῃς μοι        ^ Dx +

ἀγαθὸν πορίσας,           ^ D. |        − ∪ − ∪ −⁻

        τοῦτο κοινὸν ἔσται.

Without dactylo-anapestic in the same context, ^D is confined to Euripides—cf. its use in *Alc.* 903 = 926ff., among the fragments out of which the chorus attempts to construct a piece of consolation (all of them taken from the initial ×− ∪ −.|− ∪ −. ‖ [or ×− ∪ −. |− ∪ − +] D x |E ^, in which the fact of loss is first stated):

[285] Cf., for a possible parallel to the opening ^D.| ∪ ∪ −×− ∪ −, *Rhesus* 527 = 546 (Table IV) and, for the prepositive ὡς at the end of the period in the antistrophe, Pind. *O*10.18, A. *Ag.* 1354 and (in a similar rhythmical context) Ar. *Nub.* 804 = 700ff.: ×− ∪ − − ∪ ∪ − − ∪ ∪ − ∪ −⁻ + ×− ∪ −× (μόνας θεῶν ὡς) + × Dx− ∪ − ∪ −⁻.

ἐμοί τις ἦν ἐν γένει,                   x- ᵕ -. | - ᵕ -. ‖ - ᵕ ᵕ - ᵕ ᵕ -x | E ˆ +
                                              —D———
  ὦ κόρος ἀξιόθρηνος ὦλετ᾽ ἐν δόμοισιν,

  μονόπαις, ἀλλ᾽ ἔμπας                    ᵕ ᵡ꞊ ᴗᴗ̅ -x         +
                                              —D̲—
ἔφερε κακὸν                              x˙˙ ᵕ -. ‖ (or x꞊ ᵕ - +)

  ἅλις ἄτεκνος ὤν,                       ˙˙ ᵕ ˙˙x ²⁸⁶

    πολιὰς ἐπὶ χαίτας                    ᵕ ᵕ - ᵕ ᵕ -x
                                            —ˆD———
    ἤδη προπετὴς ὤν,                     ᴗᴗ̅- ᵕ ᵕ --| ᵕ ᵕ - ᵕ - ⁻
                                            —ˆD———

Also confined to Euripides, or Aristophanic parody,²⁸⁷ is the use of the
demarcation - | ᵕ ᵕ - ᵕ ᵕ -, with or without dactylo-anapestic analogues,
          —D———
within a movement:

    ὅθι ποικιλόνωτος                     ᵕ ᵡ꞊ ᵕ ᵕ -x
                                              —D̲—
οἰνωπὸς δράκων                           -.-.- ᵕ -

    σκιερᾷ κατάχαλκος                    ᵕ ᵡ꞊ ᵕ ᵕ -x
εὔφυλλον δάφνᾳ                           -. -. - ᵕ -. | - ᵕ -x-| ᴗᴗ̅꞊̲ᵕ ᵕ -x- ᵕ ᵕ - ²⁸⁸
γᾶς πελώριον                                                    —D̲—
τέρας ἄμφεπε μαντεῖον Χθόνιον.

    ἔτι νιν ἔτι βρέφος                   ˙˙ ᵕ˙˙x -|.|

    ἔτι φίλας                           ˙˙x -| ᵧᵕ - ᵕ ᵕ -x- ᵕ -x ²⁸⁹
                                             —D—
    ἐπὶ ματέρος ἀγκάλαισι θρῴσκων

ἔκανες ὦ Φοῖβε, μαντείων               ˙˙ ᵕ -.- ᵕ -x -| ᵧᵕ- ᵕ ᵕ -
                                             —D—
    δ᾽ἐπέβας ζαθέων


²⁸⁶ Disjunct - ᵕ -x + ˆD may appear at *Rhesus* 254 = 242ff. as well, though the highly
symmerical structure of the stanza might suggest an alternative analysis, with syncopation
(- ᵕ -.- ‖ ᵧᵕ - ᵕ ᵕ -):
                 —D—
x- ᵕ --| ᵕ ᵕ -x- ᵕ -.|D.| ᵕ ᵕ -.|D x|D x|D .|- ᵕ -.꞊ᵀᵀ⁻ᴰ̅—̅—̅—̅ᵕ̅ᵕ̅-x|- ᵕ -x-|.|
                               ˙˙x˙˙ ᵕ (꞊)-| ᵕ ᵕ -- ᵕ ᵕ -|- ᵕ ᵕ - ᵕ -⁻
²⁸⁷ Cf. the passages cited in the text, 111 with n. 120.
²⁸⁸ The scansion x-(ᴗᴗ̅)- is necessary if the responding θεᾶς μῆνιν in the antistrophe is
correct. If the antistrophe is emended to correspond exactly (e.g., by Hartung's μήνιμα
θεᾶς) the rhythm may be either x- ᵕ ᵕ - or ᴗᴗ̅- ᵕ ᵕ - (cf. the final line of the stanza).
²⁸⁹ Or, as the parallel with the following ᵕ˙˙- ᵕ ᵕ -... might suggest, ᵕ˙˙ ˙˙ᵕ ᵕ˙˙x
-| ᵧᵕ- ᵕ ᵕ -. The ˙˙ᵕ˙˙x-|.|˙˙ posited in the text is a variant on the - ᵕ -x-|.|-x-
ᵕ- discussed earlier (text, 195-96). For parallels in other prosodiac contexts, cf. *Med.*
846-49 = 856-59 (xD|- ᵕ ᵕ -x-|.|-x- ᵕ -x| x- ᵕᵧᵕ- ᵕ -x. . .) and *Rh.* 250 = 260
                                                  —A———
(above, n. 286).

τρίποδι τ'ἐν χρυσέῳ θάσσεις ἐν ἀψευδεῖ θρόνῳ

μαντείας βροτοῖς

θεσφάτων νέμων

ἀδύτων ὕπο, Κασταλίας ῥεέθρων γείτων,

μέσον γᾶς ἔχων μέλαθρον.

⏑⏑⏑‒⏑⏑‒×‒⏑‒×‒⏑‒.|‒.‒.‒⏑‒.|‒⏑‒×‒|⏞D⏞⏑⏑‒⏑⏑‒⏝⏝‒⏑⏑‒×‒|⏑‒.‒⏑‒⏑‒⁻

‒‒‒⏞D⏞

— *I. T.* 1245–58≈1270–83

Combination of dactylo-anapestic with aeolic, like combination with prosodiac, is more frequent in Euripides than elsewhere. The "anapestic" opening suggested by initial ⏑⏑‒⏑⏑‒⏑‒ is no longer confined, as in Sophocles and Pindar (Table VI) to prosodiac and heptadic aeolic, but appears in octadic aeolic as well, or alongside extended versions of itself (⏑⏑‒⏑⏑[‒⏑⏑]‒⏑⏑‒⏑‒) in short, disjunct series (*ibid.*). The heaviest concentration of such series is in *Ion* 452 = 472ff. Each one shows a different pre-clausular variation, after which the basic rhythm is introduced in a slightly different way: as part of a dactylo-anapestic extension of a preceding ‒×‒⏑⏑‒:

μόλε Πύθιον οἶκον              ⏑⏑‒⏑⏝‒⁻

'Ολύμπου χρυσέων θαλάμων       ××‒×‒⏑⏑‒|⏑⏑‒⏑⏝‒⁻

πταμένα πρὸς ἀγυιάς

−458−60 = 478−80

or, in the ambiguous form ⁻‒⏑⏑‒⁻ (x̄‒⏑⏝‒⁻ or ⏝⏝‒⏑⏝‒⁻) as heptadic aeolic following either ⏑⏑‒⏑⏑‒⏑⏑‒⏑⏑‒:[290]

ἱκετεύσατε δ' ὦ κόραι,          ⏑⏑‒⏑⏝‒⏑‒ +

τὸ παλαιὸν 'Ερεχθέως            ⏑⏑‒⏑⏝‒⏑‒ +

γένος εὐτεκνίας χρονίου καθαροῖς   ⏑⏑‒⏑⏑‒⏑⏑‒⏑⏑‒|⁻‒⏑⏝‒⁻

μαντεύμασι κῦρσαι

−468−71 = 488−91

or octadic ××‒⏑⏑‒⏑⁻⁻:[291]

---

[290] Cf., for ⏑⏑‒⏑⏑‒⏑⏑‒⏑⏑‒ in conjunction with ⏑⏑‒⏑⏑‒⏑‒ or ×‒⏑⏑‒⏑‒, Tables V, C and VI.

[291] Cf., earlier in the stanza, 455–58 = 475–77 (××‒×‒⏑⏑‒×‒×‒⏑⏑‒| ⏑⏑‒ ⏑⏑‒⏑⏑‒⁻ if the correction ὦ πότνα is accepted in 457).

Φοιβήϊος ἔνθα γᾶς                     ‿‿- ∪ ∪ - ∪ - +

μεσσόμφαλος ἑστία                   ‿‿- ∪ ∪ - ∪ - +

παρὰ χορευομένῳ τριπόδι        ×× - ∪ ∪ - ∪⁀| - - ∪ ∪ - ‾

μαντεύματα κραίνει

                                            −461−64 = 481−84

In the *Hcld.* (‿‿⁾- ∪ ∪ - ‾ serves as a disjunct coda for × × - ∪ ∪ - ∪ - × × - ∪ ∪ - ∪ - (373, 375, 754 = 765, 750 = 761 and 757 = 768, coupled in the last two instances with a further disjunct addition: × ̆× ̆ - ∪ ∪ - ‾ or ×× - ∪ ∪ - ∪ - ∪ - ‾). The rhythm is not certainly attested elsewhere, however,[292] and non-initial modulations between dactylo-anapestic and aeolic continue to be rare.[293]

The enlarged number of uses to which dactylo-anapestic is put, and their prominence among Euripidean rhythmical innovations, may be more than accidental. Dactylo-anapestic is the heroic rhythm par excellence, and dactylo-anapestic usage might be expected to reflect in some fashion the rejection, extension or transcending of tragic heroism that is in various ways a recurring preoccupation of Euripidean drama. Thus a more supple, variable, adaptable version of metric anapests develops as a principal vehicle for the monody of female passion and pathos—a tragic counterpart to be set against the epic narrative of masculine achievement and pathos. As the emotional center of gravity of a play comes to be located in its agonized or joyous amoibaia, something more is required than the confusion, helplessness or panic suggested by dochmiacs in the Aeschylean and Sophoclean manner. There is room for a passionate, exalted expansiveness, aptly conveyed by dactylo-anapestic, with its smoothly flowing, rapidly recurring regular cycles, its unparalleled capacity for repetition, and the feeling of remoteness from the everyday created by its epic associations. Mixed prosodiac, to whose iambo-trochaic sections dochmiac could be related in the same way as it was to pure iambo-trochaic in earlier drama (cf. above, 107), was a natural, if not inevitable way of introducing the new movement. The puzzling elegiacs of the *Andromache*, appearing

[292] *Or.* 838 is a possible parallel; but with βλεφάροισ<ιν> at the end of the preceding colon it becomes part of a normal ×̆×̆- ∪ ∪ - ∪ -, with the demarcation ×̆ |× found at 1004. *Hcld* 356−57 = 366−67 and *HF* 380 = 394ff. (Table VI) may be similar, but in both passages other analyses are also possible.

[293] Only *Ion* 1074−75 = 1090−91 is exceptional: ×- ∪ - - ∪ ∪ - -| ∪ ∪ - ∪ ∪ - ∪ ∪ - ∪ - × with its solitary dramatic instance of the choriambic modulation into aeolic via dactylo-anapestic found in choral lyric (text 95−96).

in the first play in which the new dochmiac manner is clearly attested,[294] may be less a hearkening back to some earlier tradition of ritual laments in elegiac metre than an initial experiment, subsequently abandoned, in the innovative use of dactylo-anapestic that is to become more and more conspicuous in Euripidean lyric. Sophocles seems to have traveled a different but parallel road with the dactylo-anapestic that is characteristic of his late plays: long tetrameter series (above, 202) "used only occasionally in choral stasima but frequently in monody and kommos . . . in contexts of passionate despair, or urgent pleading or vehement rejection" (Dale 208).

When regularity and order, as in the aeolic, iono-choriambic and iambo-trochaic forms noted earlier (202) characterize Euripidean lyric, the poet may be seeking a contrast to the disorder of the long astrophic evocations of calamity and chaos—a rhythmical accompaniment to the escapism of some of his choruses. This interpretation, however, works better for the shorter, regularly demarcated continuous sequences, suggesting as they do a simpler, older manner well attested in Anacreon and the rhythmically conservative Aristophanes,[295] than it does for the longer sequences, to which there are few parallels in earlier writers. Here one suspects that musical rather than merely dramatic considerations are at work. Certain types of epiploke are capable of being prolonged at greater length than attested earlier, but within these prolonged sequences homogeneity of cyclical movement seems to be becoming a necessary supplement to continuity of epiploke as a means of sustaining rhythmical unity. And this holds true, not only for Euripides, but for the dactylo-anapestic of Sophocles and the iambic and trochaic hypermeters of Aristophanes. A

---

[294] 830–31, 841–42, and, possibly, 863–65 ($\overline{\cup\cup}$ $\overline{\cup\cup}$–| $\cup$ $\cup$ – $\cup$ $\cup$  $\underset{\text{—D}}{-\cup\cup-}$ $\cup$ $\cup$ –x– [. . . ἐπέρασ'[εν] ἀκτάς] |do.). *Hipp.* 1268–81 already has a more consistent linking of dochmiac and prosodiac than occurs in the other tragedians:

```
do do x– ∪ –
         – ∪ –x   D    do
   do do – ∪ ∪˘˘x–
         x– ∪ –x   D    do do˄ ˄
do do do                    ‾ ∪ ∪ ‾        (?)
                x   D   do
              – ⌣⌣ D –| ∪ ∪ do ‾      (?)
```

But it lacks the characteristic Dx–| demarcation, however one analyzes the concluding dicolon.

[295] Of longer sequences in the Euripidean manner there is little trace in Aristophanes, outside non-melic hypermeters. Cf., however, *Th.* 359–66, fr. 322, and *Ran.* 240–50, one of several iambo-trochaic series found in this scene (221–67), all of which begin iambically but eventually pass into trochaic, either with the refrain βρεκεκεκὲξ κοὰξ κοάξ or with a longer trochaic sequence concluded by it.

further stage is reached once rhythmical continuity is combined with a single prevailing pattern of demarcation, extensive use of equivalent variation, and the admission of passages in other rhythms so long as they do not involve a departure from the prevailing octadic pattern. Here composition by epiploke may itself be giving way to a kind of metric composition in eight-quantity units.

Anapestic and dochmiac (above, 116–18) provide the earliest clear examples of such metric composition, and they show the same preference for a single type of demarcation, the same extensive use of equivalent variations, and, in their frequent association with each other, the same propensity for rhythmical collocations based on durational equivalence rather than epiploke. All three phenomena can be regarded as natural results of the increasing role of music in lyric composition, a role now grown to the point where it is beginning to interfere with the workings of those patterns of epiploke whose introduction it fostered three centuries earlier (above, 140–43).

Composition by epiploke is perfectly compatible with a rhythmical system whose basic elements are simply the short and long quantities supplied by the syllables of the Greek language itself, and which derives its formal structure from the arrangement of long and short syllables in recurring series. The presence of anceps alongside long and short, and the possibility of resolution, contraction and syncopation prevent recurrence from being exact; but it is largely by virtue of containing a series of syllabic quantities in an expected or familiar order that a piece of verse is felt as rhythmical. And a clear feeling for the location of a given sequence of quantities within regular repeating series makes possible the interrelation of different sequences via epiploke.

An increasingly prominent musical element in lyric composition runs the risk of disrupting such relationships insofar as it substitutes a count of equidistant rhythmical beats for a patterned sequence of quantities as the basic source of rhythm. The presence of such beats may, of course, do no more than make the durational equivalence of long to long and short to short within the pattern of syllabic quantities more exact. But it may also—and in Greece eventually did—lead to the division of the rhythmical line into isochronous units, felt as such because of the simple mathematical ratio between the durations of their component arses and theses—not because of the arrangement of their component longs and shorts into some sort of easily perceived and remembered configuration. And once it is customary to identify a given sequence—iambic, for example—by reference to the series of measures divided into arsis and thesis that it contains:

$$1\ 23, \quad 1\ 23 \quad + \quad 1\ 23, \quad 1\ 23$$
$$\times - \quad \cup - \quad \quad \times - \quad \cup -$$

it will be difficult to hear any portion of the same sequence as belonging to a different rhythm. The four quantities

$$23,\ 1\ 23 + 1$$
$$- \cup - \quad \times$$

will not be trochaic, for the trochaic metron is counted differently:

$$12\ 3,\ 12\ 3$$
$$- \cup - \times$$

But if isochronous combinations of arsis and thesis resist incorporation into different patterns linked by epiploke, they might be expected to be more tolerant of the equivalent sequences of different syllables produced by resolution and contraction. Such sequences destroy the configuration of a passage, but they do not affect the underlying beat count; and the continuous runs of shorts produced by resolution (already regarded in the earliest surviving protest [*PMG* 708] against the growing importance of musical accompaniments as characteristic of the new manner)[296] might even make the count a little easier, by giving every beat a syllable to itself.

Isochronous composition would also facilitate free association of units in one genre with those in another—dochmiac with anapestic, single cycles of aeolic with double cycles of iambo-trochaic or iono-choriambic—so long as the units were durational equivalents. And demarcation, insofar as it followed a pattern at all, could be expected to be confined to points where it would reinforce rather than disturb the articulation of a rhythmical line into its basic units.

Though the hypothesis of the increasing importance of isochronous musical rhythm would explain the late fifth-century forms under consideration and their parallels with dochmiac and anapestic, there is little evidence to suggest the actual disappearance—as against the lessened importance—of epiploke during the period. Such evidence as does exist

---

[296] The protestor maintains a succession of largely or completely resolved anapests throughout his onomatopoetic tirade against the *thorybos* and *hybris* of modern innovations (1–2), then passes into unresolved anapests and prosodiac once song's claims to supremacy are asserted (3–6). On the identity and date of the Pratinas to whom the fragment is attributed, see H. Lloyd-Jones, "Problems of Early Greek Tragedy," *Cuadernos de la Fundación Pastor* 13 (1966) 18.

involves passages which seem to display one further form of equivalent variation whose use may have a musical origin. Hellenistic theory recognizes, among other distortions of the normal time value of syllables allowed by musical rhythm, an "irrational" long syllable (here designated ᴗ̄), longer than the normal short and shorter than the normal long by what are, for the ear, indeterminate amounts (cf. *RS* 82.11–21). It is a component, both of "irrational chorees" (ᴗ̄ ᴗ ᴗ and ᴗ ᴗ ᴗ̄) which seem to have the value of iambic ᴗ˵˵ or trochaic ˵˵ᴗ (AQ 1.17 p. 37.24–38.2) and of "cretics" (ᴗ̄ ᴗ –) which count among "compressed" (*xynestrammenoi: POxy* 2687, iv.23–24) rhythms because each metron contains four rather than five *prōtoi chronoi*.[297] These cretics come into existence because "... it is possible to assign irregular time values to the first two of their three syllables":

ἐνδέχεται [τὰς

δύο τ[ῶ]ν τριῶ[ν] ξυλλαβῶν

τὰς [προτ]έρας [εἰς ἀν]ω[μάλους[298]

θε[ῖ]ν[α]ι χρό[νους] . . .

*POxy* 2687.iv.25–28

The first of the two syllables receives a longer time value than the second (*ibid.* iv.29–33), but the two no longer stand in a 2–1 ratio. Rather, they are longer and shorter parts of a diseme length or its approximation. The third quantity in the metron is longer than the other two, and the whole metron is similar to an anapest (*ibid.*, v.1–2), presumably because it is the (rough) durational equivalent of an anapest and because, like the anapest, it divides into two (roughly) equal parts.

Both irrational choree and teteseme or "anapestic" cretic may appear in certain late fifth-century texts. On occasion – ᴗ ᴗ seems actually to respond (as ᴗ̄˵˵) to iambic ᴗ –, or (as ˵˵ᴗ̆ ᴗ) to trochaic – ᴗ or – ×; as does "cretic" – ᴗ˵˵ – – ᴗ (×̣) (i.e., ᴗ̄ ᴗ˵˵ᴗ̄ ᴗ (×̣)) to dochmiac ᴗ̄˵˵˵(×̣). Elsewhere irrational forms appear where one would expect regular ones,

---

[297] Cf. iii.30–33 (three cretics said to be equivalent to an *orthios* or *trochaios sēmantos*, both of which are sequences of twelve *prōtoi chronoi* [AQ 1.16 p. 36.3–6]).

[298] The supplements in this line, as well as τάς two lines earlier, are proposed here for the first time, though all but ἀνωμάλους seem fairly certain. The latter word is regularly used in sphygmological treatises (e.g., Galen *De puls. diff.* 1.29 p. 557 Kühn) to designate pulses that do not conform to regular time patterns as determined by the art of *mousikē*. What stood in the text, however, may well have been something more exact, a synonym for στρογγύλος or κύκλιος (on the use of these terms to denote time lengths shorter than normal, see L. E. Rossi, *Metrica e critica stilistica* [Rome 1963] 45–49, 74–75 and 90–93). Texts of all the portions of *POxy* 2687 referred to here and on p. 217 are given in Appendix VII.

# TABLE X: POSSIBLE INSTANCES OF IRRATIONAL LONG IN GREEK LYRIC
## (cf. Appendix VIII)

A: ⏓ – ⏕ –

B: ⏕ –⏓
and ⏕ ⏑

C: – ⏑ ⏑ ⏑
(paeono-trochaic)

D: (⏕) ⏑ (⏕) ⏑

**A:**

Pindar *O7e*3: ⏓⏑⏕⏑|×D×D
(cf. s3: ×–⏑–‖)

S. *Tr.* 825 = 835: ⏓⏑⏑⏕⏑×⏕×⏑–×–⏑–[1]

*OC* 216, 218, 220, 222; ⏓⏑⏕×⏕×⏑–⏑–[2]

207, 237, 242, 249: ⏕×–⏑–[3]

**B:**

*Bac.* 582:
⏕⏑–.⏓⏕⏓×
600–601:
⏕⏑×|⏕–⏓×|⏑–⏓×

*Cycl.* 610–11, 615–16,
618–19, 620–21:
⏓⏑⏓⏓⏑ –|× E
(–⏑–|)

**E.**

*Tr.* 1068–69 = 1078–79:
×⏓|⏑⏓×|⏓⏑–|
⏕⏑⏕×|–⏑–⏓[4]

*Ion* 1076–77 = 1092–93:
×⏓|⏑(⏓)×|⏑⏑–
⏕⏓|⏕⏓×|⏓⏑–

*IT* 393–94 = 408–9:
×–⏑⏓×⏕⏓⏑
(or ⏓⏑⏕⏓)

*Hyps.* I,iii.10
⏕⏑⏕×⏑–⏑–

*El.* 459 = 471
⏓⏑⏕×⏑–⏑–
456 = 468:
–⏑–⏑⏑|⏓⏑⏕⏑⏑⏑–

*El.* 1245–50 = 1265–70
|⏕⏑(⏕)⏑⏑(⏕)| twice,
framing two instances of
|⏑(⏓)⏑⏑⏑⏕|
do
and followed by
⏑⏑⏑⏑⏕⏑⏑–⏑–
do

*Bac.* 135–40

⏑⏑⏑|⏕⏑⏑⏑|–⏑⏑    |–⏑⏑|⏕⏑–|⏕⏑⏑⏑[5]
⏕⏑⏑|⏕⏑⏑⏑|⏕⏑⏑⏑|–⏑⏓|
⏑⏑⏑⏑|⏕⏑⏑⏑|–⏑⏑    |–⏑⏑⏕⏑⏑⏑⏑|–
157–65
⏕⏑⏑|⏕⏑⏑⏑|–⏑⏑    |–⏑⏑
⏕⏑⏑⏑|⏕⏑⏑⏑|
⏑⏑⏑⏑|⏕⏑⏑⏑|–⏑⏑    |–⏑⏑|–⏑⏑|–⏑⏑

---

[1] Scanning ἀέλιον.

[2] Unless taken (with transposition or deletion of ἀπόγονον in 220) as instances of – ⏑⏑ – ⏑⏑ – + ⏑ ⏑ –.

[3] On the relation of these lines to 216, 218, 220, 222, cf. LMGD 138[3].

[4] Reading πρωτόβολον θ᾽ for τε πρωτόβολον.

[5] Or with τᾶς ἐρίστα ..... (cf. p. 299)

*Hel* 1501 = 1485:

*Ph.* 813 = 796:

Ar.

*Eq.* 332 = 407:

*Vesp.* 412 = 468:

1062 = 1073:

1064 = 1093:

*Lys.* 788–89 = 812–13:

*Ach.* 295 = 342:

*Vesp.* 339 = 370:

*Av.* 333–35 = 349–51;
five instances of

*Lys.* 277–78 = 262–63:

324 = 338:

*Lys.* 1284–90:

*Th.* 436 = 522:

439 = 524:

957:

*Eccl.* 1168–77:

followed by five similar tetrameters

*PTeb.* i.ii

Philoxenus Cyth. 8/821:

[6] If equivalent to the earlier ∪∪–∪∪–∪∪–∪∪– (285 = 336) in the way the stanza construction would suggest:

284–91 = 335–41:   –∪–x–∪–x–∪–‖ ∪∪–x–∪–x–∪∪–‖ ∪–x–∪–x–x–∪–‖ 12 cretics

291–301 = 341–46:   –∪–x–∪–x–∪–‖ ∪∪–∪∪–∪∪–∪∪–‖ ∪–x–∪–x–x–∪–‖ 12 cretics

or seem to be interchangeable with them in what are otherwise identical contexts. (Instances are listed, along with those of actual responsion, in Table X, A [iambic]; X, B [trochaic] and X, D [dochmio-cretic]).

The most extended passage where the possibility of such equivalence exists is the epode to the parodos of the *Bacchae:*

ἡδὺς ἐν ὄρεσ<σ>ιν ὅταν ἐκ θιάσων δρομαίων πέσῃ πέδοσε

            – ∪͞ |– ∪͞ |– ∪ ∪ |– ∪ ∪ |– ∪ –∪ ∪

νεβρίδος ἔχων ἱερὸν ἔνδυτον ἀγρεύων    – ∪͞ |– ∪͞ |– ∪͞ |– ͞͞

αἷμα τραγοκτόνον ὠμοφάγον χάριν      – ∪ ∪ |– ∪ ∪ |– ∪ ∪

ἱέμενος ἐς ὄρεα Φρύγια Λύδι᾽ ὁ δ᾽ἔξαρχος Βρόμιος εὐοῖ

            – ∪͞ ∪ |͞ ∪ ͞ ∪ |– ∪ ∪ |– ͞͞ |– ∪͞|– ͞͞

            (or ͞ ∪ ͞)

ῥεῖ δε γάλακτι πέδον, ῥεῖ δ᾽ οἴνῳ      – ∪ ∪ |– ∪ ∪ |– ͞͞ |– ͞͞

ῥεῖ δε μελισσᾶν νέκταρι          – ∪ ∪ |– ͞͞ |– ∪ ∪     (135–43)

εὔια τὸν εὔιον ἀγαλλόμενοι θεὸν     – ∪͞ |– ∪͞ |– ∪ ∪ |– ∪ ∪

ἐν Φρυγίαισι βοαῖς ἐνοπαῖσί τε      – ∪ ∪ |– ∪ ∪ |– ∪ ∪ |– ∪ ∪

λωτὸς ὅταν εὐκέλαδος           – ∪͞ |– ∪͞ |

ἱερὸς ἱερὰ παίγματα βρέμῃ σύνοχα φοιτάσιν

            ͞ ∪ ͞ ∪ |– ∪͞ |– ∪͞ |– ∪ ∪

εἰς ὄρος εἰς ὄρος            – ∪ ∪ |– ∪ ∪

ἡδομένα δ᾽ἄρα πῶλος ὅπως ἅμα ματέρι φορβάδι

            – ∪ ∪ |– ∪ ∪ |– ∪ ∪ |– ∪ ∪ |– ∪ ∪ –∪ ∪

κῶλον ἄγει ταχύπουν σκιρτήμασι βάκχα      (158–68)

            – ∪ ∪ |– ∪ ∪ |– ͞͞ |– ∪ ∪ |– ͞͞

The initial line is probably corrupt, but if it is emended to end in two dactyls or two cretics[299] the opening and concluding sections of the stanza (separated by the predominantly ionic 144–57 [above, 48]) contain twenty-seven metra (dactylic, cretic and trochaic [͞ ∪ ͞ ∪]) apiece,

---

[299] Perhaps πέσῃ <τις> or τις ἐρίπῃ. The alternative possibilities are (1) ἡδύ γ᾽ or the unemended text. In that case, however, the subject of the verb is the god himself, who must become his own *exarchos* three lines later. (2) ὃς ἄν for ὅταν. Then the subject must be the person described as ἡδύς—i.e., a worshipper "pleasing" to the god (cf. Dodds *ad loc.*)—even though the ὠμοφάγον χάριν of the next line and, presumably, the act of falling itself (the *terrae . . . petitus/suavis* of Lucretius 3.172–73) are instances of ways in which the god is ἡδύς to his followers, not vice versa. With the addition of τις, ἡδύς will stand in apposition to the subject of the final clause in the preceding antistrophe: αἷς χαίρει Διόνυσος (134).

grouped by demarcation into twos and fours, with the odd metron at the end creating a clausular trimeter or pentameter. The striking symmetry is in support of the assumption that cretics, trochees and dactyls are here durational equivalents; and the Hellenistic treatise just cited indicates one possible way in which the equivalence could have been achieved—through use of metra of the form ⌣⌣⌣⌣. Equivalence of the trochee – ⌣ – ⌣ to the cretic – ⌣ (⌣) is attested elsewhere in fifth-century verse (Table X, C). When this "trochaic" cretic (– ⌣ ⌣⌣ ) becomes an "anapestic" cretic as well (⌣⌣ ⌣⌣ ), and when its irrational longs are resolved, one has the ⌣⌣⌣⌣ ⌣ of the present passage, i.e., ⌣ ⌣ ⌣⌣⌣. A similar pair of resolved irrational longs may appear in the ⌣ ⌣ ⌣ ⌣ ⌣ ⌣ ⌣ ⌣ (i.e., ⌣⌣⌣ ⌣⌣⌣⌣ ⌣) of *Eccl.* 1169.[300]

The freedom of responsion attested or suggested in all of these passages is subject to two restrictions. The syllable following ⌣ is always short—as well as, more often than not, several others in the context. Moreover, ⌣ always stands first in its arsis, thesis or (in dactylo-anapestic) metron. One thus finds ¦– ⌣ ⌣:– ⌣ ⌣¦ where one would expect iambic ×⌣⌣:⌣ –, but not ¦×–:⌣ ⌣ –¦,[301] and ¦– ⌣ ⌣:–×¦ where one would expect trochaic ¦⌣⌣⌣:–×¦, but not ¦⌣ ⌣–:–×¦. Similarly, as *POxy* 2687 points out (see Appendix VII), ¦– ⌣–¦ for anapestic ¦⌣ ⌣ ⌣–¦ is possible (but not for dactylic ¦– ⌣ ⌣¦); and ¦– ⌣:– ⌣¦ for cretic ¦– ⌣:⌣⌣¦, but not ¦⌣ –:⌣ –¦ for cretic ¦⌣⌣:⌣ –¦.

Both restrictions on the use of ⌣ make sense in terms of the time-counting rhythm which the phenomenon of irrationality presupposes. Short syllables are preferred in the vicinity as being the nearer syllabic equivalent to the basic time-counting unit, and so making the temporal sub-structure which the long is distorted to fit more prominent.[302] And the long appears at the beginning of one of the basic units whose temporal relationship, whether of equality or simple proportion, creates the rhythm of the verse. It would have been natural for the beginnings of these units

---

[300] Cf. *GV* 360, where it is plausibly suggested that the dactyls and proceleusmatics of the monster compound found at 1169–75 are durational equivalents of the tribrachs with which the word begins:

λοπαδοτεμαχοσελαχογαλεο-      ⌣⌣ ⌣ ⌣⌣ ×̆  ⌣⌣ ⌣  ⌣⌣×̆
κρανιολειψανοδριμυποτριμματο-  ⌣̄⌣ ⌣ ⌣̄⌣×̆ ⌣̄⌣ ⌣ ⌣̄⌣×̆
σιλφιοτυρομελιτοκατακεχυμενο... ⌣̄⌣ ⌣̄⌣⌣ ×̆ ⌣⌣⌣ ⌣⌣⌣×̆

[301] Unless the "anapestic" substitutions of the comic trimeter are taken as instances of ×̆⌣– or ⌣⌣̄– (so, tentatively, *LMGD* 78–79). Against this suggestion, see Appendix VIII.

[302] Similar considerations may explain why the dochmiac ×̄⌣⌣–×̄– is so much more frequent than ×̄– –×̄–, however the octaseme scansion posited here (⌣̄ ⌣̆ ‿ – ×̆ –) may have worked, or not worked, for forms with a long syllable supplying the penultimate quantity.
                                   1 23 45 6  78

to be indicated by some modification in the normal mode of delivery,[303] and this modification could have made an initial irregularity or "irrationality" more acceptable than a medial or terminal one. However accommodated to its rhythmical context and for whatever reason, the irrational long is so located as to preclude the sequence in which it appears from forming part of epiploke. Iambic $\overline{\times}^{\smallsmile\smallsmile}\!:\!\smile^{\smallsmile\smallsmile}$ cannot be heard as part of trochaic $-\smile:-\overline{\times}|^{\smallsmile\smallsmile}\smile:^{\smallsmile\smallsmile}\times$, for then the irrational long would conclude rather than begin the thesis or arsis in which it appears. The same would hold good for a cretic $|-\smile.^{\smallsmile\smallsmile}|$ appearing as part of a bacchiac $\smile-:-|\smile^{\smallsmile\smallsmile}:-$ or an anapestic $|\smile\smile-|$ as part of a dactylic $-\smile\smile|-\smile\smile$. And the articulation into metra to which this points, would, presumably, have been characteristic of all passages in which the possibility of such irrationality was present, not simply of those in which the irrationality actually appears.

Dealing with the problem of irrational longs in late fifth-century verse leads, inevitably, to a chain of hypotheses, which might apply to other passages as well. One wonders, in particular, whether some of the rhythmical juxtapositions first attested during this period, or first attested frequently, can be adequately explained as simple extensions of an earlier asynartete manner. They may be, rather, juxtapositions of isochronous or isometric equivalents; double dactylic or double anapestic dimeters with iambic or trochaic dimeters or their eight-quantity aeolic counterparts, for example.[304] Acceptance or rejection of such hypotheses should not, however, influence one's acceptance of what is a fairly generally held idea about the relatively late introduction of time-counting rhythm into Greek

---

[303] Conceivably a slight pause before arsis or thesis, or a *sforzando* on the initial syllable which would compensate for loss of length by increase of intensity. Or the modification of the mode of execution may have been part of the instrumental or choric accompaniment: a gesture, the beginning of a foot movement, or a heavier time-marking beat. The last, if it existed, need not have been accompanied by a stress ictus in the vocal line; but there is nothing inherently implausible in the notion that ictus came to be so employed. On the incompatibility of such an ictus with rhythmical ambiguities of the sort involved in epiploke, see L. E. Rossi, "Sul problema dell' *ictus*," *AnnPisa*, ser. 2., 33 (1964) 124–26.

[304] Cf., in general, Fraenkel 185 and, for the appearance of isolated $|-\smile\smile-\smile\smile|$ or $|-\smile\smile-\smile\smile-\smile\smile-\widehat{\smile\smile}|$ in an aeolic context (not attested before the final years of the century), S. *Ph.* 1188–91 (an an$|\times\times-\smile\smile-\smile-|\times\times-\smile\smile-\smile-|-\smile\smile-\smile\smile-\smile\smile-\widehat{\smile\smile}$), OC 674–77 = 687–90 $(\times\times-\smile\smile-\smile-\times|\times-\smile\smile-\smile-\|-\smile\smile-\smile\smile-\smile\smile-\smile\smile|\times$ E$^{\flat}$), Timotheus 15/791.188–92 $(\overline{\times}\overline{\times}-\smile\smile-\smile-|-\smile\smile-\smile\smile-\smile\smile-\widehat{\smile\smile}|$ $\times\times-\smile\smile-\smile-\times|$ $\times-\smile\smile-^{-})$ and E. *Bac.* 130–35 $(\times\times-\smile\smile-\smile\smile-|$ $\overline{\times}\overline{\times}-\smile\smile-\smile\smile-|$ $-\smile\smile-\smile\smile|$ ———A——— ———A——— $\times\times-\smile\smile-\smile-|\times\times-\smile\smile-^{-}$. Note also, at Ar. *Av.* 229–41, the apparent interchangeability of $\times-\smile-\times-\smile-\times-\smile-$ (229) $\times-\smile-\times$D (231), $\smile\smile--\smile\smile--\smile\smile--$ (238) and $-\smile-\times-\smile-\times-\smile-\times$ (233, 235 and [with the deletions suggested in Dale 136] 240) as equivalent cola of eighteen units each, in regular alternation with octaseme $|$do$|$ and $|$an$|$ (singly or in pairs: 230, 234, 236, 239 and [deleting $\tau\epsilon$] 232).

lyric,[305] and the profound effect that this had on subsequent developments in the genre. Some of the specific suggestions here offered as to the character and extent of its influence on late fifth-century versification may well be wrong; but of the general tendency there can be no doubt.

Further support for these suggestions, insofar as they involve epiploke, comes from an examination of later lyric, where the influence of time-counting rhythm becomes more apparent and the area in which it is felt much wider. Epiploke virtually disappears, except from prosodiac[306] (already in late Euripides the genre which, along with dactylo-anapestic, accounts for almost all the passages in which innovation in the use of epiploke is still going on). A single prevailing pattern of demarcation and increased length of the homogeneous sequences so demarcated become hallmarks, both of lyric written for musical performance and of what metricians of a philological or grammatical bent describe as "rhythmical" composition—i.e., composition of the sort studied by the musicologists or *rhythmici*. The characteristics noted are (1) preservation of a regular alternation of arsis and thesis without interruption until the end of a piece (or until modulation into a different rhythm); (2) absence of sharp internal divisions created by regular prosodic demarcation or specifically clausular sequences such as the succession of dactyl and spondee at the end of the hexameter; and (3) unrestricted use of resolution and contraction.[307] All three characteristics can be paralleled in the long continuous sequences of late fifth-century drama, even if there is nothing there to match the 79

[305] The distinction in the text between "isochronous," musical rhythm and its predecessor is, for example, essentially that drawn by T. Georgiades in his discussion of "Zeiterfüllung" and "Zeitabstechung" as the basis of, respectively, Greek and modern Western music (*Der griechische Rhythmus* [Hamburg 1949]) and by G. B. Pighi in contrasting the "figura" of early Greek poetry with the "misura" of its successor (*Studi di ritmica e metrica* [Turin 1971] 6 and 29). For the view taken of the position of anapestic rhythm in the development of Greek lyric cf. "Inediti di E. Grassi," *Atene e Roma* 6 (1961) 159–60, where it is plausibly suggested that the conception of rhythm as an alternation between arsis and thesis first arose in connection with march anapests, to be extended subsequently to other genres.

[306] Cf. Telestes (*PMG* 805–6), Aristotle (*PMG* 842), Ariphron (*PMG* 813), Aristonous (pp. 164–65 Powell; cf. *GV* 496–97), Philoxenus (*PMG* 836), the *Meliambi* of Cercidas, and Mesomedes 1. In Philoxenus and *PMG* 806, however, sustained runs of octadic rhythm (. . . D×D×D ×. . .) recall what appears in late Euripides (text, 191–92); and Cercidas' prosodiac is so demarcated (into $|-\overset{D}{\smile}-|$ in constant alternation with $|×\underset{\smile}{\overset{D}{\_\_}}×$ see Maas 68) as to resemble the asynartetes of Archilochus and Alcaeus (text, 116) more than the form encountered in Pindar and drama.

[307] Cf., the statements found in Quintilian 9.4.46–51, *GL* 1.474.5–8, 6.41.28–42.3, 96.15–19, 374.1630–33, 585.17–586.4, 588.23–25, and DH 19 p. 84.17–18.

consecutive ionic metra of Isyllus' paean (pp. 133–34 Powell)[308] or the even longer cretic series in the Delphic hymns to Apollo (*ibid.*, 141–55). And the practice of referring to sung verse, or its formal patterns, as *rhythmoi*, by contrast with the *metra* of spoken verse, may in fact be as old as the fifth century.[309] Even the dodecaseme units, or *periodoi*, recognized by Hellenistic theory, for which there is only sporadic evidence in the lyric fragments of the period, can be plausibly regarded as belonging to a thoroughly metricized version of the composition in uniform eight-quantity cycles that is attested in long stretches of Euripidean lyric. Their clearest Hellenistic appearance is in the paean of Limenius, which modulates at its close into a fourteen-nucleus aeolic sequence[310] (36–49, p. 150 Powell) that is only slightly more regular in demarcation (always before the base, insofar as a pattern is sought), and slightly longer, than its closest Euripidean analogues.

The paean of Philodamus Scarpheus (performed in 324 B.C.) is, by contrast, a more Classical production, having—as has often been pointed out—a close analogue in Aristophanes:

---

[308] Broken only by sporadic demarcation and catalexis in the forty-sixth and, possibly, eighteenth metron.

[309] Cf. Ar. *Nub.* 636ff., where the spoken trimeter and tetrameter are called *metra* (641–42), by contrast with *rhythmoi* such as dactyl and enoplion (649–51); and, for other pre-Hellenistic texts in which the distinction is present or implied, Arist. *Poetics* 3.1448b21, with the commentary and parallel passages supplied by Else *ad loc.* Aristotle's notion of *metra* as μόρια (*loc. cit.*) or τμητά (*Rhet.* 3.8.1408b29) of *rhythmoi* anticipates the later formulations cited in n. 307.

[310] Shorter sequences occur in the paean of Aristonous (pp. 162–64 Powell: stanzas consisting of four *periodoi*, the last catalectic and the first showing thy variants ××– ◡ ◡ – ◡ –, ××–×– ◡ ◡ – and ×– ◡ – – ◡ ◡ –) and Plaut. *Bacch.* 626–33 and *Men.* 110–11 (the same variants, along with ×E and – ◡ ◡ – – ◡ ◡ –, grouped into lines of two *periodoi* each). Cf., also, the fourth-century dithyrambic fragment ascribed to Arion (*PMG* 939), which contains three modulations from dactylo-anapestic into passages (5–6, 9–11, 15–17) where ×E, ××– ◡ ◡ – ◡ –, Ex and ×– ◡ –¦– ◡ –× may function as interchangeable, isochronous units. *PMG* 655.b1 (Corinna) may consist of continuous repetition of |××–×–◡◡–◡–| but neither dating nor rhythmical analysis is certain: some of the missing line ends could have contained clausular extensions (– or ◡ – –) of the nucleus.

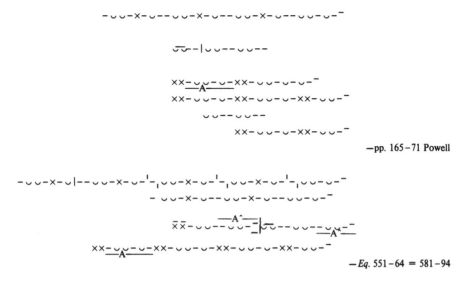

—pp. 165–71 Powell

—Eq. 551–64 = 581–94

But though the rhythmical pattern—presumably imitated from earlier models—contains sequences which might be related to each other through epiploke, the poet does nothing to bring out the relationship. The ionic of his second line is set off both by rhythm (the parallel with ◡ ◡ – – ◡ ◡ – – three lines later) and content (the ritual *Paianruf*) as a rhythmical digression.

Its counterpart in Aristophanes is, by contrast, transitional aeolo-ionic: related as ⌣⌣– – ◡ ◡ – – ◡ ◡ –. . . to the iono-choriambic that precedes and as x̄ x̄ – ◡ ◡ – – ◡ ◡ –. . . to the aeolic that follows. And the opening of Philodemus' stanza is iambo-choriambic, not the interweave of iambo-choriambic and anacreontic found in Aristophanes (above, 5). All subsequent instances of (non-prosodiac) lyric rhythm depart even further from Classical canons.

Composition in asynartete sequences, unlike epiploke, is fairly well attested in Hellenistic and later poetry. But it disappears from longer lyric structures almost without a trace.[311] What one usually encounters are

---

[311] The agglomeration of paeonic, anapestic, dochmiac, and iambic sequences found in the *fragmentum Grenfellianum* may be an exception. It is impossible, however, to know how far this mixture was made into a series of isochronous units by the sort of rhythmical distortion considered in the text; and the same applies to the apparently disjunct compositions often found in Plautus' more elaborate *cantica*. The mss. designation *mutatis modis cantica* certainly suggests *rhythmi* (text, 219) which *quomodo coeperunt currunt usque ad metabolen* (Quintilian 9.4.50) rather than the internal articulations and well-marked clausulae of Classical dramatic lyric; and the *numeri* of Plautus' epitaph may have been *innumeri*, not only in their multiplicity and variety, but in the way they defied division into clearly perceived dimeters, trimeters etc. (cf. *GL* 6.42.3: *rhythmus . . . numero numquam circumscribitur*).

single lines and cola selected and extracted from earlier lyric and then used, whether stichically or recombined into simple stanzas, in verse written for recitation rather than singing. Insofar as there is any model for the way such combinations were produced, it was probably the poetry of Archilochus and his immediate imitators. The more complicated asynartete structures that occasionally appear are perhaps elaborations on the Archilochean tradition. But they may also be efforts by non-musical artists to reproduce the impression created by reading the text of a Classical lyric. Such texts were read in the way they were originally written down—as prose. And this meant decomposing them, insofar as the location of demarcation in responding stanzas would allow, into a succession of separate rhetorical units. The prose name for such units was *kōlon* (above, 27); and its meaning underwent a natural extension once the poetic structures thus revealed began to be described (and imitated) as aggregations of discrete parts separated by diaeresis.[312]

Further analysis of the cola isolated for study and imitation in Classical texts did take place occasionally—whether in terms of the prototypical metra recognized by one of the two main non-musical schools of rhythmical theory or in terms of the processes of derivation from hexameter and trimeter recognized by the other. But such analyses were rarely of any significance for the way whole poems were written or understood. Seneca's construction of stanzas out of the elements which derivationist theory held to be the basic components of the lines Horace borrowed from Alcaeus and Sappho is a piece of Neronian radicalism that has no attested forerunners and few successors.[313] And there is even less trace of new forms created through recombination of the prototypical metra which appear in all the analyses of earlier verse carried out by the other main school.[314]

[312] As in the imitation of a tragic *amoibaion* found in *TrGF* 2F649: various asynartete combinations of trimeters and their constituent parts: the penthemimer (5, 6, 7), the posthephthemimeral $-\times-\cup-$ (5, 6, 7) and the hephthemimer itself ($\times-\cup-\times-\cup$: 4, 8, 10). Line 13 is either $\times-\cup-\cup-^-$, the iambic half-line (*hemiambeion:* cf. Cleanthes *SVF* 1.129) used stichically in parts of the *Anacreontea;* or, with deletion of one ἔα, another penthemimer. Cf., in general, Snell *ad loc.*

[313] On later analogues, presumably influenced by Seneca himself, or the theoretical treatises he followed, see L. Müller, *De re metrica* [2] (St. Petersburg 1894) 116–17 and *CP* 70 (1975) 129 (on *Carm. Epig. Lat.* 2151.15–18).

[314] The closest approach is to be found in the ionic forms considered earlier (text, 32–36), and—perhaps—in the dactylo-anapestic sequences (West 172–73) which allow equivalence between final $-\overset{\smile}{\smile}$ and $-\cup\times$ (i.e., the "acatalectic" concluding foot posited by Hephaestion [20.18–21.1] to justify his dactylic analysis of aeolic sequences ending in ... $\cup\cup-\cup\cup-\cup-$).

The two endings are equated as ... $\overset{\rule{0.4em}{0.4pt}}{-.}-$ and ... $-\cup-$ in the musical settings of Mesomedes' hymns to the Sun and to Nemesis (von Jan, *Suppl.* 48–59), but this interpretation of the equivalence need not have been the normal, or original, one.

The failure of asynartete and metric composition between them to sustain anything like the length, variety and complexity of rhythmic structure found earlier may stand as a final indication of the central importance of epiploke for lyric during the Classical period. It seems to have constituted during that period the principal means of creating a rhythmical system large enough to allow for both continuity and transformation, generic order and individual innovation, stanzaic wholeness and the sharply etched individual motif, the potential endlessness of a musical line and the finiteness of word, phrase and statement. It was, however, a phenomenon closely bound up with a particular time in musical history: born of the interaction between long-established poetic tradition and more recently naturalized, more narrowly musical arts of composition, and ultimately rendered obsolete by the elaboration which those arts received at the hands of native composers. Like so much else in the Greek cultural experience between 700 and 400 B.C., the rhythmical system based on epiploke was destined to be as short-lived as it was unique.

# APPENDIX ONE: TERMINAL – ∪ ∪ – ∪ × IN DACTYLIC

The analysis of the close of Alcman's *Partheneion* offered in the text rests on four pieces of evidence:

1) Archilochus 190, where the dicolon that appears elsewhere as – ∪ ∪ – ∪ ∪ – ∪ ∪ – ∪ ∪ + ᴇˆ shows the form – ∪ ∪ – ∪ ∪ – ∪ ∪ – ∪ – + ᴇˆ (καὶ βήσσας ὀρέων . . .).

2) Alcman 27, a poem composed, according to Hephaestion, entirely in acatalectic dactylic tetrameters—i.e., tetrameters whose fourth foot was trisyllabic: – ∪ ∪ within the poem and, presumably, – ∪ ‾ at its end.

3) Ibycus 1.282.23–26 and, possibly,

4) *POxy* 2443 fr. 1 + 3213 (Alcman; cf. M. L. West, *ZPE* 26 [1977] 38–39, where the parallel with the conclusion of Ibycus' stanza is pointed out):

Ibycus: – ∪ ∪ – ∪ ∪ – ∪ ∪ – ∪ ∪ | – ∪ ∪ – ∪ ∪ – ∪ ∪ – ∪ –
              – ‾∪‾ – ∪ ∪ – | ∪ ∪ – ∪ ∪ – ∪ – ×
                            ――A――
Alcman: – ∪ ∪ – ∪ ∪ – ‾∪‾ – ∪ ∪ | – ‾∪‾ – ∪ ∪ – ∪ ∪ – ∪ –
              – ∪ ∪ – ∪ ∪ – ∪ ∪ – ∪ ∪ | – ∪ ∪ – ∪ ∪ – ‾∪‾ ∪ – . . .
                        – ∪ ∪ – ∪ ∪ – ‾∪‾ – | ∪ ∪ – ∪ – ∪ – ‾
                                          ――A――

(The scansion of 4 assumes ἦχον for the transmitted ἔχον in the last line).

– ∪ ∪ – ∪ ∪ – ∪ ∪ – ∪ – in (1) and (3) responds to – ∪ ∪ – ∪ ∪ – ∪ ∪ – ∪ ∪ in other instances of the dicolon or strophe, hence must end in ‾× (unless one posits lengthening by prosodic demarcation in the responding passages, for which there is no support either in Ibycus' poem or Archilochean and later use of the dicolon). And if anceps is accepted here, analogy and economy favor its acceptance at the end of the tetrameters in (2) and (4). The form is explicable as, in origin, what it is in (2): a pre-pausal modification of dactylic designed to provide the necessary final long syllable without reducing (through the usual expedient of contraction) the total number of syllables. The resulting . . . – ∪ ∪ – ∪ × could have eventually come to be used before internal as well as final demarcation (1, 3, 4), or with an added quantity (the *Partheneion*), as a means of suggesting a relationship between dactylo-anapestic – ∪ ∪ –

⏑⏑(–) and aeolic –⏑⏑–⏑–(×). (The context in which the colon close or its one-quantity extension occurs is, everywhere except in Archilochus, an aeolic one.) The same "clausular catalexis with overrun" (*LMGD* 154–55) may be the origin of the choliamb: the catalectic trimeter of Archilochus (fr. 188–89, 191) interpreted as ×–⏑–×–⏑–⏑–× and lengthened by Hipponax into ×–⏑–×–⏑–⏑–×–.

# APPENDIX TWO: RESPONSION IN BACCHYLIDES 17

The metrical analysis offered in the text is similar to that of Merkelbach (*ZPE* 12 [1973] 45–55). Other recent discussions (Fuehrer 229ff., Gentili, *Serta Turyniana* [Urbana 1974] 86–100, West, *ZPE* 37 [1980] 137–42) accept more numerous freedoms of responsion, which demand a more heterogeneous rhythm. Four of the most puzzling of the transmitted responsions, however, cluster suspiciously in a very short section of the second antistrophe:

str. 1
and 2;
ant. 1: ◡ ‿ ◡◡– ◡ ◡– | ˟ – ◡– ◡–| ◡– ◡‿ ‾◡ ˘ –◡ – ◡– ◡‿ ‾‾ ◡ – ◡–
ant. 2: δόμον, ἔμολέν τε θεῶν μέγαρον τόθι κλυτὰς ἰδὼν ἔδεισε Νηρῆος ὀλβίου κόρας, ἀπὸ γὰρ ἀγλαῶν

(◡–˘˘ in responsion with ◡˘˘– is paralleled at 109, but ◡–˘˘ here necessitates the scansion ◡˘˘– for the ◡ ◡ ◡– found in the other stanzas and so the pentadic, – ◡ – ◡ (˘)(˘) ◡ – ◡ – as a concluding sequence. Without it one could analyze ◡ ◡ ◡– as ˘˘◡– and have the more normal – ◡ – ˘˘◡–˘–◡–.)

Even more suggestive of textual corruption is the way all of the irregularities disappear if one assumes that the portion of the second antistrophe which supplies the section of the rhythm indicated begins with {ἐ}μόλεν rather than δόμον:

◡– ◡ ◡– ◡◡–| ˟– ◡– ◡–| ◡–◡ – –◡ –◡– ◡– ˘˘ ◡ – ◡– ◡–
μόλεν τε θεῶν μέγαρον, τόθι κλυτὰς ἰδὼν ἔδεισε Νηρῆος ὀλβίου κόρας, ἀπὸ γὰρ ἀγλαῶν < ◡ – >

᾽Αγλαω <τάτω> ν or the like will supply the missing final syllables, and the preceding:

str. 1
and 2;
ant. 1: ˟ – ◡ – – –◡ ◡◡◡ –◡ – ◡– ◡– –◡◡ – ◡ ◡‾◡‾ ◡–
ant. 2: φέρον δὲ δελφῖνες ἐναλιναιέται μέγαν θοῶς Θησέα πατρὸς ἱππίου δόμον

can likewise be accommodated to the rhythm of the rest of the poem in various ways, e.g., by the widely accepted deletion of ἐν, combined with Θησέ᾽ ἐς ἱππίου πατρός for Θησέα πατρὸς ἱππίου δόμον (cf. *Il.* 6.47: ἐν ἀφνειοῦ πατρός . . ., 378: ἐς . . . εἰνατέρων εὐπέπλων). The transposition,

however, is harder to account for than the addition of δόμον or loss of ἐς;
and the corruption may lie in the collocation μέγαν θοῶς Θησέα, with its
unusual epithet (Fuehrer 207) and awkward hyperbaton.

If this portion of the text is dealt with along these lines, all but two of
the remaining free responsions are either easily emended (e.g., by Christ's
εὐπαγῶν for εὐπάκτων in 83, and ἰόπλοκοί <ποτε> or the like in 37),
or instances of the equivalence between pure and mixed bacchio-cretic
mentioned above (n. 187). The exceptions are, in 40, Κνωσίων κέλομαι
($- \cup - \cup \cup -$ = $- \breve{\times} - \cup -$ elsewhere in the poem) and, in 91–92
ἐξόπιθεν πνέουσ᾽ ἀήτα τρέσ- ($- \cup \cup - \cup - \cup --- $ = $- \cup - (\breve{\times}) - \cup - \cup - $
elsewhere [on the difficulties of Snell's ἐξόπιν πνέουσ᾽ ἄητᾰ τρέσ-, see
Gentili, 96–98]). These too, unparalleled as they are elsewhere in the
poem or other early pieces of bacchio-cretic, should probably be emended
also, conceivably by the transpositions κέλομαι Κνωσίων and ἐξόπιθ᾽
ἀήτα πνέουσα τρέσ-. The result would be a resolved $\overset{\smile\smile}{\times} - $ in responsion
to $- \breve{\times} -$ or $- (\breve{\times}) -$. Cf., for a partial parallel, $\bar{\times} - \cup - \ldots$ (110) in
responsion to $\cup - \cup -$ or $\overset{\smile\smile}{} \cup -$ elsewhere. There, however, it is the pure
rather than the mixed sequence which shows resolution, and the quanti-
ties involved are the initial ones in a movement.

# APPENDIX THREE:
## AEOLIC IN SIMONIDES, PINDAR AND BACCHYLIDES

The following additional examples illustrate the basic types of stanza construction discussed in the text (155–61):

A) Dactylo-aeolic.

1) Pindar, *Pae*4s

2) Pindar, fr. 169 (νόμος ὁ πάντων βασιλεύς ...)

B) Aeolic with choriambic linkage to both dactylo-anapestic and iono-choriambic:

1) Pindar, *Pae*4e

2) Bacchylides 16

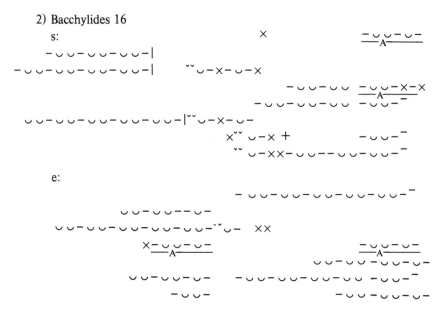

e:

[metrical scansion]

3) Pindar *N*6e

[metrical scansion]

(emending the next to last line as it appears in the second triad of the poem into conformity with the other two triads—e.g., as βοτάνα τέ ποτέ νιν λέοντος [: τέ νίν ποθ' ἀ λέοντος] | νικῶντ' ἤρεφε δασκίοις [Hermann: νικάσαντ' ἔρεψε]).

4) Pindar *O*4s1–3

[metrical scansion]

5) Simonides 16/521 (scanning the last two lines as the analogy with the closely parallel [3] would suggest)

[metrical scansion]

6) The Danae fragment of Simonides may belong here, though there are no Pindaric or Bacchylidean parallels to the whole lines of iono-choriambic which it seems to contain.

str. (*PMG* 543.7–17)                    ant. (*ibid.*, 18–27)

εἶπέν τ᾿ ὦ τέκος οἷον ἔχω πόνον

1) ×× – ‿‿ – ‿ ‿ – ‿ –
   ——A——
        εἰ δέ τοι δεινὸν τό γε δεινὸν ἦν
      οὐδ᾿ αὐταῖς ᵃ

2) – ‿ ‿ – (̈) ‿ – × – ‿ – ‿ –
        εᵗ γαλαθηνῷ δ᾿ ἤτορι κνοώσσεις
      σὺ δ᾿ αὖτε εἰς
        καί κεν ἐμῶν ῥημάτων λεπτῶν ὕπειχες οὔας

3) ‿ ‿ – × – ‿ –
ἐν ἀτερπεῖ δούρατι     κέλομαι δ᾿ εὗδε βρέφος

4) – ‿ – × – ‿ – ×(̈) ‿ – × – ‿ –
χαλκ[ε]ογόμφῳ [δὲ] νυκτιλαμπεῖ κυανέῳ [τε] δνόφῳ ταθείς
        εὑδέτω δὲ πόντος, εὑδέτω δ᾿ ἀμέτρ<ητ>ον κακόν

5) ‿ ‿ – ‿ – × – ‿ – × × – ‿ ‿ –
  —A—
      αὐλ ᵉ ᾳᾳ αν᧵ δ᾿ ὕπερθε τεᾶν κομᾶν βαθεῖαν παριόντος
        μεταβουλία δέ τις φανείη <ὦ> Ζεῦ πάτερ ἐκ σέο
        κύματος οὐκ ἀλέγεις οὐδ᾿ ἀνέμου φθόγγον

6) – ‿ ‿ – ‿ ‿ – – ‿ ‿ – × –
    ——A——
        < – ‿ ‿ – > ὅτι δὴ θαρσαλέον ἔπος

7) – ‿ ‿ – – ‿ ‿ – ×(̈) ‿ – ‿ –
πορφυρέᾳ κείμενος ἐν χλανίδι καλὸν πρόσωπον
        εὔχομαι ἦ νόσφι δίκας σύγγνωθί μοι < ‿ – ̄ >

Of the emendations necessary to produce responsion, χαλκ[ε]ογόμφῳ, κυανέῳ [τε] (s4) and <ὦ> Ζεῦ (ant5) are purely *metri gratia*. The transmitted δὲ νυκτὶ λαμπεῖ (s4), on the other hand, requires some change if it is to make sense; ἀμέτρ<ητ>ον (ant4) restores the normal poetic form (*ametron* is rare enough to be glossed with *ametrēton* in Hesychius); and ὅτι δή cannot stand at the beginning of a sentence (<εἰ δὲ κοτεῖς>, <εἰ δ᾿ ἀλίτοιμ᾿> or the like would give the combination one of its usual functions, as a means of introducing an alleged or supposed reason). The above reconstruction requires, however, either a rejection of the most plausible restoration of the corrupt opening of s2 (Casaubon's σὺ δ᾿ ἀωτεῖς), or emendation in ant2. Wilamowitz's transposition καὶ ἐμῶν κε is possible, but would introduce a unique example (from early choral lyric), of the responsion ‿ ‿ – – ‿ ‿ – = ‿ ‿ – × – ‿ –.

C. Dyadic rhythm with dactylo-anapestic expansions.

Pindar *Pae*6s

‿ ‿ – ‿ – ‿ – ‿ – ×     – ‿ ‿ – ‿ – ×
  —A—        —A—
– ‿ – ‿ ‿ –     – ‿ – ‿ – ‿ –
——B——      ——B⌣– (?)
  – ‿ – ‿ ‿ –      – ‿ –
      ‿ – ‿ –     – ‿ ‿ – ‿ (̈) ×

⌣ ‿ ‿⌣ – ‿ ‿ –⌣ ‿ ‿ – – ‿ ‿ – – ‿ ‿ – – ‿ – ‿ ‿ (̈) –
        ——B——

×−∪−∪∪−∪−
⎯⎯A⎯⎯

⎯×−B⎯∪∪−∪−×
⎯⎯A⎯⎯
×∪∪−−∪∪−∪∪∪−⎯∪∪⎯−∪∪−∪∪−
∪∪−−∪∪−∪∪−∪∪−⎯∪∪⎯−|
∪∪−∪∪−∪∪−−∪−

∪∪⎯A⎯∪−∪−∪−
⎯⎯A⎯⎯

−∪    −∪∪−

∪∪∪−∪−∪−∪−
⎯⎯A⎯⎯

∪∪∪−

−∪−∪−∪∪−

−∪∪−∪−×

e:

−∪∪−∪−∪−∪−
⎯A⎯

×−∪−∪∪−∪−     ×∪∪−∪∪−     ×−∪∪×−
⎯⎯B⎯⎯        ⎯⎯B⎯⎯        ⎯A⎯

−×−∪∪−    −∪∪−    −×−∪∪−     ×

∪−∪∪−          −×−∪∪−     ×

×−∪−∪∪−∪−    ×    −∪∪−∪∪−∪∪−∪∪−∪∪−∪−
⎯A⎯

×−∪−∪∪−∪−    ×−∪−B∪∪−∪∪−∪− ×−∪−B∪−−
                                       ⎯A⎯        ⎯A⎯

−∪∪−∪−     × −(∪∪)−∪∪−∪−    ×    −∪∪−

−∪−∪∪−∪−

−∪∪∪−          −|∪−∪∪−   −|∪−∪−∪−∪∪− −×−∪−∪∪−
                                                     ⎯B⎯         ⎯B⎯

## D. Base-nucleus alternation with initial or terminal iambo-trochaic

### 1) Bacchylides 18

∪∪−−∪∪−∪−×|×−∪∪−∪−∪−
   ××⎯A⎯    ×× ⎯A⎯    ∪−

   ××   A     ××   A     ××−×−∪−
                                  ⎯B⎯

   ××   A ‖   ××   A     ×× A⎯B⎯

   ××   A     ××   A     ×−∪−

   ××   A     ××−×−∪∪−∪−
                        =⎯B⎯

   ××   A     ∪−

### 2) Bacchylides 4

   ××−∪∪−∪−××−∪∪−∪−×
     ⎯B⎯

                                    −∪∪−∪∪−∪∪−

   ××−×−∪∪−××−∪−    (= ×−∪−−∪∪−××−∪−)
     ⎯B⎯

                             −∪∪−∪∪−∪∪−∪∪−∪∪−∪−×
                                             ⎯A⎯

   ××   A     ××   B     ∪−

   ××   B     ××   A     ×

3) Pindar, *N*2

```
××–◡◡–◡–‖×–◡◡–◡–◡– ̄
———A——      ——A——
×× A       × A ̂
×× A    ×× A    ×× A ̂
   –◡◡–×    A ̂
```

4) *N*4

```
        ——B————
×– ×—◡◡–◡––◡◡–
×   B
×   B    ××—×—◡◡–
                ——B————
××–◡◡–◡– ×–◡◡– ̄
——A——     × A —A——
×× ᴬB
×× B     × A ̂
×× A ‖   ×–◡◡–◡–◡– ̄
             ——A——
```

5) *O*9s

```
◡◡–◡◡–◡–‖×–◡◡–◡–××–◡◡–◡–◡– ̄
      ——A——   × A ̂         ——A——
×× A       × A ̂
×× A       × A ̂
×× A       × A ̂
×× A       × A ̂
×× A ‖     × A ̂
   ×–◡◡–    ××–×–◡◡–×
   ——B——      ——B——
```

E. Similar sequences of rhythmical elements in each line

1) *P*10s

(Heptadic aeolic prefaced in various ways)

```
 ̄×–◡◡– ̄
    ◡–×–◡◡–◡––◡◡––◡–
              ——A——
◡–◡◡–◡◡–×–◡◡–
    ◡––◡◡–×–◡◡––×–◡◡––×–◡
                ——B——    —B'——
    ◡––◡– ×–◡◡–◡–×
         ——A——
◡◡–◡◡–◡–×–×–◡ ̄        (cf. the very similar *Pae* xv)
          —B'——
```

2) *P*5s

(aeolic following initial iambo-trochaic, either as alternative or transition to terminal bacchio-cretic)

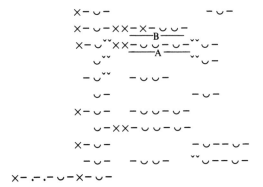

# APPENDIX FOUR: THE "ΙΑΜΒΕΡΟΣ"

The form ×–∪––|∪∪–∪∪–∪∪–‿ is usually taken (cf., however, White 350 and Fraenkel 334[1]) as iambic metron + dactylic tetrameter. The analysis fails, however, to account either for word end after the fifth quantity (present in all preserved instances of the rhythm), or the passages in Sophocles, Euripides and Aristophanes where ×–∪––|∪∪–∪∪–∪∪–‿ appears in conjunction with either ×–∪–|∪∪–∪∪–∪∪–‿ (S. *OT* 174 = 185, E. *Hipp.* 1104–5 = 1117–18) or ∪∪–∪∪–∪∪–‿ preceded by an exclamation (Ar. *Ran.* 1264ff., in a citation from the *Myrmidons*). These rhythms fit well enough with an asynartete ×–∪–x̄ + ∪∪–∪∪–∪∪–‿, substituting as they do ×–∪– or an exclamation, however scanned, for ×–∪–x̄; but they are much harder to bring into relationship with iambo-dactylic analysis. (Cf., also, *Pers.* 974–75 = 987–88: ×–∪–x̄|∪∪–∪∪–‿–‿(–) preceded and followed by an asynartete ×–∪–x + do). The only possible pre-Aeschylean occurrence of the pattern is in precisely the iambographic context (Hipponax 35) where one would expect to find such an asynartete form:

ἐρέω γὰρ οὕτω· Κυλλάνιε Μαιάδος Ἑρμῆ

if the text available to Priscian and cited by him is correct.

The absence of any certain instances of short anceps in what is here analyzed as ×–∪–x̄ can be partially paralleled by the heavy preference for long anceps in the asynartete combination –∪∪–∪∪–∪∪–∪∪ + ×–∪–... common in Sophocles; and one possible instance occurs at *Ag.* 146: ἰήιον δὲ καλέω Παιᾶνα—perhaps ×–∪–x̆ + ∪∪–‿–‿, standing in the same relationship to the pentameter that closes the stanza (αἴλινον αἴλινον εἰπέ, τὸ δ᾽εὖ νικάτω) as does ×–∪–x + ∪∪–∪∪–∪∪–‿ to the hexameter.

# APPENDIX FIVE: DISJUNCT COMPOSITION
# IN POST-AESCHYLEAN CHORAL LYRIC

The loosest form of structure contains groupings of two or three disjunct sequences, the third sometimes set off as clausular by contrasting length or rhythmical character. Sense more than form holds the groups together and makes them felt as distinct from other groupings within the stanza:

```
      -∪∪-∪- ̄                           × E^
  ∪--∪∪-∪- ̄                           × E^
  ∪--∪∪-|-∪∪-×-∪-.-∪-×
```
                                        —Ar. *Th.* 995–1000

```
    ×-.-∪- ̄          ×-∪-.-∪-∪- ̄     ××-∪∪-∪-|
    ×-.-∪- ̄          ×-∪-.-∪-∪- ̄     ××-∪∪- ̄
  -∪∪-.|-∪-∪- ̄          ∪∪-×-∪-
```
                                        —S. *Tr.* 524ff.

```
 ×-.-.-∪-×-∪-.|   ××-∪∪- ̄
   -∪-×-∪-∪- ̄      ××-∪∪-×|--|∪∪-∪∪-∪- ̄         -∪∪-∪∪-×-
 -  ∪∪--∪∪-∪- ̄            ——A——        ——A——           -∪∪-×-
                                                     -∪∪-×-×|×-∪∪-∪-.- ̄
                                                        ——A——    ——A——
```
                                        —S. *OC* 1239ff.

(Note the echo, at the end of the second group in the *OC* passage, of

```
    ××-∪∪-∪-×|×-∪∪-∪-
    ××-∪∪-∪--|∪∪-∪∪-∪- ̄
                      ——A——
```

in the preceding strophe 1211–14 = 1224–27.)

More often, however, some sort of formal principle seems to be involved as well: chiastic positioning of short and long sequences in Ar. *Th.* 969 = 974ff.:

236

$$× E | × E | × E \hat{\ }$$
$$× - \cup \cup - ‾$$
$$× - \cup \cup - ‾$$
$$× E \hat{\ }$$
$$× E \hat{\ }$$
$$× - \cup - × - \cup - × - \cup - | × E \hat{\ } \quad ;$$

diminishing length of paired sequences in S. *Aj.* 192–200:

$× D | × - \cup -.- ‾$     $× - \cup \cup - \cup -.- ‾$     $× - \cup -.- ‾$

$× × - \cup \cup - \cup - × - \cup - |$     $× - \cup -.- \cup -.- ‾$     $× - \cup \underset{A}{\cup - ×} -$     $× - \underset{A}{\cup \cup - ×} -;$

$× × - \cup \cup - \cup -$

successive approximations to a well-known rhythm (the ephymnion, with
final $× × - \cup \cup - ‾$ replaced by $- \cup \cup - \cup - ‾$) at E. *Alc.* 962 = 973ff.:

$$× × - \cup \cup - ‾$$

$× × - \cup \cup - ‾$     $× × - \cup \cup - ‾$     $× × - \cup \cup - ‾$

$× × - \cup \cup - \cup - |$   $× × - \cup \cup - \cup -$   $× × - \cup \cup - \cup - - | \underset{A}{\cup \cup - \cup -} ‾$   $- \cup \cup - \cup - | - \underset{A}{\cup \cup - \cup -} ‾ ;$

$× × - \cup \cup - \cup -$

and pattern plus pattern with elaborations at S. *El.* 504ff.:

$× \overset{\vee \vee}{\ } \cup - × -$     $× \overset{\vee \vee}{\ } \cup - × -$

$× \overset{\vee \vee}{\ } \cup - × -$     $× \overset{\vee \vee}{\ } \cup - × -$

$\bar{×} - - \bar{×} - | - × - | - × - | × - \cup - × -$

$× \overset{\vee \vee}{\ } \cup - × - | - × -$     $× \overset{\vee \vee}{\ } \cup - × - | - × -$

$× \overset{\vee \vee}{\ } \cup - × -$

(L's $\overset{\bar{×}}{\text{ο}\overset{\vee}{υ}} \overset{\vee}{\text{τί}} \overset{\ }{\text{πω}}$ $\overset{\overset{\vee}{-}\ \overset{×}{-}\ -\ |}{\text{ἔλειπες}} \overset{-\ \ \overset{×}{-}}{\text{ἐκ τοῦδ'οἴκου}}$ is retained in the second part fol-
lowing Jebb and Dawe; cf. the corresponding $\overset{×}{\text{ὡς}} \overset{\vee\vee\ \ \vee}{\text{ἔμολες}} \overset{-×\ \ \ \ -\ |\ -\ ×\ -}{\text{αἰανῆς τᾷδε γᾷ}}$ in
the first part.)

A reverse of the last pattern appears in S. *Ph.* 827 = 843ff., where the
increasing urgency of the sentiments expressed (πρὸς τί μένομεν
πράσσειν;...) leads to simplication of $- \cup \cup - \cup \cup - \cup \cup - \cup \cup |$ do into
$× \overset{\vee\vee}{\ } \cup - × -$ in the second of two similarly constructed colon groups:

– ◡ ◡ – ◡ ◡ – ◡ ◡ – ⏒⏒|do ‾                     ×˘˘◡ – × – ‾

            – × – |– x̄ – x̄ –                     – × – |– × – x̄ –                    do|an|do do

– ◡ ◡ – ◡◡ ◡◡ ◡◡ |do                             ×˘˘◡ – × –

(or do|– × – |)

                    ×˘˘◡ – × –                     ×˘˘◡ – × –

(For text and colometry, see *LMGD* 117–18, and for the type of rhythm, here and in the preceding passage, text, 107. – × – × – presumably stands in the same relation to the normal "hypodochmiac" – ◡ – ◡ – [above, 115] as does – × – to the normal cretic – ◡ –.)

Examples of disjunct composition from monodies and amoibaia are too numerous and varied to catalogue.

# APPENDIX SIX:
## "MAJOR IONIC" | – × – ⌣ –. . . AND
## | – – ⌣ ⌣ –. . . IN DRAMA

Most of the possible instances fall into the two categories of passage examined in the text (192–97), or appear in contexts which are similar in one way or another. The triple | – ⌣ – ⌣ – | – ⌣ – ⌣ – | – ⌣ – ⌣ – of, e.g., E. *Ph.* 1023–24 = 1047–49 (text, 186):

× –. –. – ⌣ – | × – ⌣ – × – ⌣ –. | – ⌣ – ⚥ –   +
           – ⌣ – ⚥ – |. | – ⚥ – ⌣ – | × E ˆ

has a non-syncopated analogue in the lines which immediately follow in that passage:

× –. –. – ⌣ – |           × – ⌣ – ⚥ – ¯       +
                     ⌣⌣ ⌣ – × – ⌣̆ | × – ⌣ – × | E   ×
                                     E  .
                                       E ˆ

or, more briefly, Timotheus 15/791.197–201:

Παιᾶν' ἐκελάδησεν,      × –. ⌣⌣ × – ⌣       +
ἰήϊον ἄνακτα . . .        × –. ⌣⌣ × – ⌣ | – × – ⌣ – × – ⌣ – | – ⌣ ⌣ – ⌣ – ¯

This anticipation of "pre-hephthemimeral" (×) – ⌣ – × – ⌣ | in an ensuing passage of iambo-trochaic is exactly paralleled elsewhere by echo of post-hepthemimeral | – × – ⌣ – from a preceding one:

             –. –. – ⌣ | – × – ⌣ –      +
                   – ⚥ – ⌣ –

                               —E. *IA* 235 = 246 and 256 = 267

×–◡–×–◡|˘˘×–◡–                    +

                    –◡˘˘◡–¯

                ˘˘×–◡–|

×–◡˘˘×–◡|–×–◡˘˘×˘˘◡˘˘◡–¯

—Timotheus 15/791.74–78

More remotely, the

×–◡–×–◡–×˘˘◡–×–◡–‖

×–◡–×–◡–×–.|–×–◡–|×–.–.–◡–|    ×–◡–.–¯    +    –◡–◡–¯

of A. *Su.* 134–40 = 144–50 may be echoed in the

                –⦶–◡–×|–◡–×–◡–|

×–◡–.|–◡        –×–◡–.  –◡–×–◡–.‖–◡–◡–¯    +    –◡–.–◡–×–◡–

of the succeeding stanza (154–61 = 168–75).

Finally, iono-choriambic –×–◡––◡◡– at S. *Ant.* 1140 = 1149 may begin with the last quantity of a nucleus—like the $\overline{-××-×-}_B$◡◡– heard within aeolic epiploke in the preceding stanza. The aeolic parallel appears in conjunction with what is perhaps an aeolic counterpart (×× $\overline{-×-}_B$|..|–) to the double syncopation that regularly precedes "major ionic" colon openings:

καί σε Νυσαίων ὀρέων        ××$\underline{-×-}_B$◡ ◡–|××$\underline{-×-}_B$|..|–  ××$\underline{-×-}_B$◡◡–××‖
        κισσήρεις ὄχθαι

                χλωρά τ' ἀκτὰ πολυστάφυλος πέμπει
ἀβρότων ἐπετᾶν
                        –×$\underline{-}_B$◡◡–‖××–×⁽˗⁾◡◡–|×Eˆ
        εὐαζόντων Θηβαΐας

                ἐπισκοποῦντ' ἀγυιάς

                                —1131–36 = 1120–25

Cf., in the iono-choriambic sequel,

παῖ Διὸς γένεθλον, προφάνηθ'        –×–◡––◡◡–|××$\underline{-◡}_A$˘˘◡–
        ὦναξ, σαῖς ἅμα περιπόλοις

                                —1149–50 = 1140–41

A similar demarcation, one quantity before an aeolic base, may be present in the "procephalic" opening of the last sequence in the stanza:

μολεῖν καθαρσίῳ ποδὶ Παρνασσίαν ὑπὲρ κλιτύν,

×+××-×̲–̲‿‿-××-×- σ͞σ-|- ‿ ‿ - ‿ - ⁻
     B

ἢ στονόεντα πορθμόν

−1142-45 = 1151-54

(For contraction in the aeolic nucleus, see what is probably ×-×̲–̲ σ͞σ-|
                                                                  B
×-×̲–̲‿ ‿ - .| E in the lines immediately preceding [1137-39 = 1146-48].)
    B

# APPENDIX SEVEN: *POXY* 2687

Two notions are basic to the author's discussion: those of (1) a pattern of time lengths (*rhythmos*); and (2) a process which is variously conceived as the "employment" (*chrēsis*) or "handling" of syllables in a given way to produce a pattern, as the "setting" (*thesis*) of syllables to given time lengths, or as the constitution of a time pattern (*rhythmopoia*) through syllables. The process may involve the employment of syllable sequences which normally require a longer or shorter time for delivery than the pattern to which they are being set allows. Overlength sequences produce a "compressed" (*xynestrammenon*) time pattern into which a more than normal amount of syllabic material has been squeezed, underlength sequences a "drawn out" (*diēirēmenon*) pattern in which the reverse has occurred. Compressings and drawings out may involve approximation rather than exact realization of a time pattern. The result are mixed (*meiktoi*) patterns composed of lengths not analyzable as even multiples of a single basic counting unit and "not accepted by the ear" (μὴ δοκιμαζομένους ὑπὸ τῆς αἰσθήσεως; cf. *RS* 82.12–13ff., on the way irrational longs create a time relationship δύο λόγων γνωρίμων τῇ αἰσθήσει ἀνὰ μέσον).

The relevant portion of the text in which these concepts appear goes as follows (supplements are those printed or suggested by the papyrus' latest editors, except for τάς in iv.25 and προτέρας and ἀνωμάλους in iv.28 [above, n. 298]):

iii.23          αἱ δὲ             The

μέλλουσαι ῥηθήσεσθαι δύναν-     ways of handling syllables which are going to be

25  ται μὲν γενέσθαι εἴ τις εὐκαί-     discussed are possible if employed in

ρως αὐταῖς χρῷτο καταμιγνὺς     appropriate conjunction

εἰς τὰς γνωριμωτέρας τε καὶ     with more accepted and

οἰκειοτέρας χρήσεις· οὐ μέν-     natural ones, though they

τοι γεγενημέναι γέ πως· λέ-     are not in any fashion ways actually used. For

30  γω δὲ τὰς τοιάσδε· ὁ ὄρθιος     example, the *orthios*

καὶ ὁ σημαντὸς τροχαῖος ἐκ     and the *sēmantos trochaios* can be constructed

τριῶν κρητικῶν δύναν-     from three cretics

ται ξυντίθεσθαι·     (i.e., ⏞‿–⏞‿–⏞‿– and ⏞‿–⏞‿–⏞‿–,

                                   thesis    arsis     arsis    thesis

                            instances of the combination of octaseme thesis and

                            tetraseme arsis found in *orthios* and *sēmantos* [cf.

           δῆλον δ' ὅ-     *AQ* 1.16 p. 36.3–6]). And it is obvious that

35 τι καὶ ἐκ τριῶν περιεχόν-
τῶν·


δύνανται δὲ καὶ ἐκ τρι-
iv.1 ῶν ἡμισέων·


ὁ αὐτὸς δε λόγος
καὶ περὶ τοῦ παιῶνος· καὶ γὰρ οὗ-
τος ἐκ πέντε περιεχόντων
δύναται ξυντίθεσθαι· δῆλον
5 δ'ὅτι καὶ ἐκ πέντε ἡμισέων.


ξυνεχὴς μὲν οὖν ἡ τοιαύτη
χρῆσις οὐκ ἂν γίγνοιτο· παν-
τελῶς γὰρ ἀλλότριον τὸ ἦθος
τῆς τοιαύτης ῥυθμοποιίας
10 τοῦ τε παιῶνος καὶ τῶν πρὸ
τούτου ῥηθέντων· εἰ δέ που


τιθεμένη ἐν καταμείξει
τοῦ ἰδίου ἕνεκα δοκιμάζοι-
το, τάχ' ἂν χρήσαιτό τις αὐ-
15 τῆι· εἰ δε μή, καθόλου διὰ τὴν προ-
εκκειμένην ἀπορίαν ἀθέ-
τους ἐατέον τὰς τοιαύτας χρή-
σεις ὅσαι μεικτοὺς τινὰς
ἐμφαίνουσι ῥυθμοὺς μὴ δο-
20 κιμαζομένους ὑπὸ τῆς αἰσθήσεως. ἐπει..
[...].αυτη[.]χρησ...[..δ]ιηι-
ρημένοι ῥυθμοὶ καὶ ξυνεστραμ-
ένοι εἰς ἐλάττους χρόνους·
25 ἐπειδήπερ ἐνδέχεται [τὰς
δύο τῶν τριῶν ξυλλαβῶν
τὰς[προτ]έρα[ς εἰς ἀν]ω]μάλους
θε[ῖναι] χρόν[ους,] λέγω δ' εἰς
ἀνίσους, τὴν μὲν προτέραν
30 εἰς τὸν μείζω ἐπειδήπερ
καὶ μακρά, τὴν δὲ ὑστέραν
εἰς τὸν ἐλάττω ἐπειδήπερ
βραχεῖα· ὅτι δε γενομέ-

they can be constituted both from three oversize (?) lengths (literally, lengths which "pro-
ject beyond" [cf. Thuc. 5.71.1 and 73] in that,
with normal delivery, like the cretics just mentioned when used in the orthios and sēmantos, they
would be too long for the space of time allotted them
by the rhythm); and that constitution is also possible
from three half-size lengths (perhaps the three
syllables in – – –, each of which would normally occupy only half the time to which it
must be drawn out to constitute part of an orthios or
sēmantos [ ⏕ ⏕ ⏕ ]). The
same applies to the paeon, for this too can be
composed from five oversize lengths
(‾⏝ – ‾⏝ – ‾⏝ – ‾⏝ – ‾⏝ – [?]) and obviously
from five half-size lengths as well (perhaps those of
the paiōn epibatos [– – – – –] according to AQ
1.16 p. 37.7–9], here drawn out, like those in
⏕ ⏕ ⏕ to double their normal length).
Continuous handling of syllables in
this fashion would be impossible, for such
constitution of time patterns is completely
foreign in character to
the paeon and the forms mentioned before
it (orthios and sēmantos). Conceivably, however,
it would be accepted as one
ingredient in a mixture, for the
sake of individual variation, in
which case one could use it; otherwise
the aforementioned difficulty is reason
for leaving alone, as a general rule,
all such handlings of syllables which
bring to the fore time patterns
heterogeneous in one way or another
and not acceptable to the ear. For
patterns composed of syllables drawn
out and compressed into shorter time
settings . . . are the ones produced by? . . .
this method of treatment—given the
fact that it is possible to give
irregular time settings to the first
two of the three syllables (in the
cretic)—I mean unequal ones, so that
the first of the two is set to the larger
time length, since it is in fact long,
and the second
to the shorter since
it is short. That the result of this

νου τούτου τὸ χρώμενον
35 οὕτως ταῖς τρισὶ ξυλλαβαῖς
v.1 ἐγγὺς ἔσται ἀναπαυστικοῦ σχή-
μματος σχεδὸν δῆλον· διὰ τί δ' οὐ
κἂν γίγνοιτο και το ἀνεστραμ-
μένον ὥστε τὴν μὲν πρώ-
5 την ξυλλαβὴν ἐν τῶι μεγί-
στωι χρόνωι κεῖσθαι την δε
δευτέραν ἐν τῶι ἐλαχίστωι
τὴν δὲ τρίτην ἐν τῶι μέσωι·
δῆλον δ' ὅτι ἡ αὐτὴ ἀπορία
10 διατείνει καὶ ἐπὶ τὴν ἀντι-
κειμένην λέξιν τῆι τετρα-
χρόνωι κρητικῆι λέξει· διὰ
τί γὰρ οὐκ ἂν ἡ δύο ἰαμβικοῖς εἰς
τὸν πόδα χρωμένη ῥυθμο-
15 ποιία [ἔχοι τὴ]ν αὐτὴν ἀγωγὴν
[ἢν καὶ ἡ δύο τροχα]ικοῖς χρω-
[μένη ῥυθμοποιία· ἀλλ' ο]ὐ γεγέ-
νηται . . .
                                    πε-
v.20 ρὶ μεν οὖν τούτου τοῦ σχήμα-
τος τοσαῦτ' εἰρήσθω· ἡ γὰρ παρὰ φύσιν τῶν ξυλλαβῶν θέ-
σις ἡ εἰς τὴν δακτυλικὴν ῥυ-
θμοποιίαν ξυντείνουσα φα-
25 νερὰ ἐκ τῶν ἔμπροσθεν·
                                        ἡ
δ'ἀπο βραχείας ἀρχομένη τῶν
ξυλλα[βῶν τά]ξις
                        οἰκεία μεν οὐ-
δενός ἐστιν τῶν ῥυθμῶν τοι-
29 ούτων . . .

handling of syllabic material (i.e., ⌣⌣-)
approximates the configuration of the
anapest is fairly obvious. As to
why the reverse should not occur

(i.e., - ⌣ ⌣̄), so that the first syllable
receives the largest time setting and

the second the shortest and the third
the intermediate one—obviously the
same difficulty extends to the verbal
segment (i.e., ⌣- ⌣-) that is the
reverse of the four-part cretic segment
(- ⌣ - ⌣). For why would the constitution
of a time pattern that uses two iambs
to a foot (presumably ⌣̄⌣̄⌣-)
not admit of the same tempo as that
which uses two trochees (- ⌣ ⌣̄⌣̆)?
But it does not in fact occur. . . .

        Enough
said, therefore, concerning this configuration, for the nature of the dactyl-

approximating setting of syllables contrary
to normal time value (i.e., - ⌣ ⌣̄; cf.
AQ 1.17 p. 37.24–26 on the irrational choree
[ἄλογος χορεῖος] which ἔοικε δακτύλῳ)
is clear from the aforesaid; and the
arrangement of syllables in which the short
comes first (i.e., ⌣- in - ⌣ - or ⌣- ⌣-, by
contrast with - ⌣ in - ⌣- or - ⌣- ⌣) is not
suitable to any of the sort of rhythms under
consideration (i.e., to the settings in
which a combination of long and short
syllable receives the time value of ⌣̄⌣̆ or ⌣ ⌣).

The meanings here suggested for *periechonta* and *hēmisea*, and the identification of the "anapestic" cretic as an example of the former may well be wrong, but this does not affect the basic point being made about the cretic and its analogues.

One of these analogues is almost certainly misidentified by the papyrus' most recent editors when they equate the *agōgē* which is permitted in the "tetrachronic" cretic verbal segment but not its reverse with the protraction mentioned earlier (ii.2–21) in connection with the cretic - ⌣ ≟ and its reverse, the "iambic" dactyl (≟ ⌣ -). There the word cretic referred to a definite time pattern; here, on the other hand, it designates a syllable sequence which *agōgē* might conceivably accommodate to any time pattern so long as it consists of four separate "lengths." And the reverse of $- \cup =\!\!\cdot$ was a rhythm that could be illustrated by poetic examples, even though excessive use of it was discouraged; $\cup - \cup -$ with the particular *agōgē* referred to here does not occur at all.

# APPENDIX EIGHT:
## IRRATIONAL LONGS IN DRAMATIC LYRIC

Table X is largely a compilation of suggestions offered in *LMGD* 56–57, 62–66, 90–91 and, for the passages in column A, T. C. W. Stinton, "Two Rare Verse Forms," *CQ* 59 (1965) 141–45. Stinton takes the sequence – ∪ ∪ – ∪ ∪ – × – ∪ – as a combinataion of dactylic – ∪ ∪ – ∪ ∪ and iambic × – ∪ –; but his alternative analysis (144) as iambic dimeter (with anomalous substitutions in its first metron) is probably preferable when the dactylic and iambic components are in verbal synapheia (as in *Ion* 1077 = 1093 and *Tr.* 1068 = 1079, both of them exactly paralleling in their internal verbal rhythm an immediately preceding dimeter); or when, as at E. *El.* 459 = 471, the colon is closely paralleled by another in the same context where dactylo-iambic analysis is excluded (– ∪ ∪ – ∪ ∪ | x̆˘∪˘∪ – ⁻ = – ∪ ∪ – ∪ ∪ | x̆˘∪˘˘∪ – ⁻ at 456 = 468).

Dale herself prefers to speak of "syllable-counting" equivalence rather than "irrationality," a formulation which allows for short syllables supplying long quantities as well as the reverse. E. *Ph.* 813 = 796 (Table X, A) is perhaps best taken in this way, since it shows – ∪ ∪ – ∪ ∪ | – ∪ ∪ – ∪ ∪ = – ∪ ∪ – ∪ ∪ | ∪ ∪ ∪ ∪ ∪ ∪ in a dactylic context. The passage, however, like other instances of "tribrachic" substitution in dactylo-anapestic cited by Dale, can just as easily be a brief modulation into a contrasting rhythm: cf. the initial variation ∪ ∪ ∪ | ∪ ∪ ∪ | ∪ ∪ ∪ | ∪ ∪ ∪ at *IT* 220, and the pre-clausular ∪ ∪ ∪ | ∪ ∪ ∪ at *IT* 208–13 (an an|an an|an an^ + an an^ + an an^ + ∪ ∪ ∪ | ∪ ∪ ∪ + an^), *Ion* 887–90 (an an^ + an an^ + an an^ + ∪ ∪ ∪ | ∪ ∪ ∪ | ∪ ∪ ∪ | ∪ ∪ ∪ + an^) and 897–901 (an an^ + an an^ + an an^ + ∪ ∪ ∪ | ∪ ∪ ∪ + an|an an^) and *Tr.* 134–37 (an|an an + ∪ ∪ ∪ | ∪ ∪ ∪ + an|an an^). The *Phoenissae* itself shows what may be ˘˘∪ – × at initial (818: ἔτεκες ὦ γαῖ'; 1498: τίνα προσῳδόν) and pre-clausular (1557: ξίφεσι βρίθων) positions in dactylo-anapestic passages. (Cf. *Hyps.* p. 47.86 Bond with the discussion in West [131]).

Even more questionable is Dale's suggestion (tentatively offered at *LMGD* 78–79) that anapestic substitutions in the comic trimeter be seen as an instance of syllable-counting equivalence between ∪ ∪ – and the tribrach ∪ ∪ ∪. There is no close correlation between the frequency and distribution of anapests and tribrachs in the trimeter to support this theory, and there is no parallel elsewhere to the posited substitution of long for short within (rather than at the start of) metron, arsis or thesis.

The comic "anapest," however analyzed, is more likely to be a phenomenon closely linked to a conversational, prose-like mode of delivery, and so at the farthest possible remove from any development which tended toward subordination of natural speech rhythms to the marking of time.

# INDEX LOCORUM

(Italicized page references are to entries in the Tables. Letter–number references [e.g., B–5] in parentheses are to headings in the table of aeolic forms on pp. 126–27).